ARIZONA

ARIZONA

A CAVALCADE OF HISTORY
Revised Edition

MARSHALL TRIMBLE

RIO NUEVO PUBLISHERS, TUCSON, ARIZONA

RIO NUEVO PUBLISHERS®
P.O. Box 5250, Tucson, AZ 85703-0250
(520) 623-9558, www.rionuevo.com

ISBN-13: 978-1-887896-43-6; ISBN-10: 1-887896-43-0
Library of Congress Catalog Card Number: 89-50790

Cover design: Lindahl-Bryant Studio, Sedona, AZ
Cover photograph: Larry Lindahl
Interior design: NewType Technology, Inc., Tucson, AZ

Printed in Canada

10 9 8 7 6 5 4 3

This book is dedicated to all my students at
Scottsdale Community College, past and present.
You have been my source of inspiration
for more than thirty years.
And to the late Honorable Barry Goldwater,
with admiration for an old friend.

Marshall Trimble
Official Arizona State Historian
November 2004

TABLE OF CONTENTS

Facts about Arizona x
Arizona Chronology xiii
Prologue xix
Chapter 1: Before the Time of Man 1
Chapter 2: Prehistoric Arizona 8
Chapter 3: Arizona's Native Americans 20
Chapter 4: Glory, God and Gold 53
Chapter 5: Rim of Christendom 61
Chapter 6: The American Entrada 74
Chapter 7: Arizona in the 1850s 88
Chapter 8: Turbulent Times: The Indian Wars 107
Chapter 9: Mining in Arizona 122
Chapter 10: Legends in Levis: The Cowboys 147
Chapter 11: Outlawry and Justice 166
Chapter 12: Steel Rails Across Arizona 184
Chapter 13: Territorial Politics, 1863-1912 194
Chapter 14: Life in The Territorial Years 210
Chapter 15: The Baby State 235
Chapter 16: The 1920s and 1930s — Boom and Bust ...248
Chapter 17: Harnessing the Great Rivers 258
Chapter 18: Politics in Arizona Since Statehood 267
Chapter 19: Recent Arizona History.............................290
Arizona's Political Figures...306
Bibliography..309
Index..323

MARSHALL TRIMBLE
Arizona's Official State Historian

Marshall Trimble grew up in the small northern Arizona town of Ash Fork. He began his career as a folk singer in the 1960s, and after Doubleday published his highly successful book, *Arizona,* in 1977, he returned to the stage, this time as a storyteller, cowboy poet and singer. He is, today, one of the state's most sought-after speakers and performers. He's taught Arizona History at Scottsdale Community College for more than thirty-five years.

This multi-talented historian can deliver everything from a serious history lecture to 45 minutes of stand-up comedy. He appears frequently on radio and television as a goodwill ambassador for the state. *Trimble's Tales* are heard daily on radio stations around the state, and his television show, *Arizona Backroads,* received a regional Emmy nomination in 2006. He answers questions about the Old West from readers all over the world in *True West* magazine's column "Ask the Marshall."

This native Arizonan is the author of twenty-one books on Arizona and the West.

In recent years Trimble has been the recipient of many honors. In 1999 he was inducted into the Phoenix College Alumni Hall of Fame. In 2000 he was selected as one of Arizona's representatives in the Library of Congress's Local Legacies. In 2002 he received the first Copper Star Award from the State Society of Arizona in Washington D.C. In 2004 the Daughters of the American Revolution honored him with their Medal of Honor for leadership and patriotism. That same year he was inducted into Scottsdale's Hall of Fame and the Arizona Veterans Hall of Fame. In 2007, the Arizona Office of Tourism presented him with a Lifetime Achievement Award for his many years of service to the state.

FACTS ABOUT ARIZONA

Arizona became a territory on February 24, 1863. Arizona became a state on February 14, 1912.

Nicknames   Valentine State, Baby State (not since Alaska and Hawaii) and Grand Canyon State.

Motto   *Ditat Deus* "God Enriches"

Population   5.1 million (2000). Arizona is ranked 20th in the nation.

State Seal   The state's traditional enterprises, ranching, reclamation, farming and mining are represented.

State Flag   Adopted in 1917, the red and gold represents the colors carried by the first Spanish explorers. Blue is one of the official colors. The 13 red and gold rays are the same as the 13 stripes on the U.S. flag. The top segment represents the rays of an Arizona sunset, and the copper star represents the state's most important industry from a historical perspective and the newest rising star in the nation. The flag was designed by Charles Wilfred Harris in 1910 and sewn by Nancy Hayden, wife of Senator Carl Hayden.

State Song   "Arizona March Song" words by Margaret Rowe Clifford, music by Maurice Blumenthal. Alternate State Song (since few know or can sing the first) — "I Love You Arizona" by Rex Allen, Jr.

State Balladeer   Dolan Ellis

State Tree   Palo Verde, Spanish for "green stick"

State Gem   Turquoise

State Colors   Blue and Gold

State Flower   Blossom of the Saguaro Cactus

State Bird   Cactus Wren

State Reptile   Ridge-nosed Rattlesnake

State Fossil   Petrified wood

State Mammal   Ring-tail Cat

State Neckwear   The Bola tie

OTHER FACTS

Arizona is the sixth largest state in the Union, with 113,909 square miles. It is 393 miles long and 338 miles wide, with 492 square miles of water.

Arizona has the largest stand of ponderosa pine in America.

Arizona's land ownership is 17.5% private; 26.7% Indian; 12.2% state and the rest is federal land.

The Grand Canyon is 227 miles long, one mile deep with an average width of 10 miles.

The highest point in Arizona is Mt. Humphreys, in the San Francisco Peaks, at 12,633 feet.

The average state elevation is 4,000 feet.

The average rainfall ranges from less than 3 inches per year in the southwest deserts to more than 30 inches per year in the White Mountains.

Oraibi, on the Hopi mesas, is reputed to be the oldest continuously inhabited city in America.

The best preserved meteor crater in America is located near Winslow. The meteor collided with the earth nearly 50,000 years ago.

The last volcanic eruption in Arizona occurred at Sunset Crater near the San Francisco Peaks around 1064 A.D. and continued until about 1250 A.D.

Arizona became a territory as part of New Mexico in 1850.

ARIZONA CHRONOLOGY

PREHISTORIC PERIOD

Circa 10,000 B.C.	Primitive Paleo Indians inhabit Arizona.
Circa 2,000 B.C.	Cochise Man begins farming primitive corn.
Circa 300 B.C.	Hohokam settle in southern Arizona.
Christian Era	Anasazi come to Four Corners area.
500 A.D.	Sinagua are farming near San Francisco Peaks.
1064 A.D.	Sunset Crater erupts.
1276-1299 A.D.	Great drought in Arizona.
Circa 1300 A.D.	The mysterious Casa Grande is built near the Gila River.
Circa 1400 A.D.	Cultural decline of prehistoric groups.

SPANISH PERIOD, 1528-1821

1528-1536	Eight-year odyssey of Cabeza de Vaca and his shipwrecked companions stirs interest in Glory, God and Gold.
1539	Fray Marcos de Niza searches for golden cities.
1540-1542	Coronado claims for Spain the vast lands that are today the American Southwest.
1582-1583	Antonio de Espejo, a miner, enters New Mexico and Arizona looking for rich minerals.

1598-1607	Juan de Oñate establishes first colonies in New Mexico. Puts Spanish "stamp" on the area.
1610	City of Santa Fe founded.
1629	Franciscans establish missions in Hopiland, the first Europeans to reside in Arizona.
1687-1711	Father Kino establishes missions in Pimeria Alta, along the Rio Santa Cruz and Rio San Pedro.
1736	Great silver discovery at *Arisonac.*
1751	Great Pima Indian Revolt.
1752	Tubac presidio established. First white community in Arizona.
1767	Jesuits expelled from Spanish realm.
1767	Franciscan Father Garcés enters Arizona.
1774	De Anza and Garcés explore route to California.
1775-1776	De Anza and Garcés take colonists overland to California. Tucson established.
1781	Yuma Revolt; Garcés murdered.
1785-1821	Spanish troops go on offensive campaigns into Apacheria. Peace treaty with Apaches; mining, ranching and missions prosper in Arizona.
1810-1821	Mexican Revolution.

MEXICAN PERIOD, 1821-1848

1821	Mexico gains independence.
1822	Santa Fe — St. Louis trade opens.
1823	Americans begin to settle in Texas.
1824	American mountain men enter Arizona to trap beaver.
1835-1836	Texas Revolution.
1837	Mexico offers bounties for Apache scalps.
1846-1848	Mexican War; Army of the West takes New Mexico and California; Treaty of Guadalupe Hidalgo ends war; vast Mexican territory ceded to U.S.

AMERICAN PERIOD, 1848-

1848	Gold discovered in California. Gila Trail becomes one of the main routes to the gold fields.
1850	Compromise of 1850 establishes Territory of New Mexico (Arizona included).
1852	Americans begin navigating the Colorado River by steamer. Army Corps of Topographical Engineers begins surveying Arizona.
1853	Gadsden Purchase gives Arizona the land from the Gila River to present boundary.
1854	First American mining (commercial) ventures.
1856	American Dragoons (cavalry) occupy Tucson; Arizonans begin petitioning for separate territorial status.
1857	Beale's camels and "Jackass Mail" stagecoach lines cross Arizona; Fort Buchanan established on Sonoita Creek.
1858	Butterfield Overland Stage Line crosses Arizona.
1861	Bascom Affair pits Army against Chiricahua Apaches; Civil War begins and Arizona military posts are abandoned.
1862	Arizona becomes a Confederate territory; Battle at Glorieta Pass, New Mexico, ends Confederate westward thrust; Battle of Picacho Pass, near Casa Grande, is called westernmost battle of Civil War; California Column occupies Arizona for Union; Battle of Apache Pass between Column and Apaches is largest in Arizona history; Fort Bowie is established in the Pass.
1863	Territory of Arizona is established. Walker Party discovers gold in Bradshaw Mountains; Weaver-Peeples party discovers placer gold at Rich Hill; Wickenburg finds rich lode at Vulture Mine.
1864	Territorial capital established at Prescott; four counties (Yuma, Yavapai, Pima and Mohave) are created. Navajo take "long walk" to Bosque Redondo, New Mexico.
1861-1886	Apache Wars.

1860s	Period of gold discoveries, Gila River, Colorado River and Bradshaw Mountains.
1869	John Wesley Powell explores Grand Canyon.
1870s-1880s	Age of Silver; open range cattle industry flourishes.
1871	Camp Grant Massacre.
1872-1873	General Crook subdues central Arizona Apaches and Yavapais.
1876	Territorial prison opens at Yuma.
1877	Silver discovered at Tombstone; copper deposits found at Bisbee.
1881	Southern Pacific Railroad crosses southern Arizona.
1883	Atlantic & Pacific (Santa Fe) crosses northern Arizona.
1888	Copper replaces gold and silver in economic importance in Arizona.
1889	Territorial capital moved to Phoenix.
1895	Phoenix linked by rail to northern and southern railroad lines.
1898	Rough riders fight in Cuba.
1902	Frank Murphy builds "Impossible Bradshaw Mountain Railroad."
1903	Salt River Water Users' Association formed, first of its kind in the nation.
1910	Arizona Enabling Act passed by Congress; Constitutional Convention meets.
1911	Theodore Roosevelt Dam completed; President Taft vetoes admission of Arizona over recall of judges; Arizona agrees to make the necessary changes in its constitution.
1912	Arizona admitted to the Union.
1914	Women gain right to vote in Arizona.
1917	WWI brings economic boom to Arizona. Labor unrest in Bisbee causes deportation of suspected radical I.W.W. Union members by locals.
1929	Great Depression lasts into late 1930s.
1936	Hoover Dam on the Colorado River is dedicated.

1941—1945	World War II brings economic boom to Arizona; Cotton, copper, cattle, farming and industry flourish.
1946	Arizona right-to-work becomes effective; industrial development and manufacturing takes on new importance. Post-WW II brings surge of population to Arizona.
1948	Motorola builds first plant in Phoenix marking the beginning of high tech industry in Arizona.
1950	Election of Governor Howard Pyle gives rise to Republican Party.
1960	Arizona Population exceeds 1 million.
1961	Stewart Udall becomes first Arizonan to serve on Cabinet (Secretary of Interior).
1963	Arizona wins Supreme Court decision in contest with California over share of Colorado River water; hopes are revived for a Central Arizona Project to bring water from the Colorado to central Arizona.
1964	Senator Barry Goldwater is the Republican Party candidate for President.
1966	Legislative reapportionment (one man, one vote). Legislative districts reapportioned to represent an equal number of people. The Republican Party gains control of the legislature for the first time.
1968	Authorization is given for construction of the Central Arizona Project; Senator Carl Hayden retires after serving Arizona in Congress since 1912.
1981	Sandra Day O'Connor becomes first woman on U.S. Supreme Court.
1984	Ernest W. McFarland dies. He was the only man in U.S. history to have served as governor, U.S. senator, and chief justice of a state supreme court.
1985	Central Arizona Project water reaches Phoenix.
1986	William H. Rehnquist is appointed Chief Justice of U.S. Supreme Court.

1987	Arizona State University football team wins Rose Bowl.
1988	Governor Evan Mecham impeached and removed from office; Rose Mofford becomes Arizona's first woman governor.
1989	Central Arizona Project water reaches Tucson.
1993	Bruce Babbitt becomes U.S. Secretary of the Interior.
1993	First Indian gaming compacts signed in Arizona.
1997	University of Arizona basketball team wins NCAA Basketball Championship
1998	Jane Dee Hull is first woman elected governor of Arizona.
1998	Arizona becomes first U.S. state to have top five state elected offices held by women: Governor Jane Dee Hull; Secretary of State Betsey Bayless; Attorney General Janet Napolitano; Treasurer Carol Springer; and Superintendent of Public Instruction Lisa Graham Keegan. The media dubs them the "Fab Five."
1998	Senator Barry Goldwater and Congressman Morris "Mo" Udall die.
1998	Arizona Diamondbacks baseball team begins play in the National League.
2000	Arizona population exceeds 5 million.
2001	Arizona Diamondbacks win World Series in seven games over New York Yankees.

PROLOGUE

Although the Paleo Indians or First Americans were known to roam this land more than 10,000 years ago, Arizona's recorded history began with the arrival of the Spanish in the 15th Century.

Rumors and legends of fabulous cities of gold provided the inspiration for the early exploration of this land the Spanish called the "Northern Mystery." The first great expedition was led by Francisco Vasquez de Coronado in 1540. Coronado spent two years searching for the mythical cities of gold and a water passage through North America. In the end he returned to Mexico City, his mission a failure. The expedition did, however, give Spain a claim to the vast regions that comprise today's American Southwest.

The Spanish avoided sending large expeditions into the region for the next 40 years. In 1583 Antonio de Espejo traveled up the Rio Grande to the vicinity of today's Albuquerque, then turned west towards Arizona. In his quest for riches Espejo reached the Verde Valley. He, too, failed in his quest to coax the wealth from the mineral-laden mountains.

Juan de Oñate, the great colonizer of New Mexico, was the next to venture into the boundaries of today's Arizona. In November 1598, he journeyed west to the Hopi mesas. Oñate hoped to explore the rich native mines in the vicinity of Jerome. He ordered a small expedition under Captain Marcos Farfán to investigate the regions around Prescott. They found rich silver ore, but it wasn't until 1604 that Oñate resumed his exploration of Arizona. That year he set out in search of the fabled Northwest Passage. Instead of finding the water passage across North America, he arrived at the Colorado River near today's Parker Dam. From there he traveled south to the Yuma Crossing. Upon finding the terrain too rough for transporting ore, a disappointed Oñate returned to New Mexico.

The next wave of explorers were Franciscan and Jesuit missionaries who came to harvest the native souls. The first Franciscan missions in Arizona were among the Hopi in 1629. The tradition-bound Hopi were not receptive to outsiders and drove the Franciscans out in the Great Pueblo Revolt in 1680.

The Jesuit entrada into Arizona came from the south in 1691. Father Francisco Eusebio Kino worked tirelessly among the Pima and Papago in the vast Pimeria Alta (Land of the Upper Pima) for nearly a quarter of a century. This remarkable "Padre on Horseback" introduced cattle raising, agriculture, religion and Spanish culture to thousands of natives in the Pimeria Alta.

In 1736, a great silver strike occurred near an Indian village called *Ali-Shonak*. Spanish prospectors rushed to the area, about 25 miles southwest of today's Nogales. *Ali-Shonak,* a Tohono O'odham word for "Place of the Small Springs," didn't roll off the Spanish tongue easily so they corrupted it to *Arizonac*. When the Anglo-Americans arrived more than a century later they changed it to Arizona — and that's what it's been ever since.

In recent years another theory has been proposed on the origin of the name. Don Garate, chief of historical interpretation for Tumacacori National Historical Park, makes a strong case for Basque origin, from *aritz* (oak) and *ona* (good), or "Good Oaks." Large numbers of Basque lived in the area, including Juan Bautista de Anza. And there is an abundance of oak trees. Many locations in South America with large numbers of Basque and abundant oak trees also bear the name Arizona, giving credence to Garate's theory.

A great Pima uprising against the Spanish in 1751 led to the building of the first presidio, or fort, at Tubac, marking the beginning of the Spanish colonial period in Arizona. Up to then a few visitas (mission stations), such as Tumacacori, San Xavier del Bac, and Guevavi were the only Spanish presence in the region.

In 1767 the Jesuits were expelled from the Pimeria Alta by King Carlos III of Spain. The following year the Franciscans took up the task of bringing Christianity to the natives. The missionaries had little success among nomadic warrior tribes such as the Yavapai,

Apache and Mohave, and the stubborn pueblo-dwelling Hopi still refused to bow to the zealous padres.

The greatest of the Franciscan padres was Father Francisco Tomas Garcés. Like Kino, he was a tireless worker and had much success among the natives. He was able to persuade the commandant at Tubac, Capt. Juan Bautista de Anza, to lead an exploratory expedition to open a land route to the new colonies in upper California. Between 1774 and 1776, Anza not only opened a road but established the colony of San Francisco as well.

The presidio was moved from Tubac to Tucson in 1775, leading to the founding of Arizona's most historic city. During this time Garcés had opened missions among the Yumas at the strategic river crossing at the junction of the Gila and Colorado rivers. Arrogant and cruel treatment of the natives by Spanish soldiers led to a revolt in 1781, which not only closed the roads to California but caused the death of Father Garcés.

Aggressive military campaigns and a program offering free rations brought about a tenuous peace with the Apaches in the late 1780s. The so-called "golden years" in Arizona followed. Mines were opened, great land grant ranches flourished and the beautiful missions of San Xavier del Bac and San Jose de Tumacacori were constructed. But the times were too peaceful to last. The Republic of Mexico was born in the early 1820s and the old treaty with the Apaches was not honored. By the 1830s, warriors ravaged the land once more. Missions, ranches and mines were abandoned and southern Arizona, with the exception of Tucson, was pretty much controlled by the Apaches.

The first Anglo-American entry into Arizona was in late 1824 when parties of mountain men operating out of Santa Fe and Taos trapped for beaver along the Gila River and its tributaries. A young adventurer named James Ohio Pattie narrated his hair-raising experiences a few years later, giving the folks in the "States" their first written account of wild and wooly Arizona. During the next few years, well-known trappers such as Bill Williams, Ewing Young, Kit Carson, Antoine Leroux, Michel Robidoux, Pauline Weaver and Joe Walker ventured into the unexplored valleys and mountains of Arizona.

When the Mexican War broke out in 1846, Col. Stephen Watts Kearny was appointed head of the Army of the West and ordered to take New Mexico, then proceed to California. Kearny and one hundred dragoons followed the Gila River to the Yuma Crossing in late 1846. Accompanying Kearny was Capt. William Emory of the Army Corps of Topographical Engineers. Emory, a brilliant cartographer and scientist, provided the U.S. government with its first scientific look at the geography, geology, flora and fauna of Arizona.

The Mormon Battalion, assigned to the Army of the West, was charged with building a wagon road from New Mexico to the California coast.

The war ended in 1848 with the signing of the Treaty of Guadalupe Hidalgo. The Mexican Republic lost nearly half her territory to the United States, including California, Arizona, New Mexico, Nevada, Utah and Colorado. Unfortunately the southern boundary line in Arizona was at the Gila River, and it wasn't possible to construct a railroad or highway through the rough mountains north of the river. James Gadsden was sent to Mexico City in 1853 to negotiate the purchase of more land. After several proposals, some of which would have provided Arizona with a sea coast on the Gulf of California, a deal was struck that came to be called the Gadsden Purchase. The southern boundary of Arizona was established at its present location, increasing its size by 29,670 square miles.

In 1850 the Territory of New Mexico was created, including the land that comprises today's Arizona. The period was marked by numerous surveys by the Army Corps of Topographical Engineers along the 32nd and 35th parallels for the construction of two transcontinental railroad lines. The most colorful of these expeditions occurred in 1857-58 when Lt. Edward F. "Ned" Beale experimented with using camels to haul goods across the arid lands.

Stagecoaches arrived in Arizona in 1857 when the San Antonio-San Diego Mail Line opened for business. The outfit was better-known as the "Jackass Mail" because during one part of the desert journey passengers were required to ride muleback.

The following year the leather-slung coaches of John Butterfield's Overland Mail began a spectacular 26-day run from Tipton, Missouri to San Francisco.

War broke out between the Army and the Chiricahua Apaches in 1861. It began when Lt. George Bascom accused Cochise, leader of the Chiricahuas, of kidnapping a white child. The army grabbed some Apaches as hostages and Cochise retaliated by seizing some employees at the stage station. After peace talks failed, Cochise killed his hostages and the soldiers hanged their Apache captives. The Bascom Affair coincided with the outbreak of the Civil War, and when federal troops were withdrawn the Apaches turned their wrath upon the settlers and miners in southern Arizona. During the next few years the Apaches kept the whites pretty much under siege at Tucson. Only the bravest dared travel through Apacheria to the settlements of New Mexico.

In early 1862, a company of Confederates under the command of Capt. Sherod Hunter occupied Tucson. Meanwhile, a large Union force under Col. James Carleton was being gathered in California to drive the Confederates out of Arizona. Detachments of Union and Confederate forces clashed at Picacho Pass in mid-April, a skirmish known as the westernmost battle of the Civil War. As the Union army advanced on Tucson, the Confederates withdrew towards Texas. At the same time, another Union army defeated the Confederates at Glorieta Pass, New Mexico, ending forever the dream of a Confederate conquest of the Southwest.

In 1863 discoveries of rich gold placers in the Bradshaw Mountains opened the land north of the Gila River to new settlers. Because of the high cost of freighting goods into Arizona by wagon, the Army Corps of Engineers, in the early 1850s, explored the possibility of using steamboats on the Colorado River. The capricious waters of the sandy-red river were found to be navigable and soon durable paddlewheelers piloted by eagle-eyed captains were hauling freight and passengers to port cities such as Yuma, Ehrenberg and Hardyville. Before the arrival of the railroad in 1877 these riverboats were Arizona's main link with the outside world.

Because of rich mineral discoveries, the Territory of Arizona was created in 1863 from the western half of New Mexico and the capital was located at Prescott, near the site of the gold diggings. During the next few years the so-called

"Capital on Wheels" shifted between Prescott and Tucson, depending on political whims, until a permanent capital was located at Phoenix in 1889.

Soon after the gold discoveries in the Bradshaw Mountains, Jack Swilling, an ex-Confederate soldier and Indian fighter, cleared out some old Hohokam irrigation canals in the Salt River Valley, and the city of Phoenix rose from the ashes of the prehistoric Hohokam Indians. As the population of this new upstart community grew so did the need for more water. For a time, prospects for the future growth of Phoenix looked dim.

In the early 1900s farmers in the Salt River Valley put their lands up as collateral and with the passage of the Reclamation Act of 1902 the construction of Roosevelt Dam was begun. When the dam was completed in 1911, the future prosperity of the Salt River Valley was guaranteed for a long spell.

The discoveries of rich bodies of silver ore in the mineral belt that stretches diagonally northwest to southeast across Arizona brought thousands of newcomers and inspired large capital investments from the East. The greatest of these silver boom towns was Tombstone. Rough and ready towns like Tombstone attracted the wide gamut of frontier society. Wyatt Earp, Nellie Cashman, Ed Schieffelin, Doc Holliday, Big-Nosed Kate and a host of others have provided historians, pulp writers and the silver screen with an unlimited source of rich, colorful material.

By the time the silver mines were playing out, America had entered the age of electricity and the vast deposits of copper made Arizona the king of the industry by the early 1900s. The demand for copper during World War I brought unprecedented prosperity to the state and created 20th Century boom towns out of places such as Globe, Jerome, Bisbee, Morenci, Ajo and Clifton.

Gen. George Crook was ordered into Arizona in the early 1870s to bring an end to the Apache Wars. Cochise and his Chiricahuas had come to terms in 1872, allowing the general to direct his full attention to the nomadic Yavapai and Apaches in the mountain ranges of central Arizona. Crook was a tough, determined warrior, both respected and feared by the hostile tribes. Following a hard-riding, relentless winter campaign in 1872-73, most of the bands surrendered and were located on reservations at Fort Apache and San Carlos. Many Apaches became unhappy with the boredom associated with reservation life, missing the glorious raids into Mexico that had been a tradition. Others resented the agents and bureaucrats sent out by Washington to minister to their needs. This tense atmosphere enabled warriors like Geronimo and Nana to lead bands of renegades off the reservation. Usually they headed for the rugged mountains of Mexico's Sierra Madre.

In 1882 Gen. Crook was returned to Arizona to put an end to these outbreaks. During the next four years, Crook used his patented mule pack trains and trusty Apache scouts on rigorous campaigns into the Sierra Madre. Although Crook was usually successful in these expeditions, Washington was getting impatient. When the untrustworthy Geronimo broke an agreement and escaped into the mountains in the spring of 1886, Crook was replaced by Gen. Nelson Miles. Miles' troops were able to bring about the surrender of Geronimo in September, 1886. Geronimo and his people were loaded onto a train and shipped to Florida.

The combination of the mining booms and the Apache Wars created a demand for beef. Fortunately, Arizona was blessed with some of the best grazing lands in America. Ranching had its beginnings in the late 1700s during Spain's "golden years" and flourished briefly following the birth of the Mexican Republic. However, Apache raiders had driven most of the ranchers off their lands by the 1840s.

Americans began ranching in the 1850s but they, too, were driven from the area when the soldiers were withdrawn at the outbreak of the Civil War. Ranching in southern Arizona began to flourish once again in the 1870s when the Apaches were located on reservations. Texas cattle were driven in by the thousands to meet the market demands.

Northern Arizona remained a sleeping giant until the arrival of the Atlantic and Pacific (Santa Fe) Railroad in 1881. Within a short time the famous Aztec Land and Cattle Company ("Hashknife Outfit") was running 60,000 cattle on two million acres of northern Arizona rangeland.

In 1886, the five Babbitt brothers bought a small cow outfit and named it the CO Bar for their hometown, Cincinnati, Ohio. Soon after entering the cattle business, the Babbitts wisely diversified into a variety of enterprises including trading posts and mercantile stores. This enabled the company to survive the hard times.

The eternal nemeses of all cattlemen — rustlers, droughts and bad markets — made the business marginal at best. The nature of the business soon demanded that cattlemen fence their lands, provide permanent water supplies and improve the breed. The era of the open range cowboy, the heyday of America's most enduring legend, was drawing to a close.

The arrival of the railroads in the 1880s brought about the greatest transformation in Arizona's economy during the 19th Century. Railroads hauled in merchandise and people and hauled out ore and cattle to the eastern markets and California.

In August, 1883 the Atlantic and Pacific reached Needles, California, completing the transcontinental line across northern Arizona.

A spur line linked Phoenix with the Southern Pacific main line at Maricopa in 1887. Phoenix would not be on the main line until 1926. The Santa Fe bought out the Atlantic and Pacific and stretched its ribbons of steel south from Ashfork to Prescott in 1892. Three years later, the line from Prescott to Phoenix was completed. The capital city was now joined by rail with both the southern and northern main lines. Historians usually mark this date, 1895, as the end of the frontier in Arizona history.

The colorful litany of Arizona's picturesquely whimsical names is a reflection of the character of the early citizens. A card game inspired the name of Show Low. When two ranchers decided the ranges were too crowded, they played cards to see who would move. Low card was the winner. "If you can show low, you win," said one. "Show low it is," replied the other as he drew the deuce of clubs, and Show Low it was. Show Low's main street, incidentally, is called Deuce of Clubs. When the entire populace in a Mogollon Rim settlement got lice, they just naturally decided to name the place Lousy Gulch. A treacherous-looking outcropping of rock hovering above a southern Arizona mining camp compelled the locals to proudly proclaim the name of their town to be Total Wreck. When folks started a community in a forlorn area in the desert east of Ajo, travelers kept asking, "Why would you want to live here?" Residents shortened it to Why.

In 1910 surveyors in Pima County mistook another mountain for Rincon Peak. When the mistaken identity was pointed out they simply named it Wrong Mountain. Prescott might have been named Gimletville and Phoenix, Pumpkinville. Fortunately, wiser heads prevailed. Tucson is a corruption of a Tohono O'odham word describing the "dark base at the foot of a mountain." The word, "Chuk-Shon," when pronounced by the Spanish came out more easily "Tucson." And that's what it became.

A hangover led to at least one silver strike. One day back in 1876 Charlie McMillan went on a wild binge in Globe. His partner, Dore Harris, didn't indulge, so the next day he gathered up Charlie and loaded him onto his trusty mule and they rode out prospecting. They hadn't traveled far when Charlie climbed down, claiming he was too hung over to go any farther. So, while Charlie slumbered, Dore took his pick and started hacking away at a nearby outcropping. Sure enough, he uncovered a rich vein of silver. Overnight a boom town materialized which was called, appropriately enough, "McMillanville," and before the ore was exhausted, over a million dollars worth of silver was taken out. McMillan became known as the "man with the million dollar hangover."

There are more fascinating names: Skull Valley, Wikieup, Dos Cabezas, Bullhead City, Sombrero Butte, Bumble Bee, Tombstone and Gunsight, to name a few. Each has a story to tell.

Arizona's people constitute a definitely pluralistic society. For hundreds of years the Navajo have occupied the steep-sided canyons, sandstone buttes and pillars that rise above the high desert plain in the vast Four Corners country. Nearby, the ancient Hopi cluster in their villages which cling precariously to the wind-swept mesas. They claim ancestry to the prehistoric cliff-dwelling Anasazi. The rugged mountains of east-central Arizona are the ancestral home of the Apaches. These determined peoples fought a long and successful war with the Spanish and Mexicans before the last elements surrendered to the U.S. Army a century ago.

The Havasupai have the distinction of being the only native peoples living in the Grand Canyon. The only way into their remote village, except by helicopter, is on foot or horseback. The river valleys are still home to the Quechan, Mohave and Pima peoples, while the Tohono O'odham (Papago) reside in the desert country near the Mexican border.

Arizona's Indians, more than any other, have been able to maintain close ties to their cultural heritage. Many reservations are located amidst incredible scenic beauty. Some are atop valuable natural resources, or have vast claims to the state's most precious commodity, water. Others occupy real estate worth millions of dollars. A perplexing problem facing tribal leaders today is finding proper solutions that would allow their people to partake of the advantages and amenities non-Indians enjoy without sacrificing their rich cultural heritage in the process.

The Hispanic people and their rich culture are an important part of Arizona's society. Although some trace their ancestry back to the 1850s, most arrived from Mexico in this century. Large numbers immigrated to the mining towns during the copper boom of World War I. Even more have come in recent years seeking jobs. Many still retain close cultural ties with Mexico. Unlike other immigrants who left Europe and settled in America, Hispanics have no oceans or other barriers keeping them from periodic return visits to their homeland. Thus, many keep their language and, like the Indians, stubbornly refuse to become assimilated in a melting pot.

Arizona's people are better described as a mulligan stew rather than a melting pot, and that is how it should be. This is a region with its own distinctive character, much the same as the Deep South, Appalachia or New England.

Arizona's land, like its people, is one of startling contrasts. All climatic life zones, from dry-tropical to arctic-alpine, are found within its borders. A 20-minute drive from Tucson, up the Mount Lemmon highway, passes from Sonoran Desert to Canadian-Alpine. Annual rainfall amounts vary from 3.4 inches at Yuma to nearly 25 inches at McNary in the White Mountains. It's not unusual for two Arizona communities to record the nation's high and low temperatures on the same day.

The elements—incessant wind, long droughts and searing heat—not to mention intractable Apaches, gunslingers and an immoral majority of unchurched, unmarried, and unwashed citizens, gave Arizona a notorious reputation that spread far and wide. Eastern journalists and writers of pulp westerns fed wide-eyed readers a steady diet of wild and wooly Arizona, contributing to its reputation as a forbidding place inhabited by rattlesnakes, scorpions, cactus, desperados and Apaches.

Negative first impressions by visiting dignitaries added to its reputation as the Devil's playground. When Gen. William Tecumseh Sherman paid a summertime visit in 1880, one of Phoenix's early-day promoters made the mistake of asking the straight-talking general what he thought of the place. "Too damn hot and dry," Sherman declared. "All she needs," the promoter said soothingly, "is less heat, more water and a few good citizens." "Huh," Sherman replied gruffly, "that's all hell needs."

Kit Carson, the legendary mountain man who lived in and loved the outdoors, once testified before Congress that parts of Arizona were so poor that a wolf would starve to death there. Few people had reason to seriously doubt the satirical words of Mark Twain when he said, "the temperature remains at a constant 120 degrees in the shade, except when it varies and goes higher." *Ditat Deus is* our state motto and means "God Enriches." It's been suggested we adopt as our alternate, "But it's a dry heat."

Arizona's nearly 114,000 square miles of land ranks it as the nation's sixth largest state. The population, about 5.1 million, places it 20th largest. About 75 percent of the people live in either Tucson or the Greater Phoenix area. Flagstaff, Yuma, Prescott, Kingman, and Sierra Vista claim most of the rest. Dozens of other communities dot the state but the majority of the people are settled in the above-mentioned areas, leaving vast reaches of wide open spaces that belong to everybody and nobody. So for all its out-of-doors ambience, Arizona is actually an urban state.

Arizona's history is marked by five milestones, all of which played a major part in the state's unprecedented growth and prosperity. The first was the discovery of vast mineral riches: gold, silver and copper. From the day that first prospector's pick turned over pay dirt during the 1850s to the present, mining has been an integral part of the state's economy. The second was the arrival of the railroads in the 1880s. The steel rails opened up the heart of Arizona for commerce and transportation. By 1895 every major community was linked by rail. The third milestone was the completion of Roosevelt Dam in 1911. With the guarantee of a water supply from the 13,000-square-mile watershed above the Salt River Valley, the future growth and prosperity of the area was assured. The fourth was the advent of the evaporative cooler, followed a few years later by air conditioning. The final milestone was World War II and the high technology that resulted from that war. During the early 1940s, thousands of soldiers trained under the clear Arizona skies and afterwards came back to live.

Industry saw advantages in relocating in Arizona: a large labor supply, mild climate and an opportunity to grow with the state. More people came, drawn by the lifestyle. Tourism blossomed into a multi-billion dollar industry, second only to manufacturing in dollars and number one in jobs. Phoenix grew from a city of sixty thousand in 1940 to more than 1.3 million in 2000. Sleepy little Scottsdale had some 400 residents at the outset of World War II; by 2000 its population had risen to more than 200,000.

The population boom has created prosperity but the price has been high. Like most major metropolitan areas, Phoenix has serious transportation and air pollution problems. More subtle, however, is the threat to Arizona's unique history and culture. Since man first walked upon this earth, migrations by larger, more dominant groups have enveloped other cultures. And the danger of that happening in Arizona is real. Much of what was old Arizona has already been "plowed under."

Former *Arizona Republic* publisher Pat Murphy pretty well summed it up when he noted:

> One of the greatest weaknesses in a state such as Arizona, where the growing population increasingly is made up of people with roots elsewhere, is that it tends to be a gathering place for

strangers with not much sense of tradition or historic perspective on their new home.

Without those values, newcomers tend to lack the spirit to preserve, to protect and to perpetuate qualities that attracted them here in the first place.

1

BEFORE THE TIME OF MAN

Arizona's Unique Geography, Flora-Fauna and Geology

Arizona's Pulitzer Prize-winning cartoonist Reg Manning once said, "If you were a giant and wanted to eat the state of Arizona, you would find that roughly it would take three large and widely different mouthfuls." Another observer was more succinct: "If ya don't like what ya see, keep on drivin'. In ten minutes it'll be totally different."

This mythical meal Manning wrote about begins in the northeast at the Four Corners (the only point in the United States where four states meet.) The first big bite would take in the Painted Desert, Canyon de Chelly and the Navajo and Hopi reservations. Next, you'd sink your teeth into the forest zone and get your fill of fiber and "greens," but don't choke on nature's grandest architectural masterpiece, the Grand Canyon. The last bite would be the desert, from Hoover Dam through the cactus belt, arcing across to the New Mexico border.

Arizona has three physiographic zones, and many contrasts within these zones. For example, the desert region of the western and southern part has islands of mountains including the Chiricahua, Pinal, Galiuro, Santa Catalina, Santa Rita and Pinaleno ranges. Mount Graham in the Pinalenos reaches 10,717 feet in elevation. In the spectacular, wind-eroded sandstone buttes, mesas and spires of the northeast zone one can find lush forests and cool mountain streams in the Chuska Mountains north of Canyon de Chelly. And the high, wide and lonesome Arizona Strip, along with the Grand Canyon, contrasts spectacularly with the largest stand of ponderosa pine in the world that makes up most of the forest zone. The three zones are roughly equal in size. The plateau zone is the largest, covering 42 percent of the state, followed by the desert with 30 percent and the mountain with 28 percent. The drainage in this vast area eventually winds its way in a southwesterly direction and ends up in the Gulf of California. Another contrast in this land of anomalies and tamales: four rivers, the Santa Cruz, San Pedro, San Simon and Little Colorado, flow northward.

The plateau zone, a giant uplifted land mass that extends into Utah, Colorado and New Mexico, includes the Arizona Strip, Grand Canyon, San Francisco Mountains, the Painted Desert, Canyon de Chelly, Black Mesa, Kaibab Plateau and Monument Valley. It is, without a doubt, the most spectacular geographic collection of scenic beauty found anywhere in the world.

The mountain zone, which is in reality a transition, makes a diagonal "S" across the state, widening as it nears the Mexican border. Some 30 different mountain ranges dapple the desert plains. Most of these are in the 4,000 to 6,000 foot range in elevation and are separated by broad valleys creating "biological islands" which isolate cool climate plants and animals.

The desert zone includes Arizona's famed cactus country and consists of broad, arid valleys flanked by stark mountains and marked by searing heat. Most of the critters (including many humans) remain nocturnal, coming out only after the sun goes down. Thanks to irrigation canals and reservoirs, civilization flourishes. About 90 percent of Arizona's population resides in the desert country.

There are deserts, and then there are deserts. Some are uncomfortably hot and others are bone-chilling cold. They share one common characteristic: they're all dry. Evaporation rates are at least twice as high as precipitation rates. A desert is usually classified as an area with less than ten inches of rainfall a year.

Historically, deserts have suffered from a case of bad public relations. Many saw them as mysterious, uninhabit-

able regions sprawling beneath a mercilous sun where everything either stabs, stings, sticks or stinks. They call deserts
fearsome wastelands, inhospitable and uninhabitable. Early
explorers accused them of savagery. Webster's dictionary
perpetuates the myth, using words and phrases such as "an
arid region lacking moisture to support vegetation; forsaken;
a region left unoccupied; waste; barren." But that has all
changed. Today, tourists tour them, scientists study them,
romantics romanticize about them. Old images aside, in the
Sonoran Desert of Arizona the land is literally teeming with
plant and animal life.

So what's so special about the Sonoran Desert? Well, for
openers, it represents the classic image of the American desert
— a realm of wonderous diversity — a sanctuary filled with the
wonder of wild things. Here in this most prolific of deserts is
found the most extensive variety of desert flora and fauna in
the world. This hard, arid land has molded life into some of the
most unusual forms on earth. It has given us a group of plants
and animals which thrive in this climate and find the desert
neither hostile nor formidable but, rather, the norm — their
home. And most important, those who have come to terms
with it find the desert a warm, friendly place.

This sandy soil, punctuated with flora bearing melodious
Spanish names like ocotillo, agave, palo verde, yucca and
saguaro, is a place where man is learning to live in harmony
with the land. In 1901, naturalist John C. Van Dyke wrote:
"The deserts should never be reclaimed; they are the breathing
spaces of the West and should be preserved forever."

Ecology, the study of plants and animals and their relationship with the environment, was developed in Arizona by
Clinton Hart Merriam in the 1890s. He proposed a theory of
life zones based on the effect of temperature on plants and
animals at different elevations. Merriam found that a change
in elevation of 1,000 feet was the same as traveling 300 to 500
miles in north-south latitude. For example, a trip from Yuma
to the top of the San Francisco Peaks would take one through
all seven life zones (dry-tropical to arctic-alpine). Desert land
accounts for 42 percent of the state and woodland-forests
cover a third. The rest is grassland. Some 3,500 species of
plants are found in Arizona's biotic communities. The forest

areas include tall trees, such as the lofty ponderosa pine, Douglas fir and spruce. The woodland community includes pinyon-juniper, scrubby chaparral such as manzanita, mountain mahogany and scrub oak. The grasslands of northern Arizona contain short grasses such as grama and bluestem while in the Lower Sonoran Life Zone, grama, curly mesquite and big galleta are abundant. Obviously, there is overlapping and life zones include more than one biotic community. The desert community includes the high desert in northern Arizona, dominated by several species of sagebrush, and the Sonoran Desert, best-known for the stately saguaro which takes nearly 200 years to reach full stature and grows to a height of 50 feet. Lesser known are the palo verde trees, prickly pear, mesquite, yucca and several species of cholla including the notorious "jumping cactus." The contrasts in land, climate, temperature and people make life possible for a wide range of plants and animals. Sixty percent of all types of wild life found in North America are found in Arizona, including ten species of big game: bear, elk (wapiti), antelope (pronghorn), big horn sheep, bison, turkey, mountain lion, mule and white tail deer and javelina.

Geographically, Arizona is in a unique location. It is a biotic extension of the Chihuahua and Sonoran deserts of Mexico, the Mojave Desert, Great Basin, Rocky Mountains, Great Plains, Mississippi Valley, Sierra Madre and Sierra Nevada. It's no wonder people come from all over the world to study this land and its people.

This arid land is not always dry. During the late 1970s and early 1980s, Arizona was hit with a series of so-called 100-year floods that wiped out several bridges in the Salt River Valley and inspired the following axiom: "If a 100-year flood happens once ever 100 years, then a 500-year flood is five 100-year floods in the same year."

Arizona's rainfall comes mainly in two seasons and from two directions. During the months of December, January and February storm systems moving eastward from the Pacific Ocean dip down and drop gentle rains on the state. These sometimes last several days. The violent monsoon season arrives in mid-July and lasts until mid-September. These storms are caused by a high pressure system centered in the

Four Corners area. Moving clockwise, the system pulls moisture up from the Gulf of Mexico. The warm desert air lifts and collides with cooler, moist air, providing brief but heavy rainfall. The spectacular display of lightning generated by these storms is something to behold. Later in the summer a hot low in Baja California can shift moisture from west coast tropical depressions into the state. These storms are the most devastating we have. Annual rainfall averages range from 3.4 inches in Yuma to nearly 25 inches in the White Mountains. Phoenix has an annual rainfall of 7.7 inches.

Scientists claim the age of the earth to be at least 4.5 billion years, long enough to make even the largest human ego seem insignificant. To give some perspective to Arizona's geological biography, let's compress it into a single year. From January to mid-August the earth evolved from its gaseous origins to a large blue-green algae in the ocean. By mid-August most of the rocks in the Grand Canyon fused. Fish swam in November and dinosaurs ruled the world in mid-December. Humans didn't walk the earth until the final 19 hours of the last day of December.

Scientists have classified major "ages." *Precambrian,* prior to 550 million years ago; *Paleozoic,* 550 to 200 million years ago; *Mesozoic,* 200 to 70 million years ago; and *Cenozoic,* the last 70 million years. Each age also has epochs and periods.

Water covered Arizona during much of the *Precambrian Age* but there was some uplifting that caused mountains to form. The area flattened out during the *Paleozoic Age.* Seas were formed. Interestingly, the Yuma area was in the high country and not covered by water. The sediment left during this period eventually gave us such natural masterpieces as Canyon de Chelly and Oak Creek Canyon. Little amphibians crawled up on shore and became the ancestors of the dinosaurs and other reptiles which were characteristic of the next age, the *Mesozoic,* "middle age," sometimes called the "Age of Reptiles."

Early in the *Mesozoic Age* the world land mass was locked into one supercontinent instead of the present seven. At the time, Arizona was located near the equator.

The seas that developed during the *Mesozoic Age* washed

in large trees from other areas and deposited them beneath tons of silt. Since the trees couldn't decay naturally, minerals in the water oozed into the woodcells and hardened. Millions of years later, the area uplifted from 3,000 feet below sea level to more than 5,000 feet above it and left us with a forest of colorful petrified logs.

This uplifting is also partially responsible for our dry climate today. As the mountain ranges of California rose, they blocked the clouds, causing them to dump their precious rainfall along the coast.

During the *Mesozoic Age* large reptiles roamed the area called the "Dinosaur Belt," extending from today's Kingman to the New Mexico line. Near Tuba City fossilized tracks of dinosaurs can be seen. Scientists disagree as to the reasons for the demise of these great beasts about 65 million years ago. Some claim a meteor collision created a huge cloud of debris that blocked out the sun for months or even years. The climate cooling resulted in the death of many types of plant and animal life. Others say an intense period of volcanic activity ejected sun-filtering dust into the atmosphere creating the same phenomenon as the meteor collision. Another group contends natural changes in the climate brought about their extinction. The great shifting and lifting of the earth's crust during the *Mesozoic Age* created faults or cracks in areas like Bisbee and Jerome, depositing gold, silver and copper. The northeastern quarter of the state uplifted as much as 2,000 feet, creating the Mogollon Rim. This raw edge of rock and faulted displacement stretches some 200 miles diagonally across the state. The Rim acts as a formidable barrier separating the Colorado Plateau from the mountain zone.

During the most recent age, the *Cenozoic,* Arizona began to take its present shape. In this time Arizona has undergone many changes. Volcanos erupted, creating mountains that gradually wore away. Dry lands became deep seas which eventually ebbed, leaving thousands of feet of many-hued sediment. Wind and water erosion etched out the softer areas and sculpted such awesome spires as those in Monument Valley. Earthquakes shook the land, buckling and cracking the surface.

Many of the state's highest mountains were the result of

molten rock cast upward from the subterranean depths of the earth. The highest and most awesome are the San Francisco Mountains near Flagstaff. Six prominent peaks form a horse-shoe towering over a broad glacier-carved valley descending to the northeast. The highest is Humphreys at 12,633 feet above sea level, followed by Agassiz, Fremont, Doyle, Reese and Abineau.

These lofty mountains once rose to heights of some 15,000 feet before nature began wearing them down to their present size. Resplendent with aspen, conifers and lush grasses, along with the ancient and gnarled bristle cone pine, they are snow-capped a good part of the year. Throughout history the San Francisco Peaks have served as beacons for travelers crossing northern Arizona. Journalists crossing in wagons and on horseback reported seeing them for days as they made their way across the pristine wilderness. Both the Hopi and Navajo regard them as sacred.places and that is how it should be.

Arizona's spectacular Grand Canyon presents geologists with a layer-by-layer record, a vertical mile of planetary history. In the inner gorge of this amphitheater of the gods lie some of the oldest rocks known to man. In the canyon one can see sandstones formed from ancient desert sand dunes. Deep in the gorge are the remains of mountain ranges that reigned majestically over this land more than two billion years ago.

Some 20 million years ago a great river, which we call the Colorado, drained the western slopes of the Rockies and meandered down through the Four Corners, then picked up the channel of the Little Colorado River valley and flowed southeasterly toward the Rio Grande. Either a lava flow or an uplift dammed the river, forming a large lake that covered most of the Four Corners region. Meanwhile an ancient river cut its way eastward through the Kaibab Plateau. In time, the river changed its course and began twisting and winding its way towards the Gulf of California. This resurgent stream has spent the last nine million years sculpting (along with some tremendous uplifting of the land) the Grand Canyon as we know it today. The timeless chasm, has been described many ways by those awed by its size and splendor. But a cowboy was most succinct. "That'd be a hell 'ov a place to lose a cow," he observed matter-of-factly.

2

PREHISTORIC ARIZONA

The monsoons struck with a vengeance during the late summer months of 1951. The rains that fell in the Huachuca Mountains of southern Arizona sent water cascading down the usually dry arroyos toward the tiny San Pedro River, sweeping everything in its path. After the waters subsided, Ed Lehner, a local rancher and amateur archaeologist, made an incredible discovery. In an arroyo behind his house, the rushing waters had washed away the banks, exposing the long-buried bones of prehistoric animals dating back thousands of years.

Lehner called in the experts from the Arizona State Museum, in Tucson, who uncovered the remains of nine elephants. Along with these beasts the archaeologists dug up the bones of a small, primitive horse, a bison and a pig-like animal called a tapir. Ashes from remains of a cookfire dated the site to eleven thousand years ago.

Other remains located at nearby Naco included a large mammoth with eight stone spear points in its head and rib cage.

The so-called Paleo Indians or First Americans that hunted the large animals probably arrived in Arizona after a long journey that began in Asia about 12,000 years ago. After the last great glacier began to recede, hunters crossed a land bridge in the Bering Strait and eventually drifted into what was then a cooler and wetter Arizona. A recent study claims there were only three distinct waves of migrations instead of the two hundred or so as formerly believed. The first migration came about 12,000 years ago; its people are the ancestors of 90 percent of today's Indians. The second was 6,000 years ago and included the Athabascan-speaking Apaches and Navajos. They drifted down from the northern plains, arriving in the Southwest about A.D. 1100. Sometime around A.D. 1400 the two groups split. The third migration came about 4,000 years ago and included the Eskimos and Aleuts.

Eleven thousand years ago, huge mammoths and mastadons standing 13 feet high at the shoulders, along with giant beavers, grizzly bears, camels, horses and large bisons, inhabited the lush, green valleys of southern Arizona. Prehistoric big game hunters set up kill sites near watering holes. Using stone knives, they charged the beast and cut the tendons on the legs so the animal couldn't escape, then killed it with spears. The economy of the First Americans centered on hunting big animals, but they undoubtedly hunted small game and gathered plant food. They were excellent stone workers as demonstrated by spearpoints found at kill sites. A characteristic of these points was a channel on each side that extended to the base. These were fastened to a light spear and thrown with an *atlatl* — a spear-launcher that extended the throwing arm about a foot and added leverage. The bow and arrow didn't arrive in Arizona until about the time of Christ.

As noted earlier, scientists still debate the reasons for the demise of these great animals. The likely reason is a change in the climate. As the region became more arid, these animals simply didn't adjust and became extinct. Also, there's no doubt the success of the hunters did much to bring about their demise.

The big game animals began to die off about 6,000 B.C. and a Desert culture slowly evolved from the First Americans. These people were more harmonious with their environment than were their predecessors, but they still hunted big game. They quit using fluted spear points and created different types for hunting small game such as rabbits and birds. They were more sedentary, gathering berries, seeds, nuts and grains then grinding them in a stone *metate* so they could be easily digested. They maintained migratory patterns but returned to the same sites. About 2,000 B.C. corn, or maize, was introduced from Mexico. Thus, these early farmers had learned, in a small way, to control their environment. These desert people were the link between the ancient elephant hunters and the prehistoric Anasazi, Patayan, Mogollon, Salado, Sinagua and Hohokam. Because many of their sites have been located in Cochise County, we call these desert dwellers the Cochise People. In recent years some people have criticized the name Anasazi because Ana means "war" in Navajo and because Anasazi can also be defined "Alien Ancient Ones," both of which have negative connotations. Many people prefer the term "Ancestral Pueblo" for Anasazi. The Hopi use *Hisatsinom*, meaning "Person of the Remote Past of Ancient Time." That being said and recognized, this book will use the more familiar term, Anasazi.

The Anasazi arrived in the Four Corners area about 200 B.C. It's possible they evolved from the Desert culture. During this early period they were called Basketmakers because of the fine storage baskets made from yucca fibers. They began to practice agriculture and pottery making about A.D. 500. They cultivated corn, beans and squash, which enabled them to settle in one location. They used an atlatl for hunting until about A.D. 700 when the bow and arrow became the dominant weapon. About this time they gave up their caves and moved into pit houses—cone-shaped, one-room structures, sunk three to five feet in the ground. In time, these houses gave way to apartment-type dwellings with common walls that we call pueblos. Some were quite large. Pueblo Bonito, in Chaco Canyon, New Mexico was five stories high, had over 800 rooms and a peak population of more than a thousand.

Religious services were conducted in a circular, ceremonial chamber called a kiva. Since the Anasazi depended on adequate rainfall to sustain their crops, most of the ceremonies were devoted to bringing rain. After the Anasazi settled down they began making pottery for cooking and storage instead of the baskets used by nomadic peoples. The style is usually white or grey with black artwork. Sometime around A.D. 1050 a dramatic change took place among the Anasazi. For reasons that remain open to speculation they moved to the tops of mesas and into the cliffs. They appear to have been trying to blend into the terrain. Were they trying to protect or hide their villages from some predator tribe?

Impressive examples of these cliff dwellings can be seen today at Navajo National Monument. Betatakin ("ledge house") can be seen from the monument. It had 200 rooms. Keet Seel ("broken pieces of pottery") dating back to A.D. 950 is the largest with 350 rooms and is one of the best preserved in the Southwest.

Archaeologists disagree over what brought about the hasty abandonment of these masonry dwellings during the last years of the 13th Century. A 23-year drought from A.D. 1276 to 1299 was certainly catastrophic. There is much evidence to indicate that the primitive farming practices mined out the soil and the need for firewood stripped the area of trees. Others claim, however, that warfare—either from within the Anasazi culture or from nomadic invaders— caused their downfall. They argue that watch towers in remote fortress-like dwellings that can only be entered by ladders support that thesis. Small T-shaped doors where intruders had to bend over to enter (and be easily clubbed) also indicated the Anasazi were threatened. Perhaps it was a combination of war-like invaders and a culture already in turmoil that caused them to abandon their pueblos in such haste.

The baffling question is this: Why would a people suddenly abandon these magnificent dwellings seemingly at the peak of their culture?

Some believe part of the Anasazi culture migrated to the Rio Grande and are the Pueblo Indians of New Mexico; and that the Kayenta Anasazi of Keet Seel and Betatakin, along with the cliff dwellers of Canyon de Chelly, moved to the Hopi mesas.

The Mogollon culture of eastern Arizona and southwest New Mexico has been overshadowed by the Anasazi and Hohokam. A mountain people, they adjusted well to their environment, living on wild game, nuts, roots, berries and seeds.

Although they did grow a high grade of corn, imported from Mexico, they didn't work hard at being farmers. Their polished brown and red pottery was the first in Arizona. The Mogollon evolved out of the Cochise culture and came into their own about 300 B.C. Their homes were usually one-room pit houses constructed of sticks, logs and branches covered with mud. They were a village people, different from the Anasazi in that the homes were in single family units widely

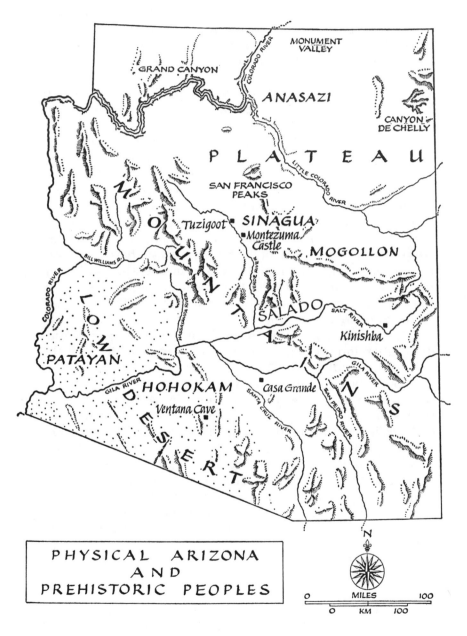

MONUMENT VALLEY

GRAND CANYON

ANASAZI

CANYON DE CHELLY

P L A T E A U

LITTLE COLORADO RIVER

SAN FRANCISCO PEAKS

Tuzigoot ■ SINAGUA

■ Montezuma Castle

MOGOLLON

M O U N T A I N S

BILL WILLIAMS R.

COLORADO RIVER

VERDE RIVER

SALADO

SALT RIVER

Kinishba ■

L O W

PATAYAN

HASSAYAMPA RIVER

GILA RIVER

HOHOKAM

Casa Grande ■

Ventana Cave ■

GILA RIVER

SAN PEDRO RIVER

SANTA CRUZ RIVER

D E S E R T

PHYSICAL ARIZONA
AND
PREHISTORIC PEOPLES

N

MILES

0   100

0   KM   100

spread along a ridge overlooking their fields. Some village sites reveal a continued existence for more than a thousand years.

By about A.D. 1100, the influence of the Anasazi caused the Mogollon to begin using masonry construction. But by and large they preferred single family units to Anasazi "condo-style." The Mogollon also borrowed cotton for weaving cloth from the Hohokam. Around A.D. 1000 their pottery changed dramatically with surrealistic designs and animal scenes along with scenes from their daily life.

The decline of the Mogollon culture came in the late 1200's, about the same as that of the Anasazi and Hohokam, and it can be attributed to invaders or drought or both. It is believed they migrated to the Casas Grandes area in Chihuahua, Mexico and left no descendants in Arizona.

The Hohokam are the "first Phoenicians." One day back in 1867 a big strapping, energetic man named Jack Swilling was riding across the Salt River Valley bound for the mining camps in the Bradshaw Mountains. He gazed out across the sprawling Salt River at the decayed mud ruins of the ancient civilization that once dwelled here. Scanning the natural contours of the land, he noticed the remains of an intricate system of canals and irrigation ditches. It was plain to see the land had once supported a large population. The canals and ditches extended out several miles from both sides of the river. He declared that if Indians had successfully farmed this valley it could be done again. Swilling wasn't the first to see the remnants of the prehistoric dwellers and it's unlikely he spent much time pondering the wherefores and whys of this mysterious civilization. The past had inspired a vision but Swilling was more interested in the present — and the future. Others would come later and attempt to sort out these traces from the past.

Eventually, scientists came to attempt to unlock the mysteries of those prehistoric "Master Farmers" — the ones we now call the Hohokam.

In January, 1888, the famous archaeologist Frank Hamilton Cushing arrived in the Salt River Valley. Cushing had been working among the Zuni Indians in the Four Corners region, when heavy snows forced him to steer further south. His wagon broke down in Phoenix and while awaiting repairs decided to explore the prehistoric ruins along the Salt and Gila rivers. Thus began the first organized study of archaeology in this part of Arizona. Since Cushing's day, other sleuths of time, especially the late Dr. Emil Haury, dean of Arizona archaeologists, have worked tirelessly to unlock the mysteries of that ancient civilization we call the Hohokam.

"How could a primitive people," archaeologists ask, "carve out an existence, develop a society and build monumental structures in such a harsh environment?"

Only the most durable artifacts survived, a few tantalizing clues, limiting the scope of our knowledge considerably. The Hohokam left no written record so we don't know how they governed, what they called themselves, the language they spoke, or what they thought. They were not as advanced as the Aztecs or Mayans but were likely the most progressive peoples in what is today's United States. Unfortunately, only a fractional amount of their culture has been found and recorded.

Who were these remarkable people who, during their peak, numbered some 20,000 to 60,000 in the Salt River and Gila river valleys before going into a mysterious rapid decline?

Most scientists believe the Hohokam arrived in Arizona from Mexico around 300 B.C. Apparently they arrived with a well-developed culture and had an immediate influence on the area and the people already living there. In time, their influence would be felt as far west as the Colorado River, east to New Mexico and north to the Flagstaff area. The 13,000-square-mile watershed above the Salt River provided a reliable water supply. During normal years the river was probably a hundred feet wide and five to six feet deep. The banks were held in check by tall stands of willow and cottonwood trees.

Digging by hand without beasts of burden (the Spanish didn't introduce oxen, horses or mules until the 16th century) they engineered the largest prehistoric irrigation project in North America. Some of these canals were 30 to 40 feet wide and 15 feet deep. For construction tools they used digging sticks and stone hoes. Large woven baskets were used to haul dirt. It's been estimated that 50 men and women could dig about 3 feet a day. More than 250 miles of gravity-fed canals were in the Salt River Valley alone. Twentieth Century engineers have marveled at the masterfully designed canals.

During construction of today's Grand Canal, surveyors followed a prehistoric ditch and couldn't improve on the grade. Other modern-day canals also followed the grade set centuries ago by prehistoric engineers using primitive instruments.

Their main crops were corn, beans, squash, tobacco and cotton. They introduced the latter into today's United States and produced fabric textiles. Unfortunately, few examples have withstood the passage of time.

The Hohokam lived in pit houses during most of their 1700-year existence. Those dwellings were submerged a foot or two below ground level, probably for coolness in the summer or warmth in the winter. The walls and roofs were constructed of logs and brush, then chinked with mud. Outdoor brush ramadas were used for corn grinding, cooking and artistry.

The ability of the Hohokam to grow abundant crops and store huge amounts of food gave them extra time for relaxation. While other, less productive prehistoric people had to scratch out a living, these industrious aborigines designed and built athletic facilities for spectator sports. A rectangular ball park was sunk about five feet into the ground and a game was played with a rubber ball and a grass hoop fastened on each side. Centuries later the Spanish found Indians in Mexico playing the same game. To make a score a player had to put the ball through the ring without using his hands. The game was low-scoring and much of the contest was devoted to wrestling and fisticuffs. When the game ended the winner got possession of the loser's clothes and jewelry — if he could catch him.

Plenty of leisure time also allowed the Hohokam to engage in arts and crafts. They developed a highly sophisticated, multi-designed clay pottery believed by many to be the best ceramic work done in Arizona at the time. Pottery is the most durable art form from the era of the Hohokam and truly demonstrates the skill of these craftsmen-artists. Ceramics of characteristic red-on-buff color were both decorative and functional. They included jars, bowls, pitchers, canteens, dippers and effigies, and ranged in size from miniatures to huge jars that could hold more than 25 gallons. The decorations displayed delicate geometric and life form designs such as horned toads, deer, snakes, lizards, and people. Made from natural materials, the clay pottery was constructed by the paddle-and-anvil method and without the aid of a wheel. For knives, tools and other utensils, chert, obsidian and jasper were used. Stone axes were made from basalt. *Monos* and *metates,* the basic grinding tools of prehistoric peoples, were usually made from porous lava material.

The Hohokam have been called by some anthropologists the prehistoric "Merchants of the Southwest." It is believed they acted as middlemen in a network of trade that extended from Mexico clear into the Great Lakes region. From Mexico, they imported small bells hand-hewn from pure native copper, and exotic birds. The latter provided colorful feathers for ceremonial events. Sea shells imported from the Gulf of California were carved and ground into rings, bracelets, pendants and figures. Using pitch as a bonding agent they designed beautiful turquoise mosaics on the backs of the shells. Life forms were etched on sea shells with the aid of juice from cactus plants. A figure or design would be drawn with pitch, then dipped in a weak acid solution. The unprotected part of the shell was dissolved by the acid leaving the raised

The mysterious Casa Grande Ruins near Coolidge, circa 1900. Photo: Arizona Historical Society, Haynes collection. Buehman Hartwell Photo.

design or figurine. About 200 years later, this process would be "discovered" in Europe. Interestingly, evidence indicates that most of the fancy jewelry and face paint was worn by the men.

Exactly why they left remains a mystery. Did the great drought of A.D. 1276-1299 drive them out? Possibly. However, their massive system of canals was substantial enough to sustain a prolonged drought. The long dry spell might have brought other more warlike peoples into the land of the Hohokam, causing a cultural decline. Perhaps the irrigation system was too efficient, causing the soil to become water-logged. Did the soil become saturated with salt, or did warlike newcomers drive them away? Did they leave the area completely or are their descendants the Pima and Tohono O'odham peoples of today? Perhaps there was a great epidemic decimating their numbers. Possibly the industrious, entrepreneural segment of the culture moved on to greener pastures leaving the less-motivated behind. The standard of living of the Pima and Tohono O'odham was far below that of the Hohokam when the Spanish arrived in the 1500s. The Spanish recorded evidence of a great cultural upheaval but they, too, were mystified.

Perhaps the key to unlocking the secrets of this great culture still lies buried beneath this modern-day metropolis of concrete, steel, glass and asphalt waiting to be discovered or uncovered by some futuristic civilization.

The Hohokam, Anasazi, and Mogollon are considered the major prehistoric cultures in Arizona. Origins of the first two are uncertain but the Mogollon are believed to have descended from the Cochise culture. The Hohokam lived in the deserts and river valleys of southern Arizona, and are recognized today as the master farmers of the Southwest. The Anasazi occupied the sandstone canyons of the Four Corners area. Although they didn't move into the cliffs until the later stage, around A.D. 1100, they are best remembered as the cliff dwellers. Both Hohokam and Anasazi are names applied by modern man. *Hohokam* is a Pima word meaning "all used up" or "the vanished ones," and *Anasazi* is a Navajo word for "ancient ones." The Mogollons lived in the rugged central mountains of eastern Arizona. Their people, and the giant escarpment that slashes across the plateau, are named for Juan Ignacio Mogollon, an early Spanish colonial governor of New Mexico.

The Sinagua Culture arrived in the Flagstaff-Verde Valley area about A.D. 500. They lived in the cliffs and in stone villages, dry-farming around the San Francisco Mountains until the eruption of Sunset Crater in A.D. 1064. The Indians returned and farmed the region, building several pueblos, the largest being Wupatki, a Hopi word meaning "Tall House." After a long drought in the latter part of the 13th Century, the area went into decline and the Sinagua might have moved to the Hopi mesas or joined their relatives in the Verde Valley. The most spectacular Sinagua pueblo was Montezuma Castle (a misnomer, since Montezuma never came near the place). The 20-room apartment house, nestled beneath a limestone overhang above Beaver Creek, was occupied between A.D. 1100 and 1400. Near Clarkdale is another Sinagua pueblo

The Tonto Cliff Dwellings, near Theodore Roosevelt Dam, circa 1900. Photo: Arizona Historical Society.

called Tuzigoot. Unlike the cliff dwellings at nearby Montezuma Castle, Tuzigoot was perched on a hilltop overlooking the Verde River. The Sinagua also lived in Walnut Canyon east of Flagstaff from about A.D. 1120 to 1250. The canyon is about 400 feet deep and the natives lived both in the canyon and on the rim. Some of their dwellings were built into the ledges where soft limestone had eroded, creating natural overhangs.

The Salado were distant cousins of the Anasazi and known for their beautiful polychrome pottery. The best example of Salado ruins are at Tonto National Monument near Roosevelt Lake. The Salado lived in cliff villages along the Salt River and farmed the narrow valleys. They intermingled and were probably assimilated by the larger Hohokam and Mogollon cultures.

The Patayan lived in the Prescott area, west of Flagstaff, and along the Colorado River in western Arizona. They farmed the river valleys, foraged for wild berries and hunted the deserts for game. It is believed they evolved into the Yuma-language peoples of western Arizona.

The Hohokam, Anasazi and Mogollon, along with the lesser-known Salado, Sinagua, and Patayan, adapted well to their respective environments. Despite many differences and great distances, there was a great deal of intermingling, sharing and trading. All the Indian cultural groups went into decline about A.D. 1250. By the time of the Spanish entrada in the 16th Century, they had mysteriously vanished, and modern man has been able to piece together only a fragment of these once-great civilizations.

The rise and decline of these ancient ones follows a pattern as old as man. Their time in the sun was brief. Their battles against the elements were epic. In this pristine wilderness they carved empires and built civilizations far superior to their contemporaries in Europe.

In the end, the elements won out. What finally drove them away? Was it drought? Was it pestilence, famine or plague? Or did the arrival of warlike Apaches and Navajos cause them to depart? Since they left no written accounts and science has unearthed only a fractional account, the complete story may never be known.

3

ARIZONA'S NATIVE AMERICANS

Arizona's native people are as diverse as the state's rich and varied landscape. At first, the Indians lived in a state of harmony with their magnificent surroundings. Their numbers were relatively few and the impact on the land was small. When an area became polluted, nomadic tribes simply moved on to a new location.

Native American religion is based upon nature and the environment. The earth is mother. The gods are those who provide rain and sun to grow crops and to feed wild animals upon which the Indians traditionally subsisted. All things come from the land, the sun, and the rain.

Arizona's native peoples have a complex relationship with the state and federal governments. For example, the Arizona Constitution prohibits the state from taxing Indian lands or property without the consent of the affected tribes. Although native peoples living on reservations were not legally recognized as citizens of the United States at the start of World War I and were thus exempt from the draft, more than 8,000 Indian men and women volunteered for service in the U.S. armed forces, and more than 25,000 Indians served in World War II as well. Still, Indians were not granted the right to vote until 1948, when the Supreme Court ruled in favor of two Yavapai men who had filed a lawsuit.

Arizona's Indians belong to one of three language groups. The Navajo and Apache belong to the Athabascan, while the Colorado River tribes and the "Pais" are Yuman. The Hopi,

Pima, Tohono O'odham (Papago), Paiute and Chemehuevi belong to the Ute-Aztecan language group. Economically, they have been classified as band, village and rancheria dwellers.

Part I

THE NAVAJO
(DINÉ: THE PEOPLE)

The Navajo are a group of Athabascan people who moved in and occupied the Four Corners region where they adopted many of the customs of the Pueblo people. Not only has much of their ceremonialism been adopted from these early Pueblo contacts, but so are their horticultural skills, rituals, origin myths and concepts of matrilineal descent. They also adopted customs such as sand painting, weaving, metate and firepit styles. Over a period of time, these separated the Navajo culture from the Apache who seldom came in contact with the Pueblo people.

The Navajo were great borrowers. Although it has been said they borrowed silversmithing from the Spanish, weaving

A Navajo Indian camp with an Apache basket in the foreground. Taken at the Grand Canyon in 1932. Photo: Arizona Historical Society.

and sheep-raising from the Hopi and hell-raising from the Utes, the Navajo dwelling was not borrowed. These earth-covered houses called hogans can be traced all the way back to the Asian world from whence they came. The customs and taboos concerning the hogan alone would fill a small volume.

For more than 300 years the *Apaches de Navahu* (Apache of the cultivated fields), or Navajo, battled with their traditional enemies: the Comanche from the Llano Estacado (Staked Plains of Texas); Spanish-Mexicans along the Rio Grande and the Utes to the north. They raided the villages on the Rio Grande for slaves, cattle, horses, sheep and goats. They also raised lots of hell with their neighbors, the Hopi. Unlike their Apache cousins, they became more adept at horticulture, growing corn, squash and beans.

The scenic land occupied by the Navajo is some of the most spectacular in the world. It ranges from the wind-sculptured, red sandstone monoliths of Monument Valley, to pine-covered mountains that reach heights of 10,000 feet, to the awesome steep-sided canyons of Canyons de Chelly and del Muerto. Here, in impervious domes where canyon walls rise a thousand feet off the canyon floor, were the sanctuaries of the ancient Anasazi and later the ancestral stronghold of the Navajo.

The Navajo people fought a long series of raid and counter-raid wars with the Spanish and later the Mexicans along the Rio Grande. When the American Army occupied the land in 1846, it was with the understanding that it would assist the local inhabitants along the Rio Grande to bring an end to the Navajo raids.

For a time, nothing much was done, and the raiding continued. In 1864 the legendary mountain man-turned-soldier Col. Kit Carson rounded up the Navajo and relocated them to a "land of milk and honey," along the Pecos River of New Mexico. Carson's orders were to shoot all who resisted but, to his credit, the old frontiersman followed a more humane approach. Carson's men burned the Navajo orchards and starved the people into submission. Old timers in the area say the Navajos always have respected Carson as a warrior, but they have never forgiven him for burning their beautiful orchards.

Carson rounded up some 8,000 Navajo at Canyon de Chelly and began the infamous 300-mile Long Walk to Fort Sumner, New Mexico. Fort Sumner, or Bosque Redondo, along the Pecos River, turned out to be a Navajo nightmare. The land was poor. Floods, droughts and insects devastated the crops. Kiowa, Comanche and Mescalero Apache bands preyed upon them. A smallpox epidemic in 1865 took the lives of more than 2,000. In 1868 a treaty was negotiated between the tribe and the federal government allowing the Navajo to return to their beloved red clay country. They could have received fertile agricultural land along the Arkansas River in Oklahoma but they chose to return to the Four Corners region. "When you understand why we came back to this bleak desert land rather than that rich farm land in Oklahoma," one said, "then you understand the Navajo."

It was not until 1923 that the Navajo organized themselves into a tribal political body. The last great chief and first tribal chairman was Henry Chee Dodge who led his people brilliantly for 70 years. In 1938 he became chairman of the newly-formed Navajo Tribal Council. Under his tutelage, the Navajo moved from the dark days of post-treaty into the modern age. Chapters, similar to Anglo precincts, were established in 1927 where leaders, both formal and informal, were recognized.

The Navajo Reservation has grown to some 25,000 square miles. The population is rapidly approaching 225,000 (in Arizona) and growing at twice the national average. But much of the land is still barren and isolated. In some areas it takes 250 acres to run one sheep for a year.

Many of the time-honored customs are strictly adhered to. The family is the fundamental unit from which all others derive. The Navajo grandmother still heads the clan although men do represent the family in public ceremonies.

The Navajo creation story has the people progressing through three previous worlds. In the First World all was black, for there was no light from the heavens. First Man and First Woman were created; their purpose was to arrange conditions suitable for the Navajo. Unfortunately, Evil Beings quarreled and cast evil spells so the People moved to the second or Blue World. Here they discovered more turmoil, because the evil ones from the first world had followed. Coyote, a cunning creature who appears frequently in native legends, persuaded the people to journey on to the third or Yellow World. But they didn't find happiness in Yellow World and when a great flood came they climbed into the fourth, or Glittering World. In the Glittering World deities called *Yay-ee-ee* instructed the people about how to live the Peaceful Way. First Man and First Woman taught them how to build and bless the hogan. The door had to face the east because that was where First Headman, who gave wisdom to the people, lived. Day, night, the sun, moon and the stars were created, along with the four sacred mountains: the San Francisco Peaks, Navajo Mountain, Mt. Taylor and Hesperus Peak. One day, First Man and First Woman found a baby girl. The baby quickly grew into the beautiful Changing Woman, representing nature and the changing seasons. She became the most beloved of all the Holy People. Changing Woman mated with the sun and gave birth to the Twins. Because dreaded monsters infested the Glittering World and Changing Woman feared they would harm the Twins, she hid them deep underground. While in the underworld the Twins found Spider Woman who liked them and taught them special prayers and chants to rid the world of the evil monsters. Then, Changing Woman and the Twins cast a spell on the huge beasts, turning them to stone.

Today those massive monsters stand frozen in time and are still seen in such places as Monument Valley.

The Navajo name for themselves is *Dine* (dineh), which means "People of the surface of the earth." Dinetah, or Navajoland, comprises 15,398 square miles in Arizona. The reservation produces more energy than anywhere else in the state. There are up to forty billion tons of coal reserves and it has the only producing oil wells in the state. The tribe receives millions of dollars annually in royalties from leases. Still, traditionally, the number of sheep and cattle owned is the determinant of wealth.

Navajo life today is changing rapidly. The desire for consumer goods is causing more people to seek wages for income. Although farming and sheepraising are still symbolically important, fewer people are living in the traditional way.

People still come from miles around, driving the modern pickups that have replaced the horse-drawn wagons of a mere generation ago, to social gatherings that last several days. These gatherings provide an opportunity for old-timers to catch up on the latest gossip and give the young folk an opportunity for courtship.

Navajo men pose for photographer. Each seems to reflect a different impression on having his picture taken. Photo: Northern Arizona University. Switzer collection.

The family is the center of all activity among the Navajo and the home of the eldest woman or grandmother is the clan meeting place. All members of the clan are responsible for the behavior of one another. When one misbehaves, others might look at him and say, "He acts as if he had no relatives." Traditionally the Navajo are a matriarchal society and the property is retained by the woman's clan. When a man marries, he leaves his clan and joins that of his wife. Divorce was relatively simple. If a man came home one day and found his saddle lying outside the hogan, there was no mistaking the message. His marriage was now history.

The trials and tribulations of marriage customs have caused many young Navajo men to resort to practical precaution. Upon getting married he *slowly* moves his sheep from his mother's herd to that of his new wife. If it looks like things aren't going to work out, he slowly eases them back home to mama.

Many of the old customs and traditions are still practiced by the elderly. When visiting an older person it is proper to let him be the first to speak. It is considered impolite simply to walk up and begin conversing. One must sit quietly for as long as it takes and in time the older person will speak. Only then is it courteous to begin speaking. When a Navajo visits another hogan he will not walk up to the door and knock. On the contrary, he will stand around outside the home quietly awaiting an invitation to enter. When it is extended he will come in; if it is not soon forthcoming he will go away. It works the same if one approaches the home in an auto. It's proper to honk the horn, then wait for an invitation.

There are many local customs and taboos among the Navajo, especially concerning the home and the land immediately surrounding them. Since the reservation is so large, many of these local taboos and customs are not always known throughout it. Examples of some well-known taboos: the door of the hogan must always face the east; the Navajo must never kill a snake or a coyote; they must never eat bear steak; a man must never look at his mother-in-law and must observe this taboo even though he lives in close proximity. This last is a matter of respect rather than rudeness and the family cooperates in the keeping of this ritual. Usually she would cover her face with a blanket when he approached and that would suffice.

The dead are not mentioned; when a person dies his clothes are sometimes put on backward and the moccasins are placed on opposite feet. This is to confuse the evil spirits who might want to follow the deceased. When a person dies inside the hogan, the body is removed through a hole cut in the north wall, and the hogan isn't used any more. The north hole is to release the spirit. However, sometimes the body is buried inside. After a death, the smoke hole is plugged, religious items are removed and the hogan is abandoned. It's possible to avoid these inconveniences by taking the person outside when death is inevitable. Since the spirits of the dead live in the north, there are no windows in the north wall of the hogan, thus prohibiting these spirits from observing the activities going on inside.

The spirits or ghosts that inhabit a dead hogan are called *chindis*. One isn't supposed to call out the dead person's name for fear the chindi will think it is being called and come. The chindi is believed to remain forever in the hogan.

Ghosts and witches are fairly common. Ghosts inhabit the world of the dead and are beyond control but witches are terrible, fearful powers among the living. They are usually called skinwalkers and they got that way by making some evil pact with the Devil in exchange for power. To gain this power they have to commit some terrible sin such as incest or the murder of a family member. The skinwalkers come out only after dark and assume the form of an animal such as a wolf. They can run at speeds of up to 60 mph and can change forms. Believers tell of following an animal track only to have it turn into human form. Other humans can't detect a skinwalker but animals, especially dogs and horses, can. When a skinwalker is killed the family quietly buries the body and doesn't report the death.

Living among the Navajo are individuals sensitive to non-physical forces. These psychics or, as they are called among the people, "hand tremblers," are known for their ability to locate missing items ranging from stolen property to downed aircraft on the remote reservation wilderness. Some of these abilities can be attributed to a vast network of informers at the disposal of the hand tremblers, but there are times when their psychic predictions defy either scientific or logical explanation.

Hozhó is the most desired quality in all things: to live to an old age; to have a close family; good health; and to be happy. To have all these is to achieve *Hozhó*.

Among the 35 major types of ceremonies is the Blessing Way, used mainly to restore or ensure harmony. When disharmony exists between man and the forces of nature the Blessing Way ceremony is a means to restore or strengthen harmony. It's used for young women at puberty, pregnant women, Navajos who have been living for an extended period away from Navajoland, and for survivors after a death in the family. The Enemy Way is another important ceremony and is given to Navajo men returning from war.

When a Navajo is ill or disturbed, there are several options available. There is the diagnostician who can locate the ailment through ESP, knowledge, or intuition. The herbalist, who might also be a diagnostician, is adroit in the use of herbs to cure most common ailments. The serious cases go to the medicine man, who performs healing ceremonies which may last for several days.

The medicine man is an important person to the Navajo. His Navajo title is *Hataalii,* which roughly translates to *Singer.* The Singer's hogan is constructed with great care and ceremony. He must go through a long apprenticeship and, during that time must learn hundreds of songs to perfection, including the precise tone in which to sing them. The Navajo believe that bodily disorders are induced by mental or emotional disturbances, and therefore illness is the result of man being out of harmony with the universe. When this happens, the medicine man will organize a "sing." Many friends will come to the "sing" in support of the patient for the gods to observe. The Navajo also believe that disease comes through the violation of a taboo. To cure the ill, sand paintings are used. The sand painting may take two to four hours to make and must follow a precise formula since mistakes are dangerous to all. However, if an outsider is watching, the medicine man will not make a perfect one but will make an intentional mistake somewhere on the painting. Creating the sand painting is not a ceremony in itself, but is related to several others, and it must be destroyed before dark.

The Navajo sweat bath is related to the preservation of health. The participants will gather hot stones and place them in the hogan. Prior to entry, each calls to the gods four times and is then allowed to enter. Following the steam bath, all take an abrasive sand bath.

THE APACHE
(INDEH: THE PEOPLE)

Historically, the Apache have been the most notorious of the Arizona tribes. Like the Navajo, they belong to the Athabascan language group. It is believed they crossed the Bering Strait land bridge some 6,000 years ago and eventually moved down into the Great Plains. A great cultural shift drove most of them from the Great Plains into the rocky terrain that was New Mexico, Arizona and Mexico. They probably arrived in the Southwest about A.D. 1100.

Around A.D. 1400 the various groups went off in different directions. The Navajo and Jicarilla Apache settled in the San Juan River basin in the Four Corners region. The Mescalero Apache occupied southern New Mexico, the Lipan Apache roamed across southwest Texas; the Kiowa Apache rode the Panhandle region of Texas; the Chiricahua settled in northern Mexico, southern Arizona and New Mexico; and the western Apache found a home in the rugged central mountains of Arizona.

They were essentially a hunting and gathering society and, by living in small bands, adjusted well to the harsh, dry climate. Unlike the community-oriented Pueblo Indians, the *Indeh* believed in the primary importance of the individual.

The name Apache is derived from the Zuni word *Apachu,* which meant "enemy." The name first appeared in the writings of the Spanish colonist Juan de Oñate around 1600. To differentiate the numerous groups, the Spanish applied regional names. Thus we have "Apache de Mescalero" for those who gathered the mescal plant for food; Chiricahua for those who inhabited the Chiricahua Mountain strongholds; the Aravaipa, Gila, White Mountain, and Tonto in those areas.

The Apache pretty well had the upper hand in their wars with the Spanish and later the Mexicans. For some 300 years they held the Spanish and Mexican encroachments in Arizona to the lands below the Gila River. Only a few interlopers dared venture into the land that was called "Apacheria." Some writers have praised the Apache as culture preservers for their efforts to contain the Spanish and their zealous missionaries. To the Spanish and Mexican authorities, Arizona was among the farthest reaches of the northern frontier. They knew of the rich minerals in the brawny, rugged mountains, but could not, or would not, put forth the investment needed to extract the riches.

It would be left to the ambitious Americans to make the

final conquest of Apacheria and it would take some 25 years of tough guerrilla warfare to accomplish the feat.

As warriors, the Apache proved to be a most difficult adversary. They usually operated in small bands, carefully concealing themselves until they were ready to spring a surprise attack. Afterwards they split up to confuse their pursuers and later rendezvoused at a prearranged location. Leadership in these Apache war bands was not inherited. Leaders were chosen for ability to locate and plunder and to get in and get out of a situation without suffering any casualties.

Among the Apache, a band was generally a small cluster of clans, and this band was the political unit. The Apache never considered themselves a single nation. Because of the harsh conditions in which they lived, small bands were the rule. Their allegiance ran from family, to clan, to band, to group, and finally and rarely, to tribe. There were no hereditary chiefs as in some tribes. However, a chief's son could rise to a leadership role by proving himself in battle or raid. If he failed, he was quickly dropped or ignored. If a band or clan encroached on another's rights, they would fight each other as quickly as they would Mexicans or Americans.

To be killed in a show of bravado was the last thing on an Apache warrior's mind. His stock in trade was stealth and cunning. Women captured on a raid were always prized, not necessarily by the wives at home but certainly by the men. A woman captive could expect a harsh life, not only from the elements, but from the jealous spouses, especially if she was attractive. If captives were too young to travel, they were usually killed on the spot. Otherwise, the Apache raised them as their own. Many captives rose to positions of influence in the band. For an adult male captive, only the worst could be expected. The Apache, perhaps taking some lessons from their enemies, had many interesting ways of making death a long, terrible ordeal.

The Apache had several great trails, usually through the river valleys leading into Mexico, where they went in search of plunder that ranged from women and children to livestock. In the years prior to the coming of the Anglo-American, Taos, New Mexico, was the main market place for the selling of captives and booty. When a woman was captured on a raid, she became the property of the warrior who took her captive. However, it was most unfortunate if she was captured by two warriors, since there was general agreement among the Apache to get rid of anything that caused animosities between the warriors of the band. Articles could be burned, horses killed, and a woman in the same position often met the same fate.

Like the Navajo, the Apache family customs are matriarchal. The son is lost to his family by marriage, and he now belongs to the clan of his wife. Should his wife die, he would mourn for perhaps a year and then usually would marry one of his wife's sisters or cousins. In marriage, the consent of the girl's parents was necessary. During courtship, one of the suitor's relatives usually did the honors of negotiating. The usual compensation to be paid to the prospective bride's father was horses. The suitor might leave several horses outside her father's wickiup and leave. If, when he returned the next day, the horses were taken and placed in the family corral it meant his offer had been accepted. If, on the other hand, they were still standing where he had left them, it meant his proposal was still being considered. If nothing was done by the second day, the prospective bride might be considered a bit stuffy. If, by the fourth day, nothing had been done to care for the horses, he was considered rejected. This was cause for great humiliation, as there were probably several of his contemporaries watching the whole proceeding as he came to retrieve his dowry. He might have lost face, but was probably better off than his horses, which had gone unattended during the courtship. If the proposal was accepted, this was cause for three days of feasting.

Following a week or two of honeymooning, the couple returned and moved into a wickiup near the wife's family. Like the Navajo, an Apache was never supposed to look at his mother-in-law, nor to speak directly to her. When she entered the wickiup or dwelling, he had to leave at once. In traveling together in a wagon or automobile, a curtain was hung between them so as not to violate the custom.

The Apache believe in a supreme being called *Usen,* who is the giver of all life. *Usen* is of no sex or place and the Apache cannot approach this god directly, but must go through some medium. This medium is revealed to an Apache through dreams and visions and may come in many forms, such as animals, insects, or elements of weather. Each Apache has his own medium, and when it is revealed to him, it becomes his guardian spirit or medicine.

Spirits, ghosts, and monsters are a vital part of life. The Apache believe that life for them began with the coming of the White Painted Woman. She is the mother of all people. According to Apache lore, one day she was lying nude in the rain. When the water entered her body, a child was conceived and he was called Child of the Water. The child grew up and made things as they now are. He conquered the monsters and made the world safe for the people (Apache). When this was done, Child of the Water and White Painted Woman instructed the people on what was good and bad in the world. This being done, the two went to their home in the sky.

The medicine man is a powerful influence among the Apache even today. He is always paid for his work — the richer the client, the longer the ritual. Many place more trust in the medicine man than in the Indian tribal leaders, whom they feel have been influenced by the white man's bureaucratic system.

An important ceremonial part of Apache tradition is the crown dancers. These dancers, who represent anonymous beings with ceremonial crowns and black face masks, perform in most of the religious festivities, especially those dedicated to girls' puberty rites.

Many young women today still participate in the Sunrise Ceremony, a sort of debutante celebration to commemorate a girl's entering womanhood. The ceremony lasts four days and requires the young lady to perform certain rituals. Older people will observe her conduct during this ordeal as it is believed that if she behaves well under this duress it is a sign that she will be able to cope with the difficulties of life.

Traditionally, the Apache practiced polygamy. The short-age of males in this warrior society made this necessary. The Apache were noted for their fidelity, so matrimonial miscon-duct was the exception rather than the rule. Chastity was rigidly enforced among the Apache. Woe to the promiscuous woman, because the custom was to slice off the nose of an unfaithful wife. Not surprisingly, adultery was rare.

When a woman was about to give birth, or as soon as labor pains set in, she was sometimes tied to a tree, hands above the head, and left in this position until the child was born. Apache women were known to give birth along the trail and be back, riding horseback, a few hours later.

Women and children participated in battle when necessary. Young girls were trained in the use of weapons the same as boys. All youths were tested for strength and durability by the elders.

Like many other tribes, the Apache had a horror of death. The dead were not spoken of, and a home where an Apache had died would be deserted. The cutting of hair and prolonged wailing were ways of demonstrating grief for a lost one. In case of murder the next of kin was obliged to take revenge.

There was, and is, a fear of enemies doing harm by voodoo. An Apache is very careful not to leave a part of himself for some adversary bent on doing evil. Such things as the leavings from defecation, hair and finger or toe nail trimmings are always disposed of in such a way as to not let them fall into evil hands.

The population of the combined White Mountain and San Carlos Apache reservations is about 25,000. They occupy some of the most beautiful land in Arizona. The recreational facilities in the White Mountains are of the finest quality. There is a large ski resort and the fishing and hunting are some of the best in the state. Along with this, the tribe owns large numbers of beef cattle, while other lands are leased to non-Indians. In an ironic twist, the Apache have become cowboys complete with addiction to rodeos and pickup trucks.

Part II
The Ute-Aztecan and Yuman Language Groups

THE HOPI

The Hopi name for themselves *(Hopitu)* means the "Peaceful People." They have lived on the three mesas in the Black Mesa Range since prehistoric times. Old Oraibi, on Third Mesa, is the oldest continuously inhabited city in America, dating back to before A.D. 1200. The Hopi are believed to have descended from ancient Anasazi, a people who have called that region home since before the time of Christ.

Their lives have not always been peaceful. Native tribes such as the Ute and Navajo were a constant threat, raiding

Walpi Village on First Mesa, circa 1920. The Hopi constructed Walpi around the time of the Great Pueblo Revolt in 1680. Photo: Arizona Historical Foundation, Tempe.

their livestock and kidnapping their people on one side while the Spanish tried desperately to impose their religion and culture on the other.

The first whites to visit Hopiland were soldiers from Coronado's expedition in 1540 during his quest for the mythical Seven Cities of Gold. Zuni Indians told the Spaniards of "seven villages to the northwest." Hoping those villages might be the Golden Cities of Cibola, Coronado sent Pedro de Tovar to investigate. Tovar's mounted troops easily overran the Hopi footsoldiers, and a tenuous peace was established. He called the place Tusayan. In their pursuit of treasure other Spanish explorers, including Espejo, Farfán, and Oñate, all visited the mesas in the late 1500s. The Franciscans established the first mission in Hopiland in 1629. Hopi leaders resisted this intrusion, but it was not until the Great Revolt in 1680 that the Spanish were driven out. Four priests were killed and the church destroyed. Beams from the church were used to construct a new kiva at Oraibi, still in use today.

It is said that each new arrival had to demonstrate some contribution before being accepted into the Hopi tribe; thus, the Hopi are a "melting pot" of different peoples. The Tewa on First Mesa are a more recent example of these arrivals. Originally from the area around Santa Fe, the Tewa began moving to Hopiland after the Pueblo Revolt in 1680. They live at Hano on the eastern end of First Mesa. The village adjoins the Hopi villages of Sichomovi and Walpi. The Tewa maintain their own customs and language. By tradition, the Tewa claim the Hopi invited them to move to First Mesa because of their reputation as fearless warriors. This would provide a buffer against the enemies of the Hopi. Although they are generally peaceful, the Hopi fiercely resisted attempts by the Franciscan missionaries to Christianize them during the 1600s. The Spanish soldiers and priests in Hopiland were all murdered during the Great Revolt of 1680. Since that time, Catholics have not been allowed to build churches on the mesas. Other church groups have found the going rough, but this has been due to their own lack of consideration. In 1901, a Mennonite church was built on the mesa near Oraibi without village consent. The church was struck by lightning not once, but twice!

The Hopi have a complicated, interwoven social structure. Like the city-states of ancient Greece, each village is a separate entity. Each individual has a particular responsibility, and each clan is designated for particular duties. The clan system is much stronger among the Hopi than among other Pueblo peoples. They are a matrilineal society, and although a man marries and lives with his wife near her clan, he still has responsibility to his own clan mother, or his "real home." Women own the home, gardens, and pueblo furnishings, while men take care of herding, farming, and activities away from the village.

Most of the villages in Hopiland are perched on top or at the foot of three barren, limestone-colored mesas that extend out on the south end of Black Mesa. Whites number the mesas "first, second and third," moving east to west, while the Hopi number west to east. Second Mesa is the only one that doesn't have to concern itself with numbering. Kivas, or underground ceremonial chambers, can be seen in all the villages and are characterized by long ladder-poles extending upward through a hole in the roof. A conservative, deeply religious people, their lives center around the kiva. Each clan in the village has its own kiva where the men go for meditation, meetings, rituals, and seclusion. A ceremonial entrance is located in the roof, although there are side doors for practical use. Most of the ritual is concerned with crops. Corn is symbolic and the most important commodity. Ceremonies begin in January and last until the crops are harvested in the late summer. Today these celebrations are usually held on weekends to accommodate Hopi living off the reservations.

The two most important rituals are the bringing of rain and the curing of illness. The rituals have been dutifully explained by numerous writers; however, it should be noted that the highly complex, esoteric functions and meanings will never be fully understood by outsiders. The high point of the year is August, when the nine-day snake dance ceremony is performed.

Each of the nine days is spent in some specific activity; the culmination comes on the ninth day with the snake dance. Rattlesnakes, along with bull snakes and red racers, are gathered from the rocky mesas and the desert land for use in the ceremony. Dancers carry both venomous and non-poisonous reptiles in their mouths, and are accompanied by so-called huggers, whose job it is to distract the snake's attention away from the dancer's face with a feather. Occasionally dancers are bitten but apparently suffer no serious ill effects from these bites. Following the ceremony, the gatherers take up the snakes and release them so that they might return underground to inform the gods of the need for rain. The San Francisco Peaks, to the southwest of the Hopi mesas, are the homes of the kachinas, the spirits of the ancestors. Each summer these kachinas return with the clouds to bring water to the thirsty land.

The kachina ceremonies are the most well-known and colorful of all Hopi rituals. The masked kachinas are actually represented in three ways. The first is the doll that tourists are fond of collecting. The purpose of the dolls is to teach youngsters to become familiar with the Hopi religion. The second representation occurs when men dress as kachinas and perform ceremonial rites in the plazas and kivas. The third way represents the spiritual kachinas, who reside high in the San Francisco Peaks but who visit the village periodically, bringing gifts to the people. Not all kachinas are benevolent. Some are ogres who handle discipline. There is even a kachina called "Navajo girl" to provide comic relief at the expense of long-time Hopi adversaries.

The supernatural kachinas live for six months in the underworld beneath the San Francisco Peaks. The other half of the year they remain near the Hopi villages.

The Hopi believe they emerged into this world from a hole in the earth called a *sipapu,* a "birthing hole" through which they emerged into this world. This sacred hole is located near the Grand Canyon. Inside each kiva is a symbolic sipapu.

Each village has its own organization, and each person has a place in the operation of a community. The clan is presided over by a woman who is designated as the clan mother. When a man marries, he moves into the household of his wife but still participates in the ceremonies of his own family.

Land among the Hopi is communal, given to the clans and apportioned to the various families who enjoy its use and then hand it down to their daughters. From the Spanish, the Hopi adopted the system of ownership whereby a man retains ownership of such property as his horses and sheep.

Each village has a number of matrilineal clans such as the Rabbit, Parrot, Snake, Bear and Spider, to name a few. According to tradition, the Hopi descended from the underworld, and each group acquired the clan name from some incident that befell it. Each clan brought with it a sacred object and the knowledge of a ceremony having power to bring rain. Therefore, all the ceremonial offices should be filled from the membership of a given clan. The Bear Clan contributes the village chief. From the Parrot Clan comes the Kachina Chief, from the Snake Clan the Snake Chief, and so on. These offices are religious rather than political, and all chiefs are priests rather than secular officials.

Intermarriage and adaptation to the ways of the white man have absorbed or overwhelmed most Native American tribes. By and large, this has not happened among the Hopis. Traditionally, they are a sedentary people, and they have maintained a strong religious and family-oriented society. This has given them an inner strength that has made them indomitable as a people. They knew how and when to bend, but never break.

The Spanish entrada in the 1600s brought an array of amenities to Hopiland. Metal tools were introduced along with furniture, weapons and glazed windows. Onions, tomatoes and peaches were added to their staple diet of corn, beans and squash. The Spaniards also introduced sheep and cattle, providing a source for wool, hides and meat. Horses and burros made packing and transportation easier. All this had a price. The Spanish also brought their religion, claiming the Hopi way was paganistic. By the 1630s missions were established at Awatovi, Shongopavi and Oraibi, along with *visitas* (mission stations) at Walpi and Mishongnovi.

The Hopi religious leaders resisted this intrusion and in 1680 succeeded in throwing out the Spanish intruders.

In 1699 the Spaniards returned and re-established a mission at Awatovi. In retaliation, Hopi raiders destroyed the village, killing the men and distributing the women and children to other villages. Awatovi was never re-settled. Only a few of its clans and rituals survive today in other villages.

During the next 200 years the indestructible Hopi battled drought, smallpox and raids from Ute, Navajo and Apache. After the United States took control of the area in 1848, army troops took up the trail against the Hopi's traditional foes but again there was a price to pay. Hopi children were forced to attend schools far away from the mesas.

A tribal council was formed in 1936 but not all the villages participated. Gradually, the protesters relented somewhat. Still, each village retains a great deal of autonomy today.

The Hopi have become famous for their arts and crafts throughout the world. The women are especially noted for their beautiful pottery and basketry, while the men have gained fame for their weaving, silver and turquoise jewelry, and in recent years painting and sculpture. Originally the

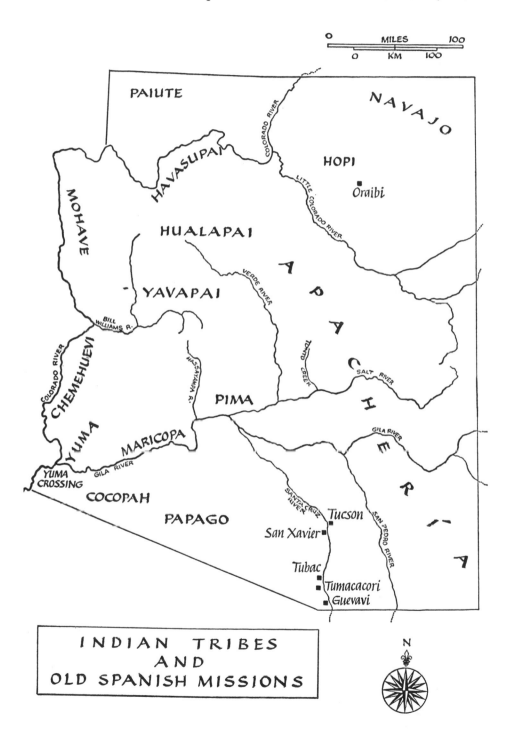

INDIAN TRIBES
AND
OLD SPANISH MISSIONS

Hopi imitated the Navajo in silversmithing. In 1938 the Museum of Northern Arizona encouraged them to develop a style of their own, which they have done to the enjoyment of all who respect and admire their creative genius.

The Hopi are known as great distance runners and perhaps the most famous of all was Louis Tewanima, the "Happy Hopi from Shongopavi." He received his early training chasing jackrabbits, and just for sport he used to run 67 miles along what is today's Arizona 87 to Winslow to watch the trains; then he'd run back home again—all in the same day.

Tewanima attended school at the famous Carlisle Indian School in Pennsylvania with the legendary Jim Thorpe. The pair made up an entire Carlisle track team. In the 1908 Olympics at London, he finished ninth in the marathon. In 1912 he won the silver medal in the 10,000-meter run at Stockholm, a record not matched by an American until another Native American, Billy Mills, won the gold in 1964.

Tewanima died in a fall in 1969, at the age of 92. Returning home from a ceremony late one evening, he took a wrong turn at Second Mesa and fell 70 feet to his death. When the Arizona Sports Hall of Fame was created, Louis Tewanima was the first athlete selected.

Today, the time-honored Hopi Way continues to survive. The population is about 10,700. Despite the encroachments of television, electric guitars and pickup trucks they cling proudly to the old ways. Hopi farmers still plant crops. Women still make decorative pottery from native soil fired with cow or sheep dung, and the ceremonies continue to dominate life in the villages as they have for centuries. It's worth believing: there'll always be a Hopiland.

THE PIMA
(ACKIMOEL O'ODHAM—RIVER PEOPLE)

One of Arizona's agrarian tribes is the Pima of the Gila and Salt river valleys. Like the Hopi, they are not as well known to the outside world via the movies and television as the Apache and Navajo. Unlike those tribes, neither the Pima nor the Hopi really took to the warpath against the whites although both tribes did know when to take their stand against white encroachments on their lands. Fortunately for the Hopi, the whites saw no future in trying to farm near the arid mesas. Such was not the experience of the Pima, who farmed the verdant lands along the Gila and Salt rivers.

The Pima, whose Indian name, Ackimoel O'odham, translates roughly to the "River People," are believed by some to have descended from those so-called "master farmers of the Southwest," the Hohokam. For hundreds of years they have farmed the Gila valley, taking time off occasionally to do battle with their traditional foes. The Pima were nearly surrounded by enemies: the Yuma and Mohave tribes to the west, the Yavapai and Tonto Apache from the north, and other Apache groups from the east.

Following a raid the Pima "Hard" or "Bitter" Man — the one chosen to lead in battle — organized a war party and went in pursuit. When the two enemy parties faced off with bows, arrows, shields and war clubs ready, the two war chiefs started things off by hurling insults at each other. Soon both armies followed suit. Then the warriors locked horns. As soon as a Pima slew an enemy he withdrew from battle and blackened his face. When the chief saw several blackened faces he called a withdrawal and claimed victory. The killers-of-the-enemy didn't make a triumphal return, but marched behind the rest of the group. Once home, they and their spouse had to go into isolation for 16 days of purification and fasting. Meanwhile, the rest of the village celebrated. The enemy scalps were raised on poles and the people danced. Later, storytellers recounted details of the battle around a fire. The celebration lasted for 16 days and nights while the slayers sat alone in the desert. At last each was considered purified and suitable to return to the village. The scalp was presented to him and it was given a special place in the home, as it was considered a source of great power in future battles.

Like most tribes, the Pima have their creation story and it differs from the scientific. In the wintertime the old man of the village told the story of how the world came to be. (According to legend, stories couldn't be told in the summer because rattlesnakes didn't like storytellers and would bite the teller.)

In the beginning Earth Doctor created the world out of a ball of dirt. Then he made the people. A rival, Elder Brother, arose and joined Earth Doctor. They, along with Coyote, got things organized.

Some wrong people came in and caused trouble so Earth Doctor and Elder Brother destroyed the world by flooding. After the floodwaters receded, Elder Brother became the ruler. Later he fell into disfavor with the people and was banished into the underworld. There he found allies (today's Pima and Tohono O'odham). He led them above ground and drove out the Hohokam who built the Casa Grande. Then Elder Brother left, promising to return someday.

The amiable Pima, who farmed the Gila watershed for hundreds of years, were the early day "welcome wagon" to many a weary traveler along the old Gila Trail. The Pima villages, oases in the desert near Sacaton, were like beacons to Spanish, Mexican and Anglo alike. Here the immigrants and soldiers enjoyed the friendly hospitality of the River People and purchased foods for the long arduous journey across the desert to California.

Unfortunately, their gracious hospitality and military assistance was forgotten after the subjugation of the Yavapai and Apache. White settlers poured into the Gila River area above the Pima villages and cut off the vital water that had made Indian crops flourish for hundreds of years. Despite pleas from both the Pima and friendly whites, the bureaucracy in Washington was incredibly slow in responding to the needs of the Pima. For a time the federal government planned to move the tribe to Oklahoma, but that plan met stubborn resistance in the Pima villages. During the 1860s and 1870s some moved to the Salt River Valley, where there was more water.

Through a comedy of errors in 1879, President Rutherford B. Hayes signed an executive order declaring the towns of Phoenix and Tempe, along with almost all the tillable lands in the entire Salt River Valley, a Pima reservation. It was one of the most generous acts toward Indians ever seen before or since, but it wasn't meant to be. After some five months of bureaucratic backpedaling the order was rescinded. The reservation was redrawn to its present boundaries.

Historically, the Pima clans were patriarchal; the women belonged to the father's family until marriage. Since most of the people in the village were related, young people had to go

Pima elder with his remarkable calendar stick. The markings record the historical events in tribal life. Photo: Southwest Studies.

outside to find a spouse. Generally, marriage was a simple matter; the prospective groom came to the home of the girl, stayed four nights and then she went to live with his clan. Divorce was easy. If the two weren't getting along, they just separated. If children were involved, it wasn't uncommon for the boys to remain with their father and the girls with their mother. Family support was shared equally, so in case of divorce the woman was capable of supporting herself. Polygamy was practiced, so a woman usually had little trouble finding another spouse, especially if she was industrious. In case of death, it was common for the survivor to become the spouse of one of the in-laws, or of some member of the deceased's extended family, such as a cousin.

The Pima number about 18,000 today and are one of the few tribes living near a large metropolitan area. Dress customs being what they were in the hot desert, in the early days of Anglo-American settlement, Pima men used to come to Phoenix wearing only a smile and a thin breechclout; causing some concern on the part of the ladies in town. The resourceful ladies of Phoenix solved the dilemma by collecting several pairs of trousers and hanging them on a tree outside of town. The tree was dubbed the "pants tree" and whenever the men entered town they donned a pair and on their way out, hung them up for the next person.

Although the tribal organization of the Pima was strong,

the villages, similar to the city-states of ancient Greece, held much political power. Each village had a chief, and one head chief presided over all the villages.

The head chief was elected by the village chiefs. As in most tribes the Pima leaders were known for their practical wisdom, as illustrated by the following:

A story is told about a time when the late Sen. Carl Hayden was sheriff of Maricopa County. A local feminist group in Phoenix was putting a great deal of pressure on the sheriff to do something about an "abominable situation," on the Salt River Reservation.

It seems the chief had several wives, and the ladies insisted something must be done about it.

They persuaded Sheriff Hayden to ride out to the chief's place and make him see the evil of his ways. Hayden visited the chief for several minutes, carefully sizing up the situation and trying to decide how best to approach the delicate subject. After awhile, he stated the nature of his visit saying that, in the white man's world, a man had only one wife. Being very careful not to offend the tribal leader, Hayden suggested that for the sake of public relations with the women of the white community the chief might be willing to give up all his wives but one. The Pima leader pondered the situation for a moment and then replied that he would comply with the sheriff's request on one condition: that Hayden choose which wives had to go and then tell them to take their things and leave. Now it was Hayden's turn to assess the situation.

History records that the sheriff decided discretion was the better part of valor. He wisely got on his horse and rode back to Phoenix. The case, as far as he was concerned, was closed.

THE TOHONO O'ODHAM
(THE DESERT PEOPLE)

The first Indians encountered by the Spanish in their entrada from the south during the 1690s were the Tohono O'odham. The Spanish called them Bean Eaters or Papago, but like most tribes they had words in their own language for themselves, *Tohono O'odham*, which means "the desert people." Living on the second largest reservation in the United States, they are now economically the poorest people in the Southwest. Their reservation runs south from below the Gila River all the way to the Mexican border. During times of drought, the arid land will hardly sustain the livestock on which much of the economy is based. In the past they grew crops by "flash flood" farming. During the summer rainy season they would move their homes to low-lying areas that were subject to flooding. When the rains came they planted their crops. Harvesting took place in the fall. Today there is still some "flash flood" farming but more modern methods of irrigation are gradually improving their life-style. The land is still devastated by periodic droughts. When the Spaniards arrived they found the O'odham raising beans, corn, and squash. The newcomers introduced many new crops and taught the natives the rudiments of farming and cattle ranching. During the winter they maintained quarters in the higher elevations of the Baboquivari Mountains, where water is more plentiful. When the saguaro cactus comes into bloom they harvest its fruit. The pulp is made into a sweet jam and the juice is fermented and used as a ceremonial drink.

The Tohono O'odham live on four reservations in southern Arizona and number about 25,000. They are the Ak-Chin near Maricopa, the San Xavier south of Tucson, the Papago-Gila Bend near Gila Bend,

A Tohono O'odham basketweaver. Large baskets such as these were used for storage. Photo: Southwest Studies.

and the big Main Reservation with headquarters at Sells. Most villages have a Catholic church and the people combine that religion with their native beliefs. Near the church is a "feast house," an open-air kitchen and dance ground where fiestas complete with song, dance and food are held. Because of the proximity to the Mexican border there is a strong Hispanic influence in the culture.

Cattle raising is one of the major industries along with agriculture and copper mining. The ancient art of basketry is important still. Tohono O'odham women weave more baskets than any other tribe in the country.

The Tohono O'odham are a communal people and their moral and religious leader was the Keeper of the Smoke, who presided over nightly meetings of the council. In early days he wielded a great deal of authority. Today, most people practice the Roman Catholic faith. The mission San Xavier del Bac near Tucson accommodates the residents living in the area as well as providing a school for the youth. The major communal activity is the annual tribal cattle roundup.

Traditionally, the Tohono O'odham have a fairly strong family unit; the sons and their families, as well as the unmarried daughters, remain with the family. Today the tribe is governed by a council of elected representatives. They are closely related to the Pima and possibly are descendants of the ancient Desert Hohokam.

THE YAVAPAI
(PEOPLE OF THE SUN)

During the early days the Yavapai Indians inhabited the rugged region from the Salt River canyon to the Bradshaw Mountains. They lived in small bands, hunted and gathered nuts and berries. Their language was Yuman and some customs were similar to their relatives, the Hualapai and Havasupai. However, their close contact with the Tonto Apache caused them to adopt many of the cultural traits of the Apache. Anglo-Americans often confused them with Apache. After the winter campaign of 1872-73, Yavapai were placed on a reservation near Fort Verde. Later, they gathered and marched on the infamous "March of Tears" to Hell's Forty Acres — San Carlos, east of Globe. A quarter of a century later they were given their own reservation at old Fort McDowell, on the Verde River northeast of Phoenix. Only about 200 chose to leave; the rest had made a life among the Apache and chose to stay in the San Carlos area.

Like the Apache, the Yavapai were fierce warriors in battle. There is still much confusion among historians over battles in the central mountains as to whether Apache or Yavapai were involved. Because of their small numbers, intermarriage has almost rubbed out the pure Yavapai lineage. Approximately 3,000 reside on reservations at Fort McDowell, Prescott and Camp Verde.

THE HUALAPAI
(PINE TREE FOLK)

The Hualapai Indians occupied a vast area ranging from the San Francisco Peaks on the east, to the Bradshaw Mountains on the south, the Grand Canyon on the north, and the Colorado River on the west. The Spanish called them *Cosninas* or *Cohonina,* referring to both the Hualapai and Havasupai peoples. Later the Anglo-Americans arbitrarily separated the two. However, they still consider themselves one people—the Pai.

The first written report of these people was by Father Francisco Garcés in 1776. Because there were few European trekkers in that part of Arizona, the next contact came in 1826 when parties of French and American trappers passed through. During the 1850s members of the Army Corps of Topographical Engineers—Capt. Lorenzo Sitgreaves and Lt. Edward Beale and Lt. Amiel Whipple—encountered bands west of Flagstaff. Near the Cerbat Mountains, a war party attacked and wounded famed scout Antoine Leroux.

The discovery of rich minerals in the Cerbat and Hualapai mountains in the 1860s brought in large numbers of prospectors and freighters. It wasn't long before war broke out. The army was called in and soon put an end to the warring ways of the Hualapai. In 1869 they settled on a reservation and lived peacefully. Today about 2,200 live on the Hualapai Reservation in northwest Arizona.

THE HAVASUPAI
(PEOPLE OF THE BLUE-GREEN WATER)

The Havasupai tribe are the only Indians living in the Grand Canyon. They number nearly 600 today. It is believed they have lived in the same area since A.D. 1100. They grew crops of corn, beans and squash along the blue-green waters of Cataract Creek and supplemented their diets with small game and berries.

The Havasupai didn't have clans; the family and extended family made up their social organization. They were a patrilineal society. Marriages and divorces weren't an issue. When man and woman reached an understanding they took up residence with her family. After a child or two, they built a home close to the man's family. The male owned the home and land and the female retained rights to the pottery, baskets and other personal items.

THE MOHAVE
(THREE MOUNTAIN PEOPLE)

The Mohave Indians were once the largest and most warlike of all the Colorado River tribes. Their name comes from the three Needles mountains near the California-Arizona border. A rancheria economic group, they lived along both sides of the river between Needles and Black Canyon, near today's Hoover Dam. Early Spanish explorers such as Oñate and Garcés met them but no missions or settlements were located in Mohave land. The first Anglos to come in contact with these Yuman-speaking Indians were mountain men such as Jed Smith, Ewing Young and James Ohio Pattie between the years 1826-1834. Relations weren't always friendly.

Only a year after a friendly visit in 1826, Jed Smith's party was ambushed and nearly wiped out by an angry bunch of Mohaves who were smarting over an earlier shoot-out with another party of trappers.

Mohave leaders were men chosen for their honor and dignity; however, the war chiefs and shamans had more influence. Their allies were the Apache, Yavapai, and Yuma. Their enemies were the Cocopah, Pima, Tohono O'odham and Maricopa. Mohave braves enjoyed warfare and were known for their prowess in battle. Their fighting was mainly hand-to hand, charging their enemy hell-for-leather with bare fists, war clubs or bow and arrow. Today about 2,200 Mohave live at the Fort Mohave reservation west of Kingman. Others share a reservation at Parker.

THE QUECHAN
(THE YUMA INDIANS)

Commonly known as the Yuma Indians, this Colorado River tribe is actually Quechan ("Another Going Down") which means "on the legendary trail by where they came." The word "Yuma" was a name given by the Spanish. It comes from *Umo,* meaning smoke, and refers to the smoky firebrands the natives used to carry to ward off pesky insects along the river.

Originally they ranged west to the Pacific Ocean and east to the mountains of Arizona. Eventually they settled on both banks of the Colorado River at its junction with the Gila.

The first mention of the Quechan was by Father Eusebio Kino in 1701, when they numbered between three and four thousand. A fierce, warlike people, they stubbornly resisted interlopers following the Gila Trail to California. In 1781 they revolted against the Spanish and closed Yuma Crossing for more than half a century. During the early American years, the 1850s, they went on the warpath again. Finally, the establishment of Fort Yuma forced them to live peacefully. Approximately 2,800 Quechan are enrolled at the Fort Yuma reservation today.

THE COCOPAH

Agriculture has always been the backbone of the tiny Cocopah tribe. For centuries they've planted their crops along the Colorado River below Yuma. The first contact with whites came in 1540 when Captain Hernando Alarcón anchored his ship at the mouth of the Colorado and went upriver in a small boat. Alarcón had hoped to rendezvous with the Coronado Expedition on its search for the fabled Seven Cities of Gold. The origin of their name is unknown.

Other Spanish explorers including Melchior Diaz, Juan de Oñate and padres Kino and Garcés visited their villages over the next 250 years.

The Cocopah numbered about six thousand in those

days and were described as being quite tall and well-built. They traveled up and down the Colorado on craft that ranged from logs to rafts large enough to carry provisions for several days. Some of these journeys were fishing expeditions down to the Gulf of California.

When the legendary steamboats began to plow their way up and down the Colorado, the Cocopah were hired as pilots, guiding the paddlewheelers through the treacherous sand bar-laced waters. Today, less than a thousand live on the Cocopah reservation at Yuma.

THE CHEMEHUEVI
(TANTAWATS: SOUTHERN MESA)

The Arizona Chemehuevi Indians reside in a chunk of land south of Parker which they share with small groups of Navajo, Hopi and Mohave. They are relative newcomers to Arizona, arriving from the Mojave Desert around 1800. About this time the Mohave Indians had driven a branch of the Maricopa tribe away, creating a vacancy. Since the Chemehuevis got along well with the Mohaves, they were allowed to take up residence. After settling along the river, they adopted customs similar to those of other river tribes. About 500 are registered at the Colorado River reservation, a place they share with Mohave, Hopi and Navajo.

THE MARICOPA
(PIPATSJE: THE PEOPLE)

The Maricopa Indians are a minority within a minority. The origin of the name Maricopa is unknown. Anglos gave the name to distinguish them from other, more warlike Colorado River tribes. They are related to the Yuman tribes of the Colorado but were constantly at odds with those groups, so they allied with the Pima. Inhabiting the lands near the junction of the Salt and Gila rivers, the Maricopa were the Indians living closest to where Phoenix is today. Earlier they resided in the vicinity of Gila Bend and before that nearer the Colorado River. Warfare drove them further and further up the Gila to their present locations. Their life-style was similar to other river tribes. Houses were made of poles and thatch covered with mud. They gathered food, hunted small game and fished. Like other Yuman peoples, they adorned their bodies with tattoos and face paint, though not to the same degree as the Quechans, Cocopahs and Mohaves.

The Maricopa are best known for their beautiful mesquite-fired red pottery. Ida Redbird, a member of the Arizona Women's Hall of Fame, was the most famous of these potters. Today, about 700 Maricopa live with the Pima, on reservations near Phoenix. About half live north of Mesa along the Salt River; the other half in the West Valley near Tolleson.

THE PAIUTE
(THE DIGGER PEOPLE)

The Kaibab Paiute are of Ute-Aztecan language stock and live in the area around Pipe Spring National Monument, just east of the Kaibab Plateau on the Arizona Strip. This small, semi-nomadic group of hunters and gatherers had scarcely ever seen a white man until a century ago.

They were poor and unable to resist the entry of Mormon ranchers and farmers in the 1860s. The Paiutes had little in the way of religious organization, and many were converted to the Mormon faith. Today, about 250 live on the Kaibab reservation near Pipe Spring.

THE YAQUI

The Yaqui are the only "non-native" Indians in Arizona. They could be called the "Apaches of Mexico," for their hostile relations with the Mexican government was similar to that of the Apaches of this country.

During the 1880s they began an exodus from Mexico, settling in southern Arizona where they were accepted as refugees. During the Mexican Revolution of 1910, many fought on the losing side and fled to the United States. Battles were fought between Mexican troops and Yaqui warriors as recently as 1926.

The Yaqui successfully resisted Spanish military intrusions into their lands but in 1609 the Jesuits were allowed to establish missions. The Catholic religion is still a very important part of Yaqui life today. Yaqui villages in Arizona today are Pascua and Barrio Libre in Tucson; Guadalupe, near Tempe; and Vista del Camino in Scottsdale. They were not granted a reservation until 1964 and were not recognized officially by the U. S. government until 1978. Their population today is about 3,000.

Their religious ceremonies are a rich blend of Catholic and native. Ceremonies such as the famed Easter fiesta are based on 17th Century Jesuit miracle plays in which evil tries to overcome good but always loses out in the end. During Holy Week masked ceremonial dancers including the *Matachines, Fariseos,* the *Deer Dancer, Chapayoka* and *Pascolas* perform a colorful re-enactment that dates back nearly 400 years.

Arizona's Indian population numbers about 385,000, third largest in the nation. Because many are far removed from urban areas, they have remained the most traditional of America's Native peoples.

What the future holds for Arizona's 21 federally recognized tribes is uncertain. In 1993, the state signed the first gaming compacts with the Indian tribes. Before then the fate of tribes rested almost entirely with the federal government, which often provided inadequate programs for native people whose barren lands left them few ways to provide for themselves. In less than a decade, gaming has dramatically changed that story. Today the tribes are better able to take care of themselves and others. The tribes use profits from gaming mainly to provide essentials such as housing, health care, education, police and fire protection, roads, and water and sewer lines.

In addition to fostering self-reliance, gaming dollars are bridging the Indian and non-Indian worlds. With a renewed commitment to self-reliance, tribes today are becoming involved in myriad businesses including recreation, skiing, mining, agriculture, sand and gravel operations, resort hotels, and industrial parks. Even so, the amenities of outside life are luring many young Indians away from their traditional values and surroundings. Some continue to resist outside assistance because of old mistrusts and misunderstandings of the white man.

4

GLORY, GOD AND GOLD

"Granted they did not find the gold; at least they found a place in which to search." So wrote Pedro de Castaneda, of the famed Coronado Expedition. One would be hard-pressed to find a more fitting name for this untamed land than that which the Spanish used: the "Northern Mystery." The grand hopes and fond dreams of getting rich without working were dashed in 1542, when Francisco Vasquez de Coronado returned to Mexico City from his unsuccessful search for the fabled Seven Cities of Gold. Two years earlier, the greatest expedition yet seen in the New World had embarked like some gaudy serpent bending its way northward in the quest for *El Dorado*. The Spaniards found, instead, unconquerable natives, vast arid lands with twisting, impenetrable canyons and brawny, rough-hewn mountains — awesome barriers one and all.

The inspiration for such a daring venture can be summed up in three words: Glory, God, and Gold.

In 1492, Spain emerged victorious from a long war with the Moors. Her fighting instincts were honed to a fine cutting edge, and the new nation was ripe for overseas conquest. In the years following Columbus' successful landing in the New World, Spanish conquistadores such as Hernán Cortés and Francisco Pizarro found unbelievable riches in Mexico and Peru. Overnight, Spain became the wealthiest nation in the world.

The success of Cortés and Pizarro inspired other conquistadores to seek fame and fortune in the New World. Legends began circulating throughout New Spain of other wondrous places far to the north, and these bold adventurers reasoned that the vast hoards of gold and silver already discovered proved the existence of more in the unexplored north.

Along with this insatiable quest for conquering new lands and seeking treasure was Spain's penchant for saving the lost souls in the New World. During these troubled times for the Catholic Church in Europe, Spain was determined to be the bastion of Catholicism. The thousands of natives in the New World provided a bountiful harvest for the zealous missionaries. There was another reason for gathering in the natives; the Spanish depended on them as a labor force. Since the vast majority of Europeans were miners, merchants, soldiers, priests, planters and ranchers, the natives were needed in menial jobs such as herders and mine workers. At the same time, Spanish culture, law, language, religion, animal husbandry and new crops were introduced to the New World.

The stage had been set for the great Coronado Expedition several years earlier, in 1528, when an exploring party was shipwrecked off the coast of Florida. Using makeshift rafts, the survivors tried to make their way back to New Spain by following the gulf shore of today's United States. They were wrecked again, this time on the Texas coast. The survivors, Cabeza de Vaca, Alonzo del Castillo, Andrés Dorantes and the latter's slave, Esteban, were taken captive by local Indians. De Vaca's prowess as a healer eventually gained freedom and respectability for the four pilgrims. They spent the next eight years walking across the wilderness of today's Texas and northern Mexico.

In 1536, the four naked, half-starved skeletons straggled into Culiacan, Sinaloa. Taken before Viceroy Antonio Mendoza, de Vaca unraveled a tale of great cities. He hadn't seen them, but he had heard stories from the natives of the existence of seven cities of gold. It's a pretty good bet that, at the same time, they claimed the weather in that land was awfully hot — but it was a wonderful, dry heat.

Mendoza attempted to suppress the rumors of gold to prevent a rush, while quietly organizing an expedition of his own. He recruited a handsome, dashing young hidalgo named Francisco Vasquez de Coronado to lead the quest. Meanwhile,

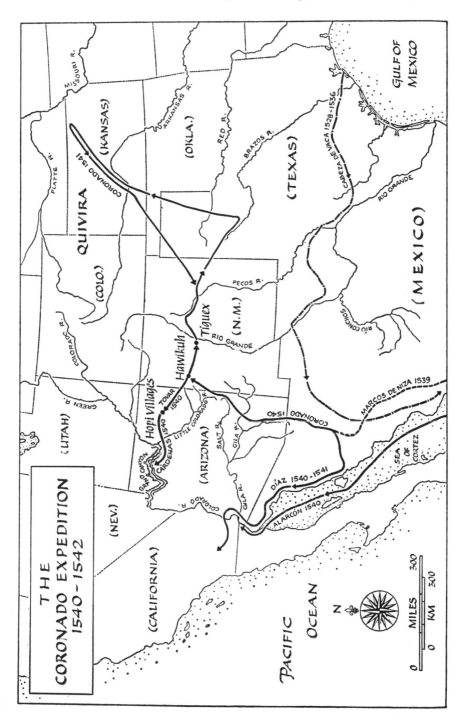

THE
CORONADO EXPEDITION
1540-1542

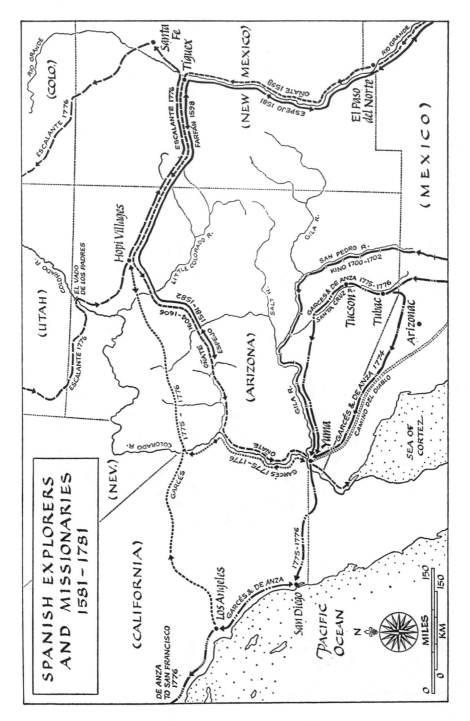

SPANISH EXPLORERS AND MISSIONARIES 1581–1781

he sent a Franciscan padre, Fray Marcos de Niza, and Esteban, the Moorish slave, north on a reconnaissance mission to verify the existence of the golden cities.

In 1539, de Niza and Esteban ventured north, crossing into Arizona, probably through the San Rafael Valley. Somewhere along the way they parted company and the Moor was sent ahead. A few weeks later Esteban arrived at the Pueblo Indian village of Hawikuh, near today's Zuni, New Mexico, and made his customary request for food and female companionship. The inhospitable natives cut his brash visit short, literally and figuratively, puncturing his body with arrows. His frightened escorts were sent scurrying back down the trail to de Niza's camp.

The 38-year-old friar hurried back to Mexico City. The further he got from Hawikuh the more his imagination began conjuring tales of great wealth in the new lands. In his fertile mind the tiny, mud and wattle village of Hawikuh grew into a city larger than Mexico City with buildings ten stories high where natives wore giant pearls, gold beads and emeralds, ate their meals out of gold and silver utensils, and decorated their doors with turquoise. When de Niza finished his tale, all Mexico City went into a gold-crazed frenzy.

In February, 1540 Francisco Vasquez de Coronado, dressed in gilded armor, rode out at the head of a resplendent army numbering nearly 300 horsemen and foot soldiers. Behind them came a thousand Indian allies followed by native and black slaves. The intrepid explorers, with Fray Marcos as their guide, trudged through the wilderness for nearly five months before arriving at Hawikuh, bone-weary and nearly starved.

Their shock and disappointment at the sight of the mud-walled village was the first of many on the journey. After a brief battle, the hungry Spaniards stormed the village and confiscated the natives' food supplies. The battle, fought on July 7, 1540, marked the first between Indians and whites in what is now the United States.

The natives quickly learned that the best way to rid themselves of the pesky Spaniards was to tell them the treasures they sought could be found elsewhere. Seven cities existed, they said, some distance to the northwest. Coronado quickly sent an expedition led by Pedro de Tovar off in that direction. Arriving at the Hopi village of Awatovi, the mounted Spaniards once again had to fight and win before the stubborn Hopi admitted them into their ungilded village. The rest of the Hopi villages surrendered, sending peace offerings and, more important, information that further west a great river flowed. Hoping this might be the eagerly sought but mythical Northwest Passage, a fabled waterway across the continent, they hurried back to report the news to Coronado. Another expedition of 25 horsemen led by Captain López de Cárdenas set out to find the river. Unfortunately, the great stream they sought lay at the bottom of the impenetrable Grand Canyon.

The Coronado Expedition, 1540-1542. Painting by Frederic Remington.

Cárdenas didn't realize it, but that reddish ribbon of water far below would one day become known as the mighty Colorado and would be the last major river in the U.S. to be explored.

At the same time Cárdenas was gazing down at the Colorado, another group of Spaniards were exploring that same river far downstream. The naval arm of the Coronado expedition, led by Hernando Alarcón, had sailed its ships through the Gulf of California to the mouth of the Colorado. Then Alarcón boarded a small craft and headed upstream to the river's junction with the Gila at the site of today's Yuma. He had hoped to link up with Coronado but when he learned from natives that the land expedition was far to the east, he buried letters at the base of a tree, carved an inscription on the trunk and returned to Mexico City.

A short time later these letters were found by still another arm of the expedition led by Capt. Melchior Diáz. Diáz and 25 soldiers had been sent in a northwesterly direction by Coronado in hopes of finding Alarcón. At the Yuma Indian villages, natives told Diáz of Alarcón's visit. He located the tree with a message on the trunk that read: "Alarcón came this far. There are letters at the foot of this tree." The letters told of the sailor's visit and return to Mexico. Alarcón was in a bit of a hurry, because worms were eating his sailing ships. Diáz explored the land around the lower Colorado, then left to rejoin Coronado. Somewhere along *Camino del Diablo,* the "Devil's Highway" (along the present Arizona-Sonora border between Nogales and Yuma), Diáz was thrown from his horse, impaled on his lance and died a horrible death.

Frustrated at his failure to find gold or a passage to the Orient, Coronado turned his attention eastward toward the Rio Grande River. He made base camp at Tiguex, a pueblo near today's Bernalillo (a few miles north of Albuquerque). At Tiguex, they spent the next two winters. Here also, they heard stories of a magical place called *Gran Quivira* from a native yarnspinner named El Turco.

Expeditions were sent east to the Pecos River, the dreaded *Llano Estacado* (Staked Plains) of Texas, and north into Kansas in a fruitless search for *Gran Quivira.* When *Gran Quivira* turned out to be another poverty-stricken Indian village of grass huts, the angry Spanish sent El Turco to the happy hunting ground. Finally, in 1542, the disappointed expedition returned to Mexico City.

Coronado was considered a failure for not finding glittering cities with streets cobbled with the golden boulders of the *madre del oro.* He died a few years later, never realizing that he'd opened vast new lands laden with riches for future explorers.

Forty years after the Coronado Expedition, Antonio de Espejo led a small group of prospectors to the Hopi villages. From there he dropped into the Verde Valley and found ore of an undetermined value. He also found warlike Indians. The only thing that held the Indians back was the fear of the four-legged critters ridden by the interlopers. Espejo returned with ore specimens and a wild tale about a lake of gold somewhere in northern Arizona.

In 1598 another explorer, miner Juan de Oñate, traveled across much of Arizona after establishing the first colony in New Mexico. One of his officers, Capt. Marcos Farfán, led a troop of eight men to the vicinity of Prescott where he found rich silver ore.

It wasn't until 1604-05 that Oñate was able to recruit an expedition and return to Arizona. He saw much of the country but didn't find a lake of gold or even an easy route to the Pacific Ocean. Local native yarnspinners did entertain him with tales of a rich island of bald-headed men ruled by a fat woman with big feet; a tribe of one-legged people; some Indians who slept in trees; others who slept under water; and a great lake where the natives decorated their bodies with gold jewelry.

Eventually, Oñate returned to New Mexico empty-handed. World events were causing Spain to re-evaluate its position in regard to control of Mexico's northern frontier. The intractable natives, especially the nomadic tribes, were impossible to defeat. They had no capital city to conquer and no generals or prime ministers to capture and negotiate a treaty on behalf of the rest. It was truly frustrating. The best way to control the area, Spain determined, was to make good Spanish-speaking Catholics out of as many natives as possible. Henceforth, missionaries would be sent out to Christianize the vast lands. By bringing these natives under the Spanish umbrella, Spain believed it could thwart attempts by the Russians, French, and English to penetrate the Spanish empire's northern frontier.

5

THE RIM OF CHRISTENDOM

The first missionaries to arrive in Arizona were Franciscans from New Mexico. Three friars and twelve soldiers arrived at the Hopi villages in 1629 and established the first permanent structures for use by non-Indians in Arizona. One of the lasting contributions of these padres was the naming of the towering San Francisco peaks, some seventy miles to the southwest, in honor of their patron saint St. Francis of Assisi. The peace-loving Hopi clustered mainly in permanent villages around and atop three arid, limestone-colored mesas. Since they didn't move from place to place like the nomadic tribes, the Spanish naturally figured it would be easy to establish missions in their villages. What they failed to consider or chose to overlook was the fact that these village people had a well-organized government and time-honored native religious practices and they didn't particularly cotton to these newcomers moving in and telling them how to live. Besides, they deeply resented the strict discipline and forced labor imposed upon them. Since the Hopi were the farthest removed from Spanish authorities at Santa Fe, they were the least influenced by Spanish customs and were able to maintain their own traditions. Other Pueblo peoples seeking to escape Spanish oppression often sought refuge among the Hopi.

Naturally, the deeply religious Hopi were openly hostile to the three Franciscan padres. Native spiritual leaders especially resented the competition. However, when Padre Francisco Porras healed a blind child, relations eased and the missionaries began to make a few conversions. In 1633, the medicine men jealous of his success, poisoned Father Porras. The fate of the other two padres is unknown. In time, other priests arrived and zealous persistence paid off. By 1675 there were three missions and two *visitas* (mission stations) in Hopiland.

During the Great Missionary Period (1610-1680), the Spanish sent padres among the natives to convert and integrate them into Spanish society — at a lower class. The natives were taught art, music, drama, language, carpentry, adobe-making and religion. They provided a labor force to sustain the Spanish settlements. The natives seemed willing to accept the Christian faith as long as they could integrate it with their own religion. However, the padres found this unacceptable and accused the natives of pagan practices. Practice of their native religion was strictly forbidden and medicine men were imprisoned or killed. The medicine men or shamans, whose very authority rested on the maintenance of the ancient rituals, also resisted the blendings of religions. Soldiers entered kivas and destroyed religious articles.

Why didn't the natives rise in revolt? They far outnumbered the newcomers. It lies in the culture. The Pueblo culture didn't lend itself to individualism — conformity was the rule. In Pueblo culture it was considered improper to perform some act that brought attention to an individual. Thus, no native took it upon himself to rise up and lead the people in revolt. Also, the Pueblo people didn't consider themselves a nation or tribe. They spoke different languages and at times were at odds with one another.

In the 1670s a great famine reduced the population to half of what it had been prior to the arrival of the Spanish. Native shamans insisted this was a warning from their gods to throw the Spanish out. Both sides braced for a showdown.

After some eighty years of oppression a leader named Popé took a stand and organized the most successful Indian revolt in American history. The great Pueblo Revolt in 1680 spelled an end to the missions in Hopiland. Popé, a shaman from San Juan, had been imprisoned but was released after a public outcry from his people. He realized this show of unity could bring an end to Spanish rule. Popé went to the northernmost pueblo at Taos and planned his revolt. The plan was for all pueblos to rise up in unison. Runners carrying knotted cords were sent as far as Hopiland, 300 miles to the west. Each day a knot was untied. The revolt was to begin when all the knots were gone. The plan worked to near-perfection. On August 9, all the Pueblo Indians in Arizona and New Mexico struck in force and, when the dust had settled, some 400 settlers, including 22 priests, had been brutally murdered. Arizona had no settlers but three of the four priests were martyred and another enslaved.

It wasn't until 1692 that Don Diego de Vargas led the re-conquest of New Mexico. Vargas and his troops swept across the Hopi mesas and extracted a promise from all the villages except Oraibi to keep the peace. Only one village, Awatovi, allowed the padres to return. Soon after, the other villages organized a war party and destroyed Awatovi, killing the men and distributing the women and children to other villages. During these years, Hopiland became the "Switzerland" or refuge for other Pueblo Indians seeking to escape Spanish rule. The ancestors of the Tewa people living on First Mesa today came to live among the Hopi at this time.

The defiance of the Hopi ended attempts to establish a foothold from New Mexico. Settlement would come from the south under the gentle hand of a Jesuit priest named Eusebio Kino.

Priest, explorer, cattleman, promoter, cartographer and defender of the frontier, Father Kino was truly a man for all seasons. During the twenty-four years spent in the Pimeria Alta (Land of the Upper Pima), the tire-

Father Eusebio Francisco Kino, the legendary "Padre on Horseback." (Picture drawn from a composite)

less "padre on horseback" rode thousands of miles to ride herd on his loyal flock. Kino rightly believed the natives were more apt to accept Christianity on a full stomach. Putting these beliefs to practice, he introduced new crops and drove the first beef cattle into what would one day become Arizona. In 1692 he extended his "rim of Christendom" into the San Pedro and Santa Cruz valleys. By 1700 a small mission was located at the Papago village of Bac. Nearly a century later, on that site, the beautiful mission San Xavier del Bac was built. In 1701 he established Guevavi mission on the Santa Cruz river east of today's Nogales. A *visita* was located nearby at Tumacacori.

Kino rode the Pimeria Alta alone for nearly a quarter of a century. His dream of locating missions along the San Pedro, Gila and Colorado rivers was never realized. Spain was deeply involved in European wars and had neither the time nor money to spend on Kino's remote Christian outposts. The humble priest died in 1711. His deathbed consisted of the usual two calf skins for a mattress, Indian blankets for covers, and his old saddle for a pillow. He was buried in the chapel of his church at Magdalena, a few miles south of Nogales.

Diorama at Tumacacori Mission of Father Kino in Arizona.

The Pimeria Alta fell into neglect during the twenty years following the death of Kino. During the 1730s, Spain was recovered enough from its wars to turn its attention to the frontier once again. Many of the Jesuits were recruited from German states, including Padres Grazhoffer, Middendorf, Pauer, Sedelmayr, Segesser, Keller, Pfefferkorn and Stiger. All were hardworking and demonstrated the zealousness characteristic of the Society of Jesus. None, however, had Kino's energy, or the ability to gain the love and respect of the natives enjoyed by the great padre on horseback. Native medicine men or shamans resented the competition and sought to undermine their efforts. The new padres were not as tolerant of native ceremonies as Kino and for Father Johann Grazhoffer it proved fatal. The padre criticized the polygamy and drinking orgies enjoyed by the natives and in 1733 someone put poison in his food.

The discovery of the rich Planchas de Plata silver strike in 1736 brought a mass migration of rough and tumble miners into the Pimeria Alta. The influx of populace upset the usually tranquil Pima. Near the silver town of *Arissona* lived a Pima headman named Luis. Earlier, Luis had helped the Spanish put down a rebellion and, as a reward, was given the lofty title "captain-general" and made a governor. His thirst for power grew and soon he was undermining the padres by spreading rumors of their cruelty to natives. At the same time, he was laying plans to drive the Spanish out and seize control of the ranches, mines and missions.

Luis set his plan in action on November 20, 1751. He lured some twenty Spaniards into his home under the guise of providing a refuge from an Apache war party, then set fire to the place. The victims either burned to death or were slaughtered while trying to escape. When word of the rebellion spread, other bands of Pima took up the cause. During the next few days more than a hundred Spaniards were killed.

Spanish soldiers were ordered to round up Luis and his followers. After a lengthy chase, the Pima warriors were cornered in the Santa Catalina mountains north of Tucson and defeated.

A year later the Spanish established a garrison, or presidio, at Tubac on the Santa Cruz river. Fifty soldiers and their families settled along the east bank of the river in 1752. For the first time in the history of Arizona, white women had taken up residence. Five years after its founding, the population had grown to some four hundred.

The final years of the Jesuit era in Arizona were marked by controversy. Spanish civil authorities, military and the padres clashed frequently over the welfare of the natives. Each blamed the other for transgressions, real or imagined. The native leaders, in turn, took advantage of this discord to further their own political interests.

Ironically, in 1767 when the ax fell on the Jesuits, it had little to do with affairs in the Pimeria Alta. With the stroke of a pen, King Carlos III expelled them from the Spanish realm. The Bourbon king wanted absolute rule, something adamantly opposed by the Society of Jesus. King Carlos had reason to fear the Jesuits were becoming too powerful, so he had them expunged. More than fifty Jesuit priests in the Pimeria Alta were secretly rounded up and deported to Spain. Some historians believe Spain removed the Jesuits from the Pimeria Alta because they feared the padres might provide strategic information about the area to their arch enemies: England and France.

The exodus of the black-robed Jesuits in 1767 was followed by the *entrada* of the brown-robed Franciscans a year later. Fray Francisco Tomás Garcés, a humble man, cut from the same cloth as the great Kino, was the priest assigned to the Arizona missions. The intractable Apaches greeted the new padre on his arrival at San Xavier del Bac with a raid that destroyed part of the adobe church.

Despite the continuous raiding by Apache war parties, the tireless Garcés worked well among the natives. He sat cross-legged on the ground with them, ate their food and, although he was only thirty years old, earned the affectionate nickname "Old Man." Another priest described the humble friar aptly, saying, "God in his infinite wisdom, must have created Garcés for the place in which he served."

Like Kino, Garcés was the consummate missionary, always in search of souls to harvest. A year after his arrival, the gregarious friar had learned to speak the Pima language fluently. In 1771, he headed west in search of a land route to

Alta, California, which would link up with the missions recently established there by the legendary Franciscan padre, Junipero Serra. Using three Indian guides and a horse, he followed Kino's old trail, *Camino del Diablo,* to the Yuma villages on the Colorado. This expedition convinced Garcés that a land route was possible.

During the next five years he accompanied Capt. Juan Bautista de Anza, commander at Tubac, on two major expeditions to California. On the second trip in 1775-1776, 240 colonist-soldiers and their families were taken to the San Francisco Bay where a new settlement was established. Most of the colonists were women and children. Only one of the thirty soldiers in the expedition was unmarried. Interestingly,

San Xavier del Bac in 1890. Photo: Arizona Historical Foundation, Tempe.

many of the original settlers in the "City by the Bay" listed their birthplace as Tubac. Garcés didn't accompany de Anza to San Francisco. Instead he remained among the Yuma Indians at the historic river crossing establishing missions.

While de Anza was taking his colonists to Alta California, Garcés set out on another of his epic journeys, this time up the Colorado River where he explored the westernmost reaches of the Grand Canyon. Heading east, he even-

Captain Juan Bautista de Anza. From a drawing based on painting by Fray Orsi.

tually reached the Hopi villages, becoming the first padre to visit in over seventy-five years. Time had not softened the Hopi stand on the white man's religion. The Hopi elders at Oraibi allowed the kindly priest to stay a couple of days before issuing a stern warning to get off the mesa. Garcés gave a short speech on peaceful co-existence and brotherhood before being forced to rapidly depart. Later he recorded the experiences in his journal and dated it at the bottom, July 4, 1776.

Later that year two other Franciscans, Fathers Silvestre Escalante and Francisco Dominguez, following the advice of Garcés, attempted to open a trade route from Santa Fe to California. The explorers trekked northwest across Four Corners into Utah around Provo before giving up and returning to New Mexico. On the way home they crossed the Colorado River near today's Page (the crossing of Vados de Los Padres is now buried beneath the water of Lake Powell) and then on to the Hopi villages before heading back to Santa Fe.

Garcés journey into the wilderness lasted eleven months and covered some two thousand miles. During his absence, the presidio at Tubac had been moved farther north to Tucson.

During the de Anza expeditions to California, the natives living at the strategic Yuma crossing were promised presents and missions in exchange for allegiance and cooperation. Their chief, Palma, was taken to Mexico City and given a hero's welcome before being baptised in the Cathedral of Mexico and given the name Salvador Carlos Antonio Palma. Chief Palma returned to his people with many promises of gifts but the Spanish failed to follow up. After his great colonizing triumph in California, de Anza was named governor of New Mexico. Unfortunately for Spain, few commanders had de Anza's ability as statesman-soldier. In August 1779 Garcés and another priest arrived at the Yuma villages without the lavish gifts promised. Chief Palma lost face and the natives grew more restive. When a group of Spanish soldiers allowed their horses to graze on the natives' valuable source of food, the mesquite trees, Chief Palma decided it was time to rid his people of the unwanted interlopers, including the padres.

The Yuma rose in rebellion against their Spanish oppressors in July 1781. One group vented their wrath on the padres at San Pedro y San Pablo Mission, killing father Juan Diaz and Matias Moreno. Moreno was beheaded with a crude ax. Most of the men were killed but the women and children were spared and later ransomed back to the Spanish. Father Garcés was taken and for a time it looked like his life might be spared. In the end, the radical element held sway over the rest and the beloved priest was martyred. Afterward his body was buried and flowers were planted on his grave by the natives. Garcés once observed, "We have failed. It is not because we haven't tried. It is because we have not understood." His words are timeless.

The Yuma Revolt of 1781 closed the land route to California for forty years. During this time, which was also the last days of the Spanish empire, settlement would be concentrated in the Santa Cruz Valley.

The Royal Regulations of 1772 called for a cordon of fifteen presidios from San Antonio, Texas, to Tubac. A red-headed Irish mercenary in the Spanish army named Col.Hugo O'Conor was given the responsibility of selecting the sites. O'Conor chose Tucson over Tubac primarily because it was

Cal Peter's drawing (conception) of the Royal Spanish Presidio of Tucson, circa 1795. View looking southeast. Photo: Arizona Historical Society.

closer to Apacheria. Construction was begun in 1775 but proceeded slowly because most of the soldiers had gone to California with de Anza. The entire arsenal consisted of fifteen muskets and carbines, twenty-two sabers, ten six-ply leather vests, and six lances. The latter was considered the best weapon for Apache warfare.

Discipline was lax at the new presidio until the arrival of Don Pedro Allande in 1777. Allande, a spit-and-polish officer destined to be one of Spain's greatest combat commanders, denounced the conditions at Tucson and took immediate measures to build a defensible fortress. He was a seasoned veteran of European wars and quickly adapted to the unorthodox manner in which the Apaches fought. Allande and his brave *soldados de cuera* (leather jacket soldiers) were encumbered by a government that wouldn't expend much money on defense. Each soldier carried a smooth-bore musket called an *escopeda*, two unreliable pistols, a lance and a short sword.

The sword and lance were designed for traditional European warfare where the opponents stood and battled hand to hand. Since each soldier was issued only three pounds of gunpowder annually (any excess came out of the soldier's meager pay), there was very little target practice.

In addition to the thick leather vests, the soldiers used a bull hide shield (*adarga*) and leather leggings (*botas*). Some visionary officers suggested these hot, heavy, cumbersome outfits be discarded and in their place create mobile, hard-hitting light cavalry like the Apaches. Spanish bureaucracy, and the fact that the old ways were cheaper, kept matters at the status quo for a while. A troublesome characteristic of the Spanish system was that it was highly centralized. It took forever to get the government to act and a radical change was almost out of the question. We acquired the term *red tape* for the ribbons that were used by Spanish officials to bind government documents.

Despite this, Allande trained his troops well and when the Apache attacks did come, the Spanish made them pay a heavy price. His relentless campaigns into the heart of Apacheria eventually led to a peace that lasted forty years. Allande was also a fund-raiser for noble causes. In one of the more poetic ironies of Southwest American history the presidio commandant, in 1777, took up a collection among his humble settlers to raise money for the American colonists fighting for freedom far to the east. A total of 459 pesos was raised for the cause — a sizable amount considering that four pesos would buy a cow and a good horse could be bought for seven pesos.

On May 1, 1782, a large war party of Apaches swooped down on Tucson. A desperate fight ensued, pitting the Spanish and their native allies against the Apaches. The Apaches' main thrust was at the front entrance and, fortunately, some of the soldiers were on the outside and caught the Apaches in a crossfire. Captain Allande and twenty soldiers made a gallant stand at the main gate. Although severely wounded, the captain refused aid and remained with his men. The discipline of Allande's men paid off and, in the face of superior firepower, the Apaches withdrew. An attack like the May Day battle was rare in the annals of Apache warfare. They usually preferred hit and run guerilla-style, raiding small settlements and running off with the livestock.

In 1784, a new Indian policy, the Galvez Plan, was formulated. Named for Viceroy Bernardo de Galvez, the plan combined aggressive military campaigns with bribery. The Apaches were encouraged to settle near trading posts where they would be rewarded with booze, food rations, and weapons (of an inferior quality). The plan worked wonderfully well and for the first time there was peace on the frontier.

The last 30 years of the Spanish empire (1790–1821) brought unprecedented prosperity to what would become Arizona. Tucson began to flourish. The population totaled 1,015 including soldiers, priests, and Indians. Of that total, thirty-seven were Spanish settlers. Gold and silver mines were opened, new settlers arrived, large herds of cattle were brought in to stock the ranges, and the beautiful missions of San Xavier del Bac and San José de Tumacácori were built, the former at the exorbitant cost of 40,000 pesos. The latter is today a national historic monument, while the former is a "living" church to the Tohono O'odham. The ornate structures, blending Moorish, Byzantine, and late Mexican architecture, are among the most awe-inspiring in America.

Mission of San Jose de Tumacacari.

The Mission of San José de Tumacácori, circa 1864. From a sketch by J. Ross Browne.

The Mexican revolution began in 1810. By this time the Inquisition and costly European wars had taken their toll on Spain. The world's richest and most powerful nation had been in decline for some time. Interestingly, Spain's support for the struggling American colonies in their war for independence from England had been extremely costly and contributed greatly to its demise.

6

THE AMERICAN ENTRADA

Mexico's struggle for independence from Spain began on September 16, 1810, when Father Miguel Hidalgo called upon the people to rally around the cause for freedom. Unfortunately, the upper crust of Mexican society failed to heed his call. Hidalgo was killed and his rebellion was short-lived.

However, the seeds had been planted and in 1821 Mexico gained its independence. During the next few years, one unstable government after another tried and failed. Many politicos died by the gun in the turmoil. During one 24-hour period, three men held the office of president — one for only 45 minutes. Finally, one man, Antonio Lopez de Santa Anna, proved cunning and strong enough to wrest control of the government, and he proved to be the worst despot in Mexico's turbulent history. He was president-dictator 11 times and over the next 30 years managed to lose or sell more than half of Mexico to its neighbor, the "Colossus of the North."

During these unstable years, the peace agreements with the Apaches were ignored and, by the mid-1830s, war parties once again swooped down on Tubac and Tucson. Ranches and mines were abandoned. Under pressure from large landowners, the government secularized church lands and sold them at public auction. All priests were required to take a loyalty oath to Mexico or get out, and all foreign-born padres were deported. The once-beautiful missions were deserted and fell into disrepair.

The citizens of Tucson, the "post farthest out," knew little and cared less about the turmoil in Mexico City. In 1824, the state of Occidente was created, made up of Sonora, and Sinaloa, including the settled areas around Tucson and Tubac. A rift soon developed between Sonora and Sinaloa; in 1831 the two split and southern Arizona became a part of Sonora.

In 1837 the Mexican Republic, in a desperate move to stop bands of Apaches from relentless attacks on settlers, began paying bounties for Apache scalps. The policy was euphemistically called *Projecto de Guerra* or Project of War. A rugged assortment of well-armed border ruffians organized into companies and rode into Apacheria hell-bent-for-leather. The best-known of these was James Kirker, a former mountain man who was reputed in a single year to have collected $100,000 in Mexican silver for his grisly business. In 1846 Kirker joined the American Army as a scout in the War with Mexico. He knew northern Mexico like the back of his hand and provided invaluable service to the Americans. The Missouri Volunteers, to which he was attached, pronounced him absolutely fearless. Mounted on a fine horse, armed with bowie knife and a silver-inlayed Hawken rifle, he cut quite a swath while showing off his horsemanship riding Comanche-style, hanging off the side of his mount while riding full speed and letting his long hair sweep the ground.

Scalphunting for government pay in Arizona and New Mexico lasted until about 1850, when the United States took control and put an end to the business. At the same time, the enterprise of selling captives as slaves was terminated.

The opening of a 900-mile trade route between Santa Fe and St. Louis in the early 1820s played a significant role in the first American penetrations into Arizona. American traders, unwelcome during the Spanish colonial period, brought in much sought-after merchandise from the United States to exchange for Mexican silver, fur and mules. American fur trappers or mountain men moved their informal operations to Santa Fe and Taos. From these villages, trapping expeditions were launched into Arizona. Few records were kept since this was still Mexican territory and the authorities and the stuffy trappers played a running cat-and-mouse game. A reckless and daring breed of men, their names read like a "Who's Who" of America's frontier history: Kit Carson, Jedediah Smith,

Joseph R. Walker, Felix Aubry, Thomas "Peg Leg" Smith, "Old Bill" Williams, Pauline Weaver, David Jackson, Antoine Leroux and a tall, strapping man from Tennessee named Ewing Young.

Ewing Young was the most entrepreneurial of these fur trappers. He came down the Santa Fe Trail with Bill Becknell in 1822 and soon became the central figure in the fur trade in the Southwest. In 1824 he led one of the first American trapping expeditions into Arizona. A soft-spoken but determined frontiersman, Young feared neither man nor beast. He was the first American to trap along the Salt and Verde rivers and the first to explore the Gila to its mouth. Among his proteges was the legendary Kit Carson. No photographs or composite drawings of Young exist and he kept no journal, since Americans were usually not permitted to trap the area. While some gave up their citizenship and became Mexicans in order to obtain a license, Young, a staunch American, refused and took his chances with the authorities.

The risks were great. Warrior tribes, the searing desert and grizzly bears took their toll. During the 1828-29 trapping season, somewhere near the junction of the Salt and Verde rivers, Apaches set an ambush, killing 18 to 24 in Young's party. During one 1,000-mile expedition into Arizona, Young gathered in some $20,000 in beaver pelts, lost a third of his men in battle and, when he arrived at Santa Fe, Mexican authorities confiscated all his furs,

Christopher "Kit" Carson, famed mountain man, scout, Indian agent and Civil War general. Photo: Arizona State Library.

claiming his license was void. It seems a new law nullifying his license had been passed while Young was in Arizona. In order to avoid having their furs impounded, the Americans cached their pelts in the mountains near Taos then smuggled them over to Bent's Fort, a trading post on the north bank of the Arkansas River in American territory.

Kit Carson, destined to become a legend in his own time, headed into the mountains as a greenhorn in the season of 1829-30. He was raised in Missouri and at the age of 17 ran away from a saddle shop where he had been apprenticed. He joined a party bound for New Mexico where he met Ewing Young. That first expedition took young Kit into the wilderness of Arizona where they trapped the Gila, Salt and Verde rivers, eventually winding up in California. Later he rode the Rockies with the great scout Thomas Fitzpatrick. No doubt, Kit was fortunate to have the best of teachers and he was a good student. A diminutive and modest man, Kit was always willing to give due credit to mountain men, less famous, who had been his mentors. During these travels he met "Pathfinder" John C. Fremont. The officer took a liking to Carson and hired him as a guide. Capt. Fremont's florid journals were filled with heroic exploits of Carson and were widely read back east, making the daring young mountain man a national idol. During the Mexican War, Carson served in the California Bear Flag Revolt and guided Gen. Stephen Watts Kearny's Army of the West across Arizona. At the Battle of San Pasqual, near San Diego, Carson again distinguished himself by sneaking through enemy lines to get help for U.S. troops who were surrounded.

In 1843, three years before the Mexican War began, Carson settled in Taos and married 15-year-old Maria Josefa Jaramillo of a prominent New Mexico family.

Part of Kit's matrimonial life is subject to conjecture. His first wife was a young Arapaho named Singing Wind who bore him a daughter. Singing Wind died soon after and left Carson with an infant daughter to raise. He reputedly married a Cheyenne woman named Making Out Road. She was a fiery young lass and they were soon divorced. Kit later denied ever having made those latter marriage vows.

In 1849 he returned to Taos, settled down briefly and

became a rancher. Four years later he was appointed Indian agent to the tribes of northern New Mexico, a position he served admirably until 1861. Kit might have lived out his life as a prosperous rancher had the government not requested his services once again. During the Civil War he led the outgunned New Mexico Volunteers valiantly against Sibley's Confederate Army at Valverde on the Rio Grande. Afterwards, Carson was promoted to brigadier general by Gen. James Carleton and sent on a campaign against the Mescalero Apaches. After defeating them, Carson was ordered to attack the Navajo stronghold at Canyon de Chelly. That same year, 1864, Carson was again ordered into the field, this time against the Kiowa.

Despite all his military successes, Carson was a reluctant campaigner. He'd lived among the Indians most of his life, understood their plight, and was a staunch defender of the red man. Carson died shortly after the Civil War and was buried at Taos. He had no formal schooling and learned to read and write later in life, yet few have matched his accomplishments or have contributed so much to the making of this great nation. During the 1850s, writer W.H. Davis said: "There is nothing like the fire-eater in his manners, but, to the contrary, in all his actions he is quiet and unassuming. He has endured all imaginable hardships with a steady perseverance and un-flinching courage."

The first written account of Arizona by an American was the journal of James Ohio Pattie. Pattie was only 20 years old in 1824 when he arrived in Santa Fe with his father. Pattie's journal, written several years after his Arizona adventure, paints a rather colored-up account of his trials and tribula-tions. It begins with the daring rescue of Jacova Narbona, the beautiful young daughter of a former New Mexico governor, from rampaging Comanche raiders. In gratitude, young James was given a license to trap the Gila. Over the next few years he faced fearsome Apaches and Mohaves, hot, blazing deserts, cougars and grizzlies. Finally, James and his father, Sylvester, were jailed as trespassers in California, where his father died. During a smallpox epidemic, James innoculated thousands and gained his freedom. He returned home to Ohio, a tired, beaten young man, lamenting, "The freshness, the visions, the hopes of my youthful days have all vanished and can never return."

Joseph Walker was another of the great pathfinders to explore Arizona. In early 1863 Capt. Joe Walker led a party of prospectors up the Hassayampa River and discovered rich gold placers in the area where Prescott would be located. Walker, despite the fact that old age was slowing him down and his eyesight was failing, was one of the most indestructible frontiersmen in American history. He stood well over 6 feet tall and weighed 200 pounds. During the 1830s he was one of the nation's foremost scouts and mountain men. In 1833 he led a winter expedition over the treacherous Sierra Nevada range, becoming the first to accomplish that feat and the first Anglo-American to see what would become Yosemite National Park.

In 1837 he was exploring Arizona in the Gila, Little Colorado and Mogollon Rim country. In 1851 Walker's explorations along the 35th parallel provided valuable information to the government about the feasibility of a transcontinental railroad across northern Arizona. A decade later he led a party of prospectors into northern Arizona, searching for gold around the San Francisco Peaks. Finding no gold, the group headed for Santa Fe to spend the winter and while in that city, Walker met Gen. James Carleton, military commander of New Mexico. Carleton suggested Walker explore the possibility of gold in the Bradshaw Mountains, and the rest is history.

Joe Walker was, without a doubt, one of the best of the legendary trailblazers. He had the admiration and respect of red men and white. He was comfortable in both cultures; in fact, was married to an Indian woman and was at home in Indian country for more than 50 years. Most remarkable, in all those years as a leader of brigades of trappers and immigrants he lost only one man. One time an old mountain man was asked by a traveler who was trying to catch up with one of Walker's expeditions asked, "Which trail did he follow?" "He don't *follow* trails," the old man replied, "he makes 'em."

Another member of this "reckless breed" was Tom "Peg Leg" Smith. Smith wasn't always minus one leg. In fact, he was born with both legs in their proper place. During a gunfight with Indians up on the Platte River in 1828, he was shot below the knee. Fearing gangrene, he helped with the amputation of his leg, seared the wound and later carved out a wooden leg for himself. Thereafter he was known as "Peg Leg." It was said he became a hellish fighter. He'd remove the leg and use it as a war club. In 1865, somewhere in the desert west of Fort Yuma, Smith found a rich lode of gold. He arrived in San Diego near death with some $1,500 worth of gold in his poke sack. He died soon after and to this day goldseekers still look for the "Lost Peg Leg Mine."

If Ewing Young was the most entrepreneurial; Peg Leg Smith, the toughest; Jim Kirker, the most gruesome; James Ohio Pattie, the manifestation of jaded youth; Kit Carson, the most famous; and Joe Walker, the one you'd want to lead your wilderness expedition; then the nominee for most colorful would be Ol' Bill Williams.

The picturesque town of Williams takes its name from Bill Williams Mountain, which towers above it and provides as beautiful a high country setting for a community as can be found in America. It's a fitting place name for Ol' Bill Williams, the "greatest free trapper of 'em all."

Bill was as colorful a man as any who ever forked a horse or mule and headed toward the setting sun. To those who knew the tireless old mountain man, he'd always seemed old —and eccentric. His drunken sprees around Taos set the standard others tried to match but never could. He rode alone into hostile Indian country.

Williams was a tall, skinny, redhead with a high-pitched voice, his body battle-scarred and worn. He was known to run all day with six traps on his back and never break into a sweat. He had a peculiar way of walking, more closely resembling a stagger, and he never walked in a straight line. He fired his long-barreled "Kicking Betsy" with unerring accuracy in what was described as a "double wobble." A "double wobble" was a technique in which the shootist let the heavy rifle "wobble" or traverse across the target and then squeezed off a shot at the precise moment the sights were on the mark. On horseback he wore his stirrups so short his knees bobbed just beneath his chin. He leaned forward in the saddle, resembling a hunchback on horseback. All these eccentricities enhanced his reputation as the Old West's most unforgettable character.

George Frederick Ruxton, an English adventurer who toured the West in the 1840s, wrote this colorful description of him:

> Williams always rode ahead, his body bent over his saddlehorn, across which rested a long, heavy rifle, his keen gray eyes peering from under the slouched brim of a flexible felt hat, black and shining with grease. His buckskin hunting shirt, bedaubed until it had the appearance of polished leather, hung in folds over his bony carcass; his nether extremities being clothed in pantaloons of the same material. The old coon's weather beaten face was sharp and thin, a long nose and chin hob-nobbing each other; and his head was always bent forward, giving him the appearance of being hump-backed. He appeared to look neither to the right nor left, but, in fact, his little twinkling eye was everywhere. He looked at no one he was addressing, always seeming to be thinking of something else than the subject of his discourse, speaking in a whining, thin, cracked voice. His character was well-known. Acquainted with every inch of the Far West, and with all the Indian tribes who inhabited it, he never failed to outwit his Red enemies, and generally made his appearance at the rendezvous, from his solitary expeditions, with galore of beaver when numerous bands of trappers dropped in on foot, having been despoiled of their packs and animals by the very Indians through the midst of whom old Williams had slipped.

They called him "Old Solitaire" for his lonesome ways (Bill wasn't that lonesome; he always seemed to have an Indian woman waiting somewhere). Fact is, he spoke several dialects and was more at home among the friendly tribes than he was with his own people. It was said he came west as a missionary to the Osage Indians but they converted *him.* He took an Osage wife, who died after bearing two daughters. So Bill headed for the mountains and became a trapper.

Bill had more lives than a cat, surviving one hair-raising adventure after another. His luck finally ran out after some 30 years in the wilds, when on March 14, 1849, a war party of Utes killed him and Dr. Ben Kern near the headwaters of the Rio Grande in southern Colorado.

Two years later, Richard Kern, a brother of Dr. Kern, was

traveling with the Sitgreaves Expedition in northern Arizona. Kern took copious notes on everything he saw and heard on the journey. During the trip Kern and guide Antoine Leroux applied the name "Bill Williams" to the 9,200-foot range. Later, the pair honored Ol' Bill again by giving his name to the river that headwaters near Hackberry. Later it was changed to Big Sandy. Today, the stream becomes the Bill Williams River after it joins the Santa Maria River near Alamo Lake on its journey to the Colorado River.

Like the Indians, with whom they sometimes lived and sometimes fought, mountain men like Williams were "nature's children." They loved the outdoors, hated fences and restrictions, respected grizzlies and rivers, and rode anything that "wore hair."

Storing the knowledge of this *tierra incognita* in their heads, they guided the storied Army Corps of Topographical Engineers on their historic surveys along the 32nd and 35th parallels during the 1850s. These paths later became the trails that led immigrants to the promised land.

It is ironic that this reckless breed of men — who went west to escape the restraints of the societies they despised — later opened the West for expansion and settlement of those beloved sanctuaries, ending a way of life that would never be seen again.

CONQUEST OF THE SOUTHWEST

During the early 1840s the cry, "Manifest Destiny," was ringing far and wide. "It is our destiny," advocates proclaimed, "to reign from the Atlantic to the Pacific." Extremists even went further, suggesting the conquest of Canada and Mexico be included. Texas, heavily populated by Anglo-American settlers, won its independence from Mexico in 1836 and would join the Union nine years later. The same year Texas entered the Union, President James K. Polk sent John Slidell to Mexico City with an offer to purchase New Mexico and California and the real estate that separated the two for 25 million dollars. The Mexicans, still smarting over the loss of Texas, refused to discuss the matter and made plans to go to war. Her French military advisors were certain this was a war Mexico would win. Both young republics, it seemed, were spoiling for a fight.

Mexicans boasted they'd plant the Eagle and the Serpent on the banks of the Potomac and their American counterparts claimed they'd hang the Stars and Stripes above the Halls of Montezuma.

The war began in some disputed land in Texas between the Nueces River and the Rio Grande. The American strategy was to send an army, under Gen. Winfield Scott, to Vera Cruz by sea and advance towards Mexico City. A second army, under Gen. "Old Rough and Ready" Zachary Taylor, would invade northern Mexico from Texas. Another small but important part of the American strategy was to send an army west, taking Santa Fe, then marching on to California. California was the real prize in this war. Col. Stephen Watts Kearny was selected to head this so-called "Army of the West." Kearny was a veteran of many years of campaigning on the frontier and was known as the "Father of the U.S. Cavalry." The Indians on the Plains called him "Horse Chief of the Long Knives." Kearny's army consisted of 300 regular cavalry; 800 boisterous, undisciplined but rawhide-tough volunteers from Missouri; and a battalion of Mormons whose mission was to build a road to California.

The Army of the West, numbering nearly 1,700, followed the Santa Fe Trail to Bent's Fort on the Arkansas River. There Kearny found some four hundred wagons loaded with millions of dollars worth of merchandise waiting to join him on the trek to Santa Fe. Because Santa Anna had closed the trade a few years earlier, Kearny believed these coveted trade goods would make the entrada of the American force easier. Kearny wisely sent one of his officers, Capt. Philip St. George Cooke, and a well-known trader, James Magoffin, to hold secret talks with New Mexico governor Manuel Armijo. It is believed that Capt. Cooke carried along a satchel full of hard cash as an added inducement. When the Army of the West entered Santa Fe on August 18, 1846, Governor Armijo and his force of dragoons had fled to Chihuahua. Kearny's conquest of New Mexico was achieved without firing a shot.

On September 22, 1846, Kearny issued a proclamation declaring American civil government in New Mexico. Included were a code of laws, a bill of rights and the appointment of territorial officials, marking the first time American government was applied to what would one day be Arizona. Kearny also promised the citizens of New Mexico military protection from the nomadic tribes that had ravaged the Rio Grande Valley for generations.

Meanwhile, in California, John C. Fremont and his ragtag band of mountain men successfully launched the "Bear Flag Revolt" and set up a provisional government. Kit Carson, already famed as a guide, was given dispatches and ordered to ride cross-country to inform Washington.

Unaware of Fremont's Bear Flag takeover, Kearny took three hundred dragoons and set out from Santa Fe on his own conquest of California. Near Soccoro, New Mexico, he met Carson and learned that the war in California was over. It really wasn't. The ex-mountain man couldn't have known that, soon after he rode out, the *Californios* counter-attacked and regained control. Kearny, in a hurry to get to California, sent his wagons and two hundred of his dragoons back to Santa Fe; then he ordered Carson to turn around and lead his small band west to California.

The Army of the West, now one hundred strong, had among its ranks two diarists, Dr. James Griffin and Capt. William Emory, and an artist, John Mix Stanley. These three men were awed by the flora and fauna encountered along the Gila River and spent many days taking copious notes. Stanley made the first detailed sketches in Arizona and Emory's scientific notes were later published worldwide. Militarily, the Army of the

Major (later general) William Emory. A soldier-scientist, he led several boundary surveys in the 1850s. His writings did much to popularize Arizona's unique flora and fauna. Photo: Arizona Historical Foundation, Tempe.

West impacted little on Arizona history. They stopped at the Pima villages and traded for pumpkins, melons, beans, and flour, finding the natives friendly and eager to help.

Kearny's force saw no action until it reached the outskirts of San Diego and learned the hard way that the war hadn't ended.

The Army of the West lost a bloody battle to the *Californios* at San Pasqual on the outskirts of San Diego. The beleaguered force was saved when a young naval lieutenant named Ned Beale, Kit Carson, and a Delaware Indian known as *Chi-muc-tah* sneaked through enemy lines and went for help. A few weeks later, Kearny regrouped and joined forces with other Americans and marched to Los Angeles where, on January 13, 1847, Gen. Andres Pico, head of the *Californios,* surrendered in the vicinity of today's Hollywood.

Following in the dust of Kearny's small army was the Mormon Battalion. Under the command of Capt. Philip St. George Cooke, the Mormon volunteers were assigned the difficult task of building a road to California. Originally numbering some 500 men, 25 women and some children, Cooke's little army started across Arizona with 340 men and 5 women; the remainder were too old, too young, or too sick for their assigned mission. Their road led farther south from Kearny's mule-back trail along the Gila. Guided by experienced mountain men Pauline Weaver, Baptiste Charbonneau and Antoine Leroux, the trail blazers detoured south around the mountains, seeking a passage wide enough for a wagon road, then turned north following the San Pedro River. The only action came near today's Benson, when they were attacked by a herd of wild bulls. Mules were gored and wagons rammed, but none of the troops was injured seriously. The so-called "first battle of bull run" lasted about an hour; nothing more than a well-placed bullet to the heart would stop the hard-charging longhorns.

On December 17, 1846, the Mormon Battalion reached the dusty little adobe village of Tucson. The Mexican commandant at first refused to allow the *Americanos* to enter without a fight to the finish. However, when Cooke persisted, he took his small army of defenders and fled south a few miles to the Mission San Xavier. So, without firing a shot, the Stars and

The Mormon Battalion arriving at the Gila River in 1846 after a tortuous journey across the desert from Tucson. Painting by George M. Ottinger, 1881.

Stripes flew for the first time over an Arizona village.

The arrival of the *Americanos* caused the locals to charge "tourist prices" for their tortillas, grain, and other supplies. Not to be outdone, the Yanks paid in scrip redeemable only in the United States.

At the Gila River, Lt. George Stoneman decided to perform a naval experiment on that shallow stream. Lashing together some cottonwood logs, he set sail with about 2,500 pounds of food and supplies. He hadn't traveled far when the craft sank. Stoneman went down with his ship, then walked ashore, declaring the river unsuitable for navigation.

The Mormon Battalion reached California in January, 1847, completing the longest infantry march in U.S. history. Shortly after the Saints hacked and sawed their way across the wilderness of Arizona, James Marshall found gold at Sutter's Mill near Sacramento, altering the course of the westward movement from a slow, natural trickle to a raging river. During the next few years, thousands of immigrants would travel the Cooke wagon road, or what would be better known as the Gila Trail.

The passage of time does little to alter paths of least resistance from one place to another. Later, the Southern Pacific, U. S. Highway 80, then Interstates 10 and 8 would transport modern-day travelers along much of the same passageway.

7

ARIZONA IN THE 1850s

War with Mexico ended on February 2, 1848 when a treaty
was signed at Guadalupe Hidalgo, near Mexico City. Mexico
agreed to give up its claims to Texas and ceded to the United
States the lands including California, Utah, Colorado, Wyoming, New Mexico, and Arizona north of the Gila River.

The Mexican Republic received $15 million in recom-
pense and the United States agreed to absorb more than $3
million in claims American citizens held against Mexico. Much
of the new boundary was north of the Gila Trail, the best all-
weather route to California. The treaty called for a boundary
to be surveyed and marked, which proved to be a serious
problem. An inaccurate map used as the final authority placed
El Paso 34 miles north and 100 miles east of where it actually
was. The American boundary commissioner, John Russell
Bartlett, and his Mexican counterpart, Gen. Pedro Garcia
Condé, seemed headed for a stalemate. The Mexicans argued
that, despite the error, the location of El Paso on the treaty
map be accepted, thus allowing Mexico a large part of the rich
Mesilla Valley. The two boundary commissioners finally reached
an agreement but the American surveyor, Andrew B. Gray,
refused to sign, declaring Bartlett was giving away some 6,000
square miles of land belonging to the United States. Since
Gray's signature was necessary to make it valid, the agreement was put on hold. Bartlett ordered Gray and Lt. Amiel
Whipple to move further on down the line and begin a survey
along the Gila River. Meanwhile, Bartlett, who was more
interested in writing a book on the area than surveying a

boundary, went on a junket to Mexico to study Indians. His travels took him clear to Acapulco, then north up the Pacific Coast to San Francisco.

Whipple and Gray surveyed the Gila until they ran out of supplies, then headed downriver to Fort Yuma. Tired and hungry, they found the fort abandoned and some 1,500 angry Indians outside. The tiny group of Americans were prepared to make their final stand on Christmas day, 1851 when a young Indian girl recognized Whipple. Two years earlier, while on another survey, Whipple had found the girl lost and wandering in the desert. He gave her some food and presented her with a small mirror before taking her back to her people. The girl had never forgotten the soldier's kindness. The ice was broken; the warriors broke into friendly grins and even assisted the weary, but relieved soldiers across the Colorado. Bartlett, a greenhorn political appointee with no knowledge of surveys, created such a controversy by his ineptitude and lack of interest that he was eventually replaced by the capable Maj. William Emory of the Army Corps of Topographical Engineers.

The boundary controversy nearly boiled into open warfare between the United States and Mexico in 1853 before President Franklin Pierce sent James Gadsden to Mexico with an offer to purchase more land. Gadsden arrived in Mexico City with five different offers. The largest, with a $50 million price tag, included a large chunk of northern Mexico that would have given Arizona a sizable seacoast. However, it wasn't meant to be and the United States eventually paid $10 million for some 29,670 square miles and access via the Colorado River to the Gulf of California. Gadsden's Treaty was signed on December 30, 1853, and ratified by Congress on June 30, 1854. The important southern transcontinental railroad line along the Gila Trail was now possible.

Mexico might have sold more land had it not wanted to maintain the land bridge to Baja California, and if a band of adventurers under William Walker hadn't made an ill-timed "invasion" of Mexico in 1853. That unfortunate incident raised the ire of Mexicans against selling any more land than was necessary to build a railroad. The U.S. Congress also was divided on the issue. Southerners wanted to acquire more land below the Mason-Dixon Line and Northerners were opposed. The final boundary survey was completed by October, 1855. On March 10, 1856 Capt. Hilarion Garcia lowered the Mexican flag at Tucson and moved his soldiers south. The following November, Maj. Enoch Steen and his First U.S. Dragoons arrived to take formal possession.

An old Arizona legend tells how the Arizonans missed out on having a seaport when engineers were surveying west of Nogales. It seems they were heading towards the Gulf of California when someone pointed out that the nearest saloon was northwest at Yuma. The thirsty surveyors did a right oblique and marked a diagonal line towards the famous river crossing. Makes a good story, but "it ain't true."

In 1850 Arizona became a part of the Territory of New Mexico. At the time there were only about 1,000 non-Indian residents. Since there weren't any white settlements north of the Gila, what was considered "Arizona" was, in reality, Dona Ana County, which extended across southern Arizona and New Mexico. The county seat was located at the small adobe village of Mesilla, along the Rio Grande. Feeling ignored by the government in Santa Fe, the citizens of Tucson began petitioning for separate territorial status almost immediately after the Gadsden Treaty was ratified. In April, 1860 an unofficial "Territory of Arizona" was created with the capital at Mesilla.

During the years preceding the Civil War, four military posts were established in Arizona. Fort Yuma, the first, was actually located on the California side of the Yuma Crossing. The hot desert was hell on humans and their livestock on their way to California. By the time they reached the crossing, most were in sad condition. To attend to these needs and keep an eye on the sometimes-warlike Yuma Indians, a post was established on October 2, 1849 and called Camp Calhoun. A year and a half later it was renamed Camp Yuma. Getting supplies to the remote post was a major problem because they had to be hauled overland across the hazardous desert from San Diego. In 1852, the first steamboat loaded with supplies plowed its way up the muddy Colorado and the future of the fort was assured.

In 1851, Fort Defiance was built in the Four Corners country to keep an eye on the Navajos who for generations had raided the Hopis and the Spanish settlements along the Rio

Grande. The isolated post was quickly dubbed "Hell's Gate" by the soldiers who were stationed there. The location of the fort was ill-planned. It was in a narrow canyon, vulnerable to attack on three sides.

On April 30, 1860 a large war party made a bold attack on the fort. Stubborn resistance from the small force of defenders was all that prevented a massacre. Afterwards some 1,500 soldiers were assigned to the post to prevent a recurrence. The Civil War caused the post to be abandoned in 1861 and the Navajos resumed their raiding.

In 1856, Fort Buchanan was established to protect settlers and miners in the mountains south of Tucson. Three years later, Fort Mojave was built on the Colorado River as a shelter for immigrants following the old Beale Camel Road across northern Arizona.

At the outbreak of the Civil War, all these posts were abandoned. Many of the officers and men who came from the South went home to fight for secession. Those loyal to the Union regrouped in California and New Mexico for the expected Confederate invasion. Naturally, the warrior tribes saw the retreat as a victory for their side and went on the warpath.

Most of this new land acquired from Mexico was *tierra incognita,* known only to a few mountain men. One of the first tasks for the U.S. Government was to explore, map and survey routes for steamboats, wagons, and railroads. The responsibility for this giant undertaking was given to the Army Corps of Topographical Engineers, an elite, handpicked group of West Point graduates. Some of their names are stamped indelibly on the face of Arizona: Sitgreaves, Whipple, Ives, Beale, and Parke.

The first of these daring explorer-scientists was Capt. Lorenzo Sitgreaves. In 1851, he led an expedition of 20 men with an escort of soldiers and guided by the legendary scout Antoine Leroux along the 35th Parallel. Their trek led some 650 miles across some of the West's most inhospitable land. During an attack by Yavapai warriors, Leroux was struck by three arrows. It was said the battle-toughened old scout suffered more from embarrassment at allowing himself to be shot than from the physical pain inflicted by the wounds. The expedition's doctor, Sam Woodhouse, operated on Leroux with only one hand. Earlier he'd been bitten on the other by a rattlesnake. The expedition suffered other hardships, including another savage attack by Yuma Indians, before reaching Fort Yuma bone weary and half starved.

The next group to run a survey along the 35th Parallel (the future route of Interstate 40 and the Santa Fe Railroad) was led by Lt. Amiel W. Whipple in 1853. A few years earlier this young officer had won his spurs surveying the Arizona-Mexico boundary following the Treaty of Guadalupe Hidalgo. Whipple's assistant on this expedition was Lt. Joseph C. Ives. Again the expedition was guided by the redoubtable Antoine Leroux.

Whipple's small band spent a cold, wintry Christmas camped at the foot of the snow-covered San Francisco Peaks. Near the headwaters of the west fork of the Verde River, they turned south, then headed west to the Big Sandy River, thence to the Bill Williams Fork and on to the Colorado. He headed north to modern-day Needles then west to the coast. His report proved that a railroad could indeed be built over the dry, mountainous plateaus of northern Arizona.

A few months earlier another expedition was led by Francois X. Aubry, the so-called "Skimmer of the Plains." Aubry and 18 men left Tejon Pass in California and rode east at a record-setting pace. Then he led a wagon train along the same route just to show the feasibility of such a venture. Hard riding was nothing new to the French-Canadian who earned his nickname by riding horseback non-stop from Independence, Missouri, to Santa Fe, a distance of 800 miles in a little over 5-1/2 days. While crossing northern Arizona in the 1850s, Aubry claimed to have encountered a tribe of warriors using rifle balls made of solid gold. He also reported selling some clothes for $1,500 in gold and swapping a broken-down old mule for a pound and a half of the precious yellow metal. Aubry sowed the seeds for several lost mine tales in the area.

Despite several shootouts with Indians, Aubry was convinced the 35th Parallel was the best place to locate a railroad. He met Whipple in Albuquerque, in October, 1853 and gave the young officer much-needed information about the region about to be explored. Soon thereafter, Aubry was killed in a saloon brawl in Santa Fe, but his journals eventually reached

Washington and provided important information to army explorers.

In 1858, Lt. Joseph C. Ives, former chief assistant to Whipple, was picked to chart the course of the unpredictable Colorado River. Steamboats had been plowing their way up the river as far as Yuma since 1852 when Capt. James Turnbull assembled a small, prefabricated sidewheeler called the *Uncle Sam.* The 120-mile trip from the mouth of the Colorado to Fort Yuma took two weeks. Progress was delayed by frequent stops for mesquite wood to fuel the 20-horsepower wood-burning engine. All hands had to go ashore and rustle up firewood. Later local natives, after overcoming their initial fear of the smoke-belching creatures, sold firewood at "service stations" along the way. Incidentally, the swift current of the Colorado sped things up a bit on the return journey. It took only 15 hours.

The strategic Yuma Crossing at the confluence of the Gila and Colorado rivers provided a wonderful business opportunity for an entrepreneur named Dr. Able Lincoln. The lure of gold in California brought thousands of immigrants along the Gila Trail and they needed a way to cross the Colorado. Dr. Lincoln built a ferry and in 1850 made $60,000 in just three months. This lucrative business didn't go unnoticed by John Glanton and his band of scalp hunters. They horned in on the enterprise and soon incurred the wrath of the Yuma Indians, who commenced to massacre the whole bunch, including the unfortunate Dr. Lincoln. Legend has it the gold stashed by Glanton and his gang was never recovered.— *quien sabe!*

Louis J.F. Jaeger reopened the ferry business a short time later and the establishment of Fort Yuma in 1852 served to protect the business from Indians and itinerant scalp hunters.

In 1853, Capt. George Johnson brought a sidewheeler dubbed the *General Jesup* to Fort Yuma. The 50-horsepower paddlewheeler could haul 50 tons of freight. At $75 a ton, the *General Jesup* was soon grossing $20,000 a month and the steamboats on the Colorado became Arizona's main link with the outside world until the arrival of the railroad in the late 1870s.

Little was known about the navigability of the Colorado

above Fort Yuma until 1858 when both George Johnson and Joseph Ives took their steam crafts up the river. The military steamer, piloted by Lt. Ives, was an iron-hulled sternwheeler called the *Explorer.* It wasn't a graceful craft, and one observer described it as a "water-borne wheelbarrow." Regardless, it did what it was supposed to do. In fact, both Johnson's civilian and Ives' military expeditions demonstrated the navigability of the silt-laden Colorado beyond today's Hoover Dam.

The U.S. Explorer in 1858. This was the first military craft on the Colorado River. Sketch by Heinrich Baldwin Möllhausen.

On the way back, Lt. Ives left his paddlewheeler and struck out east towards the Grand Canyon. With the help of some native guides, he snaked his way to the bottom, thus becoming the first white man to accomplish that feat. Ironically, his comments afterwards suggested that his visit was likely the last for a white man. "It can be approached," he wrote, "only from the south and after entering it there is nothing to do but leave. Ours has been the first and will doubtless be the last party of whites to visit this profitless locality." It's all in the eyes of the beholder.

During the next few years, steamboats with colorful-sounding names such as *Cocopah, Mohave, Esmeralda,* and *Gila* battled their way up and down the unpredictable Colorado, hauling passengers to such river ports as Yuma, Ehrenberg and Hardyville. But commerce ran east and west; unfortunately for the steamboat business, the muddy Colorado ran north and south. Still, a few steamboats continued to haul freight and passengers until the building of Laguna Dam, above Yuma, in 1907. Today, paddlewheelers churn their way through the waters of the Colorado again. This time they haul tourists on excursions around Lake Havasu or gamblers over to the casinos at Laughlin, Nevada.

The steamboat, Searchlight, docked at Yuma, circa 1880. This paddlewheeler was fairly typical of the steamboats that hauled freight and passengers on the Colorado River during the 19th Century. Photo: Southwest Studies.

A year previous to the Ives Expedition, Secretary of War Jefferson Davis selected a colorful adventurer named Edward (Ned) Fitzgerald Beale to build the first wagon road across northern Arizona. Beale, a former naval officer, was now a lieutenant in the Topographical Engineers. He was a hero of the battle of San Pasqual in 1846 and had delivered the first dispatches about the California gold discovery to Washington three years later. Beale's expedition was unique in the annals of exploration in that camels were imported as beasts of burden. The camels' amazing ability to go great distances without water, eating only the natural forage along the trail, offered a solution to the army's transportation problem in the arid Southwest. Although Beale championed his illustrious camels, his hired hands scorned them. The muleskinners couldn't speak Arabic and the stubborn beasts wouldn't learn English. The animals were said to be bad-tempered, something understandable when one considers the female only comes in heat every three years while the male is ready any time. Furthermore, the animals' bad breath would peel the hide off a gila monster and they had a habit of spitting at anyone they didn't like.

The problem was partially solved by importing North African camel drivers. Hadji Ali was the most famous. His name was quickly Americanized to "Hi Jolly." Despite problems with the foul-smelling camels, whose strange ways and appearance caused pack mules and wagon teams to panic, Beale successfully opened up his wagon road. But this romantic episode in Arizona's history came to an end just prior to the Civil War. Hi Jolly remained in Arizona, married and settled down. He is memorialized on a pyramid-shaped monument topped off with a lone camel at Quartzsite, Arizona.

"Camel Mail in Arizona," a diorama in the Arizona Heritage Museum. On July 18, 1859 on a prairie west of the San Francisco Peaks, camels arrive from California.

While Sitgreaves, Whipple, Beale and Ives were surveying routes across northern Arizona, others were marking paths along the Gila Trail or, more scientifically, the 32nd Parallel. In 1854 Lt. John G. Parke of the Topographical Engineers was sent out to explore routes between El Paso, Texas and the Pima villages near today's Sacaton, Arizona. Parke was also a veteran of the 35th Parallel country, having been with Sitgreaves in 1851. Since part of the trail blazed by the Mormon Battalion dipped into Sonora, Parke searched for shortcuts through the mountain passes inside the Gadsden Purchase. Assisted by Lt. George Stoneman, Parke mapped a route through Apache Pass, at the north end of the Chiricahua Mountains. This was the path followed a few years later by the famous Butterfield Overland Mail. The pass had too steep a grade and too many arroyos for a railroad so Parke returned a year later and located a new route north of the Dos Cabezas Mountains. The Civil War delayed the building of a transcontinental railroad for many years, but when the Southern Pacific stretched its steel ribbons across Arizona in the 1880s, Parke's old survey was followed. Today, Interstate 10 passes along the same pathway. That same year, the Texas Western Railroad Company hired Andrew B. Gray, a veteran of the Bartlett Boundary Survey, to map a route along the 32nd Parallel.

Jesse Leach built the first commercial wagon road across southern Arizona in 1858. Leach's road ran from El Paso to the San Pedro River, then turned north to the Gila River and followed that stream to Maricopa Wells, then on to Yuma. Although it was 47 miles shorter, Leach bypassed Tucson and doomed his road to failure.

In 1849, it took 166 days to travel coast-to-coast in a covered wagon. The same trip by stagecoach in the 1860s took 60 days. A decade later one could make the trip by rail in 11 days. By 1923 the time was shortened to 26 hours by airplane. A 747 jumbo jet could travel cross-country in five hours by 1975 and in 1980 the Space Shuttle made it in eight minutes.

In 1857, the first mail and passenger line across Arizona was chartered. It ran from San Antonio, Texas, to San Diego, California. The itinerary inspired one critic to mutter: "It ran from no place through nothing to nowhere." The line was better known as the "Jackass Mail" because the coaches were pulled by mules and, west of Yuma, passengers were required to ride across the sand dunes on the hurricane deck of the long-eared critters. The stage rolled by day and stopped to camp each night; because of the weather, the routine was sometimes reversed. In its one year of operation the Jackass Mail made only 40 trips across Arizona before being replaced by the legendary Butterfield Overland Mail.

"Remember boys, nothing on God's earth can stop the U.S. Mail." So said John Butterfield — and hardly anything did. Butterfield had the first reliable stage line across Arizona. He had a government-subsidized operation that ran 2,800 miles from Tipton, Missouri, to San Francisco, California. The line was quickly dubbed the Ox Bow because it swung south through Texas to Tucson, then Los Angeles and San Francisco. Butterfield was a logistical genius — building stations; hiring agents and teamsters, blacksmiths, hostelers, shotgun messengers; obtaining livestock; and running his line with clock-like efficiency. Coaches averaged less than five miles per hour on the 473-mile trip across Arizona. The Missouri to California trip took about 26 days; the fare cost $200 plus meals, which usually consisted of coffee, beans, venison, mule meat, salt pork and heaps of mustard.

Stations were located about 20 to 40 miles apart. A short distance from the station the stage driver would announce his arrival by blowing a bugle. By the time the stage rolled in the hostler had a fresh team of horses ready to hitch up to the traces. Passengers had little time to stretch their legs. With the exception of meal stops the stage was ready to move in less than ten minutes. In Arizona most of the stations were made of adobe and had protective walls in case of Apache attacks. Indians rarely attacked the coaches but the stations provided a fresh source of livestock for raiding war parties. It could be dangerous work; 168 Butterfield men died violently during those tumultuous years prior to the Civil War.

The twice-weekly stage ran 24 hours a day but the rough roads rendered a night's sleep impossible. To help pass the time, male passengers usually drank their way across Arizona, throwing their empties out alongside the trail. Modern pilots claim they can trace the old trail from the air because of all the glitter of broken glass.

In the foreground is the Concord-type stagecoach. To the rear is the open-air Celerity Wagon, more frequently used in Arizona. Photo: Southwest Studies.

The top line for the stagecoaches were the Concord coaches. They were sturdier, hand-crafted from the finest materials and assembled with more meticulous care than the most expensive of today's automobiles. All wood was first dried and sun-warped for three years so it wouldn't shrink in the hot, dry Southwest. The Concord had no metal springs. Instead there were thick leather thoroughbraces supporting the body. These let it roll rather than bounce over the bumps. The Concords were used primarily in the eastern and western ends of the line. In Arizona, the lighter "Celerity Wagon" was used. It had wooden seats that folded into beds and canvas flaps that rolled down to keep the dust out. The wagon was pulled by mules and some were so wild they had to be blindfolded before they could be hitched.

These leather-slung cradles on wheels were luxury liners compared to earlier times when men, women and children traveled afoot, on horseback or in some primitive wagon train. Newspapers as late as the 1870s still carried a long list of precautions for the prudent traveler. These included: If a team runs away, don't jump out — just sit tight and ride it out; don't discuss politics or religion with your fellow passengers; don't drink hard liquor in freezing weather; and don't grease your hair — too much dust.

The Butterfield Overland Mail was stopped only once in its 2 1/2-year history. In 1861, Cochise and his Chiricahua Apaches went on the warpath around Apache Pass and did what nothing else on "God's earth" could: shut it down.

The winds of political change swept across Arizona in the mid-1850s. On the morning of March 10, 1856, Capt. Hilarion Garcia and his company of soldiers stood at attention while the tri-colors of the Mexican Republic were lowered for the last time over the tiny presidio at Tucson. It had been two years since the United States purchased the land from Mexico, however, and Mexicans continued to man the small garrison in the interim. After the ceremonies Capt. Garcia, along with his cavalry troops and their families in the wagons behind, rode south along the dusty road leading to Mexico. A small group of Americans stood silently in front of Edward Miles' adobe dry goods store, watching the procession as it made its way through the narrow streets leading out of town. One of the spectators was a tall, strapping frontiersman from Virginia named Bill Kirkland. He was one of only 17 Americans living in Tucson at the time. The storekeeper pulled out an American flag and handed it to the Virginian. He took the flag, tied it to a small rough-hewn mesquite post, shimmied up the side of the building and hoisted the Stars and Stripes on the roof. The small crowd of Americans gathered in front of the store, let out a series of enthusiastic hurrahs, accented with the firing of Colt revolvers. The occasion marked the first time the national colors had been raised in what was to become Arizona since the land had become a part of U.S. territory.

Bill Kirkland went on to become one of Arizona's most illustrious pioneers. He established a cow ranch at Canoa, near Tubac in 1857, ran a lumber mill in the Santa Rita Mountains, operated a freighting business and was a road builder. A restless man, Kirkland kept on the move. He ranched and mined in Yavapai County, along the Mexican border on Sonoita Creek, and was a lawman at Willcox. Kirkland moved so much his friends claimed that whenever he stepped out the back door his chickens rolled over on their backs so their feet could be tied up for the next journey. Of all Kirkland's notable achievements in the new land, and there were many, the one event he was most proud was that March day in 1856 when he raised the American flag over Tucson.

Tucson, which had a population of some 1,000 during times of peace with the Apaches, had dwindled in recent years to about 100 residents in 1856 due to Apache raiding and plundering. Early American explorers reported seeing decaying ruins of once-prosperous ranches and mines.

The wheels of bureaucracy turn slowly at times and, despite these Apache depredations, Tucson's only military protection from Garcia's departure in March until Maj. Enoch Steen and his First U.S. Dragoons arrived eight months later was a small militia force of Tucsonians.

During the time between the departure of Mexican soldiers and the arrival of dragoons, a sizable party of American miners arrived in Tucson under the leadership of an adventuresome young man named Charles Debrille Poston. They were headed for the mineral-rich Santa Rita and Cerro Colorado mountains, south of the Old Pueblo. During the next few years they would mine a king's ransom in silver.

Poston's company rested in Tucson for several weeks. It was fiesta time, he wrote in his journal, and the men were allowed to "attend the fiesta, confess their sins, and get acquainted with the Mexican senoritas, who flocked there in great numbers from the adjoining state of Sonora."

A few weeks later Poston established the company headquarters at the abandoned Spanish presidio of Tubac some 45 miles south of Tucson. The old fortress was still in pretty good shape. Most of the adobe buildings were still intact, but the doors and windows had been hauled away. Work crews were sent into the pine-studded Santa Rita Mountains to cut lumber; corrals were rebuilt and soon the historic old presidio was habitable once more. A short distance to the east flowed the cool waters of the Santa Cruz River, and nearby fields provided abundant grass. As soon as word reached Sonora, large numbers of Mexicans arrived seeking employment in the reopened mines. Next Poston purchased the 20,000-acre Arivaca Ranch on the west side of the Cerro Colorado Mountains. Old mines were reopened and soon Tubac was a bustling little community.

Tubac, with its low-lined adobe dwellings and dusty streets, quickly took on the atmosphere of a pristine utopia.

Far from cumbersome bureaucracy, cluttered cities and the influence of the Catholic church, Poston would later write, "we had no law but love and no occupation but labor; no government, no taxes, no public debt, no politics. It was a community in a perfect state of nature."

The young entrepreneur had a paternalistic fondness for the Mexicans, especially the women. "Sonora has always been famous for the beauty and gracefulness of its senoritas," he wrote admiringly. The gold rush had created a mass exodus of young men to California, leaving the ratio of women to men as high as 12-to-1 in some Sonora towns. Many of these unattached ladies headed north to the new American mining camp at Tubac when they could get transportation in wagons hauling provisions. Others came on burros, and many came on foot. All were provided for. The Mexican senoritas really had a refining influence on the frontier population. Many of them had been educated at convents, and all of them were good Catholics.

Poston seems to have missed little in his observations. "They are exceedingly dainty in their underclothing, wear the finest linen when they can afford it, and spend half their lives over the washing machine."

The ladies of Sonora made a rich contribution to life in the community, not only providing companionship for the lonely miners, but assuming other responsibilities as well. "The Mexican women were not by any means useless appendages in camp," Poston noted. "They could keep house, cook some dainty dishes, wash clothes, sew, dance, and sing." They could give a good account of themselves in men's games also. "...they were expert at cards and divested many a miner of his week's wages over a game of Monte."

Poston was, in effect, the *alcalde* or magistrate, of Tubac. Accordingly, under Mexican custom, he was in charge of all criminal and civil affairs of the community. "I was legally authorized to celebrate the rites of matrimony, baptize children, grant divorces, execute criminals, declare war, and perform all the functions of the ancient El Cadi."

Young couples who couldn't afford the $25 marriage fee charged by the priests in Sonora came to Tubac where Poston not only married them for free but gave them jobs. In gratitude, many children were named Carlotta and Carlos in honor of the *patron.*

Life in Tubac went on its merry, uncomplicated way until Archbishop Jean Baptiste Lamy of Santa Fe sent Father Joseph Machebeuf to check out the spiritual condition of Tubac. The priest was aghast upon learning the marriages hadn't been blessed by a priest. He quickly ruled all marriages null and void. "My young friend," the priest told Poston, "I appreciate all you have done for these people, but these marriages you have celebrated are not good in the eyes of God."

Poston defended his actions, claiming that he hadn't charged the couples any money and had even given them an official-looking marriage certificate. The couples were then given a ceremonious salute called "firing off the anvil" (a homemade tribute made by detonating a charge of blasting powder held in check by a huge anvil so as not to cause any damage). Father Machebeuf must have felt bested by the persuasive Poston, for he agreed to do some horsetrading. The marriages would be blessed on the condition that Poston would refrain from activity customarily performed by the church. A gala celebration was held; the couples were reunited in marriage. Guests included all the little Carlottas and Carloses. According to Poston, "it cost the company about $700 to rectify the matrimonial situation."

Poston enjoyed those halcyon days at Tubac. On Sunday mornings he relaxed in one of the natural pools of the Santa Cruz River, smoking good cigars and reading six-month-old newspapers.

Tubac had little government, few laws and no taxes. Employees were paid in company scrip called *boletas.* Since none of the Mexicans could read English, each *boleta* had a picture of a particular animal and each animal represented a specific amount. A calf represented 25 cents, a rooster was 50 cents and a horse was worth a dollar.

Food for the hungry miners was hauled in from Sonora. Fresh fruit came from the orchards of the nearby mission at Tumacacori. Manufactured goods were hauled from St. Louis over the old Santa Fe Trail.

One of the freighters hauling trade goods in from Santa Fe was Charles Trumbull Hayden, father of the late Senator Carl Hayden.

In 1857, the Heintzelman Mine in the Cerro Colorado Mountains hit a rich vein that yielded $7,000 to the ton. The ore was hauled by wagon to Guaymas, then by ship to San Francisco at a hefty 50 percent profit. In the fall of that year, Poston sent a wagon train loaded with rawhide bags full of ore, a ton to the wagon, over the Santa Fe Trail to Kansas City. The ore was widely distributed, giving the eastern United States its first look at the mineral potential of Arizona.

But the good times couldn't last forever. A filibustering expedition of "liberators" led by Henry Crabb attempted to take Sonora in 1857. They were cornered at Caborca and killed, but the furor over the affair caused Mexico to place an embargo on commerce. For a while Americans crossing into Mexico did so at great risk. About the time tempers cooled, the Apaches heated up. Up to this time they had pretty much left the Americans alone, preferring to raid their traditional foes, the Mexicans. However, when a group of American newcomers (not associated with Poston's mines) joined a party of Mexicans and ambushed a band of Apaches, war was declared on all Americans in the area. In 1861 Cochise and his Chiricahua Apaches went on the warpath and bands of marauding Apaches raided throughout the Santa Cruz Valley. That same year the Civil War broke out and the U.S. government focused its attention on more pressing matters.

Federal troops were removed from the area and Forts Buchanan and Breckinridge were abandoned. Civilians, both Mexican and Anglo, were left to fend for themselves against hostile Apaches, Sonoran bandits, and Anglo border ruffians.

Poston later recalled how "the smoke of burning wheat fields could be seen up and down the Santa Cruz Valley, where the troops were in retreat, destroying everything before and behind them. The Government of the United States abandoned the first settlers of Arizona to the merciless Apaches," he complained bitterly, adding that "armed Mexicans in considerable numbers crossed the boundary line, declaring that the American government was broken up and they had come to take their country back again.

"Even the Americans, the few Americans left in the country, were not at peace among themselves. The chances were, if you met on the road, it was to draw arms and declare whether you were for the North or the South.

"The Mexicans at the mines assassinated all the white men there when they were asleep, looted the place, and fled across the boundary line to Mexico."

The Apaches laid siege on Tubac and reduced it to rubble. There was nothing left for Poston to do but grab a few personal belongings and hightail it. Poston left Arizona in 1861, barely escaping with his life. His personal loss was great. Earlier that year, a brother, John Lee Poston, had been murdered at the Cerro Colorado Mine.

The 1850s, born in hope and prosperity with the creation of the Territory of New Mexico and enriched by the bold ventures of visionaries like Poston, died in those last dark days. Dreams of building a state in Apacheland drifted hopelessly skyward, much like the billowing smoke that curled from the charred ruins of old Tubac.

A much greater conflict loomed on the horizon. Issues that could not be decided at the conference table would be settled on the battlefield. Trials and tribulations that troubled Arizona would be placed on the back burner as the energy of the young nation would concentrate on a tragic war that divided families and pitted neighbor against neighbor, brother against brother.

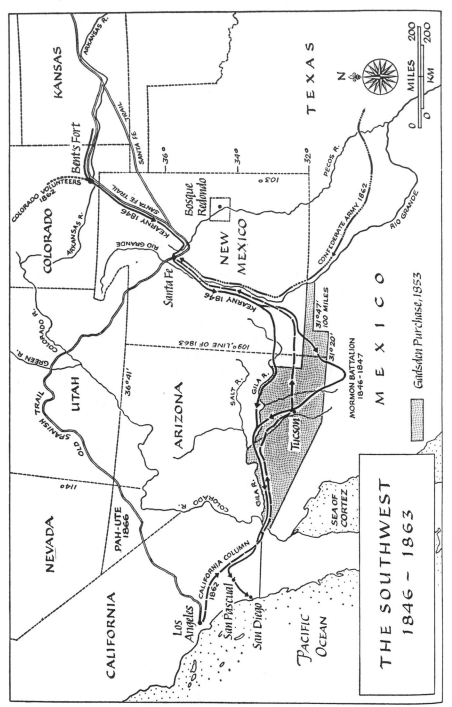

THE SOUTHWEST
1846 – 1863

8

TURBULENT TIMES

The Indian Wars

Arizona was a far cry from glorious-sounding names like Shiloh, Missionary Ridge, Gettysburg, and Chancellorsville, yet it too played a small part in the war between the Blue and Grey. Confederate President Jefferson Davis was well aware of the mineral-laden mountains in the western part of the New Mexico Territory which included Arizona. The land was also a link between Texas and what he hoped to become the Confederate state of California.

In July, 1861, three hundred Texans led by Colonel John Baylor rode hellbent-for-leather into New Mexico, taking the sleepy town of Mesilla by storm. On August 1, he declared himself governor of the "Confederate Territory of Arizona" and, since he couldn't find any Yankees to fight, opened a war of extermination on the Indians. Baylor's extermination orders got him relieved of command by Confederate leaders who considered him something of an embarrassment.

On February 14, 1862, 50 years before statehood, Arizona was officially declared a Confederate Territory. That same month, Gen. Henry Sibley led his Texas army into New Mexico. Sibley sent Capt. Sherod Hunter, a resourceful young officer, west with a company of cavalry to occupy Tucson, then turned the rest of his boisterous army north towards Santa Fe. He won a hard-fought victory at Valverde, then marched through Albuquerque and took Santa Fe, the New Mexico capital.

Sibley had served as a U.S. officer in New Mexico before the war and knew that vast amounts of critical military supplies were stored at Fort Union, a hundred miles up the Santa Fe Trail. He was determined to get his hands on them. Also, he knew that once he took Fort Union, there was nothing to keep him from marching north to Denver, then on to the Oregon Trail, effectively cutting off the entire West from the Union.

Sibley's best laid plans got waylaid by a bunch of rough-hewn miners known as the Colorado Volunteers. They marched out of Denver under the dynamic leadership of a Bible-thumping ex-Methodist preacher named John Chivington. The Coloradans, known as "Pike's Peakers" engaged the Texans at Glorieta Pass, a few miles outside Santa Fe, in late March. For three days the two armies locked horns like a pair of old Texas steers.

Finally, a young officer named Manuel Chavez, who had been raised in the area, led Chivington and his men along a ridge that led behind the Texas lines. The Pike's Peakers blew up the supply wagons and killed hundreds of horses and mules. With victory within their grasp, the Texans were forced to withdraw and were soon in a full-scale, every-man-for-himself retreat down the Rio Grande. The so-called "Gettysburg of the West" ended forever hopes of a Confederate empire in the West.

While Gen. Sibley was making dubious history in northern New Mexico, Capt. Sherod Hunter was enjoying success in Arizona. He was welcomed joyfully by the grateful citizens of Tucson when he rode into town on February 28, 1862. Most were happy to see soldiers, no matter what color the uniform. The next few weeks were spent campaigning against Apaches and expelling from the old Pueblo those who refused to swear allegiance to the Confederacy. It wasn't long before he learned that the Confederates had failed to gain control of California and a two thousand-man volunteer force led by a flinty-eyed professional soldier named Jim Carleton was heading towards Arizona. Already, advance elements were storing supplies along the Gila River.

By a series of brilliant maneuvers, Hunter created an illusion of having a much larger force than his small company of Texans. He sent small, mobile patrols out to destroy the Union supply stores. At the Pima villages near Sacaton, he arrested a miller named Ammi White who'd been processing grain and gathering supplies for the Californians. Hunter gathered fifteen hundred sacks of wheat and presented it to the Pima Indians. A few days later Capt. William McCleave and his nine-man force unwittingly rode into White's mill. The man they believed to be Ammi White was Capt. Sherod Hunter dressed in civilian clothes. After the Union soldiers relaxed their guard and informed "Mr. White" there were no other Union troops near, Hunter drew his revolver and took them prisoner. McCleave was so chagrined at his blunder he challenged Hunter to a fist fight — winner go free. Hunter, no doubt, admired the young man's spunk but politely refused the offer. Instead, he ordered Lt. Jack Swilling to escort the prisoners to Texas.

A rescue party sent out to secure McCleave got there too late but did manage to encounter some Confederates at Stanwix Station on the Gila River (near today's Sentinel) about eighty miles east of Yuma. Several shots were exchanged and a Union soldier was wounded before the two patrols broke off the battle. Some historians call this the westernmost battle of the Civil War. Others say a gunfight near the Goldwater store in La Paz on the east bank of the Colorado River holds that honor. Neither of these can be considered much of a "battle."

A better case can be made for the fight that took place at Picacho a few days later. Two Union patrols were sent south from the Pima villages in hopes of capturing the ten Confederates pickets camped there. On April 15, young Lt. Jim Barrett surprised three Confederates and took them prisoner, then carelessly allowed his own force to be ambushed. A furious 90-minute firefight took place in the thick chaparral and when the smoke had cleared Barrett and two Union enlisted men were dead and three were wounded. Two Confederates suffered wounds that would later prove fatal. The Union force retreated to the Pima villages and the Confederate pickets rode to Tucson and informed Capt. Hunter that the California army was approaching. Hunter gathered his troops, lowered the colors, mounted up and rode east.

On May 20, 1862, the California Column entered Tucson.

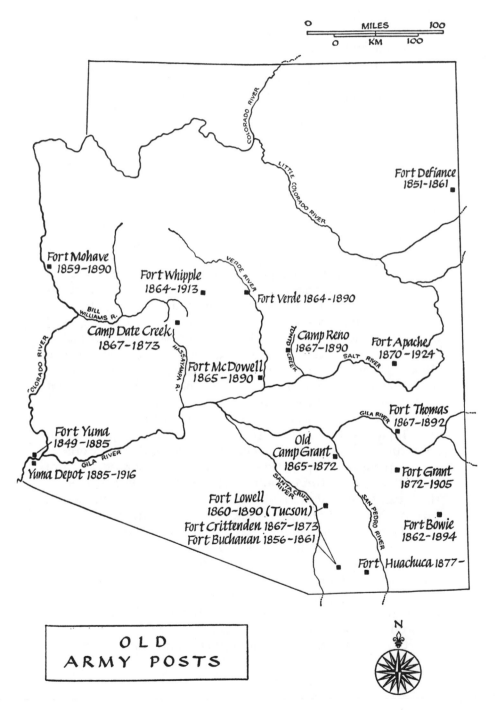

MILES

KM

Fort Defiance
1851-1861

COLORADO RIVER

LITTLE COLORADO RIVER

Fort Mohave
1859-1890

Fort Whipple
1864-1913

VERDE RIVER

Fort Verde 1864-1890

BILL WILLIAMS R.

Camp Date Creek
1867-1873

HASAYAMPA R.

TONTO CREEK

Camp Reno
1867-1890

Fort Apache
1870-1924

SALT RIVER

Fort McDowell
1865-1890

COLORADO RIVER

Fort Thomas
1867-1892

GILA RIVER

Fort Yuma
1849-1885

GILA RIVER

Yuma Depot 1885-1916

Old
Camp Grant
1865-1872

SANTA CRUZ RIVER

Fort Grant
1872-1905

Fort Lowell
1860-1890 (Tucson)
Fort Crittenden 1867-1873
Fort Buchanan 1856-1861

SAN PEDRO RIVER

Fort Bowie
1862-1894

Fort Huachuca 1877-

OLD
ARMY POSTS

N

Col. Carleton, still smarting over the exasperating young Texas captain, and needing an ego booster, delayed his entrance until June 7 so the artillery units could get set up and give him a fitting and proper cannon salute.

Col. Carleton's orders were to proceed on to New Mexico. Several weeks before he moved his forces east from Tucson, Apache scouts were sent out from the lair of Cochise and Mangas Coloradas in Apache Pass to keep an eye on the bluecoats. An advance force of 126 California volunteers under Capt. Tom Roberts was ambushed as they approached the watering hole in the pass. The Apaches held the high ground but Roberts' thirsty men fought desperately to reach the spring. The soldiers opened fire with howitzers, scattering shrapnel on the warriors strung out along the edge of the canyon rim. After several rounds of devastating fire, the Apaches picked up their dead and wounded and withdrew. Roberts' men, having endured a 19-hour march and a six-hour battle with only a cup of black coffee to sustain them, drank eagerly, then awaited the next attack.

The next day, July 16, the Apaches regained the high ground and resumed their attack on the soldiers, driving them from the spring. A supply train under Capt. John Cremony had joined the beleaguered troops who now were holed up in the ruins of the old Butterfield stage station. Once again Roberts opened up with his howitzers, scattering 12-pound spherical shot among the Apaches. When the battle ended, the Californians had regained the spring. Roberts lost only two men in the battle and claimed to have killed more than 60 Apache. Historians later revised the Apache losses to about ten.

An interesting sidelight to the battle occurred the first day, when Roberts ordered Pvt. John Teal and five other cav alrymen to ride back and alert Capt. Cremony to hurry forward with the artillery. They were ambushed by a war party of Apache and Teal was cut off from the rest. When Teal's horse was shot out from under him, he used the carcass as a breastwork and prepared to make a last stand. Teal, armed with a new breech-loading carbine, was able to keep the Apaches at bay. They kept circling, trying to draw his fire. After about an hour one rather large Apache got careless and Teal placed a well-aimed shot in his mid-section. Suddenly, the war party gave up the fight and rode off with their wounded comrade. Surprised but relieved, Teal took his saddle and bridle and walked to Cremony's camp. He didn't realize it at the time, but the warrior he'd shot was the legendary Apache chieftain Mangas Coloradas, who survived his wound but died a year later at the hands of the U.S. Army near Pinos Altos, New Mexico..

Carleton arrived at the pass a few days later and realized its strategic importance. On July 28, 1862 Fort Bowie (named after Col. George Washington Bowie) was formally established on a site overlooking Apache Spring. It was later moved to its present site a half-mile farther east. Two decades later, during the Geronimo Campaign, Fort Bowie was one of the most important posts in the Southwest. It was abandoned in 1894 and lay in crumbled ruins. The old fort became a National Historic Site in 1964.

The 1860s began some 25 years of turbulence in Arizona. The discovery of gold and silver brought a rush of prospectors and settlers into what had been previously all Indian lands, evoking an inevitable clash of cultures. Open warfare with the fierce Chiricahua Apaches began in February 1861 when army troops from Fort Buchanan, led by Lt. George Bascom, rode into Cochise's stronghold at Apache Pass and accused the Chiricahua chief of kidnapping a youngster from a ranch near Sonoita Creek. Cochise denied the charge (it turned out he was telling the truth) and, when the soldiers tried to take him hostage, he escaped and took some hostages of his own. The eyeball-to-eyeball confrontation ended when Cochise executed his prisoners. When the mutilated bodies were found, the soldiers retaliated by hanging an equal number of Apache prisoners, including some of Cochise's relatives. The angry bands under the great Apache chieftain Mangas Coloradas, until his death in 1863, and Cochise, along with several others, combined to form a formidable force and terrorized southern Arizona for the next decade.

Yavapai and Tonto Apaches living in the central mountain range saw their traditional grounds invaded by prospectors and settlers after the discovery of gold in the Bradshaw Mountains in 1863. Civilian expeditions from Prescott, Wickenburg and other settlements led by frontier settlers like King Woolsey, embarked on relentless campaigns. Unlike the Regular Army, they took no prisoners and sought vengeance an eye for an eye. The barbarism of some shocked others. A ruffian known as Sugarfoot Jack was reported to have picked up a baby during a raid and tossed it into a burning wickiup. Later, he found another toddler crying in the aftermath of battle. He picked up the child and placed it tenderly on his knee and began rocking. When the baby began to smile he drew his revolver and fired point-blank into the tot's face. The sight of such cruelty shocked the battle-toughened veterans of Indian fighting. Had he not run off, Sugarfoot Jack might have been lynched by his own men.

War creates bizarre events and one of Arizona's most unusual occurred during a shootout between two white men and an Apache war party. During the fight, one drew a bead on a warrior and squeezed the trigger. The warrior let out a scream and fell dead. Afterwards the men discovered the slain Apache was a white woman. Who she was remains a mystery.

The Navajo also resumed their raiding during the Civil War, choosing to ignore treaties previously signed. Since they regarded a treaty as binding only by the party signing it, most weren't worth the paper they were written on. Also, army commanders made a practice of handing out gifts at these signings, a practice the Navajo regarded as a sign of weakness. In 1863, Gen. James Carleton called upon the Navajo to surrender and move to a new reservation at Bosque Redondo, New Mexico. He issued orders to kill the men but take women and children prisoners when possible. Next, Carleton sent his most dependable officer, Col. Kit Carson, to subdue the Navajo. A large number retreated into their historic sanctuaries in Canyons de Chelly and del Muerto. The canyons were thought to be impregnable but, in January, 1864 Carson sent troops in from both ends and destroyed the Navajo horses and crops, breaking the spirit of the warriors. More than 8,000 surrendered and were taken on the "Long Walk" of some 300 miles to Bosque Redondo, near Fort Sumner, on the Pecos River in New Mexico.

Life was tough for the Navajo at Bosque Redondo. Hundreds died of smallpox. Cutworms and poor irrigation caused massive crop failures and, for reasons only a Washington bureaucrat could explain, they were placed among the Mescalero Apache. The two groups got along like cowboys and sheepherders. Kiowa and Comanche war parties preyed upon them. Finally, in 1868, the government realized the Bosque Redondo Reservation project was a failure and the Navajo took another long walk, this time a happier trek, back to their beloved Four Corners country where a new reservation was established.

Normally, the old scout Pauline Weaver got along well with the Indians of Arizona. Like many mountain men, he was more Indian than white, anyway. In fact, Weaver was half Cherokee. A password in the mountains during the early 1860s was "Pauline-tobacco." Weaver shared his tobacco with his Indian friends and taught them to say "Pauline-Tobacco" when approaching other whites. This would signify that the Indians were friendly. The password worked well and prevented much unnecessary killing until the area became overpopulated with newcomers who weren't aware, or didn't care about the custom. Despite the friendship Weaver was attacked by a war party and badly wounded. The old scout had spent years among warrior tribes who performed a "death song" when mortally wounded. Weaver was doing his when the Yavapais made their final charge. Unaccustomed to seeing such things, they believed he was insane and left the scene immediately. Afterwards, the tough mountain man was able to muster enough strength to get up and go home. The Yavapai apparently regretted shooting Weaver. For months afterwards they made inquiries as to the condition of their friend "Paulino."

Indian depredations were so bad around Prescott that on January 22, 1870, the *Prescott Miner* published a list giving dates and locations of 300 whites killed in the area. It was the tragic massacre of Aravaipa Apache at Camp Grant, however, that focused national attention on the Indian problem in Arizona.

On April 30, 1871, a group of vigilantes from the Tucson area attacked a band of Aravaipa Apache living near Camp Grant. The party, which included 94 Papago, 48 Mexicans, and 6 Anglos, nearly wiped out the band in a few furious moments. Most of the Apache men were away at the time so women, children, and elderly took the brunt of the attack. When the carnage was over, about 100 were dead, all but 8 were women and children. Those taken alive were given to the Papago as slaves.

The Tucsonians took great satisfaction in the success of the raid, because for years they'd been at the mercy of the fierce Apaches. Nearly every citizen had experienced the loss of a friend or family member. Juan and Jesus Maria Elias, two of the leaders, had been driven out of Tubac and three members of their families had been murdered by Apache war parties.

While the Tucsonians were celebrating, Washington politicians and Indian proponents were outraged. President Grant called the Camp Grant incident "murder" and ordered a trial. The trial was held in Tucson and, not surprisingly, the verdict was "not guilty." No jury in the Arizona Territory would find anyone guilty of killing an Apache.

In the aftermath of the Camp Grant Massacre, President Grant ordered a two-pronged program to end the Apache wars. With one hand he extended the olive branch in the person of Gen. Oliver Howard, a one-armed Civil War officer with a reputation for honesty and intregrity. Howard would negotiate treaties with the tribes. In case Howard failed, the president carried in his other hand, the sabre, as personified by the greatest Indian fighting officer in the army, George Crook.

Gen. Howard was able to link up with a lanky redhead named Tom Jeffords, superintendent of a mail line and a man who'd become friendly with old Cochise. A few years earlier, Jeffords had boldly ridden into Cochise's stronghold and negotiated a treaty with the chief to pro-

General George Crook, called the "greatest Indian fighting general" in the army. He was also one of the few to win the respect and trust of the Indians. Photo: Southwest Studies.

tect his mail riders. Cochise respected Jeffords' bravery and honesty and their friendship lasted despite the continued animosity between their respective races. Jeffords led the general into Cochise's camp where a treaty was negotiated ending the ten-year war. The Chiricahua chief made two requests: first, that his people be allowed to remain on a reservation in the Chiricahua Mountains; and second, that his friend Tom Jeffords be made Indian agent. Both requests were granted. Since all their terms were met, the Apache had, in effect, achieved their goals in the war against the army. Jeffords, a man of great integrity was nevertheless, criticized by Tucsonians as being an "Indian lover." Later, he was accused of wrongdoing by those who wanted him out of the way. Jeffords defended his policies and was vindicated by an investigation. But his critics won a victory in 1875 when the Chiricahua were moved to the reservation at San Carlos and Jeffords was removed as agent.

Following the successful negotiations with Cochise, Gen. Howard approached the Yavapai and Tonto Apache in the central mountains. They defiantly rejected the peace proposals and President Grant had no choice but to order Crook into battle.

Crook's famous winter campaign of 1872-73 was one of the most successful in military history. He sent his troops into the field, guided by Apache scouts during the time of year when most of the bands preferred to hole up in the steep, twisting canyons around the Tonto Basin.

Military columns swept through the central mountains, keeping the bands on the move. Led by the scouts, they ventured into places where no white man dared to go. Large battles, inflicting heavy casualties, were fought at Salt River Cave, near today's Canyon Lake and Turret Peak, on the Verde River north of Horseshoe Lake. The following spring, most of the bands agreed to move onto a reservation at Fort Verde.

Following his great success, Crook was promoted to brigadier general and transferred out of Arizona. For a time it seemed the Apache wars were over. Unfortunately, reservation life didn't appeal to all Apaches. Following the death of Cochise, the Chiricahua were moved from their traditional lands to the San Carlos Reservation. The Yavapai, who weren't

Apache, were taken on their own "long walk" from Fort Verde to San Carlos, or "Hell's Forty Acres," as it became known.

Before he left in 1875, Crook protested these moves, but to no avail. This consolidation was supposed to make administration more efficient. Instead, the bands fought like cats and dogs. Their animosity led to the emergence of opportunists and troublemakers like the notorious Geronimo. During the next few years the wily renegade and his followers escaped from the reservation several times and headed for their former haunts in Mexico.

During these years the government in Washington called upon churches to supply men to minister to the Indians. Interestingly, the two churches most successful in dealing with natives, the Catholics and Mormons, were not included. Still, some of these church emissaries made their mark in Arizona history. In 1874, the Dutch Reformed church sent out 23-year-old John Clum as agent at San Carlos. The morning of his arrival, the greenhorn was greeted with a row of renegade Apache heads lined up on the parade field, compliments of Apache bounty hunters. Some were over two weeks old. Undaunted, Clum remained. He was a fiery idealist, and one of his first moves was to remove army troops and organize his own Apache police. He set up a judicial system and held inspections. A check out system was installed, whereby Apache were issued rifles for hunting. Importantly, the making of Apache moonshine or *tiswin*, was forbidden. Clum's most memorable exploit as Apache agent came in 1877 when he and his Indian police rode into New Mexico and captured both Geronimo and Victorio, placed the pair in irons and returned them to San Carlos. Although relations between Clum and Gen. Crook were cordial, the agent clashed frequently with government officials and the military. After Crook was transferred out of the territory the situation deteriorated. In 1879, Clum resigned and headed for the new silverado town of Tombstone. "Every tombstone needs an epitaph," quipped the young zealot. He started a newspaper and went on to become one of Tombstone's most prominent citizens.

Victorio, the successor to Mangas Coloradas, rose to prominence during these years. He and his band went on a rampage in 1879-80, killing more than a thousand people in the United States and Mexico. A brilliant tactician, he out-foxed and defeated several army units during the campaign. Mexican troops finally cornered Victorio in Mexico and killed him and most of his band. Old Nana also gave the army fits. Reputed to be in his late 70's, the unreconstructed reb refused to settle on a reservation. Wearing a heavy gold watch chain dangling from each ear, Nana cut quite a swath as he led the army on a chase that covered over a thousand miles. He fought a dozen battles and won them all, losing only four men wounded. Finally, the artful old dodger slipped into Mexico's forbidding Sierra Madre, unscathed.

The last Apache battle fought in Arizona occurred at Big Dry Wash, a few miles north of General Springs on the Mogollon Rim, on July 17, 1882. Its genesis began several months earlier at the remote Apache settlement of Cibicue. An Apache medicine man named Nock-ay-del-klinne started a ghost dance cult by preaching a resurrection of dead Apache warriors to lead the people to glory once more. He was developing such a large following the army became alarmed. Gen. Eugene A. Carr and 117 men rode from Fort Apache to arrest the medicine man. A shootout ensued, in which the medicine man was killed. A major Apache uprising followed, Gen. Carr and his men were nearly annihilated and, for a time, Fort Apache was under siege.

Other Apache under Na-ti-o-tish went on a foray through the Tonto Basin. At Globe a number of "concerned citizens," well-fortified with local spirits, decided to ride out in pursuit. They got as far as the Middleton ranch and stopped for a siesta but forgot to post guards. The Apache crept in and stole all their horses, leaving the tarnished heroes from Globe afoot. Meanwhile, the army was also in pursuit of Na-ti-o-tish. Soldiers followed the band up on the Mogollon Rim, just north of today's Payson. The Apaches tried to set up an ambush, but veteran army scout Al Sieber was too savvy. Army troops and Apache scouts laid in a heavy barrage of firepower and when the battle was over, 20 Apache warriors, including Na-ti-o-tish, lay dead.

In September, 1882 Gen. Crook was recalled to Arizona to bring in Geronimo. Once again Crook gathered his trusty

Military pack trains were essential to the successful Apache campaigns. Techniques devised by General George Crook were still in use during World War II. Photo: Arizona Historical Society, Wister Collection.

scouts, equipped his pack trains and headed out on the campaign trail. His relentless tactics were successful once again, and by January, 1884 the Apache agreed to return to San Carlos.

When Geronimo's plunder was taken and returned to its owners, he grew bitter and began looking for a reason to gather a few braves and escape again. Following a drinking bout in May, 1885 Geronimo and a small band headed south, leaving in their wake death and destruction. Crook took up the chase, sending his hard-riding cavalry and Apache scouts in pursuit.

In March, 1886, at Cañon de los Embudos, Geronimo met with Crook and agreed to surrender. However, that evening a whiskey peddler slipped into the Apache camp and sold the band a barrel of mescal. A drunken Geronimo, convinced Crook meant to kill him, gathered a few braves and bolted once more. The latest broken agreement by Geronimo was an embarrassment for Crook. When General of the Army Phil Sheridan questioned his placing too much trust in the Apache, including the loyal scouts, Crook resigned.

Crook's replacement for the final stages of the Geronimo Campaign was another soldier of proven ability, Gen. Nelson

Miles. In other aspects, the two were quite different. While Crook was an outdoorsman with little interest in pomp and ceremony, Miles was egotistical and politically ambitious. Miles wisely continued Crook's tactics in the field while loading up the peaceful Chiricahua at San Carlos and Fort Apache and shipped them by rail to Florida.

Geronimo and his band of Chiricahua Apache prior to their departure for Florida in 1886. Photo: Arizona State Library.

In early September, Lt. Charles Gatewood and two Apache scouts, along with interpreter Tom Horn, rode into Geronimo's lair in Mexico's Sierra Madre and arranged a final surrender. Geronimo's surrender was hastened by the fact that many of his friends and relatives had been moved to Florida. He was promised two years confinement, after which he would be allowed to return to Arizona.

In the aftermath, Gen. Miles took most of the credit for Geronimo's capture and used it to advance his career. Eventually he became army chief of staff. Unfortunately, the real heroes, Charles Gatewood and his two Apache scouts, fared much worse. Gatewood was transferred to an obscure army post out of reach of the press. He died many years later, forgotten and unrecognized. The two scouts, Martine and Kayitah, were imprisoned along with the renegade Chiricahua and sent to prison in Florida. Tom Horn, a frontier legend, left the army and became a lawman, range detective and regulator, eventually moving to Wyoming where he became involved in a range feud and was accused of murdering a 13-year-old boy. Horn was hanged in 1903. His guilt or innocence is still debated by historians.

Geronimo barely escaped hanging by angry Tucsonians while on the way to a prison camp in Florida. Political strings were pulled and the train was halted at San Antonio, Texas, while President Grover Cleveland considered sending the warrior back to Arizona to stand trial. Gen. Crook learned of the situation and intervened on Geronimo's behalf. It was pointed out that Geronimo's surrender had not been "unconditional." He'd surrendered with terms and those terms included a two-year confinement in Florida. President Cleveland then ordered the prison train to resume its journey to Florida.

Always the opportunist, Geronimo was able to capitalize on his notoriety. Despite captivity, he rode in President Theodore Roosevelt's inaugural parade in 1905 and appeared at fairs, signing autographs and selling bows and arrows (he'd fit in very well with some of today's heroes). He also learned to be a pretty good poker player. One cold night in 1909, Geronimo got drunk, fell out of a wagon, caught pneumonia and died.

Although Miles had promised the Chiricahua a two-year term in Florida and then freedom to return to Arizona, they were held in Florida and Alabama for nearly a decade before being moved to Fort Sill, Oklahoma. In 1915, a few were allowed to return to southern New Mexico. Bitter memories of the Apache wars persisted in Arizona, and the Chiricahua were not wanted by Arizonans, either Indian or white. The door to their eventual return to this land had been closed for good.

9

MINING IN ARIZONA

"If ya stumble on a rock,
don't cuss it — cash it!"

The gold and silver rushes, more than anything else, created the dramatic changes that affected 19th Century Arizona. With a single lucky break a man or woman could make more money in an instant than they could lend or spend in a lifetime. So it was off to "Arizoney with my washpan on my knee." "Lynx Creek or Bust, Rich Hill or Bust, Tombstone or Bust," cried the jackass prospectors. "If ya stumble on a rock, don't cuss it, cash it," and "If ya wash yer face in the Hassayampa River, you can pan four ounces of gold dust from yer whiskers," claimed the burro men with some credibility. Wherever there was a "rumor and a hole in the ground," as Mark Twain said, "someone built a town around it." And each one claimed it was built right smack on top of the mother lode. The rusted ruins and weathered headframes are still out there — epitaphs marking the high water mark of someone's aspiration.

They gave the towns picturesque, whimsical names like Oro Belle, Placerita, and Total Wreck. Born in boom, most faded back into the adobe dust whence they came, a metropolis that didn't "metrop." Others, such as Prescott, possessed staying power and grew into thriving cities. Tombstone, "the town too tough to die," almost did. With a grand display of remarkable grit, the community hung on. The earliest residents of these boom towns were aptly described as "unmarried, unchurched, and unwashed." The streets were ankle-deep in dust in dry weather and a quagmire when wet. They weren't passable; in fact, most of the time they weren't even "jackassable." Many towns were perched on mountain slopes. "It was about as close to heaven as any of 'em got," said one. "It was no place for a Presbyterian," Mark Twain wrote wryly, "so, therefore, I did not remain one for long."

After the surface mineral played out, a new breed of men arrived: hard rock miners. Rawhide-tough, they hammered, chiseled, and dug into the innermost reaches of the mountains, revealing riches beyond the most optimistic dreams of the *conquistadores.* Such boom camps as Bisbee, Tombstone and Jerome became household words in board rooms in New York, London, and San Francisco. This new breed of miners brought their families into the boisterous, devil-may-care camps and soon the cry was heard, "We need schools, churches, law and order." And so they did. The bawdy towns began to take on respectability. Oh, they still knew how to let their hair down once in a while but, like the rest of raucous Arizona, they were starting to grow up.

The earliest mining ventures in Arizona, excepting explorations by Coronado, Oñate, and Espejo, came during the

Hardrock miners in the Tombstone District. Photo: Arizona Historical Society.

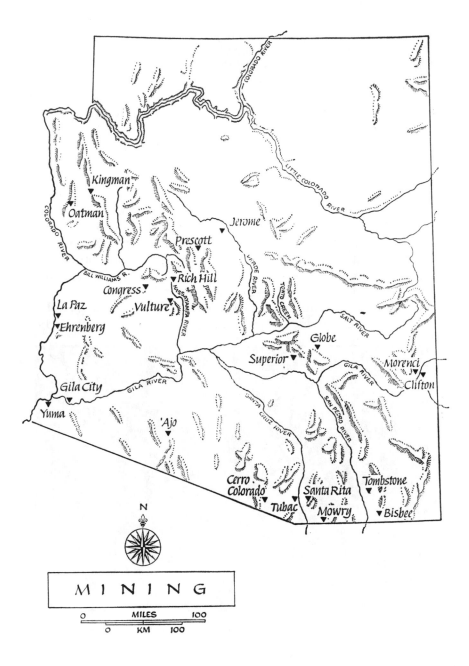

MINING

MILES
0   100
0   KM   100

mid-1700s. The famous Planchas de Plata strike in 1736 led to other discoveries in the mountains straddling the Santa Cruz River. These were abandoned a century later when the Apaches went on the warpath and drove the Mexicans out. Charles Poston, Pete Brady, Sylvester Mowry and a few others reopened those old mines in the mid-1850s but they, too, were driven out by Apache when the American troops were withdrawn at the outbreak of the Civil War.

THE GOLD RUSH

The first important gold discovery came on the Gila River about 20 miles east of Yuma in 1858, when a colorful Texan named Jake Snively swished the water in his pan and saw gold nuggets glittering in the sun. A town materialized overnight and was soon peopled with would-be millionaires who ran the wide gamut of frontier society. Gila City had everything, one visitor wrote, except "a church and a jail." Placer miners, using everything from skillets to wash pans, were panning out $20 to $125 a day in gold dust. Nuggets weighing as much as 22 ounces each were deposited at the Wells Fargo office in Los Angeles. In 1862, about the same time the gold ran out, the Gila River went on a rampage and wiped out the town. Two years later, all that was left of Gila City, according to one writer, was "three chimneys and a coyote."

Sketch of Pauline Weaver, noted trapper, guide and gold prospector. Prescott honors him as its "First Citizen." Arizona Historical Society.

The second major gold strike was made on the Colorado River at La Paz in early 1862. The ubiquitous mountain man, Indian scout and guide, Pauline Weaver, showed up in Yuma with a goose quill full of gold flakes and the rush was on. The gold was found in *Arroyo de la Tenaja* on January 12, on *El Dia de la Fiesta de Nuestra Senora de la Paz* (The Day of the Feast of Our Lady of Peace). By the time the La Paz strike was exhausted, miners using pans, rockers and sluices had taken out $8 million in gold. In 1864 the town just missed by a few votes becoming the territorial capital of Arizona.

The legendary Goldwater family's mercantile enterprise got its start in 1862 when Michael Goldwater hauled some much-needed goods across the desert from California and opened a store at La Paz. One morning in 1868 residents awakened to find the shifty Colorado River had changed its course and left the town high and dry. So they packed up their belongings and relocated on the banks of the new river course. They named the new town Ehrenberg in honor of their friend Herman Ehrenberg, who'd been killed two years earlier. Later, Mike and brother Joe Goldwater freighted goods over the dangerous wagon road to Prescott.

The fabled Bradshaw Mountains would provide the source of the greatest gold and silver discoveries during the next few years.

In 1863, noted mountain man Joe Walker led a party of some 30 prospectors up near the headwaters of the Hassayampa River. The miners' picks and shovels turned over rich deposits of gold along Granite, Lynx, Big Bug, Turkey and a host of other creeks in the area. Gen. Jim Carleton dispatched a company of soldiers to protect the miners and, at the same time, convinced the gubernatorial party of the brand new Territory of Arizona to locate the capital in the wilderness instead of at Tucson. Thus Prescott, as it came to be called, became the only wilderness capital in U.S. history.

Following on the bootheels of the Walker party was a party of prospectors led by Pauline Weaver. Weaver was heading up the Hassayampa when gold was discovered atop a lofty granite knoll in what are today known as the Weaver Mountains. Needing nothing more than jackknives to pry the nuggets loose, the prospectors gathered gold valued at more than $100,000 in just a few weeks. The richest single placer discovery in Arizona history became known, for good reason, as Rich Hill.

Early day prospectors on the Hassayampa River. Photo: Southwest Studies.

Henry Wickenburg wasn't far behind Weaver and Walker in the quest for gold along the Hassayampa. Wickenburg's bonanza turned out to be a fabulous ore discovery rather than placer. Placer gold could be mined with the toe of your boot or a jackknife. It required little capital, lots of patience and a strong back. But ore or lode gold was still attached to the rock and had to be pulverized and separated. Wickenburg's Vulture Mine was located about 11 miles from the Hassayampa, so the ore had to be hauled overland to the river where *arrastras,* or mule-powered ore crushers, had been built. He sold the ore for $15 a ton to others who hauled it over to the river. Soon a town was established and named in Henry's honor. Unfortunately, things didn't pan out for Henry Wickenburg. He sold out to some eastern financiers who promised him a piece of the action, then swindled him out of his profits. In 1905, broke and downtrodden, Henry Wickenburg took his own life.

SILVERADO

Such was Arizona's fame as a mineral bonanza that no place was safe from exploration. Even the Grand Canyon was violated by gold, silver and asbestos miners. Despite the lack of roads and frequent Indian uprisings, miners and prospectors combed the rugged mountains in search of riches. By the 1870s silver was king. The Tip Top and Peck mines in the Bradshaw Mountains south of Prescott, along with McCracken and Signal mines further west, were major producers during the mid-1870s. In 1875 a rich silver mine was located at McMillanville, north of Globe.

The richest single silver mine during these years was at Silver King, near today's Superior. It was discovered in 1871 during construction of a military road. A soldier named Sullivan found a rich specimen and showed it to friends. His enlistment ended soon after and he disappeared. Many thought he'd gone to claim his strike and had been killed by Apache. Others went in search of the "Lost Sullivan Mine." In 1875 a party of prospectors got into a skirmish with Apache, and during the battle one of their mules vamoosed. Afterward they found the mule standing atop Sullivan's mine. That eventually became the fabulous Silver King.

Many years later an old man arrived at the mine and identified himself as Sullivan. He'd gone off to California to raise money to develop his find but all his luck had been bad. He'd heard about the Silver King and had come to see it first hand. The owners took pity on the old man and gave

Ed Schieffelin, discoverer of the legendary Tombstone silver mines. Photo: Southwest Studies.

him a generous pension. Every so often a lost mine is really found. This one was worth more than $6 million in silver.

The granddaddy of all Arizona silver strikes came in 1877 when a persistent sourdough named Ed Schieffelin struck it rich on a limestone mesa east of the San Pedro River. For years Schieffelin had endured the rigors and disappointments that come with the quest for the elusive *madre del oro*. He had nothing to show for his efforts and had become something of a joke around Tucson when he decided to try his luck over in the San Pedro Valley. Apache chieftain Victorio and his warriors were on a rampage at the time and one soldier warned, "all you'll find out there will be your tombstone." Ed went anyway and eventually convinced his brother Al and a re-nowned assayer named Richard Gird to join him. Dodging Apache while he scoured the rocky crags, Ed searched and found nothing of value. His conservative sibling protested the fruitless search, preferring to give up the quest and take a two-dollar-a-day job in the mines. Then one day Ed brought in some new specimens. "You're a lucky cuss," Gird smiled as he handed Ed the results of his assay. And that's how the fabulous Lucky Cuss Mine got its name. A town grew up nearby and the folks didn't have any trouble picking a name. Ed Schieffelin had, indeed, found his Tombstone.

THE COPPER KINGS

By the time Tombstone's heyday had drawn to a close, copper, the so-called "ugly duckling" when compared to the more glamorous gold and silver mines, was becoming Arizona's most important natural resource. America was entering the age of electricity and buried beneath the gold and silver deposits lay a king's ransom in copper just waiting to be dug. The colorful jackass prospector had become a vanishing breed. His place was taken by the hard rock miner, and a new era was aborning. By the early 1900s Arizona had become the copper king of America. During World War I the industry would reach its zenith. Jerome, Bisbee, Clifton, Morenci, and Ajo boomed, and the likes of them would never be seen again. Copper towns, like their gold and silver predecessors, had a life span. Some of those early gold and silver camps lasted only

Prospecting outfit leaving Tombstone during the 1880s. Photo: C.S. Fly.

a few weeks before they became ghost towns. The life span of the copper towns was much greater, about a century. But it was only a matter of time until the inevitable demise came.

AJO

The first reported discovery of ore around Ajo was a rich deposit of silver found by Spanish miners in 1750. Charles Poston and Herman Ehrenberg prospected around Ajo in 1854. However, when Poston returned from California two years later, he set up operations at Tubac instead.

Pete Brady, another fabled Arizona pioneer, explored around Ajo in 1864. He reported finding rich silver ore deposits, and the American Mining and Trading Company was organized. The high-grade surface ore was not as rich as that found around Bisbee, Jerome, and Clifton, and technology hadn't advanced enough to operate stringers at a profit. Still, Ajo claims the distinction of having the first American-operated mine in Arizona. Despite traces of rich ore, the deposits around Ajo would lie dormant until the 20th Century.

About 1900 a smooth-talking promoter named A. J. Shotwell picked up a few ore specimens and took them to St. Louis. He had little trouble raising capital from usually skeptical Missourians. After all, this was Arizona, where every coyote hole was a potential gold mine. When these investors lost their money, another group was waiting to take their place. The second group, more doubting than the first, wanted a first-hand look at Ajo. So Shotwell wisely chose the rainy season, when water holes were full, and the investors were suitably impressed. On the way back to St. Louis, the Cornelia Copper Company was organized. But the water holes around Ajo, so necessary for mining, soon evaporated, and so did the money and the investors' enthusiasm.

In 1911 John C. Greenway, ex-Rough Rider and manager of the Calumet and Arizona Company of Bisbee, together with some business associates, then bought the Cornelia Copper Company. The reorganized and refinanced company brought in new technology and geological expertise. A huge underground reservoir of water was discovered and an open-pit operation was started. Soon Ajo became one of Arizona's richest copper camps, peaking in time for the copper boom of World War I.

CLIFTON-MORENCI

The Metcalf brothers located copper outcroppings around what would become Clifton and Morenci while working as scouts for the army. In 1872, after the Apache agreed to a peace treaty, the brothers returned to the area and filed claims on the Longfellow and Metcalf mines. In time these would be among the richest mines in the Southwest. J. N. Stevens and his brother, Capt. Jay Stevens, along with Joe Yankie, arrived and located the Montezuma, Copper Mountain, Yankie, and Arizona Central mines. That same year these men organized the Copper Mountain Mining District. Since the nearest usable railroad station was 700 miles away at La Junta, Colorado, transporting the ore was the most important concern, except for the Mimbres Apache, who claimed the area as their own.

Needing more capital to keep the Longfellow going, Bob Metcalf went to Las Cruces, New Mexico, where he made the acquaintance of Charles Lesinsky, proprietor of a stage station. The skeptical stationkeeper then showed the ore samples to his brother Henry, who was experienced in mining. Henry strongly suggested they buy into the operation. Soon the Lesinskys had a controlling interest. After the Metcalf brothers had a falling out, they sold the Lesinskys the rest of the stock.

Much of the copper ore mined in Arizona during the early 1870s was sent to Swansea, Wales, for smelting. This practice was not practical or profitable, so the Lesinskys built a crude smelter of adobe on Chase Creek, using charcoal fuel made from mesquite wood. The ore was hauled by burro from the mine down to Chase Creek. The smelted ore was then hauled by ox train over the Santa Fe Trail to Kansas City, 1,200 miles away. Many of these expeditions were attacked by Apache and Comanche, the drivers killed and the oxen eaten. The copper ingots, being of no value to the raiders, were left behind to be retrieved by the next ore train.

The Copper Mountain Mine, located west of the Longfellow, had even greater potential for wealth. In 1872 a settlement called Joy's Camp, for Capt. Miles Joy, a mineral surveyor, was established. Three years later, eastern capital was raised to expand operations, and the Detroit Copper Company was created. The Joy's Camp name was changed to Morenci, a town in Michigan.

In the late 1870s the Lesinskys built a narrow gauge railroad down Longfellow Hill to the smelter at Chase Creek. The empty ore cars were pulled up the incline to the mine by sturdy mules. On the return, the ore-filled cars, fueled by gravity, plunged headlong down the grade, with the mules getting a free ride in the empty ore cars. In 1879 the Lesinskys had the first steam locomotive hauled into the area overland from La Junta. By 1880 both the Detroit Copper Company and the Lesinskys' Longfellow Mine were reaping great profits. However, poor health and a fear of glutting the market caused the Lesinskys grave concern, so a year later they sold the Longfellow for $2 million.

In 1881, because the Detroit Copper Company was in need of investment capital, the Phelps Dodge Mining Company sent Dr. James Douglas to investigate the Clifton-Morenci area. Dr. Douglas was much impressed and wrote favorably to the New York-based firm, which put up the money for a share of the property. Then in 1895 William Church, long-time president of the Detroit Copper Company, decided to retire. He sold his stock to Phelps Dodge and gave them full control of the operation.

Clifton-Morenci would become, over the next half century, one of Arizona's greatest copper areas. Phelps Dodge would begin a massive open pit operation that would in time swallow up the picturesque city of Morenci. By the 1950s the Morenci Mine was the second largest in America and the fourth largest in the world.

GLOBE

Set against the majestic backdrop of the Pinal Mountains on one side and the Apache Range on the other is the rough-and-tumble mining town of Globe. Perched on the banks of Pinal Creek, its old buildings huddled on steep slopes, Globe was one of the great mining camps of old Arizona. Its intrepid citizens braved everything from isolation to frequent, but unwelcome, visits by Apache war parties, to carve out a community in the mineral-laden mountains.

The first reports of mineral riches came in 1864. That year, King Woolsey, a rancher on the upper Agua Fria River east of Prescott, led three punitive expeditions against Indians in the area. Woolsey's reports inspired prospectors to defy the always-dangerous Pinal and Tonto Apache bands and to stake claims. In 1870, Camp Pinal was established, 13 miles to the west of today's Globe, providing some security. Still, those lonely mountain roads leading out of Globe were not meant to be traveled by the weak of heart.

The first mine of importance near Globe was established by a party of prospectors in 1873. Two years later the Globe Mining District was formed. The origin of the name Globe is up for speculation. Three colorful legends regarding Globe would find support in the adage attributed to Mark Twain: "If it didn't happen this way, it could have happened this way." The first explanation comes from a large, round chunk of silver with lines resembling the continents of the earth. The second, a similar claim, states that prospectors found a large circular silver boulder. And the third, which hasn't anything to do with the name, says that Pinal Apache were using silver bullets and a closer investigation led to the discovery at Globe.

In 1878, the settlers moved a short distance to the banks of Pinal Creek to be closer to a source of water and called their town Globe City. Later the "City" was dropped. In 1880 Globe incorporated, but city fathers either had short memories or liked celebrations, for they incorporated again in 1905. They dropped incorporation a year later because it was too expensive, but re-incorporated in 1907. The main thoroughfare was Broad Street, which meandered along Pinal Creek with more kinks than an alley cat's tail. Old timers attribute those twists to the fact that miners and prospectors stubbornly refused to move their shanties so the surveyors could lay out a straight road.

Globe has an early history of isolation. During its first 22 years of existence, the nearest railroad was 120 miles away. In the 1870s supplies were hauled in by wagon from Silver City, New Mexico, 150 miles to the east. By 1878 supplies were brought from the new town of Florence, only 60 miles away, but the trip took five days. In 1898, the Gila Valley, Globe, and Northern Railroad was stretched along the San Simon and Gila valleys to Globe, thus allowing the mining companies to get down to serious business. The first highway to Globe was the Apache Trail (Arizona 88), built during construction of the Theodore Roosevelt Dam in the early 1900s. By 1911, a trip from Globe to Phoenix took only two days. Finally, in 1922, US 60 linked Globe with Phoenix, and the trip took only a day.

The granddaddy of all the mines in the Globe district was the Old Dominion, on the north side of town. It had a few lean years in the early days. Then, in 1895, the Lewisohn brothers of New York bought control of the company, built a new smelter and ran a railroad in from the Southern Pacific main line at Bowie. However, the mine was plagued by a persistent water problem, and pumps proved ineffective. Eventually the New Yorkers gave up on the Old Dominion and sold out. In 1903, Phelps Dodge acquired the property on the sage advice of Dr. James Douglas. Douglas put Dr. L. D. Ricketts in charge, and after a thorough overhaul of equipment, the mine started turning a profit. For the next 20 years the Old Dominion was one of the greatest copper mines in the world. The Old Dominion shut down its smelter in 1924 and closed its mine during the Great Depression. By that time it had produced $134 million in gold, silver, and copper.

Globe's spunky citizens could always be counted on to display a spirit of independence, characteristic of frontier society, in the face of bureaucracy. A story is told about the time when work on the new Central School was completed

Dr. James Douglas, mining engineer. He pioneered many mining techniques during the 19th Century. The town of Douglas is named for him. Arizona State Library.

before residents realized it was located near a house of ill repute. The law required that parlor houses not be located within 400 feet of a school. Citizens formally requested the sheriff to close the house. Another group of concerned citizens immediately petitioned the sheriff to "move the school." The sheriff obligingly measured the distance between the two structures and found that the 400-foot limit extended 4 feet into the parlor of the bordello. The matter was settled in a typical frontier problem-solving manner when the sheriff told the madam to confine all activities to the back rooms, which were within the legal limit.

Globe's citizens could be fiercely protective of their property. A French immigrant, Andre Maurel, was "the only man who ever shut down a mining company single-handed and lived to tell about it." Mr. Maurel had a peach orchard near the mine, and the miners were helping themselves to his peaches without paying. The resourceful Frenchman got even with the peach thieves one night by injecting each peach with a dose of croton oil. The company had to shut down for three days because all the workers were at home "roosting" in the privy.

The silver boom in Globe lasted only four years but, before it ended, copper was coming into great demand and the silver camp was transformed into a prosperous copper mining town. By 1886, the town was boasting that all U.S. copper coins had been minted from Globe copper.

Globe began to fade as a mining town in 1909, when richer deposits of low-grade copper ore were found seven miles west and the new upstart town of Miami was born. Local merchants led the exodus, as they rushed to establish stores in the new community.

MIAMI

Miami sits in a small valley at the foot of the Pinal Mountains. The business district is laid out on the valley floor, while most of the residences are perched on the slopes of the foothills that surround the town. Bloody Tanks Wash runs through the middle of the valley known as Miami Flat. The old Miami Copper Company and Inspiration mines, along with company offices and dwellings, were located on the north side of town near where a massive man-made mesa of bleached-out dirt lies today.

"Black Jack" Newman, a Polish immigrant, located a rich prospect in Big Johnny Gulch, which he named the Mima, for his girlfriend, Mima Tune. At about the same time, a group from Miami, Ohio, staked a claim near Bloody Tanks Wash. Black Jack wanted to name the fledgling community Mima, but the others insisted on calling it Miami. A compromise was finally reached when both sides agreed to spell it "Miami" but pronounce it "Mima."

Newman wasn't Black Jack's real name. He had a long Polish name nobody could pronounce and since he was the newest man in camp, folks called him "new man," which became Newman.

Later he sold his mine to the Lewisohn brothers of New York, but struck a deal whereby he received a commission on every pound of copper sold by Lewisohns' Miami Copper Company. With the Lewisohns and Inspiration mines, Miami, founded in 1907, faced the prosperous future with enthusiastic optimism.

The community of Miami had a rather shaky beginning, however. The Miami Copper Company and Inspiration Mines wanted a company town so they could control housing and businesses. Also, whenever an unhappy employee quit the company, it was unlikely that he could hang around to cause trouble. The businessmen in Globe weren't enthusiastic about a company town because it meant an economic loss to them. The original owners of the property at Miami Flat finally abandoned the futile project. Then along came a developer named Cleve Van Dyke, who tossed in $25,000 and bought the townsite. Then he acquired a newspaper, the *Silver Belt*, and began promoting Miami. It was too much for opponents in Globe, and the community of Miami Flat was on its way.

Inspiration began construction of a reduction plant in 1908 and by the end of World War I, the "Concentrator City," as Miami was sometimes called, had a larger population than Globe.

SUPERIOR-RAY-HAYDEN-CHRISTMAS

In 1900 the town of Superior was marked on maps as Hastings. That year the name was changed to Superior for the Lake Superior and Arizona Mine. Ten years later the Magma Copper Company was organized to take over the Silver Queen properties.

Miners dug beneath a silver cap and found an incredibly rich deposit of copper. The old Silver Queen wasn't as rich as its namesake, the nearby Silver King, but the discovery of the red metal made the Queen come up winners anyway. Magma, founded by W. Boyce Thompson, went on to become one of Arizona's greatest copper bonanzas.

The Dripping Springs Mountains, east of Superior, came in for their share of riches, too. The town of Ray sprang up around a rich discovery in the early 1880s. The Kennecott Copper Corporation bought the property in 1933 and 14 years later began open-pit operations. In the 1960s the giant pit swallowed up the twin towns of Ray-Sonora. So the company built a new town nearby and called it Kearny. Two other rich mining operations in the Dripping Springs range were at Christmas and Hayden.

BISBEE

Those brawny mountains called the Mules aren't as awesome as the Huachucas, across the San Pedro Valley on the west, or the Chiricahuas, 40 miles to the east. They're only about 30 miles long and half that distance wide, reaching the height of 7,400 feet. The rough-hewn range with its twisting, rocky canyons was a favorite sanctuary for the Apache during the 19th Century. At the southern end, a trail led through a pass and out into the San Pedro River Valley. In this steep-sided canyon were seeps and springs where men and animals could be watered. The Mexicans called the place *Puerto de las Mulas* (Mule Pass), and that's how the Mule Mountains acquired their name.

Beneath those granite mountains was a wealth of gold, silver and copper that defied the wildest imagination of even the most incurable prospector. But the mountains guarded their secrets well, and it was late in the 19th Century before a government scout named Jack Dunn stumbled across some rich outcroppings in the spring of 1877. Dunn, an Irishman, was a civilian scout with Company C, Sixth Cavalry, under the command of Lt. John A. Rucker. Company C was chasing hostile Apache and had stopped to camp in Mule Pass. Dunn went off in search of water and, in the vicinity of today's Castle Rock, found rich outcroppings of ore. He collected some specimens and showed them to Lt. Rucker and T.D. Byrne, another member of the scouting expedition. They agreed to go partners and file a claim, but the demands of the Apache campaigns kept them on the trail for the next several months.

Meanwhile, at Fort Bowie, Dunn made the acquaintance of George Warren, a 42-year-old prospector of dubious integrity. Dunn and his partners grubstaked Warren, the latter agreeing to file claims on their behalf. On his way to the Mule Mountains, Warren got sidetracked in a saloon and lost his grubstake. When the drunken prospector revealed his mission, he was quickly re-equipped but with new partners. Eventually Warren filed several claims in Mule Pass, but Dunn, Rucker and Byrne were not included.

George Warren, one of the early miners in the Bisbee area. He lost his share of the Copper Queen mine after a drunken wager. Warren bet he could outrun a horse on foot. The town of Warren is named for him and this photo was used as part of the Arizona state seal. Photo: Southwest Studies.

George Warren was a hard worker but that was the only virtue he seems to have possessed. He'd led a rough life. His mother had died when he was an infant, his father had been killed by raiding Apaches, and young George was taken captive. Later he was sold back to some miners for 20 pounds of sugar. The youth grew up among the rough-hewn miners and became something of a reprobate himself. By the time Warren met Jack Dunn, "ole John Barleycorn" had gained control.

Two years after the discovery of rich ore in Mule Pass, a drunken George Warren made a bet on a footrace, wagering his share of what was to become the legendary Copper Queen Mine. Warren firmly believed he could outrun a man on horseback, but lost the race and with it millions of dollars. He died in poverty, alone and forgotten. Years later he was reburied with a headstone honoring him as "Father of the Camp." A more lasting memorial is the nearby town of Warren, named in his honor. Another, not quite so obvious, is the miner pictured on the Arizona State Seal. The miner on the seal was taken from an old photograph of Warren, which was found hanging on the wall of a Bisbee bank.

The reputation of Warren's mining camp, nestled in what was being called Tombstone Canyon, quickly spread to the far reaches of the mining West. A smelter was erected in 1880, and the lifestyle changed from a hand-to-mouth existence to steady income. Earlier, the ore had to be freighted by wagon over to the nearest railroad, then shipped by rail to Pennsylvania for smelting.

Not all of those early-day entrepreneurs went away with their pockets full. Hugh Jones, Joe Halcro, and Hank McCoy located a claim they called the Halcro Mine, hoping for a rich silver bonanza but finding instead "copper stains." Discouraged, they mounted their mules and rode away. The next developer came along and renamed the mine the Copper Queen, and the rest is history. During the peak years of the Copper Queen, 10,000 people occupied the 640 acres of livable hillside land nearby. The Greater Bisbee area at one time supported a population of 20,000 people. It was officially called the Warren Mining District and included Bisbee, Warren, Lowell, San Jose, and a humble Mexican community called Tintown. Amazingly, the ore-bearing land lay in an area two by three miles on the surface and ran to a depth of 4,000 feet.

The Copper Queen operated day and night, mining an endless supply of rich ore. In early 1881 Dr. James Douglas paid a visit to the boom camp. The 44-year-old visionary had been commissioned by some eastern speculators to examine mining properties around Jerome and Morenci. While in Arizona, he decided to check out the place that would become known as Bisbee.

Dr. Douglas was so impressed with the area he convinced a New York-based import-export company named Phelps Dodge to go into the mining business. They purchased 51% of the Copper Queen Mine and, on Douglas' strong recommendation, several adjacent properties. Dr. Douglas was given a choice of taking a commission in cash or a piece of the action. He wisely chose the latter, acting as consultant to Phelps Dodge until 1885 when he was named president of Copper Queen Consolidated, a position he held until 1908. When Douglas died in 1918 he left behind a fortune valued at more than $20 million. Dr. Douglas, a man of rare qualities and varied interests, was trusted and respected by mine workers and investors alike for his honesty, integrity and loyalty.

In 1889 the long-awaited railroad arrived in Bisbee, ending the mule-driven hauls to Fairbank. When the Arizona and South Eastern's Engine #1 came chugging up the final stretch from Fairbank on its first run, the whole town turned out to give a rousing welcome.

Later, the Southern Pacific acquired the spur line in an exchange with the Santa Fe Railroad. When the Southern Pacific jacked up the freight rates, Dr. Douglas declared war and built a new railroad line. The resourceful president of Copper Queen Consolidated, anxious to get out from under the thumb of the Southern Pacific, succeeded in building a new and more direct line east to El Paso. Dr. Douglas renamed his railroad the El Paso and Southwestern and built a spur line joining the Santa Fe at Deming, New Mexico. In 1924 Phelps Dodge sold the line to the Southern Pacific. Old Engine #1 escaped the scrap pile and was given an honorary resting place near the Southern Pacific headquarters in El Paso.

Bisbee was named for Judge DeWitt Bisbee of San Francisco, a financial backer of the Copper Queen. Despite the fact that Bisbee eventually became known as the most cultured and gracious city between San Francisco and New Orleans, Judge Bisbee never visited it.

Bisbee was rough around the edges in those pristine 1880s. The woodframed homes were perched precariously on the steep, terraced hillsides. It was said you couldn't spit tobacco juice off your front porch without hitting your neighbor on the level below, and small children had to be tethered to fence posts lest they fall onto a neighbor's roof.

Bisbee was a two-canyon city, the main thoroughfare being Tombstone Canyon, later called Main Street, and a confluent canyon, called Brewery Gulch, coming in from the north. Tombstone Canyon became the central business district and Brewery Gulch became notorious for its saloons and shady ladies, catering to a more raucous crowd. Old-timers used to say that the farther up Brewery Gulch one went, the rougher were the saloons and the wilder the women.

Brewery Gulch got its name when Arnold Sieber (not to be confused with Al Sieber, the army scout) dug a hole in one side of the gulch and opened a brewery, embellishing the front with a bar later called Brewery Gulch. The "Gulch" went down in western history as one of America's rowdiest avenues of pleasures.

However, action began to slow down along Brewery Gulch in 1910 when prostitution was outlawed. Five years later Prohibition became law, and anyone with some wild oats to sow had to go across the Mexican border at Naco.

In 1901 investors from Calumet, Michigan, formed the Calumet and Arizona Mining Company. They hit an immense body of high grade ore which became one of the richest mines in the world, paying out $47 million in dividends. Bisbee's major mines were the Calumet and Arizona and Phelps Dodge. They thrived in friendly competition until the Great Depression, when Phelps Dodge bought out the Calumet and Arizona, which had fallen on hard times.

By 1975 the Bisbee area, one of the richest mineral sites the world has ever known, had produced a staggering wealth of $6.1 billion. It yielded nearly 3 million ounces of gold, over 97 million ounces of silver, over 8 billion pounds of copper, 304 million pounds of lead, and nearly 373 million pounds of zinc.

During World War I, the development of new techniques for reducing low-grade ore at a profit and the advent of large trucks and earthmoving equipment made open-pit mining a reality. Mountains were turned into terraced canyons. Sacramento Hill, just east of Buckey O'Neill Hill and southeast of Bisbee, was a classic example. The destruction of the cone-shaped mountain began in 1917 when tons of explosives literally blew its top off.

A new operation was begun in the mid-1950s that overwhelmed the Sacramento Pit. Called the Lavender Pit in honor of Harrison Lavender, manager of the Copper Queen Branch of Phelps Dodge, the huge pit reached a depth of more than 900 feet before it was shut down in 1974.

The most traumatic event in Arizona's labor history was the infamous Bisbee Deportation of 1917. For years a bitter power struggle ensued between the unions and the copper companies. The price of copper and company profits skyrocketed with the advent of World War I, when the allies desperately needed copper. The unions felt the time was ripe for a strike and rumblings were felt in mining towns throughout the state. One union, the Industrial Workers of the World (I.W.W.s or "Wobblies"), was more vocal than the rest, quickly gaining a reputation as a troublemaker. The copper companies, especially Phelps Dodge, waged a clever propaganda war against the union. Since Phelps Dodge controlled several newspapers, not to mention a number of legislators, it wasn't hard to arouse the general public's ire against any group that preached strike during these critical times.

The climax came on July 12, 1917, at 6:30 a.m. when 2,000 armed men with white handkerchiefs tied around their arms took to the streets of the Warren Mining District and rounded up more than 2,000 suspected I.W.W. members and sympathizers. They were herded to the baseball park at Warren, and by day's end nearly 1,200 had been loaded into boxcars and shipped to Columbus, New Mexico. By some miracle only two men died that day — one a suspected I.W.W. member, the other a vigilante.

Like so many Arizona mining towns, Bisbee exudes a rich turn-of-the-century history. The Copper Queen Hotel, built in 1902, was as opulent as any big city hostelry. Celebrants spending the night and dining in its elegant restaurant included President Teddy Roosevelt and Gen. John "Black Jack" Pershing. One early-day couple was skeptical of the four-story hillside hotel. The gentleman came back to the desk after inspecting his room on the third floor. "I can't keep that room," he asserted, "my wife's nervous and afraid of fire." The innkeeper, without any change of expression, replied, "Oh, my friend, if fire breaks out, just raise your window and step out onto the hillside."

JEROME

High above the Verde Valley sits cone-shaped Cleopatra Hill, a reddish-hued mountain on which the town of Jerome is precariously perched. The hill was a magical freak of nature, a treasure trove of gold, silver and copper. Its reputation matches that of Cripple Creek, Colorado, the Comstock Lode of Nevada, and Tombstone. Before Jerome called it quits in 1953 it was being called the "Billion Dollar Copper Camp."

Spanish explorers claimed to have found rich ore samples in the Jerome area during the 1500s. The steep-sided mountains presented formidable barriers and it wasn't until the 1870s that any serious prospecting took place. Famed army scout Al Sieber worked claims on Cleopatra Hill but gave them up without realizing their value.

In 1876, M.A. Ruffner, along with Angus and Rod McKinnon, filed claims on the site. Ruffner's claim is believed to have been what became the famous United Verde. The three relinquished their claims at a profit of $3,500 each. The property would eventually return tens of millions to another owner.

The forming of the United Verde coincided with the arrival of a railroad to Ashfork in 1882. New York financier Eugene Jerome agreed to back the United Verde venture providing they named the new town after him. Jerome, a cousin of Jennie Jerome, mother of Sir Winston Churchill, never visited the town which eventually grew to a population of 15,000.

The high cost of hauling ore over a mountain road to Ashfork caused the new owners to go belly-up in 1887. A year later Phelps Dodge sent Dr. James Douglas out with an offer of $30,000 for the property, valued at ten times that amount. Meanwhile, William Andrews Clark, a secretive Montana copper king, slipped into the area. He donned a pair of overalls and scoured the hill with a hammer, taking ore specimens. Satisfied he was standing on a bonanza, he paid the asking price. Phelps Dodge decided to meet the asking price but arrived a day after Clark closed the deal. Many years later Phelps Dodge would purchase the property at a cost of $21 million, after millions of dollars in gold, silver and copper had already been extracted.

In 1892 Clark built a narrow-gauge railroad into Jerome from Jerome Junction in Chino Valley. The line had more kinks and lazy loops than a cheap lariat. Passengers could look out the window and see the locomotive going back the other way. The hills were so steep engines could pull only five cars at a time.

By the 1890s the United Verde was paying Clark dividends of $3.5 million a year. Clark got interested in politics temporarily and ran in Montana for the U.S. Senate in 1898. He spent a million dollars in bribes to get elected but the Senate refused to seat him. He ran again in 1902, was elected and this time was given a seat. He served only one term, then returned to his business enterprises.

In 1914 Clark spent $2 million to build a smelter town four miles downhill from Jerome. At the same time he loaned $3.5 million to the Santa Fe Railroad to build a line to the new town he named Clarkdale.

Jerome had the unique distinction of becoming a two-company town in 1912 when "Rawhide Jimmy" Douglas, son of Dr. James Douglas, arrived. He bought the Little Daisy Mine and, after spending half a million without success, hit a vein of pure copper that was five feet thick. In 1916, Rawhide Jimmy's United Verde Extension mined $10 million in gold, silver and copper, more than 75% of that pure profit.

World War I brought Jerome its greatest glory. Copper sold for 30 cents a pound and the population peaked.

Jerome is a popular tourist attraction today. It's a quiet community now and that's a far cry from those halcyon days around the turn of the century when there was, roughly, one saloon for every one hundred residents.

The town took on quite a personality during those years. Payday came once a month and the mines closed for a couple of days to let the spirited miners have time to spend their hard-earned wages. Things got pretty western for a few days and the old jail, which looked more like a concrete bunker, was usually overflowing. Legend has it the jail had spikes on the floor to keep the occupants from getting a good night's sleep.

The plucky miners never let incarceration keep them from having a good time. Once, when the jail was already filled, the town constable chained 12 unruly drunks to a huge mill wheel. Undaunted, the brawny reprobates picked up the wheel in unison and hauled it to the nearest saloon where they demanded an ax to widen the door so they could get in.

Lewis St. James was the local magistrate. He was totally deaf and couldn't hear the testimony, but he seemed to know most of the defendants personally and ruled accordingly. Like most judges, he had an uncanny ability to know just how much money they were carrying and set the fine thusly.

The town dentist was Dr. Lee Hawkins. He'd never been to dental school, but folks liked him and, since his remedies were harmless, they let him practice (literally).

Jennie Banters was the town's most prominent and prosperous madam. It was said she was the wealthiest businesswoman in Arizona around the turn of the century. She was also the most resourceful. Once when the town was having one of its periodic holocausts, she went to the volunteer hose company and offered them lifetime free passes to her establishment if they'd put the fire out at her place. It was said the red-blooded volunteers rose to superhuman efforts as they charged up the hill to extinguish the flames.

Jerome's citizens never missed a chance to celebrate some festive occasion, and the Fourth of July was always the favorite. Everybody turned out to watch the volunteer hose companies run races. A great deal of pride was at stake, since fire was a constant threat in the hillside town built of wood-framed structures. The hose company judged fastest was held in the highest esteem among town folks, and won braggin' rights until the next contest.

Drilling contests were the most popular. Hard rock miners competed for some $200 in prize money—no small amount, since a miner earned only about three dollars a day. Each contestant or team had 15 minutes to drill a hole in a block of Gunnison granite. Naturally there was a lot of betting on the outcome.

Baseball, the great American pastime, always generated a lot of excitement. Fierce rivalries were established between towns such as Prescott and Clarkdale. The company bankrolled the local team and imported some of the best players money could buy. Hal Chase, banned from major league baseball for accepting a bribe, was brought to Jerome but didn't last long. One story has it he was bought off by gamblers in Clarkdale, a far cry from throwing the World Series, but no less scandalous to the rabid fans at Jerome.

Jerome never completely recovered from the stock market crash of 1929. A few years earlier, the United Verde Extension had discovered a rich body of ore directly below the town. Hundreds of thousands of tons of earth-shaking dynamite were used to wrest the ore from the mountain's clutches. Above the ground, years of choking smelter smoke had destroyed the flora on the mountain. With nothing to hold the soil, Jerome began to slide.

Despite hard times and the new catastrophe, Jerome's hardy citizens never lost their sense of humor. Mayor Harry Mader coined a new phrase when he proclaimed "Jerome is a city on the move." It was, but unfortunately all downhill.

In recent years new techniques have revitalized the old mining areas south of Tucson where miners have dug since the days of the Spanish explorers. Today, mines in Pima County and San Manuel, in Pinal County, have replaced Bisbee, Jerome, Globe-Miami, Superior-Ray, Ajo and Morenci-Clifton as copper kings of Arizona.

Those jackass prospectors and hard-rock bindlestiffs left behind a rich, colorful history and a powerful legacy. Mining was the foundation on which 20th Century Arizona would be built. As one old third-generation miner said, "Well, it's about over, ain't it. But it was sure one hell of a time, and we won't ever see anything like it again."

10

LEGENDS IN LEVI'S

The Arizona Cowboys

The men and women of the Old West are among the most cherished figures in Americana, the rugged symbols of the making of a country — independent, hard-working and self-reliant. Among these heroic figures, the most beloved and enduring are the cowboys, America's legends in Levi's. Their brash, rebellious years were short; only a couple of decades made them immortal. Yet these last American folk heroes cut a deep trail in the illustrious history of the West. "He made

Cowboys ham it up for the photographer. Photo: Arizona Historical Society.

tracks in history," wrote cowboy artist Charley Russell, "that the farmer can't plow under."

There has never been, before or since, a figure who has held the interest and imagination of so many people. Nor has there ever been a figure so misunderstood and misrepresented. The cowboy as a legitimate folk hero is really a composite. The word "cowboy" has come to represent the entire wide gamut of frontier society. Gunfighters, gamblers, outlaws and cowboys are inseparable to all but the most discerning student of the Old West. America's first "cowboys" were Tories or British loyalists during the Revolutionary War who used to hide in the brush and ring cow bells, trying to lure patriot-farmers into an ambush. Cow thieves in Cochise County during the 1880s were also known as "cowboys." The name didn't seem to gain respectability until the 1890s. The men usually called themselves drovers, waddies or peelers.

Out of a frontier history that lasted more than 350 years, Americans have taken the era of the open range cowboy, a brief 20-year span, given it immortality and called it "The West." The cowboy riding atop his trusty steed is America's answer to the knights of old. These heroic figures have come to symbolize all the manifestations of character we ascribe to the winning of the West. Their grand image represents the highest and most honorable qualities of mankind: the outdoors, freedom, individualism and defense of the oppressed. The cowboy seems so indigenous to our culture that, had he never existed, we would have invented him.

"To become a cowboy," someone wrote, "all you needed was guts and a horse. And if you had guts, you could steal a horse." They came from varied backgrounds. Kids ran away from home and walked down to the cattle country in south Texas to fulfill that dream of being a cowboy. Blacks, escaping slavery and prejudice, found what really counted on the open range was not the color of one's skin, but his ability to handle a lariat and work with horses and cattle.

Some modern-day observers have criticized the romantic image of the cowboy, claiming he was little more than an illiterate laborer on horseback, differing little from factory hands in eastern cities. The subject has been cussed and discussed among scholars at university seminars. Oftentimes overlooked is the fact that, in reality, a cowboy had much greater responsibility than other members of the laboring class. A small handful were oftentimes charged with driving a large herd up the trail to market a herd that represented the life savings of a group of ranchers. They might be called upon to defend the cattle with their lives from predatory outlaws or Indians. And they might have to risk their necks turning the herd in a stampede, or swimming dangerously swollen rivers. Many lost their lives in lonely places trying to protect their employer's investment.

Still, it was a unique way of life. With the exception of the fabled mountain men, the cowboys shared freedoms enjoyed by few others in the laboring class. Granted, they worked for bosses who might be autocratic, but away from the ranch headquarters they were pretty much their own bosses, and they had the wide open spaces to ride and plenty of clean air to breathe. It's doubtful that any of them would have traded places with a laborer in some stagnant, throat-choking factory town.

Typical turn-of-the-century cowboys. Photo: Arizona Historical Society.

Their days might be spent under a blazing sun or in a bone-chilling blue Montana norther, and their nights were spent in exhausted slumber. The body took a merciless beating from the pounding of a bronc. Skin weathered prematurely from exposure to the elements. It was a tough life and it bred an indomitable character that is deeply ingrained in our culture. Hollywood transformed the real working cowpuncher into a tight-lipped, tight-trousered puppet who was quick on the draw, straight-shooting and always on the side of right. The cowboy has been lionized, analyzed, and psychoanalyzed. We've had the lonesome cowboy, hero cowboy, anti-hero cowboy, tragic cowboy, singing cowboy, drugstore cowboy, electric cowboy, Coca-Cola cowboy, midnight cowboy, urban cowboy, rhinestone cowboy and a host of others.

The cowboy has been a rich source for humor and storytelling. Storytelling is a cherished right in Arizona and it's considered bad manners to correct a liar.

Few realize that a cowboy gave this country its first job description. The hours spent in the great out-of-doors gave them plenty of time to reflect on their work and if anyone should ask just what the job required, a cowpuncher had this stock reply:

> Cowboys is noisy fellers with bow-legs and brass stomachs that works from the hurricane deck of a U-necked cowpony and hates any kind of work that can't be done atop one.
>
> They rides like Comanches, ropes like Mexicans and shoots like Arizona Rangers.
>
> They kin spit ten feet into a stiff wind, whup their weight in wildcats, fight grizzlies bare knuckled, bite on the tail of live cougars, take on the whole Apache nation armed with one six-shooter, and ride anything that wears hair.
>
> They lives in and loves the outdoors, hates fences and respects rivers.
>
> And they's independent, too. You jest throw one of 'em into a river and he'll naturally float upstream.
>
> The only way to tame one of 'em is to cut off his head and bury it someplace where he can't find it.

Cowboys were also well-known for their extreme self-confidence. One time an unemployed puncher stopped off at a lumber camp in northern Arizona and inquired about a job. The strawboss, a big strapping hunk of a man, looked down at the wiry, 140-pound waddie and said, "Why, you look like a piece of second growth timber to me. You ever done any lumber-jackin' before?"

The cowboy looked nonplussed and replied, "Have you ever heard of the Sonoran Forest?"

The strawboss raised a hand and said, "Now wait a minute; don't you mean the Sonoran Desert?"

The cowboy nodded confidently and replied, "Yup, it is now."

Cowboys liked horses, dogs, and children and were well known for their generosity. They also had a reputation for being kind-hearted to the downtrodden.

One time over in Cochise County, a fellow was on trial for first-degree murder and he knew his goose was cooked — that is until he learned there was a cowboy on the jury. During a recess he asked the cowboy to give him a break. "Please hold out for manslaughter," he pleaded, "and I'll walk the straight and narrow. I'll never go wrong again." Well, the cowboy said he'd do the best he could. When the verdict came in, sure enough, it was manslaughter. The defendant could not believe his good fortune. He ran up to the cowboy and shook his arm like an old pump handle. "I can't thank you enough," he exclaimed, "but you must have had a hell of a time."

"I sure did," the cowboy replied, "the rest of 'em wanted to acquit you."

Rustling cattle was a serious offense in old Arizona, especially if the culprit was a stranger or a nester. However, big outfits took a more philosophical view. Two old ranchers had been neighbors for 30 years and hadn't socialized much, so one day one decided it was time to invite the other to dinner. He planned to throw the biggest barbeque southern Arizona had ever seen as a tribute to his old neighbor. Folks from three counties showed up to partake of the free beef and booze. Along about sundown the guest was feeling pretty mellow as he cut into another slice of beefsteak. "Ya know, ol' pard," he said, "we've been neighbors for 30 years and I've got a confession to make: In all this time I've never eaten one of my own cows."

The host was unflapped by the revelation. He looked out at all the tables heaped with beefsteak, smiled and replied "eat hearty, 'cause ya are now."

Throughout all the myth-making, the real working cowpuncher endures, the only one of this nation's folk heroes who can legitimately make that claim. Although they are few in number, cowboys still work cattle on the ranges in Arizona much the same as their ancestors a century ago.

The Arizona cowboy was a curious mix of the northern Plains, Rockies, California, Texas and northern Mexico cowboy culture. The influence of all these was strong, yet the Arizona cowboys, or *vaqueros,* evolved into a unique breed of their own. In a frontier that was closing rapidly at the turn of the century, Arizona offered one of the last vestiges of the freedom that was associated with being a cowboy.

Perhaps the cowboy's most distinguishable features were their wide-brimmed Stetsons, sometimes called the "John B" in honor of the manufacturer. In the Southwest it was sometimes referred to as a sombrero from the Spanish word *sombra* , meaning

"Dad" Hardiman and "Uncle" Hal Young moving the CCC horse herd near San Carlos in 1911. Arizona Historical Society.

shade. Like their other trappings, the hat was multi-purpose. It served as a water pitcher for them and their horses, to fan fires, and it kept the dust, sun and rain off their heads. They used to say, "humans dress up, but a cowboy dresses down." That hat was the first thing a cowboy put on when he got up in the morning and the last thing he took off at night. The high crown gave him the opportunity to "personalize it" or style its shape to his own liking. Expensive hats were a status symbol, and a good one would cost the better part of a month's pay. But they were so durable they lasted for years.

Most cowboys donned a pair of chaps when working cows in rough country. The name chaps is derived from the Spanish word *chaparejos* which meant "leather breeches." They saved wear and tear on a man's overalls, kept him warmer in winter and protected him from rocks, cactus and thorny brush. A few wore "hair pants" or angora chaps made from goat skin and worn with hair side out. Many preferred the Mexican "shotgun" chaps. These leggings fitted snugly around the legs and were more like a second pair of pants. They were decorated with a leather fringe on the pockets and sometimes had silver conchos running down the legs. When riding in brush country, however, the chaps with the silver conchos remained in the bunkhouse, as the cowboy didn't want to lose them in the mesquite.

The batwing type was probably the most popular. They were held on with snaps and didn't fit so tightly. Their shape, along with their big flapping leggings, gave them their name.

Trousers worn by the working cowboy were the heavy, blue denim "Levi's," when they could get them. Otherwise they wore woolen "California pants." The tighter the fit, the better. Tight pants, especially across the seat, meant fewer wrinkles to cut into the fanny. Long hours in the saddle caused the crotch of the pants to wear out first. One was able to prolong the use by stitching a large leather patch over the worn out part. Shirts were long-sleeved, colorless and made of cotton or flannel. Since there was little pocket space in the trousers, they carried essential items, such as cigarette makings, in a many-pocketed vest which was usually worn unbuttoned.

Knotted around the neck was a brighly-colored neckerchief or bandana. Most preferred the former, saying that bandanas were for farmers. The neckerchief not only served him as a "range necktie," but it also gave protection from sun and windburn. Worn as a mask, it was a dust filter in a storm

Cowboy poet Gail Gardner. He penned such classics as "Moonshine Steer"; "Dude Wrangler" and "Sierry Petes" or "Tyin' Knots in the Devil's Tail." Photo: courtesy Delia Gardner.

and could be used as a wash towel, tourniquet or sling.

Boots were of a high-shafted, two-inch heel variety, not for show, but to keep their feet from pushing through the stirrups. Those boots weren't made for walkin', but then they didn't plan to do much walkin' anyhow. Cowboys did not invent the high-heeled boots. They have been in use since the earliest Asiatic horsemen. No expense was spared when purchasing a pair. It was not uncommon for a man earning $30 a month to spent $40 on a pair of custom hand-crafted boots made of leather so fine you could "see the wrinkles in yer socks."

Another distinguishable feature of the working cow-hand's rigging was his spurs. Spurs were sometimes worn as ornaments for show, but were more important than reins when it came to maneuvering a cowpony—to signal quick action when working cows or getting over rough terrain. They weren't used to inflict pain, but more as a reminder, usually a simple movement of the leg was all that was required to get the message across.

The working cowboys were mighty particular about their "hoss jewelry," especially their saddle. After all, they spent the greater part of their waking hours seated upon it. The ranch might furnish the horses, but the saddle was nearly always the personal property of the cowhand. A good one cost about a month's wages and was worth more in dollar value than most of the horses he rode. There was a great deal of truth in the saying "a cowboy rode a $10 horse and sat on a $40 saddle." It was so much a part of the trade that "sellin' one's saddle" was a phrase used to describe getting out of the business for good.

The saddle was not only a seat, but a workbench as well. The cantle was high, to keep one's seat firmly in place and rest the back. It weighed 30 to 40 pounds, and it was built rugged to withstand the punishment. The horn was steel forged, wrapped in rawhide, then leather; and stout enough to anchor a dallied lariat with a contrary critter on the other end. The pommel might be a swell fork or slick, and the rigging and cinch a "rimfire," "centerfire" or a "three-quarter" rig, depend-ing on one's locale or preference.

The rest of the working cowboy's "hoss jewelry" was the headgear—reins, bridle and bit. Most important is the bit. The three standard types of bit are curb, snaffle and bar. Each has its own variations, but the curb is the simplest, most humane and therefore the most widely used. Some were cruel and severe, like the Spanish ring bit, but most cowboys found the most suitable bit was one that had the psychological effect of directing the horse's movement with only the slightest motion of the reins. Regardless of how severe the bit is, the real talent in making a horse perform remains in the lightness of hand on the part of the horseman.

The rope or lariat was the most important tool of the cowboy. At one time or another, each cow had to have a loop tossed around its neck. A rope enabled a 150-pound man to easily throw a 1,000-pound cow. Cowboys then and now considered roping as the feature that separated real cowhands from pretenders. Even today, good cowpunchers won't stay with an outfit long if it doesn't provide them with the opportunity to use their ropes.

The Spanish, and later the Mexicans, preferred to use a braided raw-hide *la reata* which was later corrupted into the English lariat. The *reatas* were from 60 to 100 feet long. American cowboys used a shorter grass rope like a "maguey" made from the fibers of the century plant, of a "manila," made from manila fiber. Others preferred the "seago" for their roping. The seago was short for seagoing or a maritime rope. Disdaining the longer Mexican rope, one cowboy said, "You only need one that long to catch something down in a well."

It was not the cow that made the cowboy; it was the horse. In the early days it was a range mongrel known as the mustang, those sturdy, unpampered descendants of the Spanish breed that were the greatest contributors to a cowboy's self-image. There was an aura of aristocracy, shared by the fraternity of horsemen, that bridged all cultures. The U.S. Cavalry felt a strong sense of superiority over the foot soldier, as did the horse Indian who considered fighting on foot as degrading. To the Spanish, a *caballero* was a gentleman on horseback and *chevalier* and *cavalier* meant the same to the French and British, respectively. To the cowboy, "sitting on the hurricane deck of a cowpony" made him a member of the same elite fraternity. "Nature's Noblemen," cowboy artist Frederic Remington called them. The horse was the apparatus on which the cowboy and the range cattle industry depended for survival. Without it, it would have been impossible to gather, rope, brand, and drive the millions of critters to market, which was what the range cattle industry was all about.

Those old time cowponies were not the well-bred animals seen at rodeos and at most working ranches today. During the 1600s, the Plains Indians captured a few Barbs and Arabs from the Spanish, and built an entire culture around them. Not much larger than a pony, they weighed only 700 to 900 pounds and stood 12 to 14 hands high. They looked more like a scrub of no particular parentage, but appearances are deceiving; they had undergone many changes through generations of adapting to the demands of their environment. Those broncos used by late 19th Century cowboys did not necessarily descend from the mustangs of the Great Plains as is often believed, but came from northern Mexico instead. Generally, the Hispanos were more particular about breeding good stock than the Indians, and it is likely they were the progenitors of the American cowpony. The sires were well-chosen for their bloodlines and conformation and were not subjected to the long, hungry winters that stunted the growth of the wild horses on the Great Plains.

Most cowboys regarded horses as a necessary tool of the trade and nothing more. However, extraordinary cowponies were held in high regard and provided the inspiration for much bragging during "lying hour" around the bunkhouse. Tall tales abounded about the prowess of cutting horses that could spin and turn quicker 'n a cowbrute could duck or dodge, and the term "horse sense" subsequently has become a part of the English language. It was said by many that they knew more than their rider when it came to doing the right thing at the right time. Good cow horses in an outfit were sometimes better known and longer remembered than the men who rode them.

Most had been ridden only four or five times by a bronc twister when they were turned over to the cowboy to tone up the rough edges and had to be blindfolded before being mounted. One old-timer described one of these experiences: "The horse changed ends under me and was, before I knew it, going the other way." Another said that "some of the snuffy cayuses in his string galloped a little high. The trick is to keep falling off and climbing back on again until the horse becomes bored." To meet one's shadow on the ground, in a land where you could look further and see less, a man left afoot had about as much chance as a one-legged man at a kickin' contest. It was said that the only thing a cowboy feared more than being left alone in a room with a decent woman was being left afoot in the middle of nowhere. The plight of a cowboy who was long overdue back at the ranch would be discussed in relation to what particular horse he might be riding. If it was a dependable one, nobody showed much concern. However, if the horse was "green," the available hands would ride out to look for the rider.

When a horse was sick or lame enough to call a horse doctor out, the monetary value of the horse was never a topic of discussion, nor did anybody ask how much the treatment would cost. The only thing that might be said was "save him if you can." Most of the talk centered around what a good horse he'd been, how much he'd helped the ranch and his exploits on the range. Good horses are as important to a working ranch today as years ago. Some outfits buy their replacement horses from sale barn auctions or by treaty, while others do their own breeding. There's an old adage among cow-bosses that good horses will go a long way towards holding a man to an outfit.

Texas folk historian J. Frank Dobie called the long-eared, rangy longhorn "the bedrock on which the range cattle industry was founded." No other breed of cattle has ever been as unique and no two longhorns looked exactly alike. Colors ranged from black and brown to red, white and pinto. Anyone who ever witnessed the longhorn running wild and free on the

Felix Ruelas after winning a horse race at Patagonia around 1880. Photo: Arizona Historical Society, Buehman collection.

range had to agree there was something special about the critter. They were tall and bony with an enormous horn span that reached seven to eight feet tip to tip, a coarse-haired coat, an ornery looking face, thin flanks and a swayback. They were aptly described as a "critter with four legs hitched to a set of horns." These "hairy greenbacks" were a race apart, and without them there might never have been open range cowboys. They were descendants of the racy-looking Mexican *corrientes*.

The harsh environment and geography combined to produce a unique breed—a formidable beast, unpredictable, mean and fearing nothing. They had the ability to recover much more quickly from prolonged thirst and could travel 60 miles without water, endure extreme cold and heat and were adaptable to all kinds of terrain. It was said, perhaps in exaggerated admiration, they could jump a six-foot fence standing flatfooted. During the early part of this century, the longhorn came closer to extinction than the buffalo. Today, in some regions the longhorn is making a comeback. Cattlemen are as lavish in their praise of the beast as their predecessors were, saying they calve easier, with less death loss in the first-year heifers, and there is less cholesterol in the meat compared to heavier beef.

Arizona's first cowboy was the famed Jesuit padre, Eusebio Kino. He drove the first herds of cattle into the Santa Cruz Valley from Sonora in the late 1600s. The cattle were distributed among the Pima and Tohono O'odham (Papago) peoples.

During the "golden years" of the Spanish empire, 1790-1821, rancheros stocked the ranges with large herds of cattle. Huge land grants with romantic sounding names such as Boquillas, San Rafael, Sonoita, Babocomari, Canoa, and Buena Vista occupied the best grazing lands in southern Arizona. The outfits were so large that, as the old saying goes, "you had to grease the wagon twice to get from the front porch to the front gate."

The peace treaty with the Apaches broke down in the 1830s, and by 1840 all of these beautiful ranches lay in ruins.

Ranching resumed in the 1850s after the American occupation. Such Mexican rancheros as Bernabe Robles, Pedro and Yjinio Aguirre, Juan Elías, Manuel Amado, and brothers Sabino and Teofilo Otero started big outfits and resumed ranching in southern Arizona. They were joined by Americans Bill Kirkland, Pete Kitchen and Bill Oury. These bold men held stubbornly to the land despite frequent raids by roving bands of Apaches.

During the early days of the California gold rush, herds were gathered in Texas and driven along the Gila Trail to the mining camps. In 1849, a three-dollar steer in Texas sold for $500 a head in California. A cattleman could lose most of his herd to raiders or the blistering desert and still turn a huge profit. Many cattle strayed from the herds during the drive and lost themselves among the tules along the Gila River, where they became wild as deer. Years later, after the Apache, Yavapai and Mohave were located on reservations, cowpunchers rode into the brush and gathered these wild cattle. They provided the seed crop for many a rancher who had the temerity to go after them.

The Apache Wars caused a number of military posts to be established in the Arizona Territory. By 1886, one-fifth of the entire U.S. Army was in Arizona trying to round up wily old Geronimo and his band. The military posts, Indian reservations and blossoming mining towns created a huge market for beef. By the mid-1870s, most of the tribes were on reservations and ranchers were able to graze their cattle in southern Arizona without much fear of large scale losses from raiding war parties.

However, as large herds were driven into the pristine ranges from Texas another kind of raider made his appearance: the cattle rustler. The proximity to the Mexican border and the rough, uncurried land provided an excellent refuge for large gangs of rustlers well into the 20th Century. At one point the President of the United States threatened to declare martial law on the whole territory if the rustler element wasn't restrained by local authorities.

The gangs were so well organized that cattle were stolen in southern Arizona and driven to the Tonto, Bloody, or Horsethief basins, where their brands were altered. Then they were driven as far north as Utah, Colorado or northern New Mexico, where they were sold. Then, as if not to show favoritism, the rustlers stole horses up north and sold them down south.

Ranching began to change with the arrival of men like Henry Clay Hooker in the 1870s. Hooker got his start a few years earlier by driving a large flock of turkeys across the Sierra Nevada to sell to the miners in Nevada. At the edge of a large canyon the entire herd leaped over the edge. Hooker feared the entire flock had commited suicide, but on reaching the bottom found them all in fine condition. He drove them on to Virginia City, took his profit and headed for Arizona. He bought a ranch in the north end of the Sulphur Springs Valley near Fort Grant and called it Sierra Bonita. His brand was the crooked H. Soon Hooker was known throughout the territory for his purebred cattle. His prize herds ran Hereford, Durham, and Shorthorn cattle. He once paid the unheard-of price of $30,000 for two Hereford bull calves. Hooker also had a collection of purebred stallions. His stylish ranch became the social gathering place for important visitors eager to sample western hospitality Hooker-style. Male dinner guests were required to wear a coat to the table. Of course, Hooker always kept plenty of spare ones for any emergency. Many years later the ranch became the subject of a popular stage play.

Hooker was a generous man, to white and Indian alike. When Cochise's Chiricahua Apaches were located on a reservation nearby, cattle began to disappear from local ranches. Hooker rode bravely into their stronghold and served notice that anytime they were hungry, to feel free to butcher one of his cows. The Apaches respected this kindness and Hooker's outfit wasn't bothered by raiding parties anymore.

Hooker shipped so many cattle on the rails that he was always allowed free passes. One day he climbed on board and told the conductor, "I'm Hooker, I ride free." A shapely redhead was right behind him. She smiled sweetly at the conductor and said, "I'm a hooker, too. Do we all ride free?"

The building of the Atlantic and Pacific Railroad (Santa Fe) across northern Arizona in the early 1880s inspired the first large ranching enterprises to locate there. In 1881, John Young, a son of the Mormon leader, started the Mormon Cattle Company, with headquarters at the foot of the spectacular San Francisco Peaks. A year later, he teamed with some eastern investors to form the Arizona Cattle Company or the A1 brand, as it was better known. Iron-bellied locomotives hauled thousands of cattle to market and by 1883 the price of beef was $50 a head, up $15 from just two years earlier.

Northern Arizona's most spectacular enterprise was established in 1884 when Edward Kinsley, one of the owners of the railroad, made a trip west to inspect the new line. He noted the grass-carpeted ranges between the junction of the Rio Puerco and Little Colorado rivers and Flagstaff, and declared he could raise enough cattle out there to feed a nation. Back in New York he joined with others to form the Aztec Land and Cattle Company. The company purchased a million acres from the railroad for 50 cents an acre, bought a herd in Texas and shipped it by rail to Horsehead Crossing, which was now being called Holbrook. They selected a brand which resembled a camp cook's hashknife. Since most outfits were known by their brand, the Aztec Land and Cattle Company became the "Hashknife." Eventually, the ranch ran 60,000 head on the open ranges of northern Arizona.

In 1886, five young brothers from Cincinnati, Ohio named Babbitt invested their life savings in a small cow ranch east of the new town of Flagstaff. They branded a CO Bar, for their home town, on the hides of some 1,000 cows. Within a few years the enterprising young men diversified their cattle operation into other businesses, included mercantile stores, trading posts, a bank, an opera house and even a mortuary. By the end of World War I, Babbitt Brothers was one of the most prominent corporations in the entire West. It was said the Babbitts "fed and clothed and equipped and transported and entertained and buried Arizonans for four generations, and they did it more efficiently and more profitably than anyone else."

The hell-bent-for-leather, freewheeling days of the open range came to an end in the 1880s. A series of long droughts, coupled with overstocking the ranges, spelled disaster for cattlemen. By the turn of the century, erosion and vegetation loss had destroyed what had been rich valleys where once grass grew "stirrup high." Cattle died by the thousands and many ranchers had to sell out. The ones who survived had to sell steers cheap to cut their losses and reduce the size of their herds. Homesteaders or "nesters" took legal claim to ranges cattlemen had been grazing cattle on for free. Cattlemen and their hired hands looked upon these newcomers with derision, describing them as men with faded wives, skinny mules and enough kids to start a public school. Ranges were fenced, watering holes were dug, windmills were erected, and cattlemen became more selective in their breeding. The day of the open range cowboy was over.

Weather, especially prolonged drought, was the nemesis of Arizona cattlemen. "It always rains after a dry spell," was a cowboy axiom. Arizona's capricious weather had a way of

This young Arizona cowgirl's name seems lost in history. She's identified only as the "Sunbeam Girl." Photo: Arizona Historical Society.

scattering its rainfall. It seemed always to rain on the other fellow's range while your own baked in the relentless sun. Some resorted to a higher being to bring moisture to the dry ranges. Back in the 1880s, during a particularly long period without rain, Daniel Houston Ming was asked to deliver the opening prayer at a cattlemen's convention.

"Oh Lord," he began matter-of-factly, "I'm about to round you up for a good plain talk. Now Lord, I ain't like these fellows who come bothering you every day. This is the first time I ever tackled you for anything and, if you will only grant this, I promise I'll never bother you again. We want rain, good Lord, and we want it bad, and we ask you to send us some. But if you can't or don't want to send us any, for Christ's sake don't make it rain up around Hooker's or Leitch's ranges, but treat us all alike. Amen."

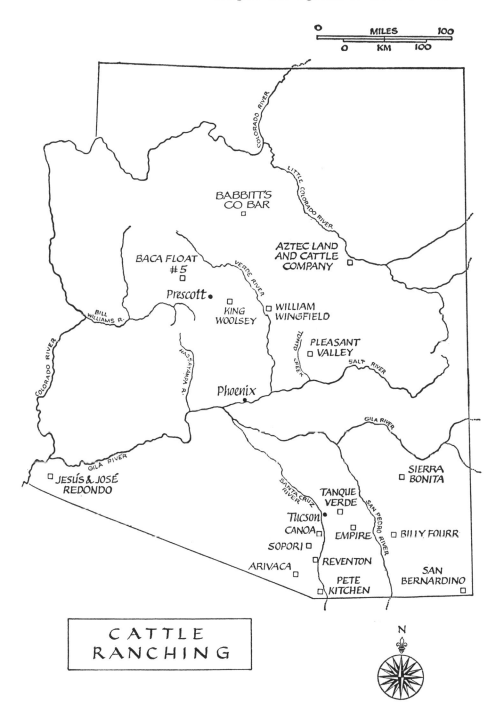

MILES 100
0 KM 100

BABBITT'S
CO BAR

AZTEC LAND
AND CATTLE
COMPANY

BACA FLOAT
#5

COLORADO RIVER

LITTLE COLORADO RIVER

VERDE RIVER

Prescott

KING
WOOLSEY

WILLIAM
WINGFIELD

BILL
WILLIAMS R.

COLORADO RIVER

HASSAYAMPA R.

TONTO CREEK

PLEASANT
VALLEY

SALT RIVER

Phoenix

GILA RIVER

GILA RIVER

SIERRA
BONITA

JESÚS & JOSÉ
REDONDO

SANTA CRUZ RIVER

TANQUE
VERDE

Tucson

CANOA

SOPORI

EMPIRE

SAN PEDRO RIVER

BILLY FOURR

ARIVACA

REVENTON

PETE
KITCHEN

SAN
BERNARDINO

CATTLE
RANCHING

N

11

GOOD GUYS AND BAD GUYS

Outlawry and Justice

The gunfighters of the West are among America's most enduring legends. They are the embodiment of every hero or villain
for all time. These overly-romanticized figures might never
have emerged had it not been for the conditions of the nation
at the time. The Civil War had ended. Fortunes, dreams and
families were scattered or lost. Many veterans of that bloody
conflict had experienced years of violence, when killing and
death had been commonplace. For those who came home
from the war to find devastation and ruin, the West became
America's great social outlet. It was a land where a man or
woman could, as Bret Harte said, "get a fresh deal all around."
But law and order hadn't kept up with the waves of settlement. Scores were often settled with six-shooters.

The West was a grand place, a vast open space filled with
beautiful, rugged mountains, crystal clear rivers, blue sky
and space—as far as the eye could see. It was a land where
dreams could be realized, where men and women loomed
larger than life. It also became a land where myths and legends
were born. It bred a society of men and women whose exploits,
real and imagined, have been immortalized in novels and
motion pictures.

Gunfighters ran the wide gamut of frontier society from
homicidal maniacs to courageous defenders of justice. The
basic tool of the trade was the Colt .45 revolver, Army Model
1873. They called it the "equalizer" because it made all men

the same size. It replaced the fighting knife as the favorite side-arm. The Colt .45 was an ideal fighting man's weapon, weighing just three pounds, with a 7-1/2 inch barrel, and it packed a wallop. It was generally carried in a leather holster, although some jammed it into their belt, while others carried it in a leather-lined coat or pants pocket.

The most feared weapon, especially in close-quarter gunplay, was the shotgun. Many peace officers carried a sawed-off 10 gauge scattergun when making their rounds in the towns' rowdy districts.

Before the advent of metallic cartridges in the 1850s, less-potent and less-reliable ball and percussion cap pistols were used. Linen or paper-wrapped cartridges of powder and a lead ball were loaded in the rifle barrel or pistol cylinder. An explosive cap was fitted over a hollow nipple. Pulling the trigger brought the hammer down on the nipple, exploding the cap. The resulting fire caused the charge in the barrel or cylinder to ignite. Wet powder or defective caps could cause a misfire. At the other extreme, all six rounds in a cylinder might go off at once. The new metallic cartridge was made with a thin copper alloy that contained both the charge and the primer with the bullet attached to the end. This gave increased firepower.

Sam Colt's new invention generated little interest when it was first produced. By 1842 his company had gone into bankruptcy. Down in Texas, however, the revolver gained wide acceptance where, up to that time Indians armed with bows, arrows and lances had the upper hand. In 1844 Capt. John Coffee Hays and his small band of Texas Rangers, armed with Colt revolvers, defeated a large Comanche war party. In the ensuing years the revolver turned the balance of power in favor of the Rangers in their epic battles with the Indians. In 1846, during the Mexican War, Hays and his Rangers were enlisted in Gen. Zachary Taylor's army. For their services, the Texans demanded and received a thousand Colt revolvers. The order rescued Sam Colt from bankruptcy and soon the Colt revolver gained world-wide fame.

When the Colt revolving cylinder patent expired in 1857, another firearm manufacturer, Smith and Wesson, bored through the cylinder making the weapon suitable for metallic cartridges, and began marketing the product. In 1869 the Smith and Wesson patent expired and Colt jumped into revolver-boring with its pistols. These, along with the sturdier Remington six-shooters, set the standard until Colt introduced its revolutionary Army model in 1873.

The favorite rifle during these years was the legendary Winchester Model 1873. This caliber .44-40 was equipped with a 12-shot, 20-inch barrel and a 15-shot, 24-inch barrel. It used a 40 grain cartridge, which packed more punch than the older 28 grain shells. In 1878, the Colt revolver, or "Peacemaker," was rechambered to a .44 caliber so one needed to pack only one kind of ammunition for both pistol and rifle.

Before the advent of smokeless gunpowder in the 1890s, black powder was used. Black powder sent up clouds of acrid smoke that is rarely duplicated in the Hollywood shoot-em-ups and added to the confusion of battle. Gunshot wounds often brought on gangrene because of chemical elements in black powder.

Incidentally, the quick draw made famous in the movies was rare. If a man suspected trouble his pistol was drawn and ready. More emphasis was placed on marksmanship than speed. "Speed is fine," said one old gunfighter, "but accuracy is final."

Most of these restless "knights in dusty leather" came to places like Arizona either to get something or to get away from something. The young territory was an excellent place where one might regain health or wealth. The remote, rough country had few roads and only limited law enforcement. Proximity to the Mexican border also contributed to the turbulence of the times. Law and order had arrived in places such as Texas, New Mexico, Kansas, Wyoming and Montana. Organized efforts to curb lawlessness in these areas pulled out the bad men. At the same time, the lure of Arizona's rich ore discoveries and sprawling new cattle ranches made the territory a mecca for outlawry.

Tombstone in the early 1880s was made up of *laissez faire* politicians, an unconcerned citizenry, defiant rustlers and a vigilance committee. All these combined to let a lawless situation get far out of hand.

Tombstone grew up next to Ed Schieffelin's fabulous silver discovery in 1877. By 1881 the area had become so populous that a separate county, Cochise, was created from the eastern part of Pima County.

A friendly, good-ole-boy-type political hack named Johnny Behan was appointed sheriff, the top political job in a county. Soon the Democratic Party machine became entrenched in local politics. Unfortunately, the sheriff was more interested in getting wealthy than enforcing the law in the county. A large, rather informal gang of rustlers led by Newman H. "Old Man" Clanton became so brazen they were stealing cows on both sides of the border in broad daylight. Rustled cows were sold to markets in Tombstone and on Indian reservations with no questions asked about brands. Prominent members of the rustler element, known locally as "cowboys," included brothers Tom and Frank McLaury; Clanton's sons Phin, Ike and Billy; Johnny Ringo, an overrated miscreant; and notorious "Curly Bill" Brocius. The free-spirited rustlers kept their ill-gotten monetary gains in circulation on spending sprees in Tombstone's casinos and saloons. They were popular with the local common folk who saw them as dashing and colorful. It's unlikely that any of these hero-worshipping locals owned cattle. Sheriff Behan, who was also county tax collector (the sheriff was allowed by law to keep a percentage of the proceeds), was more concerned with collecting taxes from the wealthy mines than chasing rustlers. If Behan wasn't in direct cahoots with the outlaws, he was certainly allowing them free rein.

On the other side of the ledger was the law and order group, the leading businessmen, including mine operators in the Tombstone area. They became a formidable force after John Clum, the crusading editor of the Tombstone *Epitaph*, uncovered a real estate scandal and was then elected mayor. Among his supporters was Wyatt Earp. Earp had been on the frontier most of his adult life and had made a reputation as a fearless lawman in the Kansas trail towns a few years earlier. Virgil Earp, an older brother and a respected peace officer, had also taken up residence in Tombstone. Both brothers were speculating on mining claims. Wyatt had also been appointed U.S. deputy marshal and Virgil would eventually become city marshal. Another brother, Morgan, and sidekick John "Doc" Holliday, a tubercular ex-dentist-turned-gambler and close friend of the Earps, also became prominent figures in the brewing feud.

A love triangle entered the plot in the person of a beautiful young lady named Josephine Marcus. She was from a wealthy San Francisco family and had come, with an acting troupe, to Arizona, where she met and became romantically involved with Johnny Behan. But they had a quarrel soon after and she found solace in Behan-rival Wyatt Earp. Earp was tall, handsome, blond, quiet and a gentleman—in short, everything Behan wasn't. Before long he had stolen her away from the sheriff. Behan's hatred grew until he openly sided with the rustler element against the Earps. Tension between the factions reached a climax on October 26, 1881 in what has become known as the "Gunfight at OK Corral." When the smoke cleared, Billy Clanton, Tom and Frank McLaury lay

Wyatt Earp. Movies and pulp fiction elevated him to legendary status. Photo: Southwest Studies.

dead. Virgil and Morgan Earp and "Doc" Holliday suffered wounds. Only Wyatt came out of the fight unscathed.

Tombstone's citizens were divided over the issue of whether it was a fair fight or cold-blooded murder. A hearing was held and the ruling favored the Earps.

The shootings didn't end, however. A few weeks later Virgil Earp was shot from ambush and permanently crippled. The following March, Morgan was shot to death from ambush. When

Sheriff Behan wouldn't or couldn't bring the assassins to justice, Wyatt and "Doc" took matters into their own hands. Within a week, three outlaws, including Curly Bill, alleged stage robber and Behan deputy Frank Stillwell, were shot and killed. Afterwards Wyatt, still mourning the murder of his younger brother, left Cochise County for good, although many claim he slipped back a few months later and killed Johnny Ringo at Turkey Creek, in the foothills of the Chiricahua Mountains.

Much has been written extolling the virtues and vices of both sides in this feud. Which side was "the good guys" is a question frequently asked. The most convincing argument is that the Earps' victims were all shot from the front and the Earps were all shot in the back or from ambush. A restless adventurer, Wyatt spent most of his life speculating in mining ventures. He and Josie remained together until his death by natural causes in 1929.

Although Wyatt Earp and his associates killed off the rustler hierarchy, violence didn't end in Cochise County. In 1887, a tough, no-nonsense ex-Texan named John Slaughter was named sheriff. Slaughter issued an edict to rustlers: "get out or get killed." He was a cattle rancher, east of today's Douglas on the old San Bernardino Spanish land grant, and had good reason to hate cattle thieves. Slaughter didn't care much for the formality of trials and he didn't talk much. It is a fact, though, that rustlers headed for other pastures during Slaughter's tenure in the sheriff's office. Ike Clanton, one of the prominent Cochise County rustlers, moved his operation to a more remote part of Arizona. He was shot and killed at Eagle Creek near Clifton in 1887, by a correspondence school detective. Doc Holliday died with his boots off, of tuberculosis in Colorado that same year.

Pleasant Valley was the setting for another famous feud. Located in the pristine cattle country at the foot of the Mogollon Rim, this was a range war, an eye-for-an-eye vendetta between families. Only one of seven brothers on both sides survived it.

Roots of the feud are obscure and still debated. Hollywood and pulp writers tried to simplify it by creating a sheepman-cattleman war. It wasn't, although sheep did play a brief part. The major figures were the Graham and Tewksbury families. Others, such as Jim Roberts, who later became one of Arizona's greatest peace officers, and members of the Blevins family also played important roles.

Drifting outlaws and rustlers began to arrive in this rugged wilderness in the early 1880s. Most agree the feud began over the stealing of livestock from an important rancher named Jim Stinson. Stinson marked his cows with a T brand that could be easily altered, and frequently was, by a number of outfits in Pleasant Valley. He accused the Grahams of stealing cows but when the case came up for a hearing, witnesses failed to appear. Stinson's foreman, John Gilleland, a good friend of the Grahams, attempted to shift blame for the larceny onto the Tewksburys. The Tewksburys and Grahams then took turns accusing the other of cattle rustling. Again, witnesses failed to show for the hearings and charges were dropped. It was downright unhealthy to take sides in a range war.

Violence reached its peak in 1887. After the Tewksburys and their friend Jim Roberts bested the Grahams in several

Commodore Perry Owens, sheriff of Apache County during the Pleasant Valley War. He is best remembered for the celebrated gunfight in Holbrook in 1887. Photo: Southwest Studies.

Jim Roberts, "Top Gun" in the Pleasant Valley War. Later he became one of Arizona's most noted peace officers. Photo: Southwest Studies.

shooting scrapes, Andy Blevins, alias Cooper, and the Grahams raided the Tewksbury ranch on the morning of September 2. Bill Jacobs and John Tewksbury were ambushed and their bodies were left to be devoured by wild hogs.

A dramatic spinoff of the war occurred just two days later when Andy Cooper was gunned down along with two others in Holbrook by the long-haired Sheriff of Apache County, Commodore Perry Owens.

Cooper had left Pleasant Valley and was visiting at the Blevins family home on Center Street, next to the railroad tracks. Witnesses later said he had been boasting in the saloons about killing two men in Pleasant Valley two days earlier. He was at the Blevins house later that day when Sheriff Owens stepped up on the front porch and attempted to serve a warrant on him for horse stealing. Andy cracked open the door and raised his revolver, but before he could fire, Owens, armed with a Winchester, put a round through the door and into Andy's midsection, mortally wounding the outlaw. From the opposite side of the room, John Blevins pushed open a door and fired at Owens, who cranked another shell into his rifle, turned and fired from the hip, wounding Blevins. A relative, Mose Roberts (no relation to Jim) leaped out a side window at the same time the sheriff moved out into the street. Before Roberts would get a shot off, the Winchester cracked once more, killing him. Meanwhile, 14-year-old Sam Houston Blevins wrestled Andy Cooper's pistol away from his mother and ran out the front door to join the fight. Before he could take aim and fire, Owens shot the youth through the heart.

The battle was brief but furious and goes down as one of the most exciting gunfights in the history of outlawry. Unfortunately, for the descendants of the Blevins family, the legacy of that event haunts them to this day.

Controversy over the gunfight continues. To most, C.P. Owens is a celebrated, legendary hero. Others considered him a hired assassin brought in by county officials to rid the area of desperadoes, but instead, gunned down the Blevins boys and Mose Roberts without giving them a fighting chance. Whichever side one chooses to believe, none can doubt the courage of Owens that day and few, if any, outside the family were sad to see Andy Cooper die with his boots on.

Two weeks after the siege at the Tewksbury ranch, Graham supporters tried another early morning sneak attack, this time at Rock Springs where Jim and Ed Tewksbury, along with Jim Roberts, were camped. Roberts had arisen early and observed the men setting up their ambush and gave the alarm. In an instant, the Tewksbury brothers were up, grabbed their rifles and opened fire. All three were expert marksmen, and when the shooting ended, one Graham partisan was dead and several were down.

At this same time, a large posse had converged upon the valley to arrest prominent gunmen on both sides. The plan was to take the Grahams first, then the Tewksburys and Roberts. The posse gathered at Perkins' Store during the night, hid their horses, and made plans to lure the Grahams into a trap. Deputies were hidden behind a five-foot stone wall near the store. They sent a couple of riders by the nearby Graham ranch, and sure enough, John Graham and Charlie Blevins rode over to check out the two strangers. When the two feudists saw the trap, they spurred their mounts and tried to make a break. A blast from a twin-barreled shotgun knocked Blevins out of the saddle, killing him instantly. John Graham was hit by rifle fire and died a few minutes later. Tom Graham, the last of the Graham clan, escaped capture.

After the shooting of John Graham and Charlie Blevins, the posse rode over to the Tewksbury ranch to make their arrests. None of the Tewksbury partisans offered any resistance.

Leaders of both partisan groups were charged in Prescott and later St. Johns. However, when witnesses for the prosecution failed to appear, charges against both sides were dropped. By now, the shooting war had about burned itself out.

Afterwards, a vigilance committee sought to rid Pleasant Valley of all bad men and rustlers. Any outsider was suspected, and a few were hanged. The vigilantes brought more terror to the Valley than the feudists.

By 1892 Tom Graham and Ed Tewksbury were the last fighting men left from the feuding families. Graham had left Pleasant Valley, married and settled on a farm near Tempe. Early on the morning of August 2, Ed Tewksbury and John Rhodes, a Tewksbury partisan, shot and killed Tom Graham on the outskirts of Tempe. Tewksbury and Rhodes were brought to trial. Rhodes claimed he was elsewhere and was released. Tewksbury was also released later on a legal technicality. Later, he became a lawman at Globe. The highlight of the trial came when Graham's widow, Anne, tried to shoot her husband's assailant. Emotions ran high in Pleasant Valley for many years afterward. Men and women who knew the real story wouldn't talk for fear of rekindling old hatreds. Losses were great. One woman lost a husband, and had four sons shot to death and another seriously wounded before the killing ended. Estimates ran as high as 50 men killed over the span of a few years. Many of those were innocent victims, caught in the violence and its ruthless aftermath.

Jim Roberts, the "top gun" in the war, became a peace officer and helped tame such towns as Congress, Douglas and Jerome. Roberts didn't drink, swear or play cards. Although he was a genuine frontier gunfighter, he didn't boast about his exploits. He'd clam up tighter'n a drum if someone asked about the Pleasant Valley War. Roberts' reputation was usually enough to keep a town peaceful. At times, though, he was called upon to use his six-shooter. One night in Jerome he approached three gunmen holed up on the outskirts of town. A young deputy came along to help. "You take the one in the middle and I'll take the other two," Roberts said quietly. Then he noticed the youngster's trembling hands. Roberts gave his assistant a fatherly look and said in a kind, but firm tone, "Get out of the way, son, and I'll take 'em all." Moments later all three desperados were down.

In the late 1920s, Roberts was constable at Clarkdale. He didn't fit Hollywood's image of an old time gunfighter. Jim didn't carry his pistol in a fancy leather holster, had no notches carved on the handle, and he didn't believe in the fast draw. This came as a disappointment to those accustomed to seeing Tom Mix and William S. Hart and other shooting stars of the silver screen. Some began to wonder if the old man who didn't wear cowboy boots and rode to work on a mule had ever been a real gunfighter.

Those doubts were put to rest in 1928 when two men robbed Clarkdale's Bank of Arizona of $40,000. Roberts, making his rounds, came around the corner just as they drove away. One fired a shot at the old lawman. Roberts drew a nickel-plated revolver out of his hip pocket, and with both hands gripping the handle, aimed and fired. The driver slumped over the steering wheel, dead. The car crashed to a halt and the other robber climbed out of the wreck and meekly surrendered. At age 70, Jim Roberts had his last shootout. He died six years later while making his rounds in Clarkdale.

Prescott was not as wild as Tombstone and Holbrook. Stalwart lawmen like George Ruffner kept a lid on the town most of the time; there were occasions, however, when violent crimes occurred, but justice was swift and severe.

One of the last men hung on Prescott's courthouse plaza was an obscure outlaw named Fleming Parker. His career as a badman was not spectacular; in fact, he might have escaped trouble with his old acquaintance, Yavapai County Sheriff George Ruffner, if the Atlantic & Pacific Railroad had treated him with more consideration. Fleming was an uncurried cowboy addicted to alcohol and the painted *filles de joie* of Whiskey Row. On the other side of the coin, he was well known over northern Arizona for his expertise with horses and his fondness for well bred animals. One day two of his string wandered onto the tracks and were killed by a passenger train near Peach Springs. When the railroad offered a measly recompense, the indignant cowboy retaliated by robbing the train at Peach Springs. Sheriff Ruffner quickly picked up the trail, and a few days later Fleming was behind bars in the Prescott jail.

Parker and Ruffner had cowboyed together in their younger days but had taken separate trails. Ruffner had gone on to become a famous sheriff, and Fleming had done five years in San Quentin for burglary before coming back to northern Arizona, where he had saved enough money to buy a string of horses. Residents were sympathetic in his dispute with the railroad, and the sheriff was an old friend. It looked for a time as though Parker would get a light sentence, until he broke out of jail and killed Lee Norris, the deputy district attorney. Ruffner got word of the break while he was at Congress investigating another crime. He immediately commandeered a train for Prescott. Meanwhile, after killing Norris, Parker and two accomplices headed for Ruffner's livery stable. Parker, who had an eye for good horseflesh, stole the sheriff's prize white gelding, Sureshot, and fled north. One of the escapees was caught at Chino Valley, and the other vanished and was never brought to justice. Ruffner, an expert tracker, quickly picked up Parker's trail. The outlaw knew his old campanion would be following, so he reversed Sureshot's shoes to throw Ruffner off track. When the animal went lame, Parker turned him loose, continuing on foot. Ruffner finally caught up with Parker north of Flagstaff, and with Parker he boarded a Santa Fe train bound for Prescott. Public opinion had shifted after the murder of Norris, and there was talk of a lynching. Sensing trouble, Ruffner took his prisoner off the train outside Prescott and sneaked in the back way to the county jail. When the welcoming committee learned of the ruse, they gathered outside the jail and demanded that Parker be turned over to them. Ruffner, armed with a twin barreled shot gun, boldly faced the mob and ordered them to disperse. The lynch mob went home, and Parker was held for trial without further incident. He was sentenced to hang at 7:30 A.M. on the morning of June 3, 1898. On the evening before the scheduled hanging, Sheriff Ruffner visited Parker and asked if he had any last request. The condemned man was not hungry, but he wondered if Ruffner would mind if "Flossie," one of the girls over on Whiskey Row, paid him a visit. The obliging sheriff found Flossie and brought her over to the jail and then said adios for an hour or so. Parker's only other request was that Ruffner carry out the sentence because he wanted to be assured that the man given the honor of cashing him in be someone he respected.

The law required that a certain number of witnesses attend the hanging, and it was standard practice to send out invitations. Ruffner had forgotten to have the invitations made up, so on the morning of the hanging, he took a deck of cards and dealt one to each witness. Nobody was admitted to the gallows area without a card from the sheriff's personal deck of cards.

George Ruffner had a long and illustrious career as sheriff of Yavapai County. When he died in 1933 at the age of seventy-one, he was the oldest Arizona sheriff in seniority and age. Many years later the National Cowboy Hall of Fame in

Oklahoma City chose him as the first Arizonan to be inducted into that select association of authentic Western heroes.

Old Sureshot never recovered completely from his ordeal with the reversed shoes so Sheriff Ruffner retired him to a farm in Phoenix at the site of what became the famous Biltmore Luxury Resort. According to the sheriff's colorful nephew, longtime Prescott historian "Budge" Ruffner, Sureshot was the only member of the family to ever reside in such opulent surroundings.

The Arizona Rangers pose for the camera during the Morenci copper mine strike in 1903. Photo: Southwest Studies.

THE ARIZONA RANGERS

While Phoenix and Tucson were growing up and becoming "civilized," the lack of good roads kept most of the territory isolated. Large gangs of rustlers were still operating in the remote mountains of eastern Arizona, having been driven into the Blue River country by lawmen from New Mexico. Cochise County was still pretty wild and wooly. The close proximity to the Mexican border made that area a fairly safe haven for obstreperous border riff-raff.

Cattle rustling, along with a series of train robberies in southern Arizona, led to the creation of a ranger force that wouldn't be bound by county lines. In 1901 the territorial assembly established the Arizona Rangers. Modeled after the famed Texas Rangers, these hard-riding young men sought to bring law and order to the border towns and remote regions of the territory. Burt Mossman, a rawhide-rough Scots-Irishman, was picked as captain. Earlier, Mossman had been brought in to run the famed Hashknife Outfit in northern Arizona. Rustlers had nearly run the company out of business. Public support seemed to be on the side of the rustlers as prosecutors had not gotten a single conviction in 14 years. Much of the rustling was being done by cowboys employed by the Hashknife. Mossman came in and whipped the ranch into shape, and his success was the primary reason Governor Nathan Oakes Murphy picked him first captain of the Arizona Rangers.

The force was small, numbering only 14 men, including a captain, sergeant and 12 privates. Mossman had his men dress like cowboys, keeping their badge out of sight until they were ready to make an arrest. Each man was provided a six-shooter and a horse. Under Mossman's regime, the Rangers operated mostly in secrecy as undercover agents, hiring out for cattle outfits. During the first year, the Rangers put 125 major criminals behind bars, killing only one man in the process. Notorious gangs led by Bill Smith and George Musgrove were chased out of the territory. During Mossman's tenure, only one Ranger, Carlos Tafolla, lost his life. Tafolla died game in a fierce gunfight when he and another officer made a desperate stand against members of the Bill Smith gang in eastern Arizona.

Mossman was as fearless as they came, never asking one of his men to do something he wouldn't. He climaxed his one-year appointment as captain with a daring capture of the notorious Augustin Chacon below the Mexican border. Chacon, mythically perceived as a borderland "Robin Hood," had boasted of killing 15 Americans and 37 Mexicans. On one of his crime sprees Chacon brutally murdered a shopkeeper in Morenci with an ax and treacherously killed a deputy sheriff under a flag of truce. He was sentenced to hang but managed to escape the gallows when a girl friend sneaked a hacksaw blade concealed in the spine of a Bible into jail.

Mossman vowed to bring Chacon in. He slipped into Mexico in the guise of a fugitive, managed a daring capture of the outlaw and returned him to Solomonville. Chacon was hanged in 1901. He was game to the end. As the hangman was preparing the noose, Chacon looked out at the gathering and smiled, "adios todos amigos" (goodby all my friends). Chacon's capture (or kidnapping) in Mexico was a violation of international law, but it was not uncommon for peace officers on both sides of the border to assist or cut the red tape in the apprehension of some fugitive.

Tom Rynning, a former Rough Rider and frontier soldier, took over the Rangers in 1902. Under Rynning the force was increased to 26 men, who pinned five-pointed silver stars on their chests. In 1903 they were used as strikebreakers at the mines at Morenci. Under Mossman, the Rangers had been the darlings of the press and heroes to the general public. These new duties, however, tarnished their image in the eyes of many. Still they were colorful, tough and rode the hard country knowing the times were a-changing and they were a vanishing breed of lawmen.

The Rangers had an interesting working arrangement with the notorious *Rurales* of northern Mexico. Led by an

Deputy Sheriff C. H. Farnsworth and Arizona Ranger W.K. Foster in 1903. Photo: Arizona Historical Society.

almost-fictional ex-Russian naval cadet named Emilio Koster-litzky, the Mexican soldier-police force dealt ruthlessly with the criminal element, rarely giving a prisoner the benefit of a trial. Cooperation between the Rangers and Rurales did much to rid the border of the lawless element. As an example, a man wanted by the Rangers might be sitting in a cantina in Cananea feeling secure. He'd have a few drinks with a pretty lady and next thing he knew, he was staring at four walls in a Bisbee jail. During the evening the girl slipped him a mickey, then a couple of Rurales tucked a gunnysack over his head, threw him over the back of a horse and delivered him to a Ranger waiting at the border.

The Rangers were, according to their charter, supposed to headquarter in the roughest town in the territory. Under Mossman they worked out of Bisbee. When Rynning took over, they moved down the road to the new town of Douglas. With its gambling halls, saloons and dance halls, Douglas quickly became the gathering place for all nefarious scalawags in the southwestern United States and northern Mexico. Capt. Rynning took a look at the place and noted: "I've been in many a rough town in my day, but from Deadwood to Tombstone I've never met up with a harder formation than Douglas was when we made the Arizona Rangers' home corral there in 1902."

Tom Rynning proved to be a capable and resourceful captain of the Rangers. He cleverly broke up a family of rustlers near Douglas by an unorthodox manner of crime detection. The Taylor family had been branding their neighbor's cows and getting away with it for quite some time until the Ranger captain got into the act. He roped a bunch of their neighbor's calves, slit open their gullets and inserted a Mexican silver coin. Then he stitched up each incision and turned them loose. He waited about six months, then rode over to Taylor's spread and, sure enough, all 13 calves had Taylor's brand. Taylor was arrested and the calves impounded in Douglas. During the trial a recess was called and the jury was led to the corral where Rynning explained what he'd done. Then he opened the gullets again and removed a coin from each. Needless to say, the verdict was guilty and the judge gave the Taylors just 24 hours to sell their ranch and get out of the territory.

The third and last captain of the Rangers was a fast-shooting young ex-soldier named Harry Wheeler. During his spectacular career, Wheeler had been involved in several heroic deeds, including a regular old wild west shootout in the Palace Saloon in Tucson. Late one night in 1904, a masked bandit named Joe Bostwick walked in through the back door and shouted, "hands up." The outlaw, wearing a long, faded coat and floppy old Panama hat, had his face covered with a red bandana with two slits for eye holes. One of the victims slipped out the front door where he encountered Ranger Harry Wheeler. "Don't go in there," he warned, "there's a holdup going on."

"All right, that's what I'm here for," Wheeler replied.

Inside, the customers were lined up against the wall with their arms fully extended, the nervous outlaw urging them to "hold 'em up higher" while he edged towards the crap table money. Suddenly Wheeler stepped through the swinging doors. Both men fired. Bostwick's big Colt .45 missed its mark but the sure-shooting Ranger fired twice, hitting the outlaw both times. The holdup man died the next day.

"I'm sorry that this happened," Wheeler told a reporter the next day, "but it was either his life or mine, and if I hadn't been a little quicker on the draw than he was, I might be in his position now."

Typically, Wheeler's remarks were made matter-of-factly and without any bravado. The great Texas lawman Jeff Milton called young Wheeler the best he'd ever seen — and in his long career, he'd seen a large number of shootists, including the legendary John Wesley Hardin.

The old days were about over and the mostly-Democratic territorial assembly was getting tired of funding what they considered a Republican governor's personal police force. Moreover, counties that were not besieged by rustlers and other desperados resented having to fund a police force that spent most of its energy dealing with trouble along the Mexican border. The Rangers were voted out of existence in February, 1909, partly because the Old West was changing and partly, as one historian put it, "because they were just too damn good and others were jealous of their accomplishments."

Outlawry in Arizona was not without its lighter moments.

A robber made off with the payroll near Flagstaff and was pursued by irate workers. During the chase he lost the saddlebags containing the loot. He was caught without the payroll and the posse was so mad they decided to hang him on the spot. They had a noose around his neck and were about to string him up when lightning struck the tree. Fearing Divine Intervention, the posse decided against taking justice in their own hands and hauled the culprit off to jail.

Bill Downing was one of the most universally disliked desperados in southern Arizona. He bullied men and beat up women. Even his fellow outlaws couldn't stand him. Early one morning in 1908, an Arizona Ranger stood outside a saloon in Willcox and ordered Downing to come out with his hands up. The outlaw, who was drinking with friends at the bar, turned and headed out the back door in hopes of bushwhacking the Ranger. He came around the corner and went for his six gun, but it wasn't there. While at the bar, one of his friends had pilfered his gun. They planted Bill's carcass in Boot Hill but he did inspire an axiom: Don't ever go fer yer six-shooter unless yer shore it's there.

At least one train robbery was directly responsible for a concerted citizen's effort to clean up the desert. In 1895 two cowboys, Joe George and Grant Wheeler, decided to up their station in life at the expense of Wells Fargo. They robbed the Southern Pacific near Cochise and tried to blow the safe open with dynamite. After two disappointing attempts, they packed the rest of the explosives around the safe. Then they took eight canvas sacks loaded with Mexican silver pesos, found in the express car, and used them for ballast. They lit the fuse and ran from the car. The explosion shook the mountains nearby and reduced the express car to splinters. Silver pesos went flying in every direction.

Horrors, the safe was empty!! The only thing of value was some 800 Mexican pesos and they were scattered over half of Cochise County. The discouraged train robbers rode away vowing to do better next time. The train backed all the way to Willcox and informed the town. Legend has it nobody volunteered to serve on the posse but instead grabbed their rakes and headed for the scene of the crime to uncover buried treasure. Legend also says that was the best-raked piece of desert landscape this side of the mansions in Paradise Valley.

12

STEEL RAILS ACROSS ARIZONA

Since the first prospector's pan swished paydirt along the Gila River in 1858, roadways following paths of least resistance were essential to get supplies in and ore out of the rugged mountains of Arizona.

In 1852, steamboats began churning their way up the muddy Colorado River. These paddlewheelers hauled freight, passengers and soldiers to busy ports: Yuma, Ehrenberg, Hardyville and others. From there, roads that weren't much more than cattle trails headed into central Arizona. These steamboats were the main supply link with the outside world until the arrival of the railroads in the late 1870s. From that time on, the days of the paddlewheeler were numbered. Historically, America's western roads ran east and west, and there wasn't much demand for riverboats that ran north and south, far from the population centers.

Naturally, there was always much cause for celebration with the arrival of a new railroad. Anyone who had crossed the desert afoot, on horseback or mule, rocked and rolled on the leather-slung thoroughbraces of a stagecoach, or jolted in a wagon without shock absorbers, was bound to appreciate the wonders of riding in a steam railroad car.

In the spring of 1877, Arizona's citizens at Yuma were anxiously awaiting the arrival of the first railroad at Yuma. Construction was delayed when the Southern Pacific, building eastbound from California, reached the Colorado River and ran into some Washington-style bureaucratic politicking. Earlier, permission had been granted from Gen. Irvin McDowell to build the bridge. However, the secretary of war overruled the department commander and refused to allow the railroad to cross a federal stream until some red tape was untangled. Permission was granted to build the bridge — they just couldn't stretch any steel rails across it.

Chinese workmen spent the hot summer months laying a grade while pile drivers were busily constructing a 667-foot bridge across the Colorado. On September 29, 1877, the bridge was complete except for the rails.

The new line ran close to the old military post at Fort Yuma, on the California side of the river. The entire garrison at the time consisted of a Maj. Tom Dunn, a sergeant, a private and a prisoner.

Major Dunn's orders were not to allow any track laying on the bridge, and the major was determined to see that the railroad remained on the California side, even if it meant putting his entire command on military alert. He surveyed the construction crew. All hands appeared to be complying with the secretary's orders.

In fact, things appeared too quiet for the suspicious officer. That evening he decided to post a sentry at the entrance to the bridge. At 11:00 p.m. the guard went off duty and, within an hour, dark, shadowy figures seemingly appeared out of nowhere. With a flamboyant display of the stealth and cunning of an Apache war party, the gandy dancers began laying track across the bridge. All went well until about 2:00 a.m., when some careless pick and shovel men accidentally dropped a rail. The resounding clatter woke up the sleeping soldiers and the four-troop garrison of Fort Yuma sprang into action. With bayonets fixed, Maj. Dunn and his men (minus the prisoner; presumably he remained in his cell) grimly stood their ground, the major bravely stationing himself on the tracks. Suddenly, a rumbling sound came out of the darkness and the major found himself staring into the headlights of an iron-bellied locomotive. Quickly determining that discretion was the better part of valor, the major and his men made a hasty retreat to the confines of the fort.

Along about sunrise the next morning, old Engine #31 came rolling into Yuma with her whistle screaming. The whole town turned out to witness the historic occasion. The locomotive crept slowly along, blowing off steam while the gandy dancers strung track ahead of her along Madison Avenue.

The Southern Pacific and the federal government each accused the other of being high-handed in the matter. Gen. McDowell was much chagrined and quickly reinforced Fort Yuma with a dozen more soldiers to thwart any further usurping of his military authority. Most folks around Yuma found the incident humorous and were glad that the railroad had, at last, arrived.

Some 1,100 Chinese and 200 Anglo construction workers began laying track eastward across Arizona. By May 19, 1879 work was halted at Casa Grande. The Chinese spread out across the territory opening restaurants, laundries and truck farms. The big silver strike at Tombstone inspired the Southern Pacific to resume laying track a few months later and by March, 1880 the railroad reached Tucson. A gala celebration was held as Tucsonians turned out to witness the event. The citizens of Tombstone presented a silver spike to ceremoniously nail down the last steel rail. There was a great deal of speechmaking, socializing and imbibing spiritous beverages. Self-congratulatory telegrams were sent to distant American cities. Some wags conceived a brilliant notion that the Pope should be notified of the historic occasion. The others agreed, and colorful Tucson Mayor Bob Leatherwood quickly penned the following wire:

> To His Holiness, the Pope of Rome, Italy:
>
> The mayor of Tucson begs the honor of reminding Your Holiness that this ancient and honorable pueblo was founded by the Spaniards under the sanction of the Church more than three centuries ago, and to inform Your Holiness that a railroad from San Francisco, California now connects us with the entire Christian World.
>
> R.N. Leatherwood, Mayor

A few minutes later, Mayor Leatherwood was interrupted by a young telegrapher who handed him a telegram and quickly departed. The mayor didn't take time to read the message but called the informal gathering to order. Then he read the "Pope's Reply":

> His Holiness the Pope acknowledges with appreciation, receipt of your telegram informing him that the ancient city of Tucson at last has been connected by rail with the outside world and sends his benediction, but for his own satisfaction would ask, where the hell is Tucson?
>
> "Antonelli"

It's highly probable the "Pope's Reply" was conjured up by more discreet and sober celebrants but it added considerably to the festivities. It is a matter of historical record that on March 20, 1955, the 75th anniversary of the railroad's arrival, the Pope did send a congratulatory message to all the folks in Tucson.

Although army surveyors had mapped out a route across northern Arizona in the 1850s, the Civil War delayed construction of any southern line. By the early 1880s, the Santa Fe had stretched a line across Kansas and into New Mexico. In November, 1881, the tracks reached Winslow. It was a long hard ride across northern Arizona. The line went west of Gallup, New Mexico down the Rio Puerco to a meeting with the Little Colorado River near Horsehead Crossing, then followed the river west to Winslow and on towards the San Francisco Mountains. Between Winslow and the San Francisco Mountains was a deep gorge called Canyon Diablo where a bridge 250 feet above the canyon floor would have to be constructed. The bridge was pre-assembled elsewhere and arrived several feet short of reaching the other side, causing further delay. West of the mountains the tracks turned northwest to pick up more watering places. Those locomotives needed plenty of water to get up a head of steam. That's why the line took a more circuitous route towards its destination at Needles, California.

By August, 1883 the Santa Fe had been extended across to Needles. The federal government provided lucrative incentives, awarding land grants of ten square miles of public land for each mile of track laid. These were odd-numbered sections and in effect amounted to twice the area if used for grazing lands.

A Santa Fe passenger train crossing Canyon Diablo, east of Flagstaff during the 1880s. Photo: Southwest Studies.

When the Santa Fe reached Needles, it encountered a huge stumbling block. The Southern Pacific had used its extensive political clout in California to obtain right-of-way, and had built a line to Needles to block any attempt by the Santa Fe to reach the coast. But the clever Santa Fe had an ace up its sleeve. Earlier it had built a line south of Albuquerque down the Rio Grande, then west to Deming. At Benson, a Santa Fe subsidiary continued a line south to Fairbank, Patagonia and on to Nogales, where it connected with a line to Guaymas on the Mexican coast.

The Southern Pacific wanted the line to Guaymas in the worst way. Realizing they'd been outmaneuvered, they agreed to do some horsetrading. The Santa Fe could have the line running west from Needles in exchange for the line to Guaymas. All parties were satisfied. The Southern Pacific could continue its monopoly on the west coast of Mexico and the Santa Fe had a line that, on November 14, 1885 reached San Diego on the coast of California.

Other lines would be stretched across burning deserts, through twisting canyons and over precipitous mountains.

These would be connecting lines to mines and towns not located along the main lines.

Phoenix had a big turnout on July 4, 1887 when the first steam engine from the Maricopa, Phoenix and Salt River Railroad arrived. At the time, the future capital rated only a branch line from the Southern Pacific station at Maricopa. Phoenix wasn't quite ready for the big time. A turntable hadn't been built yet, so after the ceremonies, the train had to make the 35-mile trip back to Maricopa in reverse.

One of the most exciting finishes to the building of a railroad line occurred at Prescott in 1886. Tom Bullock, a gregarious, smooth-talking promoter, proposed a line to link Prescott with the Santa Fe main line at Seligman. Earlier, Bullock had made a fortune building streetcar lines in New York. Now the 32-year-old entrepreneur was in Arizona seeking to make another fortune.

Prescottonians raised $300,000 for constructing the 75 miles of track. However, Bullock had to reach Prescott no later than midnight on December 31, 1886, or face a stiff $1,000-a-mile ($72,000) penalty. No sooner had construction begun than railroad cars loaded with beer were being shipped in to mobile tent saloons set up along the way. Cattlemen, angry over the railroad right-of-way across their grazing lands, had their cowboys stampede cattle through the construction site.

Meanwhile, in Prescott the betting was heavy as to whether Bullock would meet his deadline. Some folks tried to hedge their bets by vandalizing the line. Someone tried to blow up a caboose. Others set fire to a trestle, but a rainstorm doused the flames. Once, vandals tried to derail the work train by removing a section of track. The plot was foiled when the engine ran aground before reaching the damaged area.

Working feverishly against the clock, the track layers reached Granite Dells with one day to go. By the eve of the final day they were only two miles from Prescott. Odds against the Bullock line reaching Prescott on time went as high as 20 to 1. Those who had taken the bet shouted encouragement from the sidelines. Some couldn't restrain themselves and joined the work crews.

The Bullock line reached Prescott with five minutes to spare. Throngs of locals cheered as Governor Conrad M. Zulick drove a gilded spike into a rail tie painted red, white and blue. Prescott, at last, was linked by rail to the outside world.

When it was completed, Bullock's railroad was every bit as zany as the construction had been. During the first few months of operation there was no turntable at Prescott, so the trains had to run backwards the 72 miles to Seligman (Prescott Junction). The fare for passengers was ten cents a mile but a better deal could be made with members of the crew. The schedule was quite flexible. The train might stop for a few beers or a crap game at Del Rio Springs. Other stops were made along the way to allow passengers and crew to go deer hunting.

By 1891, the Bullock line was in deep trouble. Flooding washed out tracks. Ties were rotting and trestles were in need of repair. The little steam locomotive "Hassayampa" slid off the tracks and lay sprawled on its side in a sea of mud for three weeks before a team of mules came to the rescue. A big flood in Chino Wash in 1892 was the final blow. At the same time the Bullock line was going broke, a king's ransom in gold and silver was lying buried in the Bradshaw Mountains, waiting for another enterprising entrepreneur. He wasn't long in coming.

Frank Murphy was one of the most energetic and resourceful of territorial Arizona's entrepreneurial giants. Murphy, more than any other, was responsible for attracting eastern capital into the developing region. He planned a new rail line linking Ash Fork to Prescott and wisely chose higher ground. On August 17, 1892 the first spike was driven at Ash Fork as tracklayers and gandy dancers worked their way south. The 57-mile line, called the Peavine because of its twisting curves, reached Prescott on April 24, 1892.

From Prescott, Murphy continued south towards Phoenix. The line skirted the lofty Bradshaw Mountains and wound its way down into Skull Valley. From there it turned west, then south through Date Creek and close to the rich gold mine at Congress, then through Wickenburg, winding down Hassayampa Canyon and into Phoenix. The 136-mile line from Ash Fork was completed on March 13, 1895.

The linking of Phoenix to the northern main line is considered the official closing of the frontier in Arizona.

Other lines would spring out from Murphy's Ash Fork-Phoenix railroad. Branches were stretched into Clarkdale from Drake to haul ore from Jerome's fabulous mines. Murphy sold these lines to the Santa Fe in 1901.

But the railroad for which Frank Murphy will be most re-membered was the so-called "Impossible" railroad into the mineral-rich Bradshaw Mountains.

Towns and mines with colorful-sounding or lofty names like Bueno, Turkey Creek, Tiger, Oro Belle, Tip Top, Big Bug and Senator dappled the Bradshaws. A fortune was waiting for the one who could figure out a better way of getting equipment in and the ore out.

Frank Murphy, owner of several mining properties in the Bradshaws, was anxious to extend his railroad into the mountains. In 1901 he hired a crew of muscular men with backs like ironwood and began construction. The pay was a dollar a day — twice the going rate. When a dynamite blast on a cut exposed a rich vein of gold, a gold rush ensued and Murphy had to recruit another crew. On April 21, 1902 the first branch line reached the rich mines at Poland and Walker. The first week $180,000 in gold ore was hauled out. Now Murphy turned his attention to the more difficult task of building the line from Mayer to Crown King, high in the Bradshaws.

The Crown King line went east from Mayer to Cordes, then turned south into Crazy Basin. From there it was 13 steep miles and a 3,000-foot rise in elevation to Crown King. At Horsethief Canyon there were so many switchbacks it took seven miles of track to go just two miles. Experts said it couldn't be done but in late October, 1903 a steam locomotive pulled an excursion train of Prescottonians up to the summit for a look-see. From the top one could see 50 miles off into the distance.

Crown King became a bustling and prosperous commu-nity during the next few years. And it attracted its share of rascals. It was said they planted no less than 17 men with their boots on during one period.

By the end of World War I the ore was starting to run out and the good times were about over. The last train pulled out of Crown King in 1926, marking the end of an era. The rails were ripped out and the line was converted to a roadway for autos. Board planks were nailed to the tops of trestles and, for

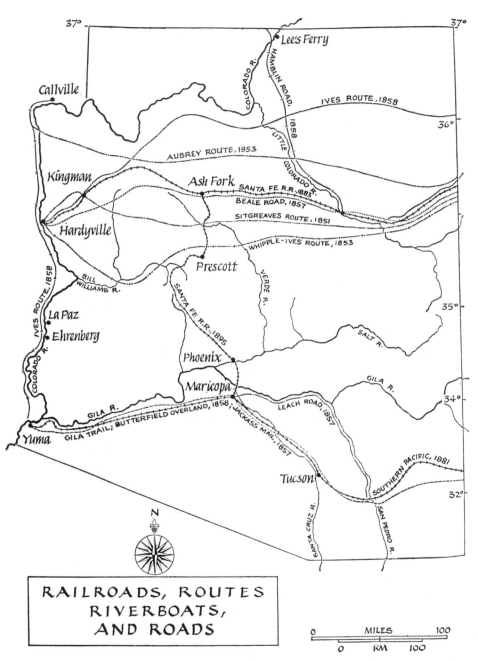

RAILROADS, ROUTES
RIVERBOATS,
AND ROADS

many years cars crossed steep arroyos on these improvised bridges. Crown King became one of those "towns too tough to die" as Phoenix residents, before the age of air conditioning, headed up that way to escape the summer heat.

Frank Murphy, a man respected for his integrity, resourcefulness and vision, would go on to other ventures. His kind were rare in the annals of this period of Arizona and the territory was better because he passed this way.

13

TERRITORIAL POLITICS

1863-1912

The Congress of the United States didn't fall all over itself welcoming Arizona into the Union in the early 1860s. When Ohio Congressman James Ashley introduced the Organic Act in 1862, he found strong opposition in both houses. The 1860 census counted fewer than 2,500 non-Indians in the area. The major complaint by politicians opposed to Arizona was that it had too few people to warrant territorial status. However, the Ohioan was convinced that Arizona's mineral wealth could help the Union cause in the war against the South. Two of the largest mining operations in Arizona were chartered in Ohio and Congressman Ashley had seen the ore specimens. During a House debate a mammoth chunk of silver was displayed. That demonstration won the day and the battle.

In reality, Arizona had been a territory (sort of) at least three times previously. The Arizonans themselves had so proclaimed it in 1860 but nobody paid any attention. The Confederate Congress claimed it two years later, as did the Union's Gen. James Carleton. All these called for a line dividing the Territory of New Mexico along the 34th parallel. Most of this area was in the old Gadsden Purchase area. However, the New Mexicans preferred a different split, one in which they would keep the rich Mesilla Valley and give the uncurried land of the Apaches further west to the upstart Arizonans. So Ashley's bill called for a line running south from the west boundary of Colorado Territory (Four Corners) to the Mexican border, and so Arizona took on a new shape — the one we're familiar with today.

Arizona's first territorial officers, circa 1863. Standing: H.N. Fleury (Governor Goodwin's private secretary); Milton B. Duffield, U.S. Marshal; and Almon Gage, district attorney. Seated: Joseph P. Allyn, a justice on the supreme court; John Goodwin, governor; and Richard McCormick, secretary. Photo: Arizona Historical Society.

After a long fight, on February 24, 1863, President Abraham Lincoln signed the statute and the territory was created.

The first territorial governor appointed was a "lame duck" congressman from Ohio named John Gurley. He died before assuming office and was replaced by another ex-congressman, John Goodwin of Maine. Among the other officials were three judges, who would form three judicial districts and sit on a supreme court; a district attorney, surveyor general, U.S. marshal and a superintendent of Indian affairs. The latter office was filled by Charles Poston, who'd played a key role in promoting the creation of the new territory.

It was assumed they'd establish the capital in Tucson, since the Old Pueblo was the only community that could actually claim to be a community. But it wasn't meant to be. Tucson had been a little too supportive of the Southern Cause.

Besides, Gen. James Carleton had a vested interest in the new gold discoveries in the Bradshaw Mountains, and had already sent troops out to establish a military post nearby. So a temporary capital was chosen which would be located somewhere near the mines.

The party left Santa Fe's comfortable environs and headed west. On December 29, 1863, certain they had crossed the boundary into Arizona, they held a ceremony. At a waterhole called Navajo Springs, the solemn oaths of office were taken and the Territory of Arizona was officially established. One of the reasons they were so anxious to have a swearing in was that Congress had decreed their pay not begin until they had taken the oath in Arizona. Afterwards, the historic moment was toasted with a home brew mixed up in the communal bath tub.

On January 22, 1864 the party arrived in Chino Valley where a temporary military post had been located. A few weeks later the capital was moved a dozen miles south, to the banks of Granite Creek. On May 30, a meeting was held in a crude log cabin and a name for the capital was chosen. Some wag suggested Gimletville but, fortunately, Richard McCormick had a better idea. McCormick, secretary of the territory, later governor and delegate to Washington, had in his possession William Hickling Prescott's classic history of Mexico. In a bit of stirring oratory for which he was known, McCormick suggested naming the town Prescott. And that's what it became. Residents did alter Mr. Prescott's name a little. Its local pronunciation is "Prescut." McCormick is also credited with drawing up the territorial seal. Then someone claimed it was stolen from the label off a can of baking soda. So, they designed a new one that included a deer, a saguaro, a pine tree and a mountain.

The story of Arizona's "First Lady" is a sad one. Soon after Prescott was founded, Richard McCormick's new wife, Margaret, came west to live with him. During the birth of their first child in 1867, both she and the baby died. They were buried in a forest grave outside Prescott one day before her 24th birthday. Rose cuttings she had brought from back east and planted at the Governor's Mansion can still be seen at the site, which is now the Sharlot Hall Museum.

Prescott was a rather crude little burg in those days. Miners' shacks were mostly ramshackle, tumble-down log cabins. Caroline Ramos was one of only two women in Prescott, and she was known locally as the "Virgin Mary." How she came about this lofty appellation is anyone's guess. She operated a popular restaurant-boarding house called Fort Misery. A sign tacked on the door read, "room and board, $25 in gold, cash in advance." The menu offered little variety but the hungry miners didn't seem to mind: Breakfast—venison and chili, coffee, bread and goat's milk; Lunch—venison, chili, bread, coffee and goat's milk; Supper—venison, chili, coffee, goat's milk and *tortillas.* On Sunday, Fort Misery was converted into a church and, when necessary Judge "Blinkey" Howard dispensed justice or "misery" there. The Governor's Mansion was the most impressive building in town. The log cabin cost $6,000 to build and was the only two-story house north of the Gila River.

Whiskey Row in Prescott is one of Arizona's best-known avenues. Around the turn of the century there were 40 saloons stretched out along Montezuma Street or, as it was better known, Whiskey Row. The first, going south to north, was the Kentucky Bar which stood on the corner of Goodwin and Montezuma. The row ended down by the Santa Fe depot at a bar called the Depot House. Thirsty cowboys, in off the range, used to start in at the Kentucky Bar and try to drink in each bar all the way down to the Depot House. And, if they were still on their feet, turn around and drink all the way back to the other end.

The earliest saloons in Prescott weren't on Montezuma but were built a block west along Granite Creek. The first one, called the Quartz Rock, was run by an army deserter who'd lost his nose in a fight.

No one knows for sure why the saloons were moved from Granite Creek to Whiskey Row. Some say it was because sober citizens got tired of hauling drunks out of the creek. Others say, and this sounds more believable, it was because the sight of that pure water made the drunks sick.

John Goodwin didn't remain governor for long. In September 1865 he was elected territorial delegate to Congress (the most coveted office in the territory, for it allowed the politico to reside in the nation's capital), and was off to Washington. Richard McCormick, secretary, was the next governor. "Little Mac" or "Slippery Dick" as friends and enemies, respectively, called the diminutive governor, worked for the betterment of the territory. He pushed for better roads, education, mining, railroads and agriculture. He also wanted to become delegate to Washington. Folks in Tucson offered their support if he would relocate the capital in the Old Pueblo. Thus begins the storied Capital on Wheels.

The capital was moved to Tucson in 1867 amidst cries of "foul" by Prescottonians. Tucson clung to it tenaciously for a decade before Prescott recovered the coveted prize. The McCormick-arranged transfer of the capital incurred the wrath of John Marion, the fiery editor of the Prescott *Miner.* Marion, a staunch Democrat, penned several scathing attacks upon the character of Mr. McCormick, who just happened to be a Republican. Marion was so anti-Republican that he sometimes lost his objectivity. He supported a Democratic candidate for county attorney despite the fact that the rascal had run off with Marion's wife.

When the First Territorial Legislature met in Prescott on September 26, 1864, the capitol building wasn't completed, so the session was held in Governor Goodwin's home. The mines were well represented with about half the delegates either miners or engineers. Jackson McCrackin was one of the miners. He first arrived with the Walker party before there was a territory. His friends at the mining camp wanted him to go in style, looking like a proper politician, so they hauled him down to a creek and gave him an old-fashioned scrubbing with lye soap and a horse brush. He was presented with a second-hand suit and sent to a barber to make his appearance respectable. Incidentally, ten years later McCrackin struck it rich over in western Arizona and wound up with a town named in his honor.

Although this first session appropriated money for education and chartered some road companies and railroads, its greatest achievement was a code of laws. It was called the Howell Code in honor of Associate Justice William T. Howell. Later in the year, however, Howell resigned and went home, saying he wouldn't serve in a district where three out of four residents went barefoot. The courthouse was an adobe shack and the rostrum was a dry goods box. Chief Justice William Turner complained to Washington there wasn't a set of law books in the entire territory.

In later years Charles Poston, first superintendent of Indian affairs for the territory and second delegate to Congress, took most of the credit for persuading Congress and the President to create the new territory. Through much self-promotion, Poston had become known as the "Father of Arizona." Poston also earns dubious credit for being the first to take an expensive and unnecessary junket at taxpayer expense. Elected as delegate to Washington in 1864, he took the scenic route through Panama at a cost of $7,000.

Charles D. Poston, mining promoter. He is recognized today as the "Father of Arizona." Photo: Southwest Studies.

Sylvester Mowry, a flamboyant ex-army officer and mining magnate, certainly deserves mention. Mowry was transferred to Arizona from Salt Lake City in 1855. A dedicated ladies' man, he incurred the wrath of Brigham Young by having an amorous affair with a daughter-in-law of the Mormon leader. Mowry was described as "conspicuous as a peacock." The army must have figured Fort Yuma was as good a place as any for the hot-blooded young "peacock." Soon thereafter, Mowry left the army and got into the mining business, acquiring the old Patagonia and renaming it the Mowry Mine. In 1860, Arizonans elected him as delegate to Congress, but since there was no Arizona Territory he wasn't seated. Mowry was a tireless promoter of territorial status. He was so boastful at one point that Ed Cross, editor of the Tubac *Weekly Arizonian,* took issue with his remarks. The two decided to shoot it out in a proper duel on July 8, 1859. They squared off with Burnside rifles and exchanged shots. Fortunately, both missed their target. When satisfied, the shootists and their supporters retired to a local saloon and consumed a 42-gallon barrel of prime whiskey. Mowry then bought his former adversary's printing press and relocated it to Tucson.

During the Civil War, Gen. Carleton arrested Mowry as a Confederate sympathizer and sent him to Fort Yuma under house arrest. Mowry's current mistress was allowed to accompany him. The Mowry Mine, south of today's Patagonia, was ransacked in his absence. He later sued for damages but died in 1871 without ever collecting.

Sylvester Mowry, flamboyant mining entrepreneur and promoter of territorial status for Arizona. Photo: Southwest Studies.

Perhaps the man most responsible for bringing Arizona Territory into the Union in 1863 was Gen. Sam Heintzelman. During the 1850s he commanded at Fort Yuma and was well-acquainted with the wealth of Arizona. Later he fought at both battles of Bull Run (or Manassas) and rose to the rank of general. He was the one with enough rank to pull the right strings in Washington. Poston outlived both Heintzelman and Mowry and subsequently took most of the credit.

General Sam Heintzelman, commanding officer, Fort Yuma. Later he led the fight for territorial status. Arizona Historical Society, Sack's Collection.

A year after Arizona became a territory, 4,573 non-Indians claimed residency. Six years later the population had grown to 9,658. All were Hispanic or Anglo except for 26 Blacks and 20 Chinese. By the 1880 census the population had grown to 41,574. Among these were 1,000 Chinese and 100 Blacks. By the time statehood came in 1912, Arizona claimed over 200,000 residents.

Arizona's original four counties—Mojave, Pima, Yuma and Yavapai—were created in 1864. A year later, Pah-Ute County was created from the northwest corner of Mojave. Most of the settlers were Mormons from Utah. Nevada was able to take Pah-Ute away from the new Arizona Territory in 1866. For a time, the settlers refused allegiance to Nevada and continued to send political representatives to Arizona. Interestingly, Nevada, Arizona and even Utah levied taxes on the poor souls. Arizona finally gave up its claim in 1871. The "Lost" Pah-Ute County is today Clark County, Nevada and its chief claim to fame is that "Bibulous Babylon of the West," Las Vegas.

During its 62-year tenure as a territory, one of the longest in American history, Arizona remained one of the least-known and least-populated regions in the nation. Arizonans began pushing for statehood as early as 1872; however, outlawry, feuds, Apache wars and lack of good roads were primary factors in delaying statehood. By the dawning of the 20th Century most of those problems were resolved, so the eastern establishment, wishing to retain the status quo, conjured up new arguments. Not enough people, they said. The gold-silver issue was another. Arizona was a silver-producing state and her representatives would support free coinage of silver. Eastern Republicans preferred the gold standard. Most important, Arizona would send two Democratic senators to Washington—something eastern Republicans couldn't tolerate.

By the 1890s powerful mining and railroad interests were backing statehood for selfish reasons. They believed, correctly, that state legislatures would be much easier to control than the federal government.

Territorial status, at best, was a trying period for Arizonans who couldn't vote in presidential elections. They could send a representative to Washington, but he couldn't vote. The legislature could pass laws but they were subject to review in Washington. As mentioned, many officials, including the governor, were appointed in Washington. Congress controlled finances and could arbitrarily take land away from a territory, as in the case of Pah-Ute County.

All in all, territorial citizens were treated like second-class citizens. The governors were appointed by the President, as were all other federal officials. Since the Republicans were in power through most of the post-Civil War years, the appointees were often party loyalists who were looking for jobs. Of the 16 appointed governors, all but three were Republicans. Some were accused of being carpetbagging, incompetent opportunists, and a couple certainly were. All things considered, however, they were an acceptable group.

The legislature, or Assembly, was bicameral, with an upper chamber called the Council and a lower chamber, the House. They met annually until 1871 and then only every other year for 60-day sessions. The pay was three dollars a day, later raised to six. During the 25 sessions, the Democrats usually held a majority.

The most interesting session was the Thirteenth, that met in Prescott in 1885. The citizens of Tucson raised a satchel full of money and told their delegates to bring home the capital, that nothing less would be accepted. Meanwhile, other delegates were getting ready to play their cards. Pinal County wanted a bridge across the Gila River, while the northern part of Cochise wanted to secede. In Maricopa, Tempe wanted a normal school while Phoenix wanted an insane asylum. Prescott, of course, wanted to keep the capital and Tucson had other plans for relocating it again.

Unfortunately, ole Mother Nature intervened. A flood on the Salt River forced the Pima County delegates to catch a train at Maricopa and travel by rail to Los Angeles, then back to Ash Fork, 50 miles north of Prescott, then take a stage back to the capital. A snowstorm held up the stage at Hell's Canyon, so one of the delegates, Bob Leatherwood, took the satchel of money, climbed onto a mule and rode hard to Prescott. By the time he arrived, all the horsetrading was over and the prizes had been handed out. Prescott retained the capital, Cochise County remained intact, Florence got a bridge over the Gila River, Tempe got a normal school and Phoenix an insane asylum. When the delegates realized that Tucson had been left out, they awarded the only thing left — a university. "Why do we need a university?" moaned one of Tucson's city fathers who, incidentally, owned a saloon. "Those students won't drink." When the downtrodden delegates returned to Tucson, angry citizens pelted them with rotten eggs and overripe vegetables. One sore loser hurled a dead cat at the hapless legislators.

The nickname, "Thieving Thirteenth," was applied by critics after the free-spending politicians, with a budget of $4,000, squandered more than ten times that amount, much of it frivolously. It should be remembered that, despite all the criticism, their accomplishments were commendable. A normal school and university were established, although it would be another decade before the first public high school would be built. A mental institution was established and railroads linking Phoenix with the Santa Fe on the north and Southern Pacific to the south were chartered.

If the Thirteenth went down in history as the "thieving," then the Fourteenth should be known as the "measly" for two reasons: they didn't do much, and one of the members got measles and shared it with the rest.

Four years after the Thirteenth Legislature convened, the Fifteenth met and, once again, the capital was up for grabs. This time Phoenix, the upstart city on the banks of the Salt

River, was making the play. To ensure victory, Maricopa County delegates made a deal with a certain lady of the evening named "Kissin' Jenny" to delay one of the Yavapai County delegates during the crucial vote. The man in question wore a glass eye, the only one in the territory. He was quite proud of that glass eye and extremely vain. He'd never go anywhere without it and the delegates from Phoenix knew it. They decided to use his vanity to their advantage.

Each evening after the assembly convened, the Prescott delegate was known to spend some time in Kissin' Jenny's boudoir. On the evening before the vote the delegate had a few drinks on Whiskey Row, then headed for Jenny's place on Granite Creek. Later, after blowing out the lamp, he carefully placed his glass eye in a water glass next to the bed, then went to sleep. Sometime during the night, Jenny got thirsty and reached over, picked up the water glass and swallowed the contents, including the eye. When the delegate arose the next morning and found his glass eye missing, he refused to go out in public.

Meanwhile, the politician's allies noted his tardiness and headed for Jenny's place to roust him out. Upon discovering the reason for his absence, they pleaded with Jenny to give up the eye but she wouldn't, or couldn't, cooperate. The one-eyed delegate was absent from the assembly that day and history records that Phoenix got the capital. So, in 1889 the permanent capital was established at Phoenix where it remains.

Legislators could be, at times, self-serving to the extreme. One time a representative lost his bankroll at a horse race so he introduced a bill outlawing horse races. His mischievous colleagues kept altering the bill until the only place left where horse racing was not allowed was on his own ranch.

When Maricopa County was created in 1871, three candidates threw their hats in the ring for sheriff. Since the office was the county's highest, competition was keen. J.A. Chenowth and "Whispering Jim" Favorite were the leading contenders while "Silent Tom" Barnum was a distant third. Barnum wasn't figured to make a serious challenge as the race between the other two grew hotter. In fact, he didn't even campaign. Chenowth and "Whispering Jim" stalked each other like alley cats, their shouting matches drawing large crowds. Then one day tempers got out of hand and both men went for their guns. "Whispering Jim" had barely cleared leather when a bullet from J.A.'s six-shooter cut him down. Favorite was no more and city fathers advised J.A. he'd better leave town. When the vote was taken, the dark horse, Tom Barnum, was the overwhelming (and only) choice for first elected sheriff of Maricopa County.

The selection of a county seat for newly-created Maricopa County was also hotly contested. Some wanted it located "way out east" of the new Phoenix townsite (where downtown Phoenix is today). Polling places were set up and supporters of both sites fought a no-holds-barred battle. Barrels of whiskey were dispensed and wagon loads of Indians were imported, given names such as Murphy, Smith and O'Leary and hauled to the various polling places to cast their votes — again and again.

This brand of rowdiness, along with the Graham-Tewksbury feud in Pleasant Valley; the Cochise County War involving the Earps, McLaurys, and Clantons; Geronimo and his band; and a host of other not-so-famous outlaws and renegades gave Arizona quite a reputation for lawlessness. Though some of the reputation was well-earned, most of it was exaggerated by writers of pulp westerns. Most Arizonans were decent, hard working, honest folks with a burning ambition to see their adopted home become a state.

The fervor with which Arizonans wanted statehood is perhaps best illustrated during the Spanish-American War. When war came in 1898, Arizonans eager to show their patriotism volunteered in droves. Colorful William O. "Buckey" O'Neill, former sheriff, newspaperman and politician, was a noted warrior in the fight for statehood. He was also one of the most popular men in the territory. The volunteers quickly became darlings of the press who dubbed them the "Rough Riders." Irrepressible Teddy Roosevelt rode with them and sang their praise.

In Cuba, the Arizonans fought with courage and intrepidity. The bravest and most gallant of them all was the dashing captain of "A" company, Buckey O'Neill. He stubbornly refused to seek cover from the fierce gunfire of Spanish soldiers. "An officer should always set an example to his men," he explained, when warned of the dangers. Miraculously, the Spanish bullets never touched him. At Las Guasimas he seemed immortal, exposing himself to gunfire, oblivious to danger. Other Arizona officers, including Col. Alexander Brodie and Capt. Jim McClintock, fell wounded. Buckey wasn't scratched. At San Juan Hill he resumed his post, oblivious to the defiant Spanish marksmen. Again, he was cautioned. "Who

Buckey O'Neill, sheriff of Yavapai County. He was the only officer in the famed Rough Riders to die in the Spanish-American War. Photo: Southwest Studies.

wouldn't gladly lay down his life to put another star on the flag?" he replied. A few seconds later a sniper's bullet cut down the young officer who was so willing to lay his life on the line to see Arizona achieve statehood.

The Arizonans returned from the war with high hopes for statehood, only to be told they weren't ready yet. Most Americans still considered the place an uninhabitable desert full of cactus, rattlesnakes and scorpions. New Mexico also was experiencing difficulty in becoming a state for similar reasons.

In 1904, a bill was passed in the United States House permitting Arizona and New Mexico to merge into one large state. The capital would be at Santa Fe but it would be called Arizona. The latter concession was to appease the unruly Arizonans. Fortunately, an amendment was added stating that both territories must approve or it wouldn't pass. The joint-statehood bill came to a vote in 1906. New Mexico voted in favor, but Arizona voted overwhelmingly against it, 16,265 to 3,141. During the debate, President Teddy Roosevelt came out in support of joint statehood, something that caused Phoenix residents to temporarily change Roosevelt Street to Cleveland.

Finally Congress passed the Enabling Act and, on June 20, 1910, President William Howard Taft signed the statehood bill authorizing Arizona to hold a constitutional convention.

The 1910 Constitution borrowed much from other states. Contrary to popular myth, it was traditional and even a little old fashioned. For example, the office of governor was weakened at the same time other states were moving towards the centralized executive system. The fathers of the constitution were evidently venting their wrath against territorial appointees. The office of governor wound up with little appointive power and heads of many committees were subject to legislative review.

Democrats dominated the convention 41 to 11, as delegates were chosen by county party meetings instead of by direct primary.

The convention was controlled by the progressive wing of the party. Such liberal measures as direct primary elections, initiative and referendum were certain to win approval. Other proposals were the recall of elected officials, prohibition and women's suffrage. The recall measure passed. Prohibition failed, 33 to 15. Women's suffrage lost, 30 to 19, despite a ten-foot long petition from Gila County and a picture post card showing a young woman and child standing next to a drunk lying in the gutter. The caption read: "This man can vote, this woman cannot."

Conservatives warned that Taft, a former judge, would veto the constitution if the recall of judges was kept in. The stubborn Arizonans refused to back down and Taft vetoed it on August 11, 1911. "Take it out and then, when statehood is granted, put it back in," the Arizonans were advised by cooler heads. A few months later another vote was taken and the recall was removed. Officers of the new state were elected in December, 1911. Finally, on February 12, 1912 the Arizona statehood bill, called the Flood Resolution for the Virginia

Congressman who authored it, was ready to be signed. Since the 12th was a holiday, Lincoln's Birthday, and the 13th was considered unlucky, Taft waited until February 14, Valentine's Day, to sign the bill.

Word reached Arizona by telegraph at 8:55 a.m. and all over the new state people took to the streets to celebrate. Church and school bells rang out, pistol shots were fired and Phoenix held a big parade. The biggest blast came in boisterous Bisbee where a charge of dynamite was set which nearly blew the top off a mountain.

A young Phoenix couple, Joe Melczer and Hazel Goldberg, delayed their marriage ceremony until word officially arrived. They wanted to be the first couple married in the "state" of Arizona. Time passed slowly. The ring bearer, an energetic three-year-old, fidgeted impatiently. Finally a messenger brought the news and little Barry Goldwater stepped forward with the rings and the state's first marriage vows were solemnized.

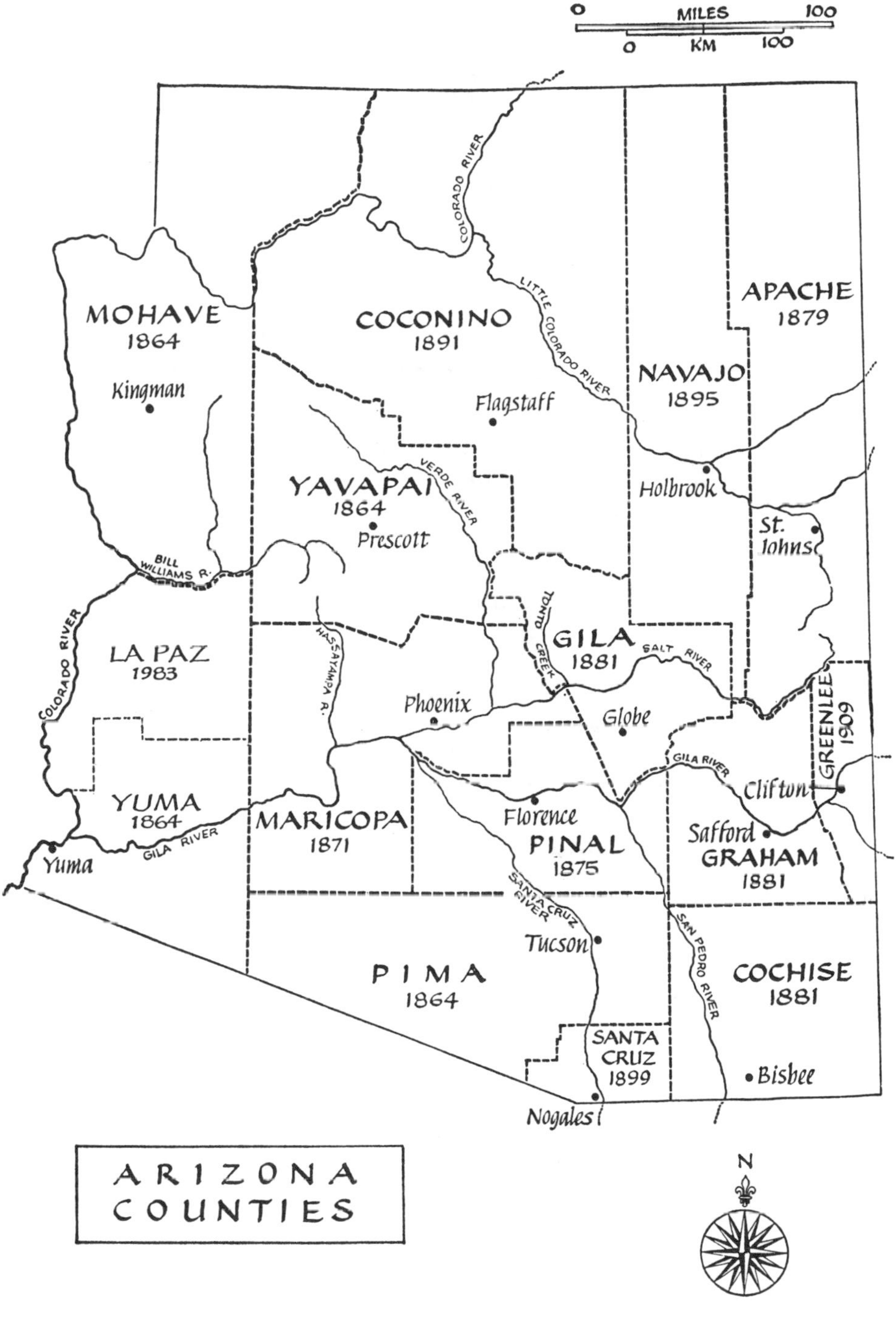

MILES

KM

MOHAVE
1864

Kingman

COCONINO
1891

Flagstaff

APACHE
1879

NAVAJO
1895

Holbrook

St.
Johns

COLORADO RIVER

LITTLE COLORADO RIVER

YAVAPAI
1864

Prescott

VERDE RIVER

BILL
WILLIAMS R.

COLORADO RIVER

LA PAZ
1983

HASSAYAMPA R.

TONTO CREEK

GILA
1881

SALT RIVER

GREENLEE
1909

Phoenix

Globe

GILA RIVER

Clifton

YUMA
1864

Yuma

MARICOPA
1871

GILA RIVER

Florence

PINAL
1875

Safford

GRAHAM
1881

SANTA CRUZ RIVER

SAN PEDRO RIVER

PIMA
1864

Tucson

COCHISE
1881

SANTA
CRUZ
1899

Bisbee

Nogales

ARIZONA
COUNTIES

N

14

LIFE IN THE TERRITORIAL YEARS

Prospectors were the first to be attracted by the lure of gold and silver in the mountains of Arizona. A lucky strike usually meant the birth of a new community. Gamblers, saloonkeepers and painted ladies made up most of the first wave. Then came merchants and, if the ore showed any sign of running deep, entrepreneurs of all kinds arrived with more plans than a politician for making the place the next San Francisco of the West.

Since the Indians living in the area had now been displaced and put on the prod, the army was called in to keep the peace. Sometimes they protected the whites from the Indians. Frequently though, it was the other way around. Somebody had to feed all the hungry newcomers, along with the Indians who, with promises of beef rations, had been relocated to reservations. So, ranchers and farmers settled near sources of water, grew crops and raised beef cattle. If the prosperity continued, a railroad was sure to lay down tracks. The railroads also opened up the land to new markets. Goods and people arrived in relative ease and comfort. Cattle and ore could be shipped to markets in California and eastern states by rail.

Nellie Cashman was one of the most remarkable people to come into Arizona during the territorial years. Her story reads like a Beadle dime novel, yet she represents the spirit of the intrepid pioneers who came to Arizona far better than the more-publicized figures of her time. A native of Ireland, she stood only five feet tall, had lustrous dark eyes and soft, feminine features. She was quite a lady, in a most unlady-like profession: prospecting. For some 50 adventurous years she trekked all over the West from Mexico to Alaska. Nellie and her sister immigrated to America from Ireland when Nellie was only 23. They settled in San Francisco where her sister married Tom Cunningham, another good Irish Catholic, and had five children over the next few years.

In 1877 Nellie joined the gold rush to the Yukon. Two years later she opened Delmonico's Restaurant in Tucson. The great silver rush brought her in 1880 to Tombstone, where she ran the Russ House, a boarding house for miners. That year, her sister died and Nellie was left to raise the five children.

Nellie was already a legend when she arrived in Arizona. During a scurvy outbreak in the Yukon she brought in vegetables to counter the effects of the disease and earned a lasting nickname, "Angel of the Mining Camps." Wherever she traveled

Nellie Cashman, "Angel of the Mining Camps." She was a prospector, humanitarian and entrepreneur. Prospecting and wanderlust took her from Mexico to the Arctic Circle. Photo: Arizona Historical Society.

Nellie was doing charitable deeds for folks down on their luck. She solicited assistance from ladies like "Black Jack," queen of the red light district, and from mining magnates. One time in Tombstone, when a mining official was in danger of being lynched by striking miners, Nellie rescued the man and drove him in her buggy to safety at Benson. Another time she befriended five men sentenced to hang for the "Bisbee Massacre." Some "entrepreneur" was erecting a grandstand and planned to sell tickets to the hanging. The condemned men asked Nellie to do something, because they didn't want it to become a public spectacle. The night before the hanging she organized a wrecking crew and dismantled the grandstand.

Nellie Cashman had a thirst for adventure, loved to make money and was very good at it. She made several fortunes but gave most of the money away. Her family claimed she made money just to support her true vocation — charity. She raised and educated her sister's five children, but never married. Not that she didn't receive many proposals. During a prospecting expedition in the hot desert of Mexico, she and her companions ran out of water. Alone, Nellie set out on a long, hot search. She found a Spanish mission and returned with enough water to save her friends' lives. When she was nearly 80, Nellie mushed a dog sled team 750 miles across Alaska's frozen land.

Nellie died in Alaska on January 4, 1925, just a year after her record-setting dog sled trip that earned her the title "Champion Woman Musher of the World". For a lady only five feet tall, in a land where people were measured, not by sex, color or creed, but by what they could do, Nellie Cashman certainly assayed out as a giant.

THE RISE OF PHOENIX

The Salt River Valley lay unclaimed for nearly 500 years. At the close of the Civil War in 1865, Fort McDowell was established near where Sycamore Creek joins the Verde River. Lt. John Y. T. Smith, mustered out of the army about that time, decided to stay on as a hay contractor and post sutler. He'd seen the fields of wild hay growing on the flood plains of the Salt River 18 miles to the southwest and decided to set up a hay camp. The place became known as Smith's Station and was located on the road he built to Fort McDowell (near 40th and Washington streets of today's Phoenix).

Originally, John Y.T. Smith was just plain John Smith, but he grew tired of meeting so many other people with the same name. Later he became active in territorial politics and when he ran for the territorial assembly in 1874, a newspaper editor commented unfavorably on a man with "a name like John Smith" running for office. Smith didn't have a checkered past, and John Smith was his real name, so he went to the legislature and legally added the middle initials "Y.T.," which stood for "Yours Truly."

In September, 1867 Smith's Station was visited by Jack Swilling, 37-year-old ex-Indian fighter, adventurer, hellion, former Confederate officer, Union scout and most recently, a member of the famed Walker party which had discovered gold in the Bradshaw Mountains. Swilling was quick to note the opportunities for irrigating the rich, fertile soil by cleaning out the old Hohokam canals and ditches. He went to Wickenburg, a thriving mining community on the Hassayampa River 50 miles to the northwest, and organized a company called the Swilling Irrigation Canal Company. The gregarious redhead also raised $400 to fund the project, then recruited a party of 16 strong-backed visionaries and headed for Smith's Station.

Swilling and his companions arrived in December, 1867 and began the laborious task of cleaning out the old canals. They started at the north bank of the Salt across from Tempe but hit caliche and rock, so they moved down the river to today's 40th Street and the riverbed near Smith's Station.

By March, 1868 the wheat and barley crops were in, and the population had reached 50. Swilling's Ditch, as the watering system was called, ran northwest across the desert for one-and-a-half miles, then curved back toward the

Jack Swilling, colorful "Father of Irrigation in the Salt River Valley." Photo: Arizona Historical Foundation, Tempe.

river. Eventually it would be called the Town Ditch and would run along the north side of Van Buren across to about 27th Avenue. During its heyday the ditch was multi-purpose: it was used to bathe in, drink, irrigate, and do the laundry in. One newspaper complained that saloonkeepers washed their spittoons in the ditch when nobody was looking. Nobody could have known at this time that from these humble beginnings the Salt River Valley would develop into one of the richest agricultural regions in the world. The first permanent farm in the valley was started by Frenchy Sawyer. That site is marked by a small plaque on the southeast corner of Washington and 24th streets.

The federal census of 1870 recorded a population of 61 women and 164 men. The ages of this hardy group ranged from 21 to 30. Among the populace were 96 who listed themselves as farmers. There wasn't a single doctor, lawyer, banker or teacher in the whole community.

On October 20, 1870 a committee of citizens gathered to select a townsite. Among the members of the selection committee was Bryan Philip Darrell Duppa, better known as "Lord" Duppa, reported to be a British lord who'd been something of an embarrassment to his family and had been exiled to the colonies. In reality, he was no "lord" at all. In those days on the frontier anyone with a British accent and an education was presumed to be nobility. He was well-educated and his family were prominent landowners in England. Duppa was a loner and unpopulated Arizona suited him just fine. Like many on the frontier, the 37-year-old adventurer was strongly addicted to ardent spirits. Duppa was also a well-traveled, man who spoke five languages fluently. His friends complained, so the story goes, that he was hard to understand because he remained in a drunken state most of the time and spoke all five languages at once.

Sometime between 1868 and 1872 "Lord" Duppa built a two-room adobe house at 116 W. Sherman, three blocks south of today's Central Avenue underpass. Today that simple little casa with a roof of cottonwood beams overlaid with salt-cedar poles and covered with arrowweed and mud, seems overwhelmed by the towering skyscrapers of downtown Phoenix. It is the oldest house still standing in the capital city and is the most obvious link with the city's historic past. Duppa favored locating the townsite about four miles west of Smith's Station, near today's Central Avenue and Van Buren Street. Actually, there were three proposed sites. One group wanted to locate at the northeast corner of 16th and Van Buren; one at 32nd and Van Buren; and the third on a mesquite-covered parcel between 7th Street and 7th Avenue, the site finally chosen. The vote of the committee resulted in a victory for the "down-towners" over the "eastsiders." That's why the center of Phoenix is at its present location and not further east. Jack Swilling, who wanted the 32nd Street site, was so angry at the voting results that he fired a round of birdshot, scoring a direct hit on one of those who had voted against him.

Swilling, a generous, big-hearted man, was the product of the violent frontier and had a past as colorful as a Navajo blanket. Originally from South Carolina, he had fought in both the Mexican and Civil wars and had been involved in several shooting scrapes with Apaches and Comanches. At one time his skull had been fractured by a gun barrel, and he was carrying a bullet in his left side from another shootout. Because his old injuries caused a great deal of pain, he took morphine and whiskey to dull the pain, and at times became a little crazy. He would die in a Yuma jail in 1878, accused of a crime he didn't commit.

Not long after the townsite had been selected, a citizen came down from Wickenburg and planted the first tree, a cottonwood, on Washington Street. The first lot, located on the southwest corner of 1st and Washington streets, sold for the sum of $103. More than 60 lots, with prices ranging from $20 to $140, were sold by the end of the day.

The next task for the settlers was to choose a name for their new town. Several were proposed, including Stonewall, Salinas, Pumpkinville and Millville. The eccentric "Lord" Duppa is credited by some historians with providing the inspiration for the name "Phoenix," while others give credit to his friend Jack Swilling. Phoenix was named for the mythical Egyptian bird that rose from its own ashes and flourished again. Thus, on October 26, 1870 the tiny community of adobe houses, reborn from the ashes of the great Hohokam civilization, had a name. In 1871 Maricopa County was organized, and Phoenix became the county seat.

In 1872 Phoenix opened its first school. Fewer than 20 youngsters showed up for the opening class, which was held in a one-room adobe building with a mud-thatched roof. It did boast the first wooden floor in town. The first teacher was a lady named Ellen Shaver. The pretty young schoolmarm didn't last long. None did in a town full of lonesome bachelors. John Yours Truly Smith promptly took her for his wife.

In 1877 funds had been appropriated for the construction of roads that would link Phoenix with the outside world. Not much more than dusty cattle trails extended toward Globe, Prescott, Wickenburg, and Yuma. By 1880 a road stretched south across the Salt and Gila rivers to Maricopa, linking Phoenix by stagecoach to the new Southern Pacific Railroad. It was a dusty, jostling stagecoach ride from Maricopa to Phoenix, but the local people were happy and tolerant just to be so close to a railroad.

In 1879 Sam Lount opened the first ice-making plant. He sold his ice for seven cents a pound. By 1880 Phoenix, zesty and full of optimism, boasted a population of 1,708.

Since both transcontinental railroads missed Phoenix, it looked as though the isolated community on the banks of the Salt River was destined to remain small and unimportant. Tucson had the railroad and all the amenities that came with it. At the time, not even the most prophetic could foresee what was about to take place in what would become known as the Valley of the Sun. Agriculture would be the key to Phoenix's growth, but it would take men of vision and fortitude to bring it about. Someone had to figure a better way to water the thirsty desert. Historically, lands located north of a canal were considered worthless. To change this, one had to build bigger and better canals.

In 1885, William J. Murphy took on the difficult task of building the 35-mile-long Arizona Canal, a project both massive and speculative, to open up irrigation north of the Grand Canal. The company that contracted with Murphy went broke, so he took his pay in bonds. Self-interest groups tried to block his efforts with political obstacles, but Murphy was undaunted.

In June, 1887 Murphy was able to meet his deadline,

completing the project with just two hours to spare. The Arizona Canal was a reality, and agriculture on a much larger scale would now be possible. There were now four canals north of the Salt River, but delivery systems were poor and there was a lot of water loss. Murphy organized the Arizona Improvement Company and built a cross-cut canal connecting all four canals, minimizing water loss and improving delivery. Phoenix was now able to challenge Prescott and Tucson, perennial rivals for the territorial capital, and two years later Phoenix succeeded in getting the capital.

Before the days of a Capitol building, legislators met in the Maricopa County Court House. The beautiful new Capitol building on West Washington Street was dedicated in 1901. On top of the huge domed structure was a weather vane called "Winged Victory," designed as the figure of a beautiful woman. Cowboys in town on a spree used to race horseback out to the Capitol and take pot shots at the celestial creature on the dome. A story is told that prevailing winds at certain times of the year caused her to face west, thus turning her backside to those approaching the Capitol steps. Apparently a few stuffy legislators took personal affront at this indignant lack of respect and had the lady welded in place facing the entrance. A few years ago the building underwent a remodeling and "Winged Victory" was freed again to expose her shapely backside whenever the winds dictated.

THE MORMONS IN ARIZONA

The first Mormon colonists from Utah arrived in Arizona in early 1854. The Navajos were on the warpath at the time and the Saints were driven out a year later. Between 1858 and the early 1870s, Jacob Hamblin, the Mormons' greatest trail-blazer, made several reconnaissance missions, locating river crossings, water holes and suitable trails. By this time the Navajos were at peace, thus making attempts at colonization safer. However, the greatest enemy facing the newcomers was the harsh, arid land and the fickle moods of the Little Colorado River.

Mormon settlements at Kanab (Utah), Pipe Spring and Lees Ferry were designated as bases from which to launch new colonies in Arizona. The primary mission of the church during

Jacob Hamblin, the Mormon's "Buckskin Missionary." He explored much of northern Arizona during the 1850s and 1860s, opening up the region for colonization by Mormon pioneers. Photo: Arizona Historical Society.

these years was expansion. Under the dynamic leadership of Brigham Young, the Mormons were determined to establish a far-flung empire from their Utah base west to California, south to the Salt River Valley and eventually to Mexico.

A reconnaissance expedition was sent to the Little Colorado River Valley in 1873 to make a feasibility study for colonization. The scouts reported it unsuitable. A Norwegian missionary, Andrew Amundsen, pretty well summed up the bleak land. His spelling left a little to be desired but the meaning was clear: "From the first we struck the little Collorado...., it is the seam thing all the way, no plase fit for a human being to dwell upon." Amundsen concluded his report rather succinctly, calling it, "The moste desert lukking plase that I ever saw, Amen."

Despite this foreboding declaration, an expedition of some one hundred colonists left Utah in early 1873, headed for the Little Colorado determined to make a go of it. They arrived on the Little Colorado in late May after a miserable, wind-blown journey down Moenkopi Wash. By this time the river was drying up. One journal entry referred to it, disparagingly, as "a loathsome little stream...as disgusting a stream as there is on the continent."

Iron-willed and purposeful as they were at the outset, the dispirited colonists soon packed their gear and returned to Utah. Undaunted, Brigham Young was determined to establish colonies in the valley of the Little Colorado River. Three years later he tried again, this time with success.

A major figure in the Mormon colonization along the river was a fiery, red-headed frontiersman named Lot Smith. Smith is perhaps best remembered for his daring guerrilla attacks on U.S. Army supply trains during the so-called Mormon War in 1857. In 1876, a mission was established at the ancient Hopi community at Moenkopi and, over the next two years, Smith and other church leaders such as William C. Allen, George Lake and Jesse D. Ballinger led parties of colonists to the lower Little Colorado River Valley to the sites of today's Joseph City, Sunset Crossing (Winslow) and Holbrook. Townsites were marked, irrigation ditches were dug, dams erected, and crops were planted. The Mormons had, at last, taken permanent root in Arizona.

The four colonizing parties, each numbering about 50 people, established camps and named them for their respective captains. Soon thereafter the names were changed. Lake's Camp became Obed; Smith's Camp was changed to Sunset, for the river crossing nearby; Ballinger's Camp became Brigham City; and Allen's Camp, St. Joseph. (Since St. Joseph, Missouri, was also on the Santa Fe line, St. Joseph was changed in 1923 to Joseph City).

As a precaution against Indian attacks, all four communities constructed forts of cottonwood logs and sandstone. These were self-contained units including communal mess halls and housing. The average size was about 200 feet square with walls reaching a height of seven to nine feet. Elevated guardhouses stood at the corners. Each had shops, cellars, storehouses, and wells in case of prolonged siege.

Sunset and Brigham City were short-lived communities located on opposite sides of the Little Colorado near the site of present-day Winslow. In 1878, the two hard luck communities were ravaged by floods which destroyed the year's crops. Obed suffered the same fate. Within a year, malaria and flooding caused the colonists to pull up stakes. However, the sturdily built sandstone fort survived and was used as a stock corral by the Hashknife Outfit until it was torn down in 1895.

St. Joseph was the only one of the four communities to survive. Despite numerous crop failures and dams destroyed by the rampaging Little Colorado, the gritty colonists won their battle against the elements. Today it holds the honor of being the oldest Mormon settlement in the Little Colorado River Valley.

A colonizing attempt by a group of Bostonians coincided with the Mormon settlements in 1876. Two years earlier, Samuel W. Cozzens had published a book called *The Marvellous Country* in which he extolled the agricultural virtues of northern Arizona (which he hadn't actually seen). In February, 1876, a party of some 50 Boston colonists headed for the Little Colorado River near today's Winslow. The Mormons had arrived earlier and already planted their crops. So, the New Englanders headed 70 miles west to the San Francisco Peaks area where they planned to start their own agricultural empire. It didn't take long to figure out that Flagstaff enjoys nine months of winter and three months of fair-to-middlin' sledding. These would-be sodbusters did provide a lasting memorial before moving on to warmer climates. On July 4, 1876 they skinned the bark off a tall pine tree and celebrated America's centennial with a flag-raising, thus providing inspiration for the name, Flagstaff, which later was to become northern Arizona's most important city.

During the late 1870s, the Mormons extended their colonization with a little chain of outposts up the Little Colorado to Woodruff, Snowflake, Taylor and Show Low. In 1880 the towns of St. Johns, Springerville, Eagar, Nutrioso and Alpine were settled. As more of the Saints took up the call to colonize, dozens of other smaller settlements were established in the Mogollon Rim country. The industrious Mormons managed to overcome the many obstacles, including scarce water, poor top soil and short growing seasons, along with loneliness and isolation, to carve out a life in the wilderness of northern Arizona. They established a large dairy ranch called, appropriately enough, the Mormon Dairy at Mormon Lake, near Flagstaff. To supplement income in a cash-poor society some people freighted goods into mining camps and army posts, while others took jobs as cowboys or on construction crews for the Atlantic and Pacific (Santa Fe) Railroad which was building a line across northern Arizona in the early 1880s.

In 1877, 84 colonists left St. George, Utah for the fertile Salt River Valley. The first settlement was located on the flood plain of the Salt. They built an adobe enclosure near today's North Mesa Drive and Lehi Road and called it Fort Utah. Later it was changed to Utahville, Jonesville then finally Lehi. A year later another group arrived and moved up on the tableland above Lehi. Their town was called Mesaville, then Hayden and Zenos. By 1888 the settlers united on the name Mesa.

Differences of opinion on the treatment of Indians at Lehi caused Philemon Merrill to take several families and move further south. They established a settlement on the San Pedro River in Cochise County and called it St. David. Ironically, this community isn't far from where members of the Mormon Battalion, many of whom helped colonize Arizona, had taken part in the "Battle of Bull Run" more than 30 years earlier.

Around 1880, another large group of Mormons settled in the upper Gila Valley where they found rich farmland. Safford eventually became the trade center for small communities such as Eden, Thatcher, Bryce, Pima and Solomonville.

Mormon settlers, unlike most of the immigrants to Arizona during this period who came for mining and its related activities, concentrated their efforts in agriculture. They supplied the mining regions with farm products and established a cordon of settlements to aid other Mormon colonists. Eventually, the Mormons would extend their colonies into Mexico where many of their descendants still reside.

It was customary in the Mormon religion to have the marriage vows "sealed" in a temple. Until 1926 when the Arizona Temple was built in Mesa, the nearest one was at St. George, Utah. Young couples, already married by the local bishop, traveled by wagon over the long, rough trails across the mountains to the Colorado Plateau, crossing the Colorado River at Lees Ferry, then across the high, wide and lonesome Arizona Strip, west to St. George. After the ceremony, the stock was rested a few days, then hitched up for the long trek home. The journey could take weeks and most certainly provided an opportunity for the newlyweds to get to know each other under the most adverse conditions. The route became known as the "Honeymoon Trail."

The practice of polygamy brought social and legal troubles upon the Mormons, both from without and within. During the mid-1880s many Mormons took parts of their extended families and moved to Mexico. In 1890 polygamy was outlawed; however, the established families were allowed to continue living in polygamy. During the Mexican Revolution of 1910, the settlements of Colonia Dublin and Colonia Juarez in Chihuahua were abandoned and many Mormons returned to Arizona. Afterwards, they returned and through hard work and determination rebuilt the shattered communities. Today the towns are again prosperous — a testament to the industrious Mormons.

Polygamy continues today in a remote section on the Arizona Strip where a fundamentalist splinter group resides. In 1953 Mojave County officials complained that young girls were being forced into plural marriage and numerous women were applying for welfare, many of whom listed the same man as their husband. That led to a dramatic raid by the Arizona Highway Patrol (Department of Public Safety) on the border town of Short Creek. Women and children were rounded up, put on buses and brought to the Phoenix area, where they were placed in foster homes. The men were taken to Kingman where they posted bail and returned home. Several months later the state's case fizzled and the women and children were taken back to Short Creek. Because of all the publicity, the people of Short Creek changed the name of their community to Colorado City. Wanting nothing more than to be left alone, they continue to live as they have in the past.

PIONEER JEWS IN ARIZONA

The contributions of ethnic groups have oftentimes been overlooked in the cavalcade of Arizona history. Blacks, Russians, Cornish, Serbs, Slavs, Mexicans, Chinese, Japanese, Italians and a host of others arrived in Arizona during territorial days with nothing but the shirts on their backs. They overcame prejudice, battled hard times and put forth much sweat and toil. Many of these found Arizona to be a veritable land of milk and honey. Perhaps most frequently overlooked have been the Jews.

Jews played as much a part in the settlement of the territory as any group. They owned and operated banks, mines, ranches, saloons, stores and hotels throughout the territory.

Michael and Joseph Goldwater arrived at the boom town of La Paz during the gold rush days in the early 1860s and operated a store, supplying everything from whiskey to Bibles. Later they hauled freight to Prescott. Eventually the Goldwater mercantile stores would prosper and grow, becoming one of the Southwest's leading chain of department stores. The town of Nogales was originally named Isaacson for Jacob Isaacson, a Russian Jew who opened the first store there. Mayer was named for Joseph Mayer who established a stage station, saloon and store there in 1882. Solomonville was named for Isador Solomon.

Wyatt Earp's celebrated third wife, Josie Marcus Earp, was the Jewish daughter of a San Francisco merchant family. Around 1900 Emil Ganz of Phoenix started what eventually became First Interstate Bank of Arizona. Isador Solomon established the Gila Valley Bank which eventually became Valley National Bank. Most of the retail stores were started by Jews. Diamonds, one of Phoenix's most prominent, was opened around the turn of the century by Nathan and Isaac Diamond. During that same period, Sam Korrick opened Korricks (now Broadway). In Tucson, Albert Steinfeld and William Zeckendorf hauled freight between Bisbee and Tucson. They were key figures in the famous Copper Queen Mining Company. Alex Levin settled in Tucson just after the Civil War and started Levin's Park, a three-acre entertainment park, four years later. For years it was the social meeting place in Tucson. Among Levin's descendants are violinist Natalie Echavarria, singer-actress Luisa Espinol and popular singer Linda Ronstadt.

Isaac Rosenzweig started out in Phoenix as a pawnbroker. Today Rosenzweig's is one of the best-known jewelry stores in the state.

The great majority of the Jews arriving in Arizona during territorial days were men and if one wanted to marry he either sent for a mail order bride or married a local, non-Jewish girl. Under Jewish law, a woman must be Jewish for the children to be recognized as Jews. An interesting story is told about how Isaac Rosenzweig sent for a mail order bride. Since he'd never met the woman he covered his bet by telling Baron Goldwater the young lady was for him. He figured that if the lady in question wasn't suitable he'd pawn her off on his friend. Well, the mail order bride turned out to be something special and Rosenzweig kept her for himself. Baron eventually married Josephine Williams, a pretty, strong-willed young nurse who'd traveled to Arizona for her health. She was Episcopalian and, according to Jewish law, their offspring were Christian despite their Jewish heritage. Their son Barry went on to be Arizona's most famous native son.

A rather tall tale is told on Senator Barry Goldwater during his younger days when he wanted to play golf at an exclusive country club. On being told Jews could not play on the course Barry, an avid golfer, replied, "But I'm only half-Jewish; can I just play nine holes?"

EARLY BLACKS IN ARIZONA

Much of the early history of Blacks in Arizona focused on the military. Four Black regiments, two cavalry and two infantry, were created after the Civil War and sent west to fight Indians. Because of their dark skin and wooly hair, the natives called them "Buffalo Soldiers." Black troopers took the name as a compliment and bore it with considerable pride. The military record of the Black units in Arizona, especially the Ninth and Tenth Cavalry, was exemplary. They fought in some of the roughest campaigns across formidable geography, yet their record on desertion and discipline outshone other army units.

Ben McClendon was with the Weaver-Peeples party of prospectors that found rich deposits of gold near the Hassayampa River in 1863. Ben found his own bonanza a year later in the desert west of Wickenburg. He would come into town and stay until his money was gone, then head for his secret mine once again. He was believed to have been killed by Apaches a few miles from Wickenburg. Ben died without ever revealing the location of his mine. Prospectors still search for Ben's lost bonanza.

During the 1880s, a cowhand known only as Jim once took on the great John L. Sullivan in a prize fight in Tombstone. Jim didn't win the fight against the skilled boxer, but did manage to stagger the champ with a roundhouse blow.

A number of Black cowboys left their mark on Arizona, including John Swain who worked many years for John

Slaughter's San Bernardino Ranch on the Mexican border. Perhaps the best-known Blacks in territorial Arizona were Bill and Ann Neal. Bill Neal, better known as Curly Bill, rode with William F. "Buffalo Bill" Cody during the Indian wars on the Plains. Later he came to Tucson and worked as a cook, learning the hospitality business from the ground up. Next, he opened a freight business, supplying fuel for the charcoal smelters at nearby mines and hauling ore on the return trip. He married Ann and the pair added a cattle ranch to his prospering enterprise. The ranch, near Oracle on the north slopes of the Santa Catalina Mountains, was soon running thousands of cows with Neal's 3N brand stamped on their hides. In 1895 they opened a resort, the Mountain View Hotel in Oracle, a favorite summer getaway for Tucsonians. During the winter, visitors to Arizona were hauled out to the resort on the Neals' stagecoaches. Ann managed the hotel, while Bill handled the ranch, freight business and other enterprises. The pair were pioneers in what was later to become Arizona's number one job-producing industry, tourism.

LUMBER: ARIZONA'S FIRST MAJOR MANUFACTURING INDUSTRY

Edward Ayer, a prominent lumberman from Chicago, arrived in Winslow in 1882. Construction delays on the Atlantic and Pacific railroad bridge at Canyon Diablo, a few miles further west, forced him to get off at Winslow. He traveled by wagon to the ponderosa pine country around the San Francisco Mountains. At Flagstaff he founded the Ayer Lumber Company and hired an Irishman named Dennis Riordan as manager. Riordan talked his brothers, Timothy and Michael, into joining the lumber business. The company, thanks to its close proximity to the largest stand of ponderosa pine in the world and the Atlantic and Pacific Railroad right next door, became a thriving enterprise.

In 1887 the name was changed to Arizona Lumber and Timber Company. Michael and Timothy Riordan bought the company from Ayer. In 1903 Timothy built a dam at the end of a long cienega southeast of Flagstaff and named the lake that formed behind it Lake Mary in honor of his oldest daughter. The enterprising Riordan brothers also built Flag-

The Arizona Lumber and Timber Company supplied railroad ties, telephone poles and lumber for the towns that sprang up in northern Arizona. Lumbering was Arizona's first major manufacturing industry. Photo: Arizona Historical Society.

staff's first electric plant. The Riordans were a close-knit family. In 1904 Mike and Tim built an opulent log mansion and named it *Kinlicki*, Navajo for "red house." The spacious home had separate living quarters at each end for the respective families and a common area in the center which was shared. Since the Riordans were among Flagstaff's most prosperous citizens, the home was a favorite social gathering place.

In 1927 tragedy struck both families on the same day. Timothy's 26-year-old daughter Anna contracted the dreaded disease polio. Members of both families took turns over the next few days administering artificial respiration to the stricken young woman. The house was placed under quarantine and nobody was allowed to leave. An iron lung was ordered by rail but failed to arrive in time to save her life. That same night, Mike's 30-year-old son Arthur passed away. The bodies of Anna and Arthur were placed in the center of the Riordan family mansion to lie in state as mourners from all over northern Arizona came to pay last respects.

Today Northern Arizona University sprawls adjacent to the old mansion, which was nearly torn down a few years ago to build a parking lot. Fortunately, the structure was able to avoid condemnation proceedings when descendants of the lumbering dynasty allowed it to become a state park.

LEISURE TIME IN TERRITORIAL ARIZONA

Have you ever wondered how Arizonans spent their leisure time before the advent of lakes, fast highways, tailgate parties, singles bars and health spas?

Don't be fooled by those stoic faces in the old photograph album. Leisure time might have been limited compared to today but, if those plucky territorial folks knew something about the good old-fashioned work ethic, they also knew how to have a good time.

They had singles bars in those days, too, but not the "body shops" we're familiar with today. The saloon was customarily a favorite social gathering place. Here, men could imbibe, take in a game of chance, or engage in a short-term love affair upstairs with one of the ladies of easy virtue. More important, it was a place where one could catch up on the latest news of the day, meet up with someone from home, or strike up a profitable financial deal.

Not all the pockets of gold were located alongside narrow gulches. A good deal of it was found in prospectors' trouser pockets, and there were experts who knew how to remove it. These opportunists performed with all the zeal of a snake oil

A faro game in progress at Morenci. Photo: Southwest Studies.

salesman with a brand new concoction. It was called mining the miner, or separating some sucker from his poke sack.

There was a limitless market in selling intimacy to lonely, love-starved men. The colorful ladies bore a litany of picturesque nicknames like Squirrel-tooth Alice, Crazy Horse Lil, Frenchy Moustache, Lizette the Flying Nymph, and Little Gertie, the Gold Dollar. These aliases weren't just to mask their identity. Sometimes they referred to some unique physical characteristic. As long as a town prospered, they stayed, but when the mines played out they were among the first to sense the economic crisis and move on.

Reasons for entering the profession were as varied as the women themselves. Some came from respectable families, while others were escaping from malevolent husbands. Some became prostitutes as a lark or from some sense of adventure; others were forced into it. A few lucky ones married some respectable gent and left the profession. Others went into business for themselves and some even became quite wealthy. Most, however, fell victim to the hazards of the trade, became strung out on drugs and booze, or died and were buried in lonely, unmarked graves.

Public acceptance can be fickle. These ladies were, at first, welcomed by love-starved men, but as the community matured they were ostracized and restricted to "districts." Those notorious shady ladies sold companionship in a variety of settings ranging from ramshackle cribs to opulent mansions.

In saloons and burlesque theaters, they were required to mingle with the customers and hustle drinks when they weren't performing. Tombstone's Bird Cage Theater, located on the south side of Allen Street, was typical. The evening's entertainment began with a variety of burlesque shows titillating the audiences with risque vaudeville acts. Private booths with drawn curtains in the balcony were reserved for the big spenders. A stairway backstage leading up to the balcony allowed the girls the opportunity to earn an extra few dollars for a few intimate moments behind closed drapes.

Between performances the girls worked as waitresses. For each round of drinks a girl was given a token worth one bit or 12-1/2 cents. At the end of the evening she could redeem her tokens for cash. As the evening wore on, the chairs and tables were moved back against the walls and the place was turned into a dance hall.

Allen Street was the main thoroughfare through Tombstone, and during the early 1880s it was one of Arizona's most notorious Babylons. Like the town itself, the street had a split personality. The south side was devoted to respectable businesses such as stores and restaurants. But the north side of the street was hell with the lid off. The sounds of boisterous laughter, rinky-tink piano music and the spinning of roulette wheels could be heard 24 hours a day.

Respectable women were afraid to walk down the dusty boardwalks on the north side for fear they might be mistaken for the opprobrious Blond Marie, Dutch Annie or Rowdy Kate.

Each community had its popular Sodom and Gomorrah. During the 1890s there were more than 600 saloons in the territory. Beer was brewed locally. However, most of the whiskey was imported from the "states." Empty beer bottles, planted bottoms up, provided Phoenix with its first "paved" street. Tucson had the Legal Tender and the Congress Hall. The latter boasted of a nightly shooting scrape. Clifton had the Blue Goose; and Jerome had the Fashion. The Cowboy Saloon in Douglas was one of the rowdiest on the Mexican border. Globe boasted the Gold Coin, and Pearce had the Bucket of Blood. Washington Street was where most Phoenicians gathered to imbibe. One establishment, the Palace, dubbed itself proudly "the only second-class saloon in the territory." Some form of reverse advertising, no doubt. Bisbee's famous Brewery Gulch had saloons that ran all the way up Zacatecas Canyon.

The most raucous kinds of entertainment were curtailed in the early part of the 20th Century. Gambling was outlawed in 1907. Seven years later the "prohibs" got control, and after one last glorious spree on New Year's Eve, Arizona went "dry" until 1933. Undaunted, those who wanted to imbibe had no trouble finding illegal booze. During the 1920s, Tucson alone had some 150 bootleggers. Residents of Bisbee made the short drive across the Mexican border to Naco, where the liquor flowed and the gaming casinos ran 24 hours a day.

During the latter part of the 19th Century, traveling

theater groups added a touch of cultural class to the entertainment-starved communities of remote Arizona. Silver-rich mining towns like Tombstone could afford to hire the best. Boom-town citizens considered themselves as refined as their eastern cousins and set about to prove it by inviting well-known acting companies to perform in Schieffelin Hall and the Bird Cage Theater.

Still, an occasional lack of social grace and cultural refinement was displayed, much to the embarrassment of the town's more refined citizens. During the 19th Century, "Uncle Tom's Cabin" was one of America's most popular plays. This dramatic story of the antebellum South brought tears from even the most hardened viewers of melodrama. During the scene in which fearsome bloodhounds were pursuing little Eliza on a frozen river, a drunken cowboy in the audience stood up, drew his revolver and shot one of the dogs. Members of the audience, incensed with this interruption on the part of the uncouth knight-in-dusty-leather, pounced upon him and there was talk of a lynching. Fortunately, a lawman was present and hauled the young caballero off to jail. The following day a sober, repentant cowboy apologized to the troupe and offered his favorite horse as a stand-in for the deceased canine.

When professional acting troupes were not available, the locals organized their own amateur shows. Nearly every community had at least one theater company.

Church socials and picnics were always a favorite pastime. Even more popular were Sunday afternoon baseball games. Fierce rivalries developed between Globe and Miami, Bisbee and Douglas, Clifton and Morenci, and betting was always heavy. For several years, rivalry existed between Tombstone's hard rock miners and the soldiers at Fort Huachuca. Providing umpires was the responsibility of the hosts and there was a definite home team advantage. A notable exception was during the brief tenure of the Reverend Endicott Peabody, who founded St. Paul's Episcopal Church at Tombstone. When Peabody was called upon to umpire the baseball games, he could be counted on to "call 'em fair and square." The preacher was also an amateur boxer who had taken on some of Tombstone's finest pugilists. Players usually thought twice before questioning his calls. He also used his talents as leverage to increase the size of his congregation by requiring boisterous miner-athletes to attend church services.

Phoenix residents in the late 19th Century took their pleasure in picnic outings in the desert or a buggy ride up on the Salt River to go swimming on a Sunday afternoon.

One popular form of vigorous activity, enjoyed by Phoenix residents today, goes back to territorial days — climbing up the rocky precipice at Squaw Peak.

These hard-working people with limited leisure time made the most of the national holidays. The Fourth of July was the favorite. Nearly every community had a colorful parade. The town's marching band led the way, followed by volunteer hose companies decked out in their fire-fighting apparel. Later in the day, the firemen from rival companies would hold match races to see who could pull the hose carts the fastest. Competition was fierce as the winner had braggin' rights for the coming year.

In cattle country, folks gathered from miles around to have a barbeque at some ranch. Ranch hands from various outfits competed against each other in roping and bronc-riding events. Friendly wagers were placed on the contestants, adding to the excitement. These makeshift affairs, done without the arenas, heralded the beginnings of professional rodeos.

Mining communities, always bursting with energy, went all out on Independence Day. From dawn to dusk celebrants blew up cast iron anvils with small powder charges, held wrestling and boxing matches, ran footraces, tugs of war and various other competitive events. The highlights of the day were the drilling contests. Rawhide-tough, hard rock miners competed against each other and the clock for 15 minutes to see who could drill the deepest hole in a block of solid granite.

There was, as might be expected, a great deal of personal and civic pride involved in these contests. Miners came from as far away as Butte, Montana to compete. Spectators gathered by the thousands to watch and wager their hard-earned money on the outcome. During the heyday of these drilling contests, 1890 to 1916, mining companies sponsored their best drillers and put up prize money for the winners. Local merchants donated other prizes.

Huge blocks of Gunnison granite, a fine-grained and uniformly hard rock, were shipped in for the events by railroad or freight wagons. Wooden platforms were erected to place contestants and judges above street level, and to give the crowd a clear view.

In all, there were three drilling contests: One was single jack, or one man swinging a four-pound hammer and turning his own drill bit. The second was the double-hand drilling with two men working as a team, one swinging an eight-pound hammer and the other turning the bit. They would alternate every 60 seconds, and the exchange required a great deal of teamwork and finesse. It was said that a good team could actually gain a stroke on the exchange. In the straight-away contest, one man would swing the eight-pound hammer and the other would hold the bit for the entire 15-minute contest. As the hole deepened and the drill bits became extremely hot, the turner would grab a new one.

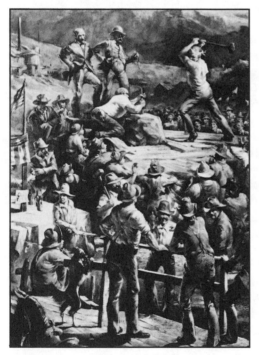

The most memorable of these drilling contests occurred on July 4, 1903, at Bisbee. Championship teams from Idaho, Montana and Colorado gathered in the plaza in front of the Copper Queen Hotel to compete for $800 in prize money. That was no small amount, considering the average hard rock miner earned only $3.50 a day.

Fred Yockey started things off by winning the single-jack contest, drilling a hole 26-3/8 inches

"Miners' Holiday," a pen and ink by Bill Ahrendt, illustrates the popular drilling contests.

deep in 15 minutes. Yockey struck his four-pound hammer an amazing 140 blows per minute. It has been called the greatest exhibition of hammering ever seen. The record set that day in Bisbee has never been broken.

Next was the double-jack team of Ed Chamberlain and Carl Make. They'd never been beaten. Despite herculean efforts of others to unseat the pair, it was to no avail. They were a flawless team working in perfect rhythm. At the end of 15 minutes a new world record was set at 46-3/4 inches.

The perennial champion of the straight-away was Sel Tarr, the so-called John L. Sullivan of drilling. He, too, had never been beaten. The large crowd began to sense an upset as Bill Moss, a mountain of a man who swung a mighty hammer with all the force of the mythical John Henry, finished with a 35-1/2-inch hole.

Tarr's turn was next and his drill turner was good friend Ed Malley. The muscular six-footer began to swing his hammer at 70 blows per minute, but, as the hole began to deepen, he increased his rate to an amazing 85 strokes. The waterman splashed cool water into the hole to keep it clean and cool the hot drill bit between the mightly blows from Tarr's hammer. Steam rose from the hole as Malley rotated the bit. On the exchange of the 13th bit, Tarr's hammer glanced off and struck Malley on the forehead. A blinding profusion of blood poured off onto his hands and into the hole. It would violate the strict code of steel-driving men to stop under any circumstances, and Malley hung in there gripping and turning. A mixture of sweat, water and blood splashed on contestants, judges and spectators alike as Tarr continued his relentless pace. When time was called and the hole was measured, Sel Tarr had established a new world's record of an amazing 38-5/8 inches.

Drilling contests are still held in towns such as Bisbee today, but the old records aren't in danger of being broken. The events are more of a tribute to the past, honoring that hardy breed of hard-rock drillers.

So, next time you're looking through the old family album, consider this: the stolid countenance of grandma and grandpa might be caused by tight corsets and stiff paper collars. And it just might be possible that, after they finished sitting for the photographer, they switched to some less formal attire and jogged up Squaw Peak.

The dawning of the 20th Century brought little change to rural Arizona. A pair of Levi's cost 75 cents, beef was 10 cents a pound, a haircut went for two bits, and you could purchase a suit of clothes for five dollars. In 1908 Tucsonians petitioned the city council for an ordinance against spitting on sidewalks. Ah, civilization was rapidly encroaching.

15

THE BABY STATE

In 1912, after years of political hassle over statehood, free silver, bigotry, hostile Indians and outlaws, Arizona prepared to take its place as the 48th state in the Union — The Baby State. The First Arizona State Legislature in 1912 gave women the right to vote eight years before suffrage was obtained nationally. Two years later, Arizona went "dry" as Prohibition was voted in. Bootleggers entered into a period of great prosperity.

Women asserted themselves as never before. In 1914 Rachel Allen Berry and Frances Willard Munds were elected to the Arizona House and Senate, respectively. Berry was the first woman in the nation to serve in the House, and Munds was the second in the nation to serve in the Senate. In 1915 a pretty, barnstorming, daredevil pilot named Katherine Stinson made Arizona's first air mail delivery at Tucson.

That same year Nellie Trent Bush became a riverboat pilot on the Colorado River, the only woman ever to do so. In 1920 she was elected to the Arizona Legislature and served there for 16 years. In 1921 she entered law school at the University of Arizona. There she met Lorna Lockwood, a native of Tombstone. Women's liberation was still light years away, even on a university campus. Once Bush and Lockwood were banned from law school classes when the subject of rape was being discussed. Nellie protested to the dean, asking if he'd ever heard of a case of rape that didn't involve a woman. The women were allowed back in class. Nellie later took up flying and became one of Arizona's first licensed pilots. During the

Colorado River controversy in the 1930s, she allowed the Arizona National Guard to use her steamboats to "invade" California. In gratitude Governor Ben Moeur named her "Admiral of Arizona's Navy."

Lorna Lockwood, a native of Tombstone. She was the first woman to be Chief Justice of a state supreme court. Photo: Arizona Hall of Fame.

Lorna Lockwood had a distinguished career in law. She served 14 years on the Arizona Supreme Court. In 1965 she became Chief Justice, the first woman to hold that position in the United States.

The livestock business took a rather odd twist around the turn of the century when ranchers started trading in their cows for ostriches. Women's fashions dictated the move. Only two ostriches survived the first shipment into Arizona, but fortunately one was male, the other female. Soon the huge eggs began to hatch. Later, one rancher paid $16,000 for 21 pairs of breeding birds and two years later doubled his money on the sale of chicks. In 1910, 4,023 ostriches had their feathers plucked and the crop was valued at $1,365,000. Ostrich farms became as common as today's convenience markets. Feathers sold for around $75 a pound. Extremely ornery when provoked, ostriches could be harder to handle than cattle. An adult might weigh up to 300 pounds and stood 8 feet tall. They could run up to 60 miles per hour in 25-foot strides. Shippers had to place hoods over their heads in transit to discourage escape. And "ostrich-boys" really had their hands full if the bunch started to stampede. Eggs were harvested both for incubation and eating. It was said an ostrich egg was equivalent to 33 hens' eggs. Ostrich meat was coarse and stringy, but in 1914 at least one restaurant advertised "Roasted Ostrich" on its menu.

Towards the end of World War I ostrich feathers went out of fashion on ladies' hats and dresses. Ostrich ranching, a major industry in the Valley for several years, died out.

During these years, horseless carriages became affordable to the common man. Earlier, in 1910, the Touring Club of America was proposing an "Ocean to Ocean" highway that would pass through Prescott and Phoenix. A Chalmers 40 automobile sold for $2,750. More reasonable was the Ford Model T touring car which went for $700. For an extra 80 bucks you could have a windshield, speedometer, canvas top and headlights. Horse and mule enthusiasts stubbornly resisted the newfangled contraptions and took great delight in ridiculing the auto at every opportunity. "Get a horse," they shouted gleefully when they passed a motorist stuck in some mud hole. Despite the reliability problems with cars, drivers could claim a few advantages also. "You only have to feed 'em when you use 'em," they insisted.

Although the first automobile was patented in 1885, Arizona's first auto didn't arrive until 1899. The "gas buggy," as it was called, caught on quickly after Dr. Hiram Fenner of Tucson "cruised Main" with his *Locomobile*. No doubt, horse and buggy advocates in this Spanish-speaking area thought it was well-named. Since service stations hadn't arrived on the scene, auto owners purchased gas and oil at a local drug store. Major repairs were performed by a blacksmith. Because dealerships were a dream of the future, the horseless carriages were purchased at bicycle shops.

Since the earliest days of the territory, roads, or lack of them, have been a major problem. When Arizona became a state in 1912 highways were little more than cattle trails. A series of road races were staged between 1908 and 1914 to promote better highways. Daredevil drivers such as Louis Chevrolet and Barney Oldfield competed for the title "Master Driver of the World" in the "Cactus Derby," a 500-mile race over dirt roads between Los Angeles and Phoenix. The three-day race also offered a $2,500 purse and competitors left $50,000 worth of parts strewn across the desert trying to claim that prize. The contestants in road races weren't always men. In 1910 the *Arizona Gazette* sponsored a race from Prescott to Phoenix. The winner was Harriet Fay Southworth, wife of a Prescott physician. Driving a Ford, she beat out seven other drivers in a time of 6 hours, 33 minutes. When she wasn't racing cars, Harriet Fay performed in amateur theater shows in Prescott. A daughter, Dorothy Fay, later married the famous Hollywood singing cowboy, Tex Ritter.

In 1916, an "ocean to ocean" caravan crossed Arizona's desert and mountain roadways promoting highways. Yet, by 1930 there were still less than 300 miles of paved highway in the state. In 1944, the Federal Highway Act established a national system of highways leading to the completion of Route 66 across northern Arizona and Route 80 across the southern part of the state. In 1956 the Interstate Defense System, a controlled-access, multi-lane-freeway building program, began.

When Arizona became a state in 1912, fewer than 2,000 vehicles were registered. By 1920, the number had increased to nearly 35,000. A decade later the figure was just under 125,000 vehicles. In 2002, 4.7 million vehicles were registered (including cars, trucks, trailers, and golf carts) and Arizona had 52,245 miles of highways.

In 1917 public drinking cups and common-use towels were banned. That same year the legislature established a $10-a-week minimum wage for women and adopted the design for the state flag. Many protested, claiming it looked too much like the Japanese flag.

The more things change the more they stay the same: Phoenix newspapers in the early 1900s took issue with drunk drivers, complaining they should be locked up in the state pen. They also wrote extensively about other contemporary subjects such as race relations, drug traffic, gun control and women's liberation. There was a prediction by some scientists that life on planet Earth would cease to exist because nitrogen was being taken from the atmosphere to make fertilizer. On July 27, 1913 the Phoenix chief of police decried the rise of women's skirts, claiming he would enforce a city ordinance that forbade a woman to expose more than 2 inches of ankle.

The main issue here wasn't the length of the hemline, but rather, the newest rage from Paris, the slit skirt. A local entertainer, Beatrice Gonzales, called the chief's bluff by strolling down Washington Street in a dress that had a slit that nearly reached her knee. A crowd of reporters and spectators gathered to witness the occasion but no arrests were made. It was reported the dress concealed much more than it revealed.

In the age of high technology we've gotten accustomed to big screen television and VCR's right in our homes. But back in the early 1900s people were mystified by the wonders of motion pictures.

A young cowboy from the CO Bar Ranch out north of Flagstaff drifted into town one day to the local movie theater. He watched the screen, in wide-eyed amazement, as several young women began to remove their clothing prior to getting into a swimming hole. Then a freight train crossed in front of them and obscured the interesting parts. After the train passed and the smoke from the engine cleared, the lovely ladies were safely attired in their swim suits. Undaunted, the cowboy rushed out and bought several more tickets. When the attendant asked why, the cowboy replied "I don't know much about these new-fangled picture shows, but I do know something about freight trains. At least one of them's gonna be late and I aim to be there when it happens."

GUNS ALONG THE BORDER

Arizona had been in the Union a little over two years when World War I began in Europe. For Arizonans the war really began with the Mexican Revolution of 1910. The fighting had a major impact on border states such as Arizona. At times it created a special diversion for citizens in Douglas, Bisbee, Naco and Nogales, while on the other hand it provided a training ground for green U.S. soldiers prior to entering the war in Europe.

In 1911, revolutionaries under Tucson-born Gen. Martin "Red" Lopez surrounded an army of *federales* at Agua Prieta, across the border from Douglas. The defenders fortified themselves along the U.S. border, forcing the revolutionaries to fire towards the American town. Stray bullets from the battle oftentimes sent Douglas residents scurrying for cover. One

Adobe buildings couldn't withstand the fierce gunfights during the siege of Naco in 1914. Photo: Arizona Historical Society.

enterprising hotel owner nailed corrugated sheets of tin on the walls of his establishment and, with tongue-in-cheek humor, dubbed his business the "Bullet-proof Hotel." Spectators gathered eagerly atop railroad cars or any lofty vantage point to see the action.

In 1914, Gen. Francisco "Pancho" Villa attacked *federales* loyal to Venustiano Carranza at Naco, Sonora. Again the *Carranzistas* were entrenched with their backs to the U.S. border forcing residents of Naco, Arizona, to pile sandbags on their southern exposure. Black soldiers from the Ninth and Tenth Cavalry, stationed along the border, planted red flags along the unmarked border in hopes of keeping the battlers in Sonora. During the next two months, some 54 Americans were wounded, most of them by stray bullets.

On one occasion some *federales* were firing into the American side, prompting Cochise County Sheriff Harry Wheeler to ride between the warring factions carrying a white flag. The former Arizona Ranger captain persuaded both sides to relocate. The two armies apologized for any inconvenience they might have caused and moved their battle to another site.

During the siege of Naco, Sonora, Villa's men dragged a small cannon up a mountain overlooking the town and lobbed shells from on high. The damage was slight because, with each shot, the recoil caused the cannon to roll down the slope, causing long delays between firings.

Another time a band of revolutionaries loaded a railroad boxcar with explosives and tried to push it into the federales' lines. The boxcar jumped the tracks and exploded harmlessly. It did put on a spectacular fireworks display for the *turistas* gathered on the American side.

Villa was way ahead of his time when it comes to promotional stunts. Once he persuaded a Hollywood film company to make a war picture starring him and his army. He promised to stage his battles only during hours when the light exposure was good for the cameras. The film was shot but was a flop at the box office. Evidently real warfare wasn't realistic enough for moviegoers.

Pancho Villa was, in some ways, too wedded to 19th Century warfare to win 20th Century battles. During the Battle of Celaya he stubbornly

Francisco "Pancho" Villa, revolutionary leader during Mexican Revolution of 1910. Photo: Arizona Historical Society.

insisted on sending his famed cavalry, the "Dorados," against the barbed wire and machine gun emplacements. But at times he was also a visionary. Once he hired an American aviator to train his young pilot-recruits for aerial warfare. Since there weren't any airfields, the plane used a rocky cow pasture. During a demonstration landing, the pilot, Ed Parsons, touched down on the uncurried turf. The craft bounced violently before coming to a halt in a boiling cloud of dust. When the air cleared, Villa's fledgling young pilots had disappeared into the wild green yonder. Villa's "air force" never got off the ground.

During the early years of the revolution, Villa had been friendly towards the United States. However, in October, 1915 President Woodrow Wilson, seeking stability in war-torn Mexico, threw his support behind Villa's arch-rival Carranza. When Villa attacked Agua Prieta, Wilson allowed the *Carranzistas* to board American trains and travel inside the United States to intercept the *Villistas*. When Villa launched a night attack against Agua Prieta, huge searchlights were turned on, blinding his troops. Hundreds of *Villistas* were slaughtered by machine-gun fire. Supporters of Villa naturally blamed the *Americanos* for the defeat suffered at the border town.

That same year, Villa captured Nogales, Sonora, and had a shootout with American soldiers. Anticipating trouble, Col. William Sage deployed American sharpshooters along International Street. When Villa's hungry soldiers threatened to cross the border in search of food, a 30-minute gunfight broke out. Several *Villistas* were killed before order was restored.

In 1918, Nogales became the scene of more violence when a Mexican arms smuggler was shot while sneaking across the border. Tempers flared and armed citizens from both sides of the border opened fire. Mexican and American troops arrived on the scene and they, too, began exchanging gunfire. The two sides battled for four days before Arizona Governor George Hunt and his Sonoran counterpart, Plutarco Calles, arranged a truce. More than 30 Americans were killed and some 80 Mexicans, including the mayor of Nogales, Sonora, died in the fighting.

Supporters of Pancho Villa, still smarting from his defeat at Agua Prieta and blaming the Americans for their setbacks, launched a bold raid into the United States at Columbus, New

Mexico in March 1916. In a surprise early-morning raid, 17 American soldiers were killed. U.S. troops rallied quickly, inflicting heavy casualties on the *Villistas* before chasing them back into Chihuahua. As a result of this action, President Wilson ordered a punitive expedition under Gen. John J. "Black Jack" Pershing into Mexico to capture Villa.

For nearly a year, Pershing's men kept Villa on the run but never succeeded in catching him. In Mexico the elusive revolutionary became something of a Robin Hood who made fools of the *gringos*. In Arizona he was more of a bogeyman.

After the Arizona National Guard was mobilized and sent to the border at Douglas, rumors began to circulate that Villa was hiding in Arizona and was going to blow up Roosevelt Dam. Others claimed he was planning a bank-robbing spree in Phoenix, Mesa and Tempe. The Arizonans quickly organized home guard units. A local bank furnished rifles and ammunition for training, while ladies prepared for the impending battle by taking Red Cross instruction.

If the problems along the Mexican border did nothing else, they prepared the citizens and soldiers for a much tougher war overseas. Revolutions in Mexico would continue right into the late 1920s.

The turbulence created along the Mexican border, coming at the same time America was preparing for war against Germany, was not just coincidental. It was later learned of the existence of a so-called Plan of San Diego, orchestrated by the Germans, that called for a general uprising of all Mexican border states against the United States. Germany's strategy was to keep U.S. troops occupied along the Southwest borders and keep them out of the war in Europe. In March 1917 the Zimmermann Note was intercepted by British naval intelligence. The note, written by German Foreign Secretary Arthur Zimmermann, outlined a plan of action to be taken in the event of war between the United States and Germany. Germany proposed an alliance that, in return for its support, would return Arizona, New Mexico and Texas to Mexico after the war.

When contents of the Zimmermann Note were made public, emotions against Germany ran high. Up to then, many Arizonans hadn't been overly concerned with the war in Europe.

Arizonans went off to World War I with a patriotic zeal that had come to characterize its frontier-bred citizens. Governor Tom Campbell offered to resign his office and raise a company of "Rough Riders." The state contributed more soldiers, sailors, and marines per capita than any other, and fewer were rejected because of physical disabilities. The Arizona National Guard, the 158th Infantry Regiment, served with valor and after the war was chosen as President Wilson's special honor guard during the Paris Peace Conference.

Overseas, several Arizonans distinguished themselves in combat. Marine Private John Henry Pruitt of the Verde Valley singlehandedly captured 40 German soldiers and killed several others. He was killed in action at Mont Blanc in 1918. Phoenix native Frank Luke, Jr. served in a combat zone for only 17 days and flew just 10 combat missions. In that short time Luke became a legend among aviators, shooting down 14 German observation balloons and 4 aircraft. On September 29, 1918, in just 10 minutes, he knocked down three balloons and two planes. Because they were so well guarded by anti-

Frank Luke of Phoenix shot down 18 German planes and observation balloons during World War I and became the first aviator to win the Congressional Medal of Honor. He died in combat on September 29, 1918. Photo: Southwest Studies.

aircraft guns and fighter planes, attacks on balloons were considered more dangerous than regular aerial combat missions. That same day, Luke's plane was shot down behind enemy lines. He crash-landed, then stepped out of the craft, drew his revolver and shot it out with German infantry troops. He died in a hail of gunfire and was given a hero's burial by the Germans. Both Pruitt and Luke were awarded the Congressional Medal of Honor for their bravery.

In other aerial combat, Lt. Ralph O'Neill of Nogales and Major Reed Chambers of Fort Huachuca shot down five and seven German planes, respectively. Both earned the coveted right to the title "ace" given to pilots with five or more kills. Mathew Juan, a Pima Indian from Sacaton, was the first of 321 Arizonans and also the first Native American, to die in the War.

On the home front, the patriotic fever sent a four-man posse into the remote Galiuro Mountains to bring in a pair of suspected draft dodgers. Two brothers, Tom and John Power, allegedly refused to register for the draft. The posse surrounded their cabin on a foggy February morning in 1918 and, supposedly without warning, opened fire, killing Jeff Power, the boys' father. In the ensuing gunfight, three posse men were killed. A fourth managed to escape. Details of the gunfight are still debated today. The brothers, with the aid of a friend, Tom Sisson, fled towards Mexico with a posse of some 3,000 men hot on their heels. It was the largest manhunt in Arizona history. They were captured by U.S. soldiers

Mathew Juan, Pima Indian, was the first Arizonan and first Native American to die in combat in World War I. Photo: Southwest Studies.

just below the Mexican border and turned over to the posse after being given assurances the three men would not be lynched. The young men had already been tried and convicted in the press. Long lines of curious spectators came to see the desperados, so local authorities put them on public display in cages. Their conviction at Clifton was a foregone conclusion and the three were locked up in the state prison at Florence.

Despite the circumstances surrounding their gunfight and the killing of their father, the two brothers served 42 years in prison before they were released in 1960. Their accomplice, Sisson, died behind bars in the mid-1950s. Each time they came up for parole, relatives of the slain lawmen persuaded authorities to keep them in prison. A year prior to the gunfight, Arizona had outlawed the death penalty; otherwise the three men would have been executed. A year later, because of the incident, the death penalty was reinstated. Their 42-year term was by far the longest ever served in an Arizona prison.

Patriotic fever wasn't the only kind that swept through Arizona during World War I. The Great Spanish Flu Epidemic besieged the citizens of Arizona and the rest of the nation, and before the virus was controlled in 1919, more than half a million Americans succumbed. During the height of the epidemic, social gatherings and sporting events were prohibited and even pool halls were closed to prevent folks from gathering unnecessarily. Schools around the state were converted into hospitals while citizens in Phoenix and Tucson were required to wear gauze "flu" masks in public. A special police unit arrested those going in public unmasked. Anyone offering a friendly handshake was looked on with apprehension or suspicion. In early 1919, the virus mysteriously changed its target and went after pigs and chickens, leaving a decimated human race in its destructive wake.

World War I brought much prosperity to Arizona. Prior to the war, the economy was in a downturn. At the outbreak of the war in 1914, business propered again until the German U-boats closed the shipping lanes. America's entry into the war on April 6, 1917 had a dramatic, positive effect on the state's economy. Copper, cotton, cattle and lumber, along with the horse and mule business, boomed. In 1918 farmers around Scottsdale could earn enough on one cotton crop to pay off the mortgage. Pima, a long-staple high-grade cotton fiber developed on the Pima Indian Reservation, was used as a fabric on airplanes and in the new balloon tires. Cotton quickly became the major crop in Arizona and today remains the king of agriculture in the state.

The cotton boom also brought significant sociological changes to Arizona during these years as many farmers converted semi-grazing lands, previously used for dairy cattle, to cotton fields. For the next several years, a large number of transient cotton pickers swarmed into the state and, when there wasn't any work, became a burden on welfare programs.

The "Great War to End All Wars" ended on November 11, 1918. The news reached Arizona in the middle of the night. Despite the late hour, citizens staged impromptu parades and pep rallies. Church and school bells rang, pistols were fired, and fireworks were set off. For those who hadn't suffered a personal loss in the war, these were the best of times. The economy was booming and employment was high. There was no reason to believe the good times weren't here to stay.

16

THE 1920s AND 1930s

Boom and Bust

The bottom fell out of the copper market in post-World War I America. The red metal which had brought 27 cents a pound in 1916 slipped to 12 cents by 1921. A new social phenomenon, buying on the installment plan, came into vogue in the late 1920s and folks loaded up on washing machines, radios, toasters, and cars, causing copper prices to rise again.

When World War I ended, cotton prices also took a plunge because the government had a huge surplus on hand. Many cotton farmers went belly up when the 1920 crop went unsold. By the late 1920s, sturdy three-wheeled tractors were rapidly replacing mules on farms. The early models had spiked iron wheels which were soon replaced by rubber-tired "tricycles." The nation's highways were filling with trucks and cars, creating a brand new market for long staple cotton which was used to strengthen the rubber tires. As early as 1928, Arizona was producing more than 40 percent of the cotton in the entire Southwest. During the cotton boom, when prices rose to $1.25 a pound, residents became part-time farmers as nearly every backyard and vacant lot in Phoenix became a cotton field.

On June 23, 1920, a real estate ad appeared in the *Arizona Republican* (today's *Arizona Republic*) offering for sale a three-room frame house for $1,500. Another advertised a six-room, double-brick house with a garage, near a streetcar line, for the grand total of $3,000. Bargain hunters could pick up a two-room home for $800 with only $200 down. These halcyon days marked the beginning of Phoenix's first real estate boom.

John Sandige, longtime Phoenix builder and developer, was the innovator behind these "wonder homes." He called them "shell houses." Sandige would subdivide parcels of land, then build small frame houses with just the bare essentials — roof, floor, walls, doors, windows, cupboards, plumbing and wiring — and also the kitchen sink. The concept was to build enough so that families could move in and do the finish work themselves.

A Sunday drive near Prescott's Thumb Butte. Photo: Arizona Historical Foundation.

By the mid-1920s, Phoenix boasted a population of 42,500. Two railroads served the area, along with 30 miles of streetcar tracks, 50 miles of paved roads, 85 miles of sidewalks, 9,363 telephones and 12 public parks. The city limits were Sixteenth Street on the east, Nineteenth Avenue on the west, McDowell Road on the north and the Salt River on the south.

Prohibition, which came to Arizona in 1914 and lasted until late 1933, was still in effect but the liquor flowed freely. Moonshiners in the mountainous parts of the state had plenty of natural cover to conceal their operations. In the desert, stills were buried in the sandy bottoms of arroyos. Government agents, armed with steel reinforcing rods, probed the sands in hopes of tapping into some hidden still. Agents used the plumbing system in a large Phoenix hotel as a way to dispose of confiscated moonshine. The process was abruptly ended when it was realized that hotel employees had figured out a way to tap into the line and had gone into the liquor business.

A raid on a whiskey still at Clifton during prohibition. Photo: Arizona Historical Society.

The air age, as far as the general public was concerned, arrived in Arizona on November 28, 1927, when Phoenix and Tucson welcomed Aero Corporation of California's Standard Air Lines. Seven-passenger Fokkers with a cruising speed of 120 mph left Los Angeles at 8 a.m. and arrived at Phoenix at 1:30 p.m. Fare in those days was $32.50 one-way. The planes had few amenities; or as one pilot put it, "no water, no toilet, no food, no nuthin'." He might have added, no radio and no navigational equipment except a compass. The plane made one stop at Desert Center, California where a gas station operator had scraped out a runway next to his business. The planes could stop to let their passengers visit the restrooms and drink a cold soda pop while the attendant filled the gas tank.

The first municipal airport in Phoenix was located at 59th Avenue and Christy Road (McDowell Road). It was so far out in the boondocks that pilots frequently couldn't locate it and landed instead at fields closer to Phoenix. The old Central Field at Central and Mohave later became the Phoenix Municipal Baseball Park. Another airstrip was at 24th Street and Van Buren near the mental hospital (which seemed somehow appropriate in those pristine days of flying).

Construction began on an 80-acre parcel of desert land, to be called Sky Harbor, on November 16, 1928. It was dedicated on Labor Day, 1929. Sky Harbor, better known as the "Farm," was way out in the country. The pavement and streetcar tracks ended at Eastlake Park on 16th Street and Washington. The rest of the trip was over what was better described as a dusty cattle trail. Despite that, 8,000 people braved the heat and dust to attend the dedication ceremonies. The biggest threat to safety didn't come from too much air traffic; cattle had to be cleared off the runway before a plane could land.

On November 23, 1927, the new air age arrived in Tucson with the dedication of the largest municipal airport in the United States. Col. Charles A. Lindbergh, the first man to fly solo across the Atlantic, threw the switch on the rotating beacon on Dedication Day in front of 20,000 spectators. A cactus-replica of Lindbergh's "Spirit of St. Louis" airplane was constructed for the historic occasion. The full size model was made mostly from saguaro and ocotillo. Barrel cactus was used for the cylinders and the propellor from prickly pear. The new airport, called Davis-Monthan, was a joint-use facility with the City of Tucson paying 80 percent and the military picking up the rest. The army also built its own hangars and other structures. During this same period municipal airports were also built at Douglas and Flagstaff.

Few people outside of Arizona (few people outside of Cochise County, for that matter) have ever heard of Naco. Actually, there are two Nacos, one on each side of the Mexican border 10 miles south of Bisbee. During Prohibition these two neighbors, like most small border towns, were by day sleepy, quiet villages. The streets were dusty and unpaved. But after dark the similarity ended. Naco, Sonora bistros lighted up like Christmas trees, beckoning to pleasure seekers, much the same as the sirens tempted the followers of Ulysses.

Today, both Nacos are quiet and the rip-roaring days are only a fading memory. Few can remember that Naco, Sonora, was once a familiar haunt for the notorious Pancho Villa and other revolutionaries. Even fewer know that Naco, Arizona claims the distinction of being the only community in the continental United States to have been bombarded from an airplane by a foreign power. It all happened back in 1929 during the Topete Revolution. The *federale* troops were entrenched on three sides of the town with their backs to the American border while the rebel force occupied the surrounding countryside. One skirmish occurred when a number of the *federales* garrisoned at Naco switched sides, joining the rebels, and were planning to take the town — after the gambling house closed and Bisbee residents went home, of course. Incidentally, changing sides was a rather common occurrence during these revolts. Generals were known to reverse the cause of their armies if the price was right.

Now the stage was set for the air attack. It began when a roguish barnstorming pilot named Patrick Murphy offered his services to the rebel forces. "I can blow the *federales* right out of their trenches," he boasted. The revolutionary leaders were quick to seize upon the opportunity to extricate the well-entrenched federal troops from Naco, so the soldier of fortune and his nondescript biplane became the Rebel Air Force.

The bombs used in these air raids were primitive affairs. Sometimes all the pilots had in the arsenal were leather pouches loaded with explosives, scrap iron and sundry items. They were ignited by a fuse which was left peeking out through the opening at the top of the bag. The bombardier was usually a young, cigarette-smoking hireling whose primary responsibility was to light the fuse with his cigarette and simply drop the suitcase-size pouch over the side. Whether or not these bombs did any real damage is a matter of conjecture; however, they did provide much entertainment for the spectators on the American side of the border. Whatever it was that inspired

Murphy to bomb Naco, Arizona has remained a historical mystery. Several of his missiles landed in Arizona, one going through the roof of Newton's Garage and destroying a Dodge automobile parked inside. Another blasted a store owned by Phelps Dodge. The raid ceased when one of the locals stepped outside with a 30.06 Springfield rifle and shot Murphy's plane down, thus ending another harrowing adventure on the Arizona scene. Murphy was picked up and jailed at Nogales for a time, then disappeared from the pages of Arizona history.

Some of the remnants of these turbulent times are still in evidence on the Arizona side. There is the "Bullet-proof Hotel," a tongue-in-cheek appellation applied to the rooming house that had been armor-plated with corrugated tin. Standing forlorn in a state of ruin behind the customs station today is a red brick building, the old Phelps Dodge store, the target of the Naco *Blitzkreig* of 1929.

The Depression of the 1930s brought hard times to Arizonans. Its devastating effects took longer to be felt in Arizona

Fixing a flat on the open road in 1926 was a three-man job. Service stations were few and far between. Photo: Arizona Historical Society.

than in much of the nation, but it held on for a longer period. Federal work projects such as the Civilian Conservation Corps (C.C.C.) helped by hiring unemployed young men to build bridges, roads, and recreational facilities around the state. These camps were semi-military in structure and helped prepare the men for duty in the war that followed. By 1940, there were 27 C.C.C. camps located throughout Arizona.

School districts suffered during these years as the number of transients and migrant families increased, placing a larger burden on the schools which were, at the same time, laying off teachers to cut back on costs. There was even serious discussion about closing the college at Tempe until the good times returned.

Cotton was hit particularly hard by the Depression and prices dropped to as low as four cents a pound in 1938. Cattlemen and sheep men saw their markets drop from nine cents a pound in 1929 to three cents four years later. By 1939, the price had risen to only seven cents. The price of wool went from 36 cents to nine, then back up to 20 cents during those same years.

The population of Arizona decreased by some 50,000 people between 1932 and 1936 as people packed their belongings and moved on. Many of these came from the copper towns. In 1929, national copper consumption dropped by 25 percent and, when a huge amount of Arizona copper was dumped on the market against foreign competition, the price dropped to six cents a pound. Nearly all the copper mines in the state were either closed or cutting way back on production between 1931 and 1934. The Clifton-Morenci mine didn't open again until 1937. Unable to produce by-products such as gold, silver, zinc, and lead, which paid much of the overhead in copper production, companies had to cut even more jobs. The copper industry would never again see the glorious days of prosperity it had come to know during World War I. Nor would it ever again wield the mighty power and influence on politics and business in the state.

Ironically, some of Arizona's greatest resorts were built during the depression years. Resorts for winter visitors to the Salt River Valley actually began in Scottsdale back in 1909, with the opening of the Ingleside Inn. The fabulous San Marcos

Camping in the wilds in 1938 was a far cry from the amenities of today. Photo: Arizona Historical Society, Winn collection.

Hotel in Chandler opened three years later. Wealthy socialites from the East usually came west by train. Most stayed the entire winter, enjoying picnics in the desert, playing golf on desert courses that used oiled greens instead of grass, riding horseback, and basking in the sun. Before long the Valley was booming with resorts. Dude ranches such as the K L Bar and Remuda in Wickenburg, along with the Flying V and Tanque Verde at Tucson, offered tourists an opportunity to experience the "wild and wooly" West, first hand. Thus, the "unsung hero" of Arizona industry — tourism — was born. Among the best known in the Salt River Valley were Jokake Inn, which opened in 1925, the Westward Ho in 1928, the Arizona Biltmore in 1929, and the Camelback Inn in 1936. In 1928, the luxurious El Conquistador Hotel opened in Tucson. The "Arizona Mission" architecturally designed hotel was a community effort, as locals purchased nearly $350,000 of stock in the enterprise. Unfortunately, the grand hotel never really panned out for its investors. In 1968 it was finally torn down and the El Con shopping center was built on the site. Isabella Greenway's Arizona Inn, built in 1931, offered a quiet elegance and was more successful. These resorts were the exclusive playgrounds of the rich and famous during the depression years. However, the good times were coming and before long even ordinary folks would be able to afford to spend some time in the sun.

The Great Depression was in full bloom by 1932 and hard times had fallen on the rural community of Mesa. It was the height of the Christmas shopping season and local merchants were feeling the pinch. Not only was business slack but it looked as if the annual Christmas parade was going to be a big flop.

John McPhee, colorful editor of the *Mesa Tribune*, looked upon the dismal scenario and was determined to inject some spirit into the holidays. The popular McPhee loved promotional schemes and he came up with an idea to save the Christmas parade —an idea that dazzled the town merchants with its brilliance.

"Why not," he asked, "hire a parachutist to dress up in a Santa suit and jump from an airplane? Then he can lead the annual Christmas parade through town."

Never before had Santa dropped from the sky dangling beneath a billowing canopy.

Now remember, parachuting was considered a dangerous stunt in those times. For that matter, aviation was still in the realm of adventure. Lindbergh had crossed the Atlantic solo only five years earlier. Well, the merchants loved the idea. Their eyes sparkled with gleeful anticipation. They could already hear jingle bells, or better yet, the jingle-jangle of change dropping into their cash registers.

McPhee persuaded an itinerant stunt pilot to make the jump in a rented Santa suit and all seemed well — that is, until the morning of the big event when the stunt man failed to appear. McPhee finally located his flying Santa screwing up his courage in a local tavern. In fact, he had screwed it up so tight that he couldn't get off the bar stool. The merchants were worried. "What now?" they asked.

"Fear not!" said the irrepressible editor. "I'll borrow a department store dummy Santa and have the pilot circle over the town, then push the dummy out the door. I will then appear in a Santa suit and lead the parade. No one will know the difference."

An ingenious idea, the merchants agreed.

On the day Santa was to take the plunge, a large crowd gathered near an open field on the outskirts of town, and the merchants waited anxiously. The sputtering of the tiny airplane's engine heralded Santa's arrival and the crowd gazed skyward.

Suddenly there he was — Santa himself, standing in the doorway of the aircraft. The people cheered enthusiastically. Then Santa, with parachute attached, was dropped from the plane according to plan and began a free-fall descent to earth.

Down he fell.

Down he tumbled, end over end.

Down, like the proverbial lead balloon, the limp, unopened chute streaming behind like a wisp of smoke.

Down came the dummy in the department store Santa suit—splat!—on the edge of a field in front of hundreds of horrified spectators.

Undaunted by the sudden turn of events, McPhee came out in his own Santa suit anyway and rode in the parade as if nothing had happened. But the public wasn't buying, literally or figuratively. Children went about in a daze, and downtown merchants gazed around their empty stores in dismay. McPhee was about as welcome as a coyote in a hen house.

He left town for a few days, hoping all would be forgotten, but it wasn't. He would always be remembered around Mesa as "the man who killed Santa Claus," a fact that was highlighted in his obituary nearly 40 years later.

17

HARNESSING THE GREAT RIVERS

During the latter part of the Nineteenth Century, James Addison Reavis, the self-styled "Baron of Arizona," almost pulled off one of the grandest real estate scams in Arizona history. Reavis learned to forge documents as a young soldier during the Civil War. He wrote his own furlough papers and, when he tired of soldiering, wrote himself a discharge. Later he improved his forgery skills while selling real estate in Missouri.

During this time he became aware of Spanish land grants in the Southwest and saw a chance to make millions of dollars. This fertile-minded, ex-streetcar conductor from St. Louis created a phony land grant that stretched from today's Sun City on the west, all the way to Silver City, New Mexico on the east — nearly 12 million acres. The vast expanse included the fertile Salt River Valley. The fraud was eventually exposed and Reavis was sent off to prison for a couple of years.

After his internment, the "Baron" returned to the Phoenix area. A few years earlier he'd been one of the most hated and feared men in the territory, despised by those who stood to lose their hard-earned land. Now he was just a pitiful, broken, and penniless old man. He walked the streets of downtown Phoenix telling anyone who'd listen of the wondrous potential for irrigating and farming the Salt River Valley.

His tired eyes sparkled as he described a new and grander scheme: the expansion of canals and ditches to water the thirsty land. But no one cared to listen and Reavis soon went away. In retrospect, had Reavis turned his visionary schemes and talent to honest endeavors, he might be an honored figure today.

The old "Baron" was right. The Salt River Valley was an agricultural paradise. It was nestled at the heart of some 13,000 square miles of watershed. However, the Salt River, which meandered through the valley, was as fickle as a stud at a snortin' post. One year it'd run over its banks and flood all the way into the center of Phoenix; the next year would be so dry the cows were giving powdered milk.

In 1891, a flood spread the banks of the Salt River eight miles wide, washing out the railroad bridge at Tempe. Later in the decade, water was so scarce that folks were loading up their belongings and moving on to California. It was said a cactus wren wouldn't attempt to fly across the Salt River Valley without packin' a sack lunch. Those who stayed to await better days patroled their irrigation ditches on horseback, armed with Winchesters. During the drought, brief but furious flash floods washed out dirt diversion dams, and farmers watched the precious water escape into the Gulf of California.

As early as 1889 a dam site at the junction of Tonto Creek and the Salt River had been chosen, but nothing came of the venture. Two years earlier, the Arizona Canal began carrying water, opening up new lands for farming and leading to the founding of new communities such as Scottsdale. Still, citizens were at the mercy of the temperamental Salt River. Events in the 1890s dramatized the need for a dam to store water and control flooding, but nothing much was done until 1902 when Congress passed the Newlands, or National Reclamation, Act. The act provided the federal monies to build irrigation projects in the West. The Salt River Valley was a natural choice because a community with canals and ditches was already in existence and was fed by a vast watershed.

Before the dam could be built, the federal government wanted a guaranteed repayment plan. Valley movers and shakers — among them Benjamin Fowler, Dwight Heard, John Orme, and William J. Murphy — persuaded some 4,000 landowners to put up their lands as security. Since the federal government refused to deal with individual landowners, it was necessary for local citizens to unite and form an association. Thus was born the Salt River Valley Water Users Association, later shortened to Salt River Project, whose duties would include management of the massive operation.

Theodore Roosevelt Dam, completed in 1911 at a cost of $10 million. Salt River Project paid the debt in full to the federal government by 1955. Two hundred eighty feet high, it is the world's highest masonry dam. Photo: Salt River Project.

Italian stonemasons were imported to construct what was to become the world's highest masonry dam. A 500-foot tunnel was dug to divert water, and a town named Roosevelt was established which allowed no gambling halls or saloons — a rarity in the West. Other businesses located there with the understanding that their tenure would be brief, since the town would eventually be buried beneath the waters of a huge lake. Apache road builders, under the supervision of famed scout Al Sieber, hacked out a road up to the dam site. Sieber was killed in a construction accident. He'd fought in the Civil War and survived many a shooting scrape during the Apache Wars, only to die when a loose rock came tumbling down and crushed him. Roosevelt Road was later renamed the Apache Trail. In 1987 it was formally dedicated as the first State Historic Road.

Tonto Dam became Theodore Roosevelt Dam, completed in 1911 at a cost of $10 million. The old Rough Rider, who'd led the Arizonans on the famous charge up San Juan Hill more than a decade earlier, traveled out to make the dedication address. With the completion of Roosevelt Dam, the future of the Salt River Valley was assured. Incidentally, the federal debt was repaid in full in 1955.

Over the next few years Horse Mesa, Mormon Flat, Stewart Mountain, and Granite Reef dams would be built on the Salt River, and Bartlett and Horseshoe dams on the Verde River to provide water storage and electricity. They combined to turn this arid land into a desert oasis.

Although the harnessing of the Salt River relieved much of the water problem in central Arizona, most folks looked to the mighty Colorado River, "The West's last great waterhole," as the future source of water. Ninety-five percent of the state's area drained into the river, and it was felt that the river should return at least a part of it. The state made up about 45 percent of the river's drainage basin and contributed about a third of the river's water. Arizona wasn't the only state interested in taking a share of the mighty Colorado. Our gluttonous neighbor to the west, California, wanted a lion's share, although it contributed not a drop. Also, Colorado, New Mexico, Nevada, Utah, Wyoming, and the Republic of Mexico all made claims to the river's annual 17.5 million acre feet of water.

In 1921 a commission was established to draw up a plan for harnessing the river. It met in Santa Fe and, by the end of 1922, completed its work, which became known as the Santa Fe Compact. All the states' legislatures, except Arizona's, ratified the agreement. Governor George W.P. Hunt opposed the bill because it didn't specify how California, Nevada, and Arizona would divide the 7.5 million acre feet allotment. Hunt had other reasons, purely partisan, for opposing the Santa Fe Compact. It had been conceived during the previous Republican administration under Governor Tom Campbell and Hunt didn't want to be upstaged. Also, his friend Fred Colter had a far-fetched plan called the Highline Canal, which proposed building a series of dams along the Colorado River in northern

Arizona and pumping the water through huge tunnels across the Colorado Plateau, over the Mogollon Rim and into the upper Verde River. Colter spent a personal fortune on the project that, although visionary, didn't come to pass. Colter's Highline Canal had a sound concept and did serve as a model for the modern Central Arizona Project.

During political campaigns, Hunt used the emotional issue of the Colorado River controversy so often as a method of rallying the voters to his cause that critics claimed, "although Jesus walked on water, Hunt *ran* on the Colorado."

In 1928 Congress passed the Boulder Dam Reclamation Act over the protests of Arizonans. The act called for the building of Hoover Dam on the Colorado River. What rankled Arizonans was that the plan also called for the building of the All-American Canal to deliver water into California's Imperial and Coachella valleys, but made no provision to deliver water into Arizona. Arizona appealed the case to the U.S. Supreme Court and lost. President Herbert Hoover put the plan in motion in 1930.

Hoover Dam was located in 800-foot-deep Black Canyon, between Arizona and Nevada, prompting critics to claim that although California profited from the project, "she didn't give a dam site for it."

Chief engineer on the job was Frank Crowe, whose goal in life was to build the largest dam in the world. In 1931 he put 3,000 men on the job. The temperature in that canyon exceeded 120 degrees and the rocks were hot enough to fry eggs. Daring workers hung by cables hundreds of feet above the canyon floor drilling holes with jackhammers and clearing debris before concrete could be poured.

For the next two years, workers dumped 16-ton buckets filled with concrete into forms every 60 seconds. Crowe, nicknamed "Hurry Up" by his hired hands, designed a complex lighting system so they could work around the clock. At its peak, 5,000 men were employed. A total of 96 died on the hazardous job. Crowe, living up to his nickname, completed the job in 1935, two years ahead of schedule, and for a time his dam was the largest in the world. Today it ranks 52nd. Lake Mead, which formed behind the dam, is still the largest man-made reservoir in the Western Hemisphere.

The construction of Parker Dam on the Colorado River in the early 1930s gave birth to one of Arizona's most embarrassing episodes in its long rivalry with California. Governor Ben Moeur became infuriated with California's power-play politics. Because Parker Dam was specifically designed to deliver water to California, Governor Moeur sent the Arizona National Guard to the east bank of the river and prohibited the construction workers from "touching the sacred soil of old Arizona." The guardsmen eagerly set up machine gun emplacements aimed at California. The gesture got the attention of the wary workers and Secretary of Interior Harold Ickes called a temporary halt to the project.

One night a party of guardsmen borrowed a couple of relic steamboats from a colorful river pilot named Nellie Bush and, under cover of darkness, headed towards the "enemy" shores of California. Unfortunately, the "Arizona Navy" got tangled in some cables and had to be rescued by the "enemy." The incident made the nation's newspapers and caused a few red faces among some sabre-rattling Arizonans. Shortly thereafter, the U.S. Supreme Court got into the act and ordered Governor Moeur to bring his troops home.

The thirsty farmers along the Gila River thought their water problems were over in 1930 with the completion of Coolidge Dam. But it seems the surveyors had explored the site during an unusually wet year. The dam was built, but a lake failed to materialize behind it. A verdant field of weeds, however, did manage to subsist rather comfortably. At the dedication ceremonies, cowboy humorist Will Rogers looked it over and quipped, "If that was my lake, I'd mow it." Incidentally, San Carlos Lake did not fill to capacity until the late 1970s.

The scarcity of water in the Southwest was cause for occasional violence and much litigation during territorial years. Men protected their precious water and flimsy brush dams with shotguns and rifles. Eastern sections of the United States never had to contend with such an unreliable water supply. American settlers to this region were accustomed to the riparian doctrine of water law, which held that a landowner was entitled to do as he pleased with water running through his property. He could allow others to divert water from his land or he could deny them. Obviously, such practices were unrealistic in these arid lands. When Gen. Stephen Watts Kearny occupied New Mexico in 1846, he proclaimed a code of water law based on Spanish law. The code allowed for the irrigation of lands not adjacent to the streams and recognized public use of lakes, ponds, streams, and rivers. This principle proclaimed: "first in time, first in right" and protected early settlers from some upstream newcomer diverting their water. It also decreed that the exclusive private use of water was forbidden, and that the water must be used in a beneficial way. This principle evolved into the Doctrine of Prior Appropriation and Beneficial Use and is the basis for Arizona water law today.

When the Territory of Arizona was established one of the first orders of business was the creation of a code of laws. The Howell Code of 1864, named for Justice William T. Howell, used Spanish water laws for a model. During the next few years the code was refined, because many interpretations were vague and it allowed water users to use the law as they saw fit.

During the 1890s the foremost authority on irrigation law was Judge Joseph H. Kibbey, who would later become governor of the territory. In 1892 he ruled that water rights were permanently attached to the land. This meant that the sale of water rights was forbidden except in regard to a specific piece of ground. Up to then, canal companies had considered water rights separate from the land. Kibbey's decision stopped rich farmers from buying up land in order to obtain the water rights. The landmark decision was a major victory for farmers.

In 1903, in another landmark decision, Kibbey ruled that domestic water had dominance over agriculture. During times of water shortage the needs of the public must prevail over farming.

In 1910, another significant decision, the Kent Decree, named for Judge Edward Kent, clarified water rights on every parcel of land in the Salt River Valley. Generally, the decree states that the land where the water was first used has the first right to water flowing in the river or stream. When water was low, only the lands with the earliest water rights could make use of the normal flow. Even if it necessitates drying up of a stream, the water can be consumed as long as it is not wasted. "Arizona streams are public, but the right to use of water is valid only when the rights of prior claimants are not violated.

Latecomers must defer to earlier appropriators," it declared. Even today those who hold the older lands are entitled to the normal flow water ahead of the latecomers.

The grand plan to bring water into central Arizona began back in the 1920s. The Santa Fe Compact allotted the state 2.8 million acre feet. (An acre foot would cover one acre a foot deep.) However, canals such as the 390-mile All-American channeled water, including Arizona's share, to California. During the years following construction of the canal, Californians found many devious ways to obstruct the Central Arizona Project (C.A.P.). It was hinted that the project would create a huge financial and industrial complex that would compete with eastern interests. Also, it was said that large utility companies resented the cheaper hydroelectric power that would be generated. Despite these tactics, severe droughts during the 1940s and the great increase in population after World War II dramatized the need to bring the plan to fruition.

In 1963, the U.S. Supreme Court divided the water allotments among California, Nevada, and Arizona. California lawyers and politicians were defeated in their attempts to have the million-acre-foot flow from the Gila River count as part of Arizona's allotment. At last, the Supreme Court had approved the state's right to the water and the U.S. Senate approved the C.A.P. bill. Construction of the massive project began in 1968 above Parker Dam. Through a series of pumping stations, water was to be lifted and passed through a tunnel in the Buckskin Mountains, then carried through an aqueduct 190 miles to the Phoenix area, then another 143 miles to Tucson. The expected date of arrival at the Old Pueblo is 1991. The stretch to Phoenix was dedicated on November 15, 1986. During an average year, 1.5 million acre feet of water will be channeled into the interior of the state. The C.A.P., estimated to cost $3.6 billion, is the most expensive water project ever built. About three-fourths of the money must be repaid by Arizonans by such means as higher property taxes and increased water fees.

Today, Arizonans are consuming water at about twice the replenishment rate. This is being done by overdrafting or mining the underground water reserves. For example, Tucson citizens are drinking water that fell to the earth 10,000 years ago. How extensive these reserves are is anybody's guess.

Currently Arizona relies on groundwater for 60 percent of its consumption. The state's renewable water supply (rainfall, snow etc.) is 2.8 million acre feet. The C.A.P. should provide another 1.5 million acre feet per year. That totals 4.3 million acre feet. Presently, residents are consuming more than 5 million acre feet annually for a net loss of nearly a million acre feet a year. A family of four uses about one acre foot annually. (Incidentally, the Columbia River in the Pacific Northwest dumps 280 million acre feet of water into the Pacific Ocean annually.)

To offset Arizona's gap, agricultural land is being gradually retired. Some critics would like to see it gone completely. They tend to forget that agriculture developed and paid for the water in the first place. And agriculture employs, directly or indirectly, more than 80,000 people in Arizona. Currently, on a statewide basis, agriculture uses 85 percent of the water supply. Municipalities and industry use 8 percent. Mining uses 4 percent, and the other 3 percent is for so-called "other" uses. Effluent (treated waste water) will be used more in the future for irrigation. As agricultural lands are retired and urban lands are developed, the amount of agricultural water will decrease.

The Central Arizona Project is designed to bring about 1.5 million acre feet of Colorado River water per year to Pima, Pinal, and Maricopa counties. CAP carries water from Lake Havasu near Parker to the southern boundary of the San Xavier Indian Reservation southwest of Tucson. It is a 336-mile-long system of aqueducts, tunnels, pumping plants, and pipelines and is the largest single resource of renewable water supplies in the state of Arizona.

Because of eastern opposition, this could be the last major water project in the West. Regarding the artificial watering of this land, the old argument remains: "No price is too high." Or should we live within the limits of our environment?

It is an article of faith that Arizonans have long regarded water as their most precious commodity. A few years ago President Jimmy Carter was cutting back on funds for water development projects in Arizona. He was confronted by straighttalking Senator Barry Goldwater who said, "Mr. President, there are three things a westerner will fight over: Water, gold, and women—in that order."

18

POLITICS IN ARIZONA SINCE STATEHOOD

Throughout the territorial years and until post-World War II, politics in Arizona was controlled pretty much by the Democratic Party. Still, some gubernatorial races were tight. The one in 1916 between Democrat incumbent George W.P. Hunt and Republican Tom Campbell was so close the courts had to finally decide the winner. At first Campbell seemed to have won by a mere 30 votes. But Hunt stubbornly refused to concede.

Both men took the oath of office in separate ceremonies on January 1, 1917. Campbell operated from his home while Hunt remained in the capitol building. The state treasurer, a Democrat, refused to honor checks signed by Campbell. Hunt demanded a recount, but he again came up 30 votes short. Hunt went to court, but was ruled against by Superior Court Judge Rawghlie Stanford (a fellow Democrat and later governor of the state). Still, Hunt wouldn't surrender the office of governor. He appealed to the State Supreme Court and won on grounds that many Arizonans had marked their ballots for a straight Democratic ticket, then voted for Campbell. Obviously, the Democrats were sending a message; they were voting for every Democrat on the ballot *except* him. Campbell served in office 11 months without pay before Hunt came in officially and finished the term. Campbell, the first native Arizonan elected governor, later served two terms, 1919-1923 (governors served two-year terms in those days).

When Arizona became a state in 1912, voters elected George W.P. Hunt, president of the 1910 Constitutional

Convention, as their first governor. Hunt was a consummate politician and would eventually be elected to office for seven terms. Humorist Will Rogers once referred to him as "Arizona's perennial governor." Opponents were less kind, calling him "King George VII." Hunt's rise to prominence was spectacular. He arrived in Globe in 1881, penniless and riding atop a burro. Blessed with a Horatio Alger-like work ethic, he was by 1900 one of the wealthiest men in the territory.

Governor George W.P. Hunt, first governor of the state. He would serve a total of seven terms. Photo: Southwest Studies.

The two elected Senators were Henry F. Ashurst, an ex-cowboy from Coconino County and a former territorial delegate to Congress, and former territorial delegate Marcus A. Smith. Former Maricopa County Sheriff Carl Hayden won the lone seat in the House.

Hunt was perhaps the most liked—and disliked—politician of his time, and he was colorful. His rotund body, bald head and walrus-like mustache made him unforgettable. Friends and enemies had a variety of nicknames but he preferred "Old Roman." Hunt had risen to wealth through sheer hard work and determination, working at jobs like grocery clerk, miner and restaurant worker. He was a Progressive and, therefore, battled constantly with his fellow Democrats in the conservative-minded legislature. Hunt was a clever politician. Although he shared much in common with large mine operators, he projected himself as a friend of the working man. "My front door is always open to the working man," he liked to say. "Yeah," his enemies replied, "but his back door is always open to the mining companies."

Hunt knew how to charm the ladies, too. He'd send his assistants out to purchase cases of jams and jellies and then peel off the labels. Out on the campaign trail, he'd pull one out of his pocket and present it to a housewife saying, "my wife was making jelly the other day and she wanted you folks to have a jar." While traveling around the state in a touring car Hunt would keep notes on towns he visited and people he'd met. On his return, he'd refer to those notes to refresh his memory. "How's that sick cow?" he might ask, referring to some obscure conversation from a past visit. Constituents were amazed at his recall and it counted at the polls.

In 1919 Hunt let it be known he was planning to run for Democrat Mark Smith's Senate seat. Smith's friends persuaded President Woodrow Wilson to appoint Hunt to some position as far away from Arizona as possible. The story is told that Wilson spun a globe to the opposite side of the world and found Siam. Then he appointed Hunt minister to that east Asian kingdom. While in Bangkok, Hunt corresponded regularly with his old friends in Arizona and returned home more popular than ever. As it turned out, Smith was defeated in the general election by Republican Ralph Cameron and his long career came to an end. He was an ex-Tombstone lawyer and one of Arizona's most colorful characters. Dashing and handsome, he was called "Mark the Idol" by his adoring fans. Naturally, his opponents altered that to "Mark the Idle."

John C. Phillips was the only other Republican (Tom Campbell was the first) to win the governorship between 1912 and 1950. He was elected in the Hoover landslide of 1928. Ironically, Philips had once worked as a stone mason on the construction of the State Capitol. He served as chief of state for only one term. Republicans were blamed for the stock market crash of 1929 and were swept out of office the following year. Hunt, now an old warhorse, returned for his seventh and last term. The vote was close, however; Hunt received 48,875 votes to 46,231 for Phillips.

Arizona's "Depression governor" was a country doctor from Tempe named Benjamin Moeur. During Doc Moeur's two terms the state was so nearly broke it couldn't finance badly needed programs. Contemporaries recall that the crusty governor possessed one of the most profane vocabularies this side of a muleskinners convention. But all agree he had a heart as big as his native Texas. During lunch hour Moeur would conduct free medical clinics for the needy in the rotunda at the capitol. The kind-hearted doctor used to send out Christmas cards to his impoverished patients marked "paid in full" for any medical debts incurred that year. One time when a construction worker at a dam project was injured, Moeur climbed into a concrete bucket and was hoisted up to the accident site to aid the stricken man. It was said ole Doc Moeur had delivered more than 10,000 babies during his long medical career and they all grew up and voted for him, thus ensuring his election.

By early 1933, 26 Arizona banks had already failed. Soon after taking office that same year, Governor Moeur declared a "bank holiday" to save those which hadn't gone under. To keep people from losing their land, Moeur cut property taxes 40 percent during his first term. New taxes on luxury items such as liquor (Prohibition ended in 1933) beer, wine and tobacco were imposed, along with a state income tax. Although the new taxes kept the state solvent during hard times, Moeur's political opponents were successful in a mud-slinging campaign to bring about his defeat in the primary election of 1936.

Two other men, Rawghlie Stanford and Robert T. Jones, served as governors during the 1930s. Stanford, a former judge, was better suited to the judicial branch of government. He later served a distinguished career on the State Supreme Court. Jones was a stand-in after the favorite, C. M. Zander, was killed in an airplane crash. Jones was better suited to ranching or running a western store, which he did for many years after leaving office.

Sidney P. Osborn was governor during World War II, one of the great transition periods in the state's history. Some observers consider him the best governor in Arizona history. He is the only governor to be elected to four consecutive terms. Osborn, a native son, had deep roots in the history of Arizona. His grandfather, John Osborn, was one of the founders of Phoenix and his father, Neri, was a page in the first territorial legislature back in 1864 at Prescott. He was the youngest delegate to the Constitutional Convention in 1910 and, upon Arizona's admission to statehood, became the first secretary of state. In 1934 he ran for the U.S. Senate against Henry F. Ashurst and lost. Osborn wasn't deterred by political defeat. He ran for governor three times and lost (1918, 1924 and 1938). The fourth time was the charm, and in 1940 he finally achieved a lifelong dream. His greatest achievement as governor was the ratification of the Colorado River Compact in 1944. Arizona had been the only one among the upper and lower basin states not to sign the 1922 Santa Fe Compact. Osborn pointed out to the legislature that Arizona's right to the 2.8 million acre feet of water from the Colorado River would not be forthcoming until the state ratified the compact. The legislators agreed and the compact was approved, opening the way for the eventual construction of the Central Arizona Project.

The election of Republican Howard Pyle in 1950 marked the beginning of the two-party system in the state. The new industries brought on by World War II created a great influx of

people from Republican midwestern states. Waiting in the wings were Republican candidates Paul Fannin, Jack Williams, John Rhodes, and Pyle. Fannin was elected governor in 1958 and served in that office until he was elected to the United States Senate in 1964. Williams, a popular radio personality, was mayor of Phoenix before his election as governor in 1966. Pyle, another popular radio personality, had as his campaign manager a venturesome young man named Barry Goldwater. Two years after helping Pyle win the governorship, Goldwater challenged Senator Ernest W. McFarland.

Governor Howard Pyle. His election as governor in 1950 marked the beginning of the rise of prominence of the Republican Party in state politics. Arizona Historical Foundation, Tempe.

McFarland was Senate Majority Leader at the time and was figured to be unbeatable. Goldwater won in one of the most stunning upsets in Arizona history. Goldwater's open honesty and charismatic personality, along with his conservative political views, made him a popular political figure throughout the nation. In 1964, he was the Republican Party's nominee for president, the only Arizonan ever to reach such lofty political heights.

The Democratic Party had been a powerful force in Arizona since the early days of the territory. However, since most administrations in Washington during the post-Civil War years were Republican, most of the appointees also were from the GOP. Most Arizonans were Democrats, so there was some natural resentment towards the territorial governors. So, when Arizonans drew up their constitution just prior to statehood, they weakened the governor's office considerably by taking away most of the executive appointive powers. Those restrictions kept the office mostly ceremonial until the 1970s when the 1910 constitution was remodeled. Many state government agencies were reorganized and grouped into "super" departments with directors appointed by the governor. Thanks to these changes, state government became much more efficient.

For the first half century following statehood, Democrats controlled the legislature. This didn't always help their fellow Democrats in the governor's office. Liberal governors such as Hunt battled continuously with conservative Democrats who frequently formed coalitions with Republicans. This caused one political sage to comment that the state had "three parties: the Democrats, Democrats and Republicans." Facing little strong opposition from Republicans, Democrats frequently broke up into factions. Powerful business interests such as mining, cattle, agriculture, and the railroads had much greater influence with the legislature than the governor.

During the early years of statehood, Republicans, although a minority party, were fairly competitive in political races. However, the Republican Party took the brunt of the blame for the Great Depression of the 1930s and, by 1942, nearly 90 percent of Arizonans were registered Democrats. In 1950 Howard Pyle had to overcome a nine-to-two registration disadvantage to win the governor's office. That same year the Democrats won all 19 Senate seats and 61 of 62 House seats.

The rise of the Republican Party from the early 1950s was dramatic, to say the least. Just 30 years later they had become the majority party in the state. The Democrats didn't give up easily. "We didn't have any damn Republicans in this state," one old Democrat grumbled, "until they invented air conditioning."

The 1966 "one man, one vote" decision by the U.S. Supreme Court had, perhaps, the greatest impact on Arizona politics. State legislatures were required to reapportion districts to represent an equal number of people. In Arizona, the ruling apportioned 15 senators and 30 representatives—half the members—to Maricopa County, which had half the population. Pima County was given 6 senators and 12 representatives. The rest were divided among the rural counties. Prior to 1966 the rural counties could form formidable coalitions against Pima and Maricopa counties. A good example was in 1954 when the Senate was reapportioned to 28 members, two from each county. Although Pima and Maricopa counties had over 70 percent of the population, the top three Senate leadership positions were controlled by the rural counties. Today, the state is divided into 30 districts with 30 senators and 60 representatives.

Just as the Republicans reached the pinnacle of prosperity in Arizona, all-out war broke out within the party. It began in the fall of 1986.

The election of arch-conservative Evan Mecham to the office of governor in 1986 initiated the one of the most turbulent periods in Arizona history. Mecham was a longtime political maverick who had gained notoriety by attacking the establishment. Born and raised in a small Mormon community in Utah, he moved to Arizona after World War II and opened an automobile agency in Glendale.

He ran unsuccessfully for the U.S. Senate in 1962 and lost to the legendary Carl Hayden. Two years later, he made his first run for governor. He lost in the primary to Richard Kleindienst and, during the campaign, made bitter attacks on members of his party that contributed to Kleindienst's loss to Democrat Sam Goddard in the general election.

Mecham ran three more unsuccessful campaigns for governor in 1974, 1978 and 1982. However, in 1986, he pulled off a stunning upset in the primary, then won a three-way race in the general election. As governor-elect, he vowed to rid the state of its "ruling elite" and declared war on drugs, organized crime, and corruption in government.

Once in office, Mecham and his administration lacked the ability to put their populist ideas into practice. They refused to seek help from the attorney general, state agencies, or the legislature and hired people who lacked the minimum credentials for their jobs. Victory had come as such as surprise that nobody knew what to do next.

With both feet planted firmly in mid-air, Mecham was in deep trouble from the start. One of his first acts was to rescind Martin Luther King Day, saying that the civil rights leader didn't deserve the holiday. He made remarks that offended women, Jews, Asians, and Hispanics. Over time he expanded his enemies list from "a few dissident Democrats and homosexuals" to include the media, most of the legislature, the Department of Public Safety, and anyone else who criticized him. He saw his critics as part of a plot to derail him by organized crime and business and political leaders.

Mecham had as many opponents as allies, and six months after his election they began trying to oust him. By November 1987, they had collected enough signatures to force a recall election. Before the election could take place, Mecham was indicted on six felony counts related to a $350,000 campaign loan. The charges against him included obstruction of justice and misuse of a protocol fund. After two weeks of hearings, the House voted 46 to 14 to impeach Mecham.

On April 4, 1988, the Senate found Mecham guilty on two counts and forced him to step down. It was the first time in 59 years that a United States governor had been impeached and removed from office. On June 16, a jury found Mecham innocent on criminal charges of violating campaign laws. The ex-governor saw this acquittal as a vindication and moral victory.

Rose Mofford, a Democrat, served out the balance of Mecham's term.

Rose Mofford, Arizona's first woman governor, is a native of Globe where her father was a copper miner. She was the youngest of six children, the daughter of Austrian immigrants. An outstanding athlete, Rose Mofford earned All American status in women's amateur softball and was later inducted into the Arizona Softball Hall of Fame. She was also a star basketball player, turning down a chance to play professionally with the All-American Redheads. She began her career as a secretary in the state treasurer's office and served as an assistant director in the Department of Revenue before becoming secretary of state and governor.

Throughout her long career in government, Mofford was known as resourceful, efficient, and reliable. During the turbulent days before and after the Mecham impeachment, she vowed to keep a low profile and heal the wounds created by the turmoil. Some critics claimed she kept too low a profile, allowing her staff to shield her from the press. However, when necessary, Mofford proved she was up to the task. She moved quickly and decisively to rid state government of Mecham appointees who continued to stir up trouble at the capitol. Wisely, she relied on the talents of longtime associates at the capitol, including members of former governor Babbitt's team, to steer the ship of state back on course.

The contrast between Rose Mofford and her successor, J. Fife Symington III, could not have been more stark. Unlike the Democratic, native-born Arizonan Mofford who had spent most of her professional life in the public sector, the Republican Symington was a relative newcomer to Arizona who rose to prominence as a real estate developer.

Born in New York City, the great-grandson of steel tycoon Henry Clay Frick, Symington grew up in Maryland as a child of wealth and privilege. After earning a bachelor's degree from Harvard in 1968, Symington joined the U.S. Air Force and served a tour of duty in Viet Nam, where he was awarded the Bronze Star for meritorious service. He separated from the Air Force in 1971, having attained the rank of Captain, and in 1976 he founded the Symington Company, a Phoenix-based commercial and industrial real estate development firm.

While many other prominent developers were forced into bankruptcy when the real-estate market crashed in the late

1980s, Symington not only survived but prospered. In his gubernatorial campaign, Symington asserted that his evident business acumen more than made up for his lack of political experience. Governor Symington was a supply-sider who believed that tax cuts were the key to economic growth. Indeed, under his administration, Arizona's economy quickly rebounded from recession and the growth rate soon outpaced the national average. The state treasury recorded surpluses year after year.

As Arizona's economy was roaring, Symington's personal fortunes took a decided turn for the worse. In 1995, shortly after he was inaugurated for a second term as governor, Symington was forced to declare personal bankruptcy. The following year, federal prosecutors served him with a 21-count criminal indictment.

In a 17-week trial culminating in February 1997, a federal jury convicted Symington on seven counts of bank and wire fraud for lying about his wealth on the financial statements he gave to creditors between 1986 and 1991. The jury deadlocked on eleven other counts and acquitted him on three. During the trial, it was revealed that Symington had received $200 million in loans from his mother as he tried to keep his struggling development business from going under.

Symington, who continued to serve as governor while under federal indictment, was forced to resign when the jury rendered its verdict. In February 1998 he was sentenced to prison and fined, but his conviction was overturned on appeal in June 1999. In January 2001 President William J. Clinton, in one of his last official acts, granted Symington a Presidential pardon.

Symington handed over the reins of office to the Republican Secretary of State, Jane Dee Hull. A native of Kansas City, Hull came to Arizona when her husband, Dr. Terry Hull, accepted an appointment with the public health service. While her husband tended the sick on the Navajo Nation, Arizona's future governor taught school. In 1964, the couple moved to Phoenix, where Dr. Hull practiced medicine for more than three decades and now works as a consultant.

Hull became active in the Republican Party and ran for a seat in the legislature, and became the first woman to serve as Speaker of the House. Later, she gained the distinction of becoming the first Republican Secretary of State after fifty years of Democratic Party control.

As governor, Hull worked to improve educational standards and funding and healthcare coverage and services for the working poor. She also worked to accommodate economic development in the state while preserving the Arizona's natural beauty through her Growing Smarter initiative.

In the years immediately following the Mecham impeachment, the state faced further embarrassment when seven members of the state legislature were charged with accepting bribes to vote for legalized gambling in Arizona. The Phoenix Police Department videotaped the legislators taking bribes from undercover officer Joseph Stedino. Six of the legislators resigned and the seventh was expelled by fellow senators. Ironically some of them had been instrumental in the Mecham impeachment. The scandal became known as "AzScam."

Former Senate President Stan Turley was another state legislator who had an outstanding career in politics. As a State Senator, he played a key role in helping to develop the Arizona Water Code of 1984. In 1976 President Jimmy Carter nearly killed the Central Arizona Project that would bring water into metropolitan Phoenix and Tucson. The federal government demanded Arizona develop a code to control water use. Governor Raul Castro appointed a twenty five member State Water Commission to come up with recommendations. The group included Senator Turley, environmentalists, and representatives of agriculture, the utilities, the mining industry, and urban areas. Each had a different agenda, and a compromise seemed impossible. With strong backing from Governor Bruce Babbitt and under the leadership of Turley and Burton Barr, the group met every Saturday for five months and came up with a plan "no one liked, but that all could live with," which became the Arizona Water Code of 1984. The passing of the code was the "finest hour" for the commission, the legislature, and the governor.

Turley earned high marks for his straightforward approach to many issues and was respected by both Democrats and Republicans. His sense of humor allowed him to diffuse many a crisis, and his friendliness and laid-back style sometimes belied the fact that he was as tough as the hardscrabble ranch country he grew up in. Turley truly defined the "golden years" of the state legislature.

Despite recent political turmoil at home, Arizona has, by proud tradition, been well represented in Washington. When Arizona became a state in 1912 some speculated it would take decades before the area matured enough to have an impact on the national scene. Yet from the very onset of statehood Arizona and America were well served. In 1911, former Maricopa County Sheriff Carl Hayden was elected as the new state's only representative in the U.S. House. Hayden was elected to the Senate in 1926 after seven terms in the House. He served another seven terms in the Senate before retiring in 1969. Hayden's 57 years in Congress gave him the distinction of serving more years in that body than any other

person in American history. At the time of his retirement, Hayden was president *pro tempore* of the Senate and third in line for the presidency. He was a quiet man who accomplished great deeds for the state without much fanfare and hoopla. Hayden's seniority allowed him to chair important committees, yet he never flaunted his authority. Colleagues referred to him as a "work horse" in contrast to the more visible "show horse" politicians. Hayden's crowning achieve-

Senator Carl Hayden when he was sheriff of Maricopa County. In 1911 he was elected to Congress and served until 1969. Photo: Arizona Historical Foundation, Tempe.

ment was the approval of the Central Arizona Project in 1968. During the years of John F. Kennedy's presidency *Time* magazine referred to the venerable senator as the "last link between the New Frontier and the real one."

Henry F. Ashurst was elected to the Senate in 1911. Ashurst, a former northern Arizona cowboy who spent lonely hours reading Shakespeare, was one of the most colorful speakers in Washington. Colleagues called him the "Silver-Tongued Orator of the Colorado" or "Five-Syllable Henry." Ashurst could be flexible when necessary. Once he changed his mind on an issue. "Well, Henry, I see you have seen the light," a fellow Senator kidded. "No," Henry replied, "I have merely felt the heat." His long and distinguished career in the Senate came to a close in 1940 when he was defeated by Ernest W. McFarland in a stunning political upset. "Mac" as he was known far and wide, also had a distinguished career. In 1952 he was elected Senate majority leader. Unfortunately for him, the job kept him in Washington and he was defeated by a political newcomer, Barry Goldwater. Mac came home and ran for governor, defeating Republican Howard Pyle in 1954. He ran for his old Senate seat against Goldwater again in 1958 but lost. A decade later he became Chief Justice of the State Supreme Court. Thus, he is the only person in Arizona to hold the "triple crown of politics" in Arizona—legislative, executive, and judicial.

Lewis Douglas, member of a famous mining family, rose to political prominence in the 1920s. Douglas, son of "Rawhide" Jimmy Douglas and grandson of Dr. James Douglas, was a native of Douglas. After serving in World War I he returned to Arizona and started a career in banking and mining. When Carl Hayden ran for the Senate in 1926 Douglas ran for Arizona's lone House seat and won. In 1933 he resigned to become Franklin D. Roosevelt's budget director. Economically and politically conservative, he resigned over policy differences with the President a year later. He remained active in business and educational interests until 1947 when President Harry S. Truman appointed him ambassador to Great Britain, a post in which he served until 1950. Douglas returned to Tucson and was active in civic

Isabella Greenway, the only woman to represent the state in the U.S. Congress. Photo: Arizona Historical Society.

and business affairs until his death in 1974.

In 1933, when Lewis Douglas resigned his seat in Congress to become Franklin D. Roosevelt's budget director, a special election was held to fill the post. Isabella Selmes Greenway won the election and thus became the only women ever to represent the state in the U.S. Congress. Greenway was an old friend of the Roosevelts; they had been guests at the Greenway ranch near Williams and she had been a bridesmaid at the wedding of Franklin and Eleanor. This relationship, no doubt, helped her as a Congresswoman.

In 1923 Isabella married Gen. John C. Greenway, former Rough Rider in the Spanish-American War and mining magnate. After his death in 1926, she ran their XX (Double X) Ranch near Williams, was part owner of an airline and operated the Arizona Inn, a guest ranch in Tucson. A dynamic, colorful lady, Greenway chose not to run for re-election in 1936.

In 1952, the same year Goldwater defeated McFarland, Republican John Rhodes won the congressional seat for District 1. Rhodes was re-elected each term until his retirement in 1983. During Rhodes' career in the House, he won great respect from both parties for his honesty and integrity. Rhodes and Goldwater were two of the three Republican leaders who met privately with President Richard Nixon and called for his resignation in August, 1974. For almost a decade before his retirement, Rhodes served as House

Minority Leader. During the political turmoil following the impeachment and removal of Governor Mecham in 1988, Rhodes accepted a draft as Republican candidate in a recall election. It was a difficult position for the elder statesman. Mechamites accused him of undermining their candidate and dividing the party. Moderates believed Rhodes was the only candidate with enough integrity to save the party. The state was spared more political bloodletting when the State Supreme Court cancelled the recall election. While some

John Rhodes served in Congress from 1953 to 1983. He was House Minority Leader from 1974 until his retirement nine years later. Arizona Historical Foundation, Tempe.

candidates complained loudly, Rhodes, his duty done, returned quietly to private life.

Stewart Lee Udall, member of a pioneer Mormon family in St. Johns, was first elected to Congress in 1954. Udall became the first Arizonan to serve in a Presidential Cabinet in 1960, when John F. Kennedy appointed him Secretary of the Interior. He continued in that post during the Lyndon Johnson administration and is considered one of the best to have held that position.

When Stewart Udall left Congress to join Kennedy's team in 1961, his seat was taken by his younger brother, Morris. "Mo" as he was better known, was re-elected to office each term and continued to serve courageously, despite a difficult struggle with Parkinson's disease. During the 1976 presidential primaries he made a determined run for the Democratic nomination before losing out to Jimmy Carter. Mo Udall, who died in 1998, will likely go down in history as one of Congress's most respected and beloved members.

Bruce Babbitt, a grandson of one of the legendary five Babbitt brothers who came to the Flagstaff area in the 1880s and created a family dynasty, became governor in 1978 following the death of Governor Wesley Bolin. Bolin for many years was Arizona's secretary of state and one of its most popular politicians. When Governor Raul Castro resigned in 1977 to become ambassador to Argentina, Bolin became governor and Rose Mofford was appointed secretary of state. When Bolin died suddenly on March 4,1978, Attorney General Babbitt, third in succession (Mofford wasn't elected secretary of state so she was ineligible), became governor. The young governor believed in strong executive leadership and made the office of governor highly visible. Babbitt, a Democrat, quickly earned the respect of the Republican-controlled legislature and, although he set a record for vetoes, the governor and the legislature worked well together. It's difficult to judge "who was best" as there are too many intangibles, but Babbitt certainly rates as one of the best governors in the history of the state. He was elected to office in 1978 and 1982. Babbitt unsuccessfully sought the Democratic nomination for president in 1986 and was appointed Secretary of the Interior in

Bruce Babbitt, scion of the mercantile-ranching dynasty in northern Arizona, was governor from 1978 to 1987. Thoughtful and intelligent, Babbitt elevated the office of governor to one of high profile. Photo: Courtesy of Bruce Babbitt.

1992, serving two terms on President Clinton's cabinet. At the time, speculation ran high that he would become a U.S. Supreme Court justice. Had he been appointed, Arizona would have had three citizens on the high court.

In 1981, Sandra Day O'Connor, member of a pioneer Arizona ranch family in Greenlee County, became the first woman justice on the United States Supreme Court. Sandra Day, whose grandfather, Henry Clay Day, started the Lazy B ranch in 1880, grew up wanting to be a cowgirl but changed her mind somewhere along the way. After graduating from Stanford Law School in 1952, where a fellow Arizonan, Chief Justice William Rehnquist, was a classmate, she married lawyer John O'Connor. After a tour of military duty they settled in Phoenix. In the 1960s she became active in politics and served in the state senate. In 1973 she was elected majority leader, the first woman in the United States to hold that position in a state legislature. Two years later she was a superior court judge and in 1979 was appointed to the State Court of Appeals. She was still serving in that position when nominated to the United States Supreme Court.

Two Arizonans sit on the nation's highest court. Chief Justice Rehnquist was the first to serve. After graduation from Stanford Law School, Rehnquist moved to Phoenix. There he practiced law until 1969,

Supreme Court Justice Sandra Day O'Connor. In 1981 she became the first woman on the U.S. Supreme Court. Photo: Courtesy Sandra Day O'Connor.

when he became an assistant U.S. attorney general. Two years later, President Richard Nixon nominated him to the Supreme Court. In 1986, during the administration of Ronald Reagan, he was appointed Chief Justice. At the inauguration of President George Bush on January 20, 1989 these two Arizonans had the honor of swearing in the President and Vice President Dan Quayle.

In 1992 Joe Arpaio was elected Sheriff of Maricopa County, the nation's fourth largest sheriff's office. He quickly earned a reputation as "America's Toughest Sheriff."

Arpaio had a long career in law enforcement that included working as a police officer in Washington D. C., and Las Vegas, and a federal narcotics agent. A specialist in undercover operations, he infiltrated drug organizations in the Middle East, Central and South America, and elsewhere.

As sheriff, Arpaio started the nation's largest Tent City for inmates and attracted worldwide attention by creating chain gangs that save Maricopa County thousands of dollars in labor costs annually. His male chain gang and the world's first female chain gang clean streets, paint over graffiti and bury the indigent in the county cemetery. He established a get-tough policy by banning coffee, smoking, pornographic magazines, movies, and unrestricted television in jails. "This is not a country club," he reminded inmates. Arpaio also created the world's largest volunteer posse, which has 3,200 members who do search and rescue missions, patrol shopping malls and assist in traditional police work. His no-nonsense approach has made him one of the state's most popular politicians. He had an 85 percent public approval rating in 1996 and strongly considered running for governor in 1998 and 2002 but opted to remain in law enforcement.

A rising star in Arizona and on the national political scene is Senator John McCain. He gained national attention during the 1988 presidential campaign when his name was mentioned prominently as a running mate for George Bush. National attention is nothing new to the Arizona Republican. McCain, a Navy pilot and the son of a Navy admiral, was shot down on his 23rd bombing mission over North Viet Nam in October, 1967. He was seriously injured when he

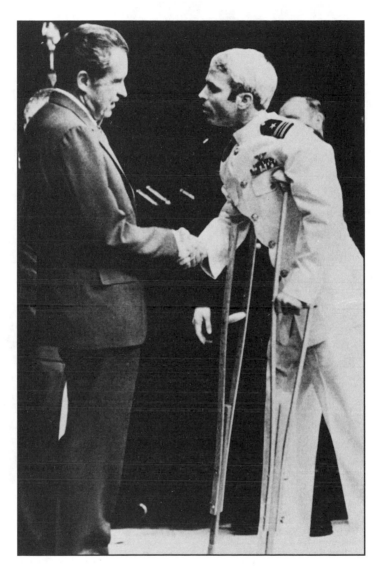

President Richard Nixon greets Lt. Com. (later U.S.Senator) John McCain during a reception at the State Department for former prisoners of war on May 24, 1973. Photo: U.P.I.

Senator Barry Goldwater and his wife Peggy in 1964, the year he was the Republican Party nominee for President. Photo: Arizona Historical Foundation, Tempe.

ejected from his Skyhawk dive bomber over Hanoi. The young pilot was knocked unconscious, his right leg was broken, his left arm was pulled out of its socket, and the right arm was broken in three places. More dead than alive, McCain was beaten and bayoneted before being thrown into the infamous Hanoi Hilton prison. Miraculously, McCain survived. During months of solitary confinement his hair turned white and his weight dropped to less than a hundred pounds. Because McCain's father was an admiral, the North Vietnamese tried to use him for propaganda purposes. However, the tough little pilot refused to cooperate with his captors. For this he was nearly beaten to death. On March 15, 1973, after 5-1/2 years of captivity, McCain came home. During the next few years he delivered speeches about his POW experience and served as the Navy's liaison with the U.S. Senate.

McCain retired from the Navy, married Cindy Hensley of Arizona and moved here in 1981. Soon thereafter, he made a bid for the congressional seat of retiring John Rhodes. His quick wit, charisma, and war-hero status, along with a pretty wife, made him an instant success with Arizonans. Critics claimed he hadn't lived in the state long, but it was quickly pointed out by supporters that most other Arizonans hadn't lived here long, either. McCain, reared in a Navy family that was always on the move, replied to critics that the longest residency he'd ever spent was at the Hanoi Hilton. That seemed to silence the opposition. When McCain entered the race in March 1982 only 3 percent of the voters knew his name. But McCain campaigned tirelessly and captured the GOP nomination against three well-heeled opponents. In the general election he went on to get 66 percent of the vote. McCain immediately earned the admiration of his Washington colleagues, and was elected president of the GOP freshman class in 1983. His dynamic energy, engaging personality and ability to tackle tough issues won high marks. In 1984 he stood for re-election and captured 78 percent of the vote. McCain's popularity in Arizona was growing, too. He returned home nearly every weekend, making speeches and participating in community work projects. When Barry Goldwater retired in 1986 from the Senate, McCain went on the campaign trail and won the Senate seat easily.

The most recognized Arizonan the world over is Senator Barry Goldwater, whose career in the United States Senate spanned four decades. Had Goldwater never entered politics he would likely have become world renowned—as a photographer, or adventurer, or both. Perhaps even as a golfer: He won the amateur division of the 1934 Phoenix Open. A member of a pioneer mercantile family that arrived in Arizona during the 1860s gold rush, Goldwater took over the family business after his father's death in 1929. During World War II he served as a pilot and eventually rose to the rank of major general in the Air Force Reserve. During his time, Barry flew every type of supersonic fighter plane in the military.

Shortly after Goldwater arrived in the Senate in 1953 it was evident he would become one of the movers and shakers. A strong advocate of a powerful defense, he would eventually chair the powerful Armed Services Committee. He became the spokesman for the conservative movement that had its beginning in the 1950s and resulted in the election of Ronald Reagan as President in 1980.

Goldwater had planned to run against John F. Kennedy in the 1964 presidential race. The two discussed traveling around the country in a series of debates. The issues and differences between the two were clear, and each had a great deal of respect for the other. Unfortunately, on November 22, 1963, an assassin's bullet ended Kennedy's life and altered the course of history. Goldwater made up his mind not to run after Lyndon Johnson succeeded Kennedy. He knew the country would never put a third person in the presidency in less than a year. But a group of Republicans convinced him to run anyway. Despite the fact that he was a heavy favorite, Johnson ran one of the dirtiest campaigns in political history. Although he polled 27 million votes, Goldwater was badly beaten. There was a party victory, however. Western Republicans had finally wrested control of the party from the eastern wing.

Goldwater remained active and when Senator Carl Hayden retired in 1968, Goldwater ran and was returned to the Senate, where he remained until his retirement in 1986. For many years the deeply respected and charismatic Goldwater was one of the most revered figures in America.

Arizonans can be justly proud of those sent to Washington to look after our interests and the nation's as well.

19

RECENT ARIZONA HISTORY

Future historians will likely divide Arizona's history into two parts: prior to World War II and after. Anyone arriving before the war will be designated a "pioneer," much the same as back around the turn of the century anyone arriving before the railroad was a pioneer—and before that, anyone arriving before Arizona became a territory in 1863 was given pioneer status. The unprecedented growth that overwhelmed the state after World War II went far beyond the most optimistic (depending on one's point of view) predictions. Back in 1920, one not-so-farsighted banker predicted that, if Phoenix kept growing at such a phenomenal rate, it would surely have a population of 100,000 by the year A.D. 2000.

The advent of air conditioning certainly made a remarkable difference in the quality of life in the desert regions. Earlier, folks beat the hot summer nights by moving their beds outside and wrapping themselves in a wet sheet. Lazy summer days were spent swimming in canals and irrigation ditches. People often ask long-time natives how they stood the searing summer heat before air conditioning. The stock reply is "We didn't know any better."

Perhaps a hundred years from now a giant dome may cover cities like Yuma, Tucson and Phoenix, keeping the temperature at a constant 72 degrees. Every Wednesday at 4:00 p.m. it will rain for 25 minutes, and picnic plans are made accordingly. Then some wag will wonder how people stood it back in 1990. "Imagine," they'll ask, "how anyone could have lived back then." Today's toddlers, by then white-bearded old-timers, can stick their thumbs in their belts and proudly proclaim, "I reckon we just didn't know any better." In honor of that projected occasion, we might today consider erecting a monument to all the brave ladies who climbed into an automobile on a hot summer day in the parking lot of a shopping center, wearing a short skirt and nothing between them and a hot, black vinyl seat cover except sheer pantyhose. A century from now folks will be awed by such formidable courage.

While on the subject of monuments, one should be built for Sam Lount, who established the first ice plant in Phoenix back in 1879. Blocks of ice placed in front of electric fans served as Arizona's first air conditioning units. The sight of an ice wagon meandering through the neighborhood meant immediate respite from the heat for generations of youngsters. They trailed along behind the ice wagon eagerly snatching small chunks of ice to chew on. Mr. Lount's ice plant certainly made the long, hot summer more bearable.

Those who could afford to, spent their summers in California. Others sought refuge from the heat in the cool climes around Prescott. The Santa Fe Railroad made a stop at Iron Springs, a small community nestled in the granite rocks west of Prescott. The place became a veritable "little Phoenix" in the summertime. Working husbands commuted, spending weekends with the family, then catching the Monday morning train for Phoenix.

A story is told by tattling old-timers that each August, Phoenix night spots such as the bar at the Adams Hotel filled with husbands on the make. It was quite a windfall for indiscreet secretaries and grass widows desiring to be wined and dined. This hot time in the old town cooled considerably when air conditioners and swimming pools came on the scene and families began spending the summers at home. Summer nights in Phoenix became noticeably quieter.

The last vestiges of the Great Depression were broken on December 7, 1941 when Japanese planes made a sneak attack on American forces at Pearl Harbor, in Hawaii. Casualties were high. The Pacific fleet was nearly destroyed.

Nearly half of those killed at Pearl Harbor were aboard the *Arizona* when two torpedoes and seven bombs struck the battleship. The crippled ship sank in minutes, killing 1,177 of the sailors and Marines on board.

In May of 1942 the U.S. Navy avenged the Pearl Harbor attack at the battle of Midway, which turned the tide of the war in the Pacific. In that engagement, Ensign John C. Butler, a recent graduate of Buckeye High School piloting a Dauntless dive bomber off the carrier *Yorktown*, was killed in action while sinking a Japanese carrier. A few weeks earlier Butler had flown cover for the carrier *Hornet* that carried Col. Jimmy Doolittle's B-25's for their famous bombing raids on Tokyo. For his heroism at Midway, Ensign Butler was awarded the Navy Cross, a decoration second in prestige to the Congressional Medal of Honor. In December, 1943 the Navy named a new destroyer, the USS *John C. Butler*, after him. The destroyer fought in six major campaigns, including Iwo Jima and Okinawa, becoming one of the most decorated ships in the war.

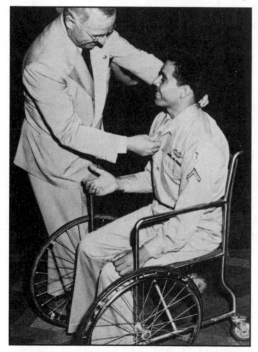

President Harry S. Truman congratulates Pfc. Silvestre Herrera in ceremonies at the nation's capital. Herrera was the only Arizonan to win the Congressional Medal of Honor in World War II. Photo: Arizona Hall of Fame.

Arizona's greatest war hero in World War II was Army Pfc. Silvestre Herrera of Phoenix. On March 15, 1945 his outfit was pinned down by German machine gun fire. The guns were protected by minefields, but that didn't stop young Herrera. Twice he mounted one-man assaults on the machine gun nests. On the first assault, he captured eight enemy soldiers. In the second assault, a mine exploded and blew off both his feet.

Herrera continued to fight, pinning down the German troops until his comrades were able to mount an attack. For his bravery, Herrera was awarded the Congressional Medal of Honor, the nation's highest award.

The 158th Regiment, Arizona National Guard, was mobilized in 1940 and sent to Panama for jungle training. They became a crack jungle-fighting outfit and earned the nickname "Bushmasters" for the deadly snake that inhabited the jungles of Panama. During the war the 158th fought in Gen. Douglas MacArthur's famed "island-hopping" campaigns of the war in the Pacific. Japan's propaganda queen, "Tokyo Rose," called them the "Butchers of the Pacific," a left-handed compliment. Gen. MacArthur said of the Bushmasters, "No greater fighting combat team has ever deployed for battle." At the war's end the 158th served with the occupational army in Japan. The Arizona boys brought the colors home again in 1946.

Another group of heroes of the Second World War were the Navajo Code Talkers. During the fighting in the Pacific,

The 158th Regiment, Arizona National Guard, on jungle training maneuvers during World War II. The outfit was given the nickname "Bushmasters" for the deadly jungle reptile. Photo: Southwest Studies.

Japanese soldiers, speaking fluent English, were intercepting messages and creating chaos with deceptive information, costing the lives of American servicemen. Navajos, enlisted in the marines, developed a special code using their language. The code of the Navajos was never broken and it's believed the Code Talkers saved the lives of thousands of soldiers and marines in the war.

Navajo Code Talkers in the South Pacific during World War II. They devised a secret code using the Navajo language that the Japanese couldn't break, saving the lives of thousands of G.I.'s and marines. Photo: USMC.

Ira Hayes, a Pima Indian from Bapchule, was one of the marines photographed while raising the flag on Mount Suribachi during the battle for Iwo Jima in 1945. The photograph became one of the most famous ever taken in battle and Hayes quickly became a national hero. After the war, he lived in Chicago and Hollywood, then returned to the reservation. His fame and recognition didn't pass with the ending of the war, but Ira had a tough time adjusting to peacetime life. He began to drink heavily, making the front pages of newspapers each time he was thrown in jail. Then one winter morning in 1955, he was found dead in a small irrigation ditch near his home. Ira Hayes was given a hero's burial in Arlington National Cemetery. A large monument depicting the historic flag- raising was dedicated at Arlington a year before he died.

Ira Hayes, Pima Indian. Hayes became a national hero after being photographed with a small group of marines hoisting the American flag on Mt. Suribachi, Iwo Jima, during World War II. Arizona State Library

Hayes is the last one in line in the photo, the one reaching out—a poignant gesture of his own life.

World War II brought tens of thousands of soldiers and airmen into Arizona to train for combat overseas. Between 1939 and 1945, nearly 150,000 Americans trained in Arizona. Some 60,000 of them were pilots, and in addition several thousand Chinese and British flyers earned their wings over Arizona's deserts.

The year-round mild weather was a prime factor, and bases were located from Kingman to Douglas. The deserts of southwest Arizona became a huge training ground for Gen. George Patton's soldiers prior to the invasion of North Africa. The weather was so hot that a bottle of beer under 100 degrees was considered a "cold one."

The largest prisoner of war escape from a U.S. compound occurred at Papago Park, east of Phoenix, on December 23, 1944. Some 1,700 German prisoners were held at the camp, many of them hardcore Nazis. Their captors believed the camp was escape-proof because the ground was too hard for digging tunnels. Despite this, the prisoners dug a 180-foot long tunnel over a three-month period, 8–14 feet beneath the surface. The excess dirt was casually deposited around the compound. At 9 P.M. on a cold, rainy night, while the other prisoners threw a loud party as a diversion, 25 prisoners including a 43-year-old U-boat skipper,

Capt. Jurgen Wattenberg, made their escape.

Three prisoners, nicknamed the "crazy boatmen" by their comrades, built a raft in hopes of floating down the Salt River and eventually getting to Mexico. Much to their surprise, the Salt, like most of Arizona's rivers, turned out to be a dry stream.

Over the next several weeks, all the prisoners except Capt. Wattenberg were rounded up. He hid out in a cave near Squaw Peak, north of Phoenix. Wattenberg was finally captured after he walked into Phoenix and, in a heavy German accent, asked for directions to the railroad station. That was his undoing. A suspicious gas station attendant called police and Wattenberg was arrested and returned to the POW camp.

War-related industries poured into Arizona during the 1940s as manufacturing came in to help balance the state's economy which, up to that time, was based primarily on cattle, copper, citrus and cotton. The salubrious weather, low-cost labor and relatively low taxes were the prime motivating factors. Before the war, people used to come to Arizona for a two-week vacation, but job opportunities were so limited they couldn't consider moving here. That all changed with new industries moving to the state. The Garrett Corporation, located in Phoenix, became one of the leaders in manufacturing parts for B17 bombers. Today, Garrett still builds components for the government and commercial aerospace applications, employing thousands at the Garrett Turbine Engine Company, Garrett Airline Services, Garrett General Aviation Services, and Garrett Fluid Systems Company plants. In 1988, these companies merged with Allied-Signal Aerospace.

In 1941, Goodyear Aircraft Corporation established a large plant west of Phoenix to build main assemblies for combat aircraft. The company evolved into Goodyear Aerospace Corporation as a part of Goodyear Tire and Rubber. In 1987, the Aerospace Corporation was purchased by Loral Corporation and became Defense Systems Division—Arizona of Loral Systems Group. The plant, located at Litchfield Park, employs nearly 2,000 people. During the war, Alcoa built a plant in west Phoenix which was later sold to Reynolds Aluminum.

During the post-war years, most of these corporations continued their operations in Arizona. Thousands of servicemen, sent here to train, returned after the war with their families to make their homes. In 1949, Dan Noble opened the first of several Motorola electronics plants in the Phoenix area. Other corporations, including General Electric, Hughes Aircraft, Sperry, Honeywell and IBM, followed Motorola to Arizona, offering the state a more balanced and diversified economy. Officials made a great effort to provide incentives for "clean air" industries to relocate in the state. In 1955, for example, the state repealed a sales tax on manufactured products for sale to the federal government. The day after the tax was repealed, Sperry Rand made plans to relocate its electronics aviation division plant and research center to Phoenix. By the 1960s, manufacturing had become the state's number one income-producing industry. Metropolitan Phoenix is now the nation's third largest high-tech area. Success breeds success. Large companies such as Greyhound, American Express, Phelps Dodge and Circle K located their corporate headquarters in Phoenix. With the new industries came more people. Tucson business and labor leaders weren't as aggressive as Phoenix. During the 1960s the "Old Pueblo" continued to lack a strong industrial base. By the late 1970s, however, that had all changed as Gates-LearJet, IBM and National Semiconductor opened plants.

The population of Arizona in 1940 was less than 500,000. Tucson boasted just under 37,000 residents while Phoenix had a population of just over 65,000 in a 9.6-square-mile area. By 1950, Arizona claimed 750,000 residents. Phoenix and Tucson had grown to 106,818 and 45,454 respectively. By 1960 the census reported a population of 439,170 in Phoenix and more than 212,000 in Tucson. More construction was done in the greater Phoenix area in 1959 than in all the years 1914 to 1946 combined. By 2000 greater Phoenix had grown to about 3 million residents and Tucson to more than 400,000. Some 80 percent of the state's entire population reside in either metro Phoenix or Tucson.

By and large, developers were in control. Urban sprawl jumped the canals and leap-frogged out into farm lands and cactus-strewn desert, devouring everything in its path. In

1950, Phoenix covered 17 square miles. By 1984, the sprawl had extended to 375 square miles. Between 1970 and 1988 the Phoenix metropolitan area registered a net gain of 246,000 newcomers. Arizona State University went from a small teachers college in the 1940s to one of the nation's largest institutions of higher learning, with more than 53,000 students. In 1960, communities such as Sun City, Green Valley, Carefree, Fountain Hills and Awatukee didn't even exist.

Yuma was an important riverport until the arrival of the railroad in 1877. The famed Yuma Crossing was the gateway to California for thousands of 19th Century travelers. Today Yuma Crossing State Historic Park provides an informative and living historical trek into those days of yesteryear. The abundance of sunshine and water has made Yuma a mecca for tourists and retirees. It is the winter home of the San Diego Padres baseball club, attracting thousands of fans from the coast during spring training. In the 1990s legalized gambling helped to make Yuma the third-fastest growing city in the United States after Las Vegas and Naples, Florida.

Flagstaff, since its beginning in 1881, has been the commerce and cultural center of northern Arizona. The rugged central mountains isolated the city from southern Arizona until the completion of Interstate 17 in the 1960s. Like other Arizona cities, Flagstaff has experienced unprecedented growth during post-war years. In 1950 the population was only 7,663. Over the next four decades the number of residents in Flagstaff and the nearby communities grew to nearly 55,000.

Northern Arizona Normal School opened its doors in 1899 with a faculty of two and a handful of students. In 1966, it became Northern Arizona University, providing even greater enrichment and prestige to the region. Historically, lumber, livestock and the railroad formed the backbone of Flagstaff's economy. Today, tourism plays a key role. Along with being the crossroads for U.S. 89, Interstates 17 and 40, this "City of Seven Wonders" is located near several of northern Arizona's most scenic attractions, including the San Francisco Peaks; the Grand Canyon; the Petrified Forest-Painted Desert; Wupatki National Monument-Sunset Crater; and Walnut Canyon National Monument.

Prescott, the first territorial capital, was an important ranching, freighting, military and mining center in the early days. The "Mile-High City's" mild year-around climate has made it one of the most desirable places in America to live. This mixed blessing has impacted the population to a large degree as Prescott grapples with many of the same problems as Phoenix and Tucson.

Arizona's soaring population has doubled every 20 years since 1920. Growth and the "good life" provided the inspiration for the low-density urban sprawl. Unfortunately, this was achieved with little extensive planning or effective regulation.

People like the informal, no-necktie, out-of-doors culture and lifestyle. And Tucson, Phoenix and Yuma are friendly, warm cities (especially in June, July and August). "Newcomers are always welcome," one transplant suggested. "That's because everyone else is a newcomer, too." It's getting difficult to find a real native Arizonan, but many lay claim to being almost-natives after a short residency. They're always happy to explain all the changes they've seen during their tenure. Some residents, many of them recent arrivals, aren't so sure. They'd like to "lock the gate" on any more newcomers.

Many "modern-day pioneers" move to Arizona after first visiting as a "snowbird," an affectionate (sort of) sobriquet given our fair weather friends who visit in the winter, crowding the roadways but enriching the state's economy. Others came for conventions, liked the place, and decided to take up residency. High-tech jobs serve as a magnet. Statistics show a high percentage of ambitious, educated people who list quality of life and career opportunities as reasons for their migration to Arizona. In the late 1970s, of family heads moving to the Phoenix area, 44 percent were under 35 years of age. Only 12 percent were over 65. The vast majority were skilled workers or managerial and professional people. And growth feeds on growth. Family members, neighbors and friends follow one another, beating a path to sun-kissed Arizona. Still, many people of retirement age are moving to the sunbelt. Retirement communities around southern Arizona will play an even more important role economically and politically baby boomers begin reaching the retirement age.

Another major reason for the state's population and economic growth was the adaptation of its great natural resources to the nation's changing needs and interests. Americans in the post-war era had more leisure time and more money to spend. Arizona possessed one of the country's three distinctive winter resorts and year-round playgrounds. Tourism, the state's second largest industry, pumps billions of dollars annually into the state's economy and provides more jobs than any other industry. Economic downturns seem to have less effect on tourism. For example, one of the Salt River Valley's greatest resorts, the Camelback Inn, was built during the depth of the Great Depression when, despite hard times, tourism continued to flourish.

Thousands of snowbirds flock to Arizona during spring training to watch their favorite major league baseball team tune up for the coming season. The economic effects of baseball alone are tremendous.

Why do they move to Arizona? Most say it's for the lifestyle. Not long ago, the desert was perceived as a forbidding place with desiccating heat, inhabited by uncurried cowboys, bewhiskered prospectors, painted Indians, cactus, coyotes, rattlesnakes, and scorpions. There was a perception that everything either stung, stabbed, stuck or stunk. Today, it means a laid back lifestyle, wide open spaces, year-round sports and recreation, and spectacular scenery. The great majority of newcomers are well-educated, goal-oriented young people—"yuppies," if you wish. Most have much to contribute. Many newcomers can offer expertise learned from past experience with the problems associated with growth. One has good reason to be optimistic about the future of Arizona, and its problems are not insurmountable. The urban areas of Tucson and Phoenix have serious problems to tackle, such as transportation and the pollution of water and air. Social problems associated with a highly mobile and transient society are troublesome. Metro Phoenix and Tucson along with cities like Prescott, Flagstaff and Yuma can learn from the mistakes of older urban areas. Resistance from limited growth groups continues. The great challenge facing all is a pragmatic balance between quality of life and growth.

Rural communities are also faced with problems not unique to Arizona. Young people see more opportunities in the cities. They leave the old home town for the bright lights, thus draining the small towns of future leadership in business and civic areas. Arizona's business and government leaders need to encourage and provide incentives to industry to locate in rural counties. This would counter unemployment problems such as the closing of mines in recent years and reduce the exodus of young people.

Rural Arizonans have always harbored a natural resentment toward city folks. And, like their forebears who pioneered this land, they are downright independent. Don Dedera, who writes about rural Arizona, tells about a flatlander from Phoenix who stopped at the little community of Chino Valley and asked a local woodcutter if he took orders for firewood. He stared at the city slicker long and hard, then replied, "Well, I do have some firewood cut and sometimes I sell it. But, mister, I don't take orders from nobody."

Arizona is, contrary to popular myth, an urban state. As mentioned, some 80 percent of the people live in the greater Phoenix or Tucson areas. Other populous areas such as Yuma, Sierra Vista, Prescott, and Flagstaff account for another large portion of the population. This, the sixth largest state in the Union with 113,956 square miles, has only about 45 persons per square mile.

Home rule, long cherished by Arizonans, has been elusive. Arizona came into the Union in 1912 chomping at the bit for home rule. Ironically, it was a time when the federal government was asserting more control over the states. Arizonans perceived themselves as self-reliant and independent, but quickly learned the realities of life in the 20th Century. The building of dams and highways could not have been accomplished without massive federal aid. Today in Arizona, the federal government spends about two dollars for every one dollar collected. The federal government owns 54 million acres, including Indian lands held in trust, in the state and is by far the largest landowner.

Some philosopher wrote, "Those who dream most, do most." Arizona has long been a place of inspiration to dreamers. During the 1960s the Army Corps of Engineers proposed a

14-foot deep concrete-lined aqueduct to curb flooding in Scottsdale's Indian Bend Wash. City officials protested the move, insisting on something more aesthetically pleasing and creative. The result was a flood control project that included lakes, ponds, athletic fields, golf courses and recreation facilities. Today, these facilities are used by hundreds of residents on a daily basis, and, not surprisingly, the project is now a badge of pride to the Army Corps of Engineers.

During the 1960s students in the College of Architecture at Arizona State University conceived a visionary plan that would transform the unsightly and normally dry Salt River bed into a garden of paradise. The Rio Salado Project, as it was called, caught the attention of Valley leaders. The plan called for a 25-year effort to fill a series of lakes and waterways, similar to the Indian Bend Project but on a much grander scale. Flanking the river would be recreational parks, housing, cultural centers and commercial development.

The imaginative but costly plan generated wide support and was finally brought before the voters in November 1987. But the project was voted down. Rio Salado was defeated at the polls primarily because taxpayers didn't want to pay the high costs of construction. It was perceived by too many people as benefitting developers at the expense of taxpayers. If the project is revived in the future the brunt of the cost will have to be borne by the private sector. The failure of the Rio Salado Project brought back memories of the early 1970s, when voters turned down a freeway through downtown Phoenix. After a delay and a modification of plans, voters approved the measure. Perhaps at some future date, the Rio Salado Project will be modified and, like the cross-town freeway, be revived.

Before the arrival of Central Arizona Project water, Tucson relied on underground water. In the early 1980s agriculture was using 75 percent of the water, while accounting for only 2 percent of the work force. That is rapidly changing. It seems likely that urban sprawl will eventually engulf all the remaining farm land in the Tucson area.

Along with the phenomenal growth of metropolitan Phoenix have come problems typical of any major city—air quality and transportation.

The problem of dealing with air quality is further complicated by the physical setting of the Salt River Valley. The Valley lies in a basin and doesn't have consistent prevailing breezes to blow the polluted air elsewhere. The "pollution season" occurs from October through March, when carbon monoxide and particulates are at a peak. During high-pollution days the elderly, young children and those with respiratory or heart conditions are advised to curtail outdoor activities. Motorists are urged to car pool or take the bus. Usually about 20 of these unhealthful days are recorded between October and March. During this period toxic carbon monoxide is at its worst because of temperature inversions—stagnant cold air trapping pollutants close to the ground. Carbon monoxide, emitted mostly from autos, cannot be seen or smelled. The ugly brown cloud that hangs over the Valley is made up of particulates. Arizonans refer to it as "smust," a combination of smog and desert dust.

The first freeway in Phoenix skirted the west side of the city and was part of the old Black Canyon Highway. During the mid-1950s four-way stop signs halted traffic at each major cross street. By the 1960s the Black Canyon, or Interstate 17, had become a reality. Because the inner city was becoming too congested, the Papago Freeway was planned as the city's first cross-town freeway. The plan had been drafted in 1960 during a time when planners claimed greater Phoenix would need 300 miles of freeway by 1980. It was to be elevated, causing critics to describe it as looking; more like a "Coney Island roller coaster than a desert freeway." Ugly freeways in older, more developed cities had gone out of fashion and this provided fodder for opponents to muster enough strength to stop it.

The Papago Freeway came to a screeching halt in 1973. Although the elevated freeway was ill-conceived, it seemed destined to gain voter approval. Then Eugene Pulliam, owner and publisher of the Valley's two largest newspapers came out against it. The "twins," as the *Arizona Republic* and *Phoenix Gazette* were known affectionately and otherwise, issued a barrage of daily editorials, cartoons and freeway horror stories. The voters took heed and rejected the Papago Freeway by a three-to-two margin. Planners went back to the drawing board and two years later a new plan, this time a below-grade freeway, was submitted for a vote. Voters approved it by a narrow margin and the Papago Freeway, at last, was on its way to reality. Further delays slowed down construction however. Hohokam villages dating back to A.D. 500 were discovered in the freeway's path. Then came legal challenges to the route. The slow-molasses construction project stretched into the mid-1980s, and the original projected cost of $50 million in 1969 rose to $700 million.

In 1985, having lost much federal funding because of the delays, Maricopa County voters approved a 20-year, half-cent sales tax to build a 233-mile Salt River Valley freeway system. This was cut to 146 miles in 1995. Plans included two major loop routes, 101 and 202. A third loop, the 303, is slated for the future. Two years later construction began on Loop 101, 202 and Arizona 51, the Squaw Peak Expressway. The latter would link the Maricopa Freeway with Loop 101 in Paradise Valley. In 1990 the western leg of I-10 was completed extending through the West Valley and linking up with Loop 101. Construction of another loop, the 303, was begun that would eventually extend all the way to I-17. Also, during the1990s the 202 through central Phoenix was extended past Scottsdale and Tempe into Mesa and back to the I-10 freeway at Chandler.

In April 2002 Loop 101 was completed when the final stretch in north Scottsdale was opened, allowing motorists to travel by freeway from Chandler in the East Valley all the way through Scottsdale, Phoenix, to the interchange at I-17, and beyond to Peoria, Sun City, Glendale and to I-10 in the West Valley.

If all this sounds confusing, it made a lot of sense to the drivers commuting during the strangling rush hour traffic. The Salt River Valley freeway system will be one of the best in the nation after its completion, scheduled for 2007.

In the future Arizona's native peoples are likely to experience further effects of the far-reaching change that began on May 12, 1992, when the federal government loaded the Fort McDowell Indian Community's slot machines into rented moving vans, intending to haul them from the reservation. Armed agents were positioned atop the gaming center, and other agents in riot gear stood nearby to ensure the machines' seizure.

The agents were unprepared for the resistance they met from Fort McDowell Yavapai Nation. At the exit the Yavapi had gathered to block the road. Members of one of the smallest and poorest Indian tribes stood in defiance of the federal and state governments. Community members—unarmed men and women, young and old—made a stand that symbolized the continuing plight of Indian people in their struggle for self-determination.

After three weeks, the government backed off and decided to negotiate gaming contracts with all the tribes in the state. The stand taken by the Fort McDowell Yavapai Nation was a moral and political victory for all Native Americans. After the signing of the first gaming compacts in 1993, many tribes went from rags to riches. Casinos began to bring economic prosperity to reservations at Ak-Chin, Fort McDowell, Payson, Hondah, Parker, Yuma, San Carlos, Pasqua-Yaqui, Cliff Castle, Mohave Valley, Prescott, Salt River-Pima and the Gila River.

Along with gaming has come a Supreme Court decision giving huge amounts of water to the tribes, which could make the tribes major power brokers in allotment of water to Arizona cities. Early in the 21st Century the federal government is expected to sign the largest water allotment in U. S. history. Ten Arizona Indian tribes are expected gain control of more than one million acre-feet of water per year, enough to serve the residential needs of more than five million people, or roughly the entire population of the state. An acre foot is enough water to cover one acre with one foot of water. That's about 326,000 gallons, enough to serve a family of five for a year. The tribes are expected to be assigned 1.3 million acre feet, and the total annual residential and industrial water use in the state is 1.8 million acre feet. The tiny Ak-Chin Indian Community is already providing water for the huge Del Webb Anthem development north of Phoenix. The Salt River Pima Community leases water to Phoenix and Scottsdale.

Still other changes are affecting leisure activities in the state. In 1995, Major League Baseball awarded a franchise to the Arizona Diamondbacks. The team began playing in the National League and three years later defeated the New York

Yankees in the World Series in 2001, bringing the state its first world championship in professional sports. Arizona now has the National Hockey League's Phoenix Coyotes, the National Football League's Arizona Cardinals, and the National Basketball Association's Phoenix Suns. Coach Lute Olson and his University of Arizona's basketball team made history in 1997 when they brought home the state's first-ever NCAA national basketball championship, defeating Kentucky 84-79 in the title game.

Arizona is no longer developing through its traditional five C's—Cattle, Copper, Climate, Cotton and Citrus. Today, Computers, Construction, Cargo and Communication have taken their place; the only constant is the Climate that brings tourists.

Tourism is one of the state's largest and most important industries, employing over 400,000 people and producing $30 billion annually, or some 25 percent of the state's revenue. Studies show tourists spend $7 for every dollar the state spends on tourism promotion. Without tourism property taxes would be 50 percent higher. Domestically, Arizona is the 5th most popular state to visit. Internationally, it's the 7th most popular.

Statistics about Arizona tend to become outmoded as fast as they are reported. In 1990 the population of the state was 3,665,268. By 2000, it had risen to 5.1 million. In 1950 Phoenix was the 95th largest city in the US. By 2000 it was the 6th largest. Metropolitan Phoenix has 3 million people. The tiny Gilbert in the East Valley had 1,600 people in 1960. By 1990 it had grown to 29,149. Ten years later it had reached a whopping 110,000 people.

Why do people come? In a word, "lifestyle." Arizona is a great place to live, work and play. The Salt River Project Economic Report of 1990 listed the state's assets in this order: healthy climate; open spaces; job opportunities; lower living costs; natural beauty; friendliness of the people; abundance of natural resources; good community colleges; and minimum danger of physical hazards such as earthquakes, tornadoes, fires or floods. Not included in this report was that it *does* get a little warm in the deserts during the summer, but it's a dry heat … and you don't have to shovel it.

No area can claim true greatness without a strong commitment to education and the arts, both visual and performing. And developers need to end the shortsighted practice of trying to make Arizona look like "back home." Lakeside villages have no place in the desert, nor does the proliferation of lush "alien" greenery. Because of high pollen counts, people no longer come to Arizona to cure allergies. Tucson led the way a few years ago when an ordinance was passed prohibiting the planting of pollen-producing olive and mulberry trees.

There's still a lot of wide-open breathing space in Arizona. A few short miles from cities of concrete, glass and steel, cowboys still work cattle, much the same as their great-grandfathers did a century ago. Native Americans still view the world through 2,000 -year-old eyes. We are the caretakers of this great land. Future generations will judge us by our deeds, both good and short-sighted. Let's hope when they tally up the score, we come up winners.

During America's first 100 years as a nation, pioneers moved ever-westward to new frontiers. When it became too crowded or the soil was mined out, they moved on to virgin land. Those days are gone forever. We have to learn to live with the problems we create. The knowledge gained from studying mistakes of the past can help to provide a brighter future. Will Rogers said it best: "The Indians never got lost because they were always looking back to see where they'd been."

ARIZONA'S POLITICAL FIGURES

Governors of Arizona

TERRITORIAL

John N. Goodwin (1824-1887)	Republican	1863-1865
Richard G. McCormick (1832-1901)	Republican	1865-1869
Anson P.K. Safford (1828?-1891)	Republican	1869-1877
John P. Hoyt (1841-1926)	Republican	1877-1878
John C. Fremont (1813-1890)	Republican	1878-1882
Frederick A. Tritle (1833-1906)	Republican	1882-1885
C. Meyer Zulick (1838-1926)	Democrat	1885-1889
Lewis Wolfley (1839-1910)	Republican	1889-1890
John N. Irwin (1845?-1905)	Republican	1890-1892
Nathan O. Murphy (1849-1908)	Republican	1892-1893
Louis C. Hughes (1842-1915)	Democrat	1893-1896
Benjamin J. Franklin (1839-1898)	Democrat	1896-1897
Myron H. McCord (1840-1908)	Republican	1897-1898
Nathan O. Murphy (1849-1908)	Republican	1898-1902
Alexander O. Brodie (1849-1918)	Republican	1902-1905
Joseph H. Kibbey (1853-1924)	Republican	1905-1909
Richard E. Sloan (1857-1933)	Republican	1909-1912

STATE

George W. P. Hunt (1859-1934)	Democrat	1912-1917
Thomas E. Campbell (1878-1944)	Republican	1917
George W. P. Hunt (1859-1934)	Democrat	1917-1919
Thomas E. Campbell (1878-1944)	Republican	1919-1923
George W. P. Hunt (1859-1934)	Democrat	1923-1929
John C. Phillips (1870-1943)	Republican	1929-1931
George W. P. Hunt (1859-1934)	Democrat	1931-1933
Benjamin B. Moeur (1869-1937)	Democrat	1933-1937
Rawghlie C. Stanford (1878-1962)	Democrat	1937-1939
Robert T. Jones (1884-1958)	Democrat	1939-1941
Sidney P. Osborn (1884-1948)	Democrat	1941-1948
Dan E. Garvey (1886-1974)	Democrat	1948-1951
Howard Pyle (1906-1987)	Republican	1951-1955
Ernest W. McFarland (1894-1984)	Democrat	1955-1959
Paul Fannin (1907-2002)	Republican	1959-1965
Samuel P. Goddard (1919-)	Democrat	1965-1967

John R. ("Jack") Williams (1909-1998)   Republican   1967-1975
Raul H. Castro (1916-)   Democrat   1975-1977
Wesley H. Bolin (1908-1978)   Democrat   1977-1978
Bruce E. Babbitt (1938-)   Democrat   1978-1987
Evan Mecham (1924-)   Republican   1987-1988
Rose Mofford (1922-)   Democrat   1988-1991
J. Fife Symington (1945-)   Republican   1991-1997
Jane Dee Hull (1935-)   Republican   1997-2003
Janet Napolitano (1957-)   Democrat   2003-

Arizona Territorial Delegates to Congress

Charles D. Poston (1825-1902)   Republican   1864-1865
John N. Goodwin (1824-1887)   Republican   1865-1867
Coles Bashford (1816-1878)   Independent   1867-1869
Richard C. McCormick (1832-1901)   Unionist   1869-1875
Hiram S. Stevens (1832-1893)   Democrat   1875-1879
John G. Campbell (1827-1903)   Democrat   1879-1881
Granville H. Oury (1825-1891)   Democrat   1881 -1885
Curtis C. Bean (1828-1904)   Republican   1885-1887
Marcus A. Smith (1851-1924)   Democrat   1887-1895
   1897-1899
   1901-1903
   1905-1909
Nathan O. Murphy (1849-1908)   Republican   1895-1897
John F. Wilson (1846-1911)   Democrat   1899-1901
   1903-1905
Ralph H. Cameron (1863-1953)   Republican

United States Senators from Arizona

Marcus A. Smith (1851-1924)   Democrat   1912-1921
Henry F. Ashurst (1874-1962   Democrat   1912-1941
Ralph H. Cameron (1863-1953)   Republican   1921-1927
Carl T. Hayden (1877-1972)   Democrat   1927-1969
Ernest W. McFarland (1894-1994)   Democrat   1941-1953
Barry M. Goldwater (1909-1998)   Republican   1953-1965
   1969-1987
Paul J. Fannin (1907-)   Republican   1965-1977
Dennis DeConcini (1937-)   Democrat   1977-1995
John McCain (1936-)   Republican   1987-
John Kyl (1942-)   Republican   1995-

United States Representatives from Arizona

Carl T. Hayden (1877-1972)	Dist. 1	Democrat	1912-1927
Lewis W. Doublas (1894-1974)	Dist. 1	Democrat	1927-1933
Isabella S. Greenway (1886-1953)	Dist. 1	Democrat	1933-1937
John R. Murdock (1885-1972)	Dist. 1	Democrat	1937-1953
Richard F. Harless (1905-1970)	Dist. 2	Democrat	1943-1949
Harold A. Patten (1907-1969)	Dist. 2	Democrat	1949-1955'
John J. Rhodes (1916-)	Dist. 1	Republican	1953-1983
Steward L. Udall (1920-)	Dist. 2	Democrat	1955-1961
Morris K. Udall (1922-1998)	Dist. 2	Democrat	1961-1991
George F. Senner, Jr. (1921-)	Dist. 3	Democrat	1963-1967
Sam Steiger, Jr. (1929-)	Dist. 3	Republican	1967-1977
John B. Conlan (1930-)	Dist. 4	Republican	1973-1977
Eldon Rudd (1920-2002)	Dist. 4	Republican	1977-1987
Bob Stump (1927-)	Dist. 3	Democrat-Republican	1997-2003
John McCain (1936-)	Dist. 1	Republican	1983-1987
James McNulty (1925-)	Dist. 5	Democrat	1983-1985
James "Jim" Kolbe (1942-)	Dist. 5	Republican	1985-2003
	Dist. 8	Republican	2003-
John J. Rhodes III (1943-)	Dist. 1	Republican	1987-1993
Ed Pastor (1943-)	Dist. 2	Democrat	1991-2003
	Dist. 4	Democrat	2003-
Karen English (1949-)	Dist. 6	Democrat	1993-1995
Sam Coppersmith (1955-)	Dist. 1	Democrat	1993-1995
J. D. Hayworth (1958-)	Dist. 6	Republican	1995-2003
	Dist. 5	Republican	2003-
Matt Salmon (1958-)	Dist. 1	Republican	1995-2001
John Shadegg (1949-)	Dist. 4	Republican	1995-
Jeff Flake (1962-)	Dist. 1	Republican	2001-2003
	Dist. 6	Republican	2003-
Rick Renzi (1958-)	Dist. 1	Republican	2003-
Trent Franks (1957-)	Dist. 2	Republican	2003-
Raul Grijalva (1948-)	Dist. 7	Democrat	2003-

BIBLIOGRAPHY

GENERAL READING

Boyer, Mary G. *Arizona in Literature.* Glendale, CA.: A. H. Clark, Co., 1935.

Cline, Platt. *They Came to the Mountain: The History of Flagstaff* Flagstaff: Northland Press, 1976.

Corle, Edwin. *The Gila; River of The Southwest.* New York: Rinehart, 1951.

Farish, Thomas E. *History of Arizona.* 8 Volumes. Phoenix: Manufacturing Stationers, 1920.

Faulk, Odie. *Land of Many Frontiers.* New York: Oxford University Press, 1968.

Faulk, Odie. *Arizona: A Short History.* Norman: University of Oklahoma Press, 1970.

Fireman, Bert. *Arizona: Historic Land,* New York: Knopf, 1982.

Goff, John. *Arizona Biographical Dictionary.* Cave Creek: Black Mountain Press, 1983.

Goff, John. *Arizona: An Illustrated History of The Grand Canyon State.* Northridge, CA: Windsor Pub., 1988.

Granger, Byrd. *Arizona's Names: X Marks the Place.Tucson:* Falconer Pub. Co., 1983.

Harris, Richard. *The First 100 Years: A History of Arizona Blacks.* Apache Junction: Relmo Publishers, 1983.

Hill, Myles and Goff, John. *Arizona's Past and Present.* Cave Creek: Black Mountain Press, 1975.

Hink, Heinz: Mason, Bruce; and Halacy, Dan. *Arizona: People and Government.* Tempe: HMH Book Co., 1975.

Hinton, Richard. *Handbook to Arizona.* San Francisco: Payot, Upham and Co., 1878. Reprinted Tucson: Arizona Silhouettes, 1954.

Hollon, W. Eugene. *The Southwest Old and New.* New York: Knopf, 1961.

Johnson, Wesley. *Phoenix: Valley of The Sun.* Tulsa: Continental Heritage Press, 1982.

Lamar, Howard. *The Far Southwest 1846-1912.* New York: W.W. Norton & Co., 1970.

Lavender, David. *The Southwest.* New York: Harper and Row, 1980.

Martin, Douglas. *Yuma Crossing.* Albuquerque: University of New Mexico Press, 1954.

Maxwell, Margaret. *A Passion for Freedom: The Life of Sharlot Hall.* Tucson: University of Arizona Press, 1982.

McClintock, James. *Arizona.* 3 Volumes. Chicago: Clarke Publishing Co., 1916.

McElfresh, Patricia Myers. *Scottsdale: Jewel in the Desert.* Woodland Hills, CA. Windsor Publications, 1984.

Miller, Joseph. ed. *The Arizona Story.* New York: Hastings House, 1952.

Miller, Joseph. ed. *Arizona: The Last Frontier.* New York: Hastings House, 1956.

Miller, Joseph. ed. *Arizona Cavalcade.* New York: Hastings House, 1962.

Miller, Joseph. ed. *Arizona: A State Guide.* New York: Hastings House, 1966.

Quebbeman, Frances. *Medicine in Territorial Arizona.* Phoenix: Arizona Historical Foundation, 1966.

Schweikart, Larry. *A History of Banking in Arizona.* Tucson: University of Arizona Press, 1982.

Sherman, James and Barbara. *Ghost Towns of Arizona.* Norman: University of Oklahoma Press, 1969.

Smith, Dean. *The Goldwaters of Arizona.* Flagstaff: Northland Press, 1986.

Sonnichsen, C. L. *Tucson: The Life and Times of an American City.* Norman: University of Oklahoma Press, 1982.

Trimble, Marshall. *Arizona: A Panoramic History of a Frontier State.* New York: Doubleday and Co., 1977.

Trimble, Marshall. *Roadside History of Arizona.* Missoula: Mountain Press, 1986.

Trimble, Marshall. *Diamond in the Rough: An Illustrated History of Arizona.* Norfolk: Donning Pub. Co., 1988.

Varney, Phil. *Arizona's Best Ghost Towns.* Flagstaff: Northland Press, 1980.

Wagoner, Jay. *Arizona's Heritage.* Salt Lake City: Peregrine Smith, 1977.

Walker, H.P. and Bufkin, Don. *Historical Atlas of Arizona.* Norman: University of Oklahoma Press, 1979.

Wallace, Andrew. *Sources and Readings in Arizona History.* Tucson: Arizona Pioneers Historical Society, 1965.

Weir, Bill. *Arizona Handbook.* Chico, CA. Moon Pub., 1981.

Wellman, Paul. *Glory, God and Gold.* Garden City: Doubleday and Co., 1954.

Woody, Clara and Schwartz, Milton. *Globe, Arizona.* Tucson: Arizona Historical Society, 1977.

Wyllys, Rufus K. *Arizona: The History of a Frontier State.* Phoenix: Hobson and Herr, 1950.

CHAPTER 1—BEFORE THE TIME OF MAN

Chronic, Halka. *Roadside Geology of Arizona.* Missoula: Mountain Press, 1983.

Comeaux, Malcolm. *Arizona: A Geography.* Boulder, CO.: Westview Press, 1931.

Olin, George. *Mammals of the Southwest Deserts.* Globe: Southwest Parks and Monuments, 1975.

Olin, George. *Mammals of the Southwest Mountains and Mesas.* Globe: Southwest Parks and Monuments, 1975.

Olin, George. *House in the Sun.* (Flora and Fauna of Arizona). Globe: Southwest Parks and Monuments, 1977.

CHAPTER 2—PREHISTORIC ARIZONA

Haury, Emil. *The Hohokam.* Tucson: University of Arizona Press, 1976.

Kidder, Alfred. *An Introduction to the Study of Southwestern Archaeology.* New Haven: Yale University Press, 1962.

Martin, Paul and Plog, Fred. *The Archaeology of Arizona.* Garden City: Doubleday/Natural History Press, 1973.

Noble, David Grant. *Ancient Ruins of the Southwest.* Flagstaff: Northland Press, 1981.

Pike, Donald. *Anasazi: Ancient People of the Rock.* Palo Alto: American West, 1974.

CHAPTER 3—ARIZONA'S NATIVE AMERICANS

Acuff, Guy. *Akimult Aw A Tham, The River People: A Short History of the Pima Indians.* Casa Grande: Casa Grande Centennial Ed., 1979.

Dutton, Bertha. *Indians of the American Southwest.* Englewood Cliffs: Prentice Hall, Inc., 1975.

Forbes, Jack. *Apache, Navajo and Spaniard.* Norman: University of Oklahoma Press, 1960.

Forbes, Jack. *Warriors of the Colorado.* Norman: University of Oklahoma Press, 1965.

Goodwin, Grenville. *The Social Organization of the Western Apaches.* Chicago: The University of Chicago Press, 1942.

Goodwin, Grenville. *Western Apaches, Raiding and Warfare.* Tucson: University of Arizona Press, 1971.

Lockwood, Frank. *The Apache Indians.* New York: The Macmillan Co., 1938.

Ogle, Ralph. *Federal Control of the Western Apaches.* Albuquerque: University of New Mexico Press, 1940.

Russell, Frank. *The Pima Indians.* Tucson: University of Arizona Press, 1975.

Santee, Ross. *Apacheland.* New York: C. Scribner's Sons, 1947.

Spicer, Edward. *Cycles of Conquest.* Tucson: University of Arizona Press, 1963.

Terrell, John Upton. *The Navajos.* New York: World Publishing, 1970.

Terrell, John Upton. *Apache Chronicle.* New York: World Publishing, 1972.

Underhill, Ruth. *The Navajos.* Norman: University of Oklahoma Press, 1967.

Waters, Frank. *Book of The Hopi.* New York: Viking Press, 1964.

CHAPTER 4—GLORY, GOD AND GOLD and
CHAPTER 5—RIM OF CHRISTENDOM

Bannon, John. *Bolton and the Spanish Borderlands.* Norman: University of Oklahoma Press, 1964.

Bannon, John. *The Spanish Borderlands Frontier.* New York: Holt, Rinehart and Winston, 1970.

Bolton, Herbert. *Coronado: Knight of Pueblos and Plains.* New York: Whittlesey House, 1949.

Bolton, Herbert. *Spanish Exploration of the Southwest.* New York: Barnes and Noble, 1952.

Bolton, Herbert. *Rim of Christendom.* New York: Russell and Russell, 1960.

Bolton, Herbert. *The Padre on Horseback.* Chicago: Loyola University Press, 1963.

Brinkerhoff, S., and Faulk, O. *Lancers for the King.* Phoenix: Arizona Historical Foundation, 1963.

Castañeda, Pedro de. *The Coronado Expedition.* Chicago: Rio Grande Press, 1964.

Dobyns, Henry. *Spanish Colonial Tucson.* Tucson: University of Arizona Press, 1976.

Hammond, George P. *Don Juan Oñate, Colonizer of New Mexico.* Albuquerque: University of New Mexico Press, 1953.

Jones, Okah. *Los Paisanos: Spanish Settlers on the Northern Frontier of New Spain.* Norman: University of Oklahoma Press, 1978.

Kessell, John. *Kiva, Cross and Crown.* Washington, D.C.: National Parks Service, 1979.

McCarty, Kieran. *Desert Documentary: The Spanish Years, 1767-1821.* Tucson: Arizona Historical Society, 1976.

Officer, James. *Hispanic Arizona, 1536-1856.* Tucson: University of Arizona Press, 1987.

Terrell, John Upton. *Pueblos, Gods and Spaniards.* New York: The Dial Press, 1973.

Wagoner, Jay. *Early Arizona.* Tucson: University of Arizona Press, 1975.

CHAPTER 6—THE AMERICAN ENTRADA

Carson, Kit. *The Autobiography of Kit Carson.* Lincoln: University of Nebraska Press, 1966.

Camp, Charles. ed. *George C. Yount and his Chronicles of the West.* Denver: Old West Publishing Co., 1966.

Cleland, Robert G. *This Reckless Breed of Men.* New York: Knopf, 1950.

Favour, Alpheus. *Old Bill Williams, Mountain Man.* Chapel Hill: University of North Carolina Press, 1936.

Gregg, Josiah. *Commerce of the Prairies.* Chicago: R.R. Donnelley and Sons, 1926.

Hall, Sharlot. *Pauline Weaver.* Prescott Booklet, 1929.

Holmes, Kenneth. *Ewing Young: Master Trapper.* Portland, OR.: Binfords and Mort, 1967.

Lavender, David. *Bent's Fort.* Garden City: Doubleday and Co., 1954.

Leonard, Zenas. *The Narrative of Zenas Leonard.* Norman: University of Oklahoma Press, 1959.

Officer, James. *Hispanic Arizona 1536-1856.* Tucson: University of Arizona Press, 1987.

Parkhill, Forbes. *The Blazed Trail of Antoine Leroux.* Los Angeles: Westernlore Press, 1965.

Pattie, James Ohio. *The Personal Narrative of James Ohio Pattie of Kentucky.* Ed. by Timothy Flint. (reprint) Philadelphia:, 1962.

Weber, David. *The Taos Trappers: The Fur Trade in the Far Southwest.* Norman: University of Oklahoma Press, 1966.

CHAPTER 7—ARIZONA IN THE 1850s

Ahnert, Gerald. *Retracing the Butterfield Overland Trail Through Arizona.* Los Angeles: Westernlore Press, 1973.

Bartlett, John R. *Personal Narrative.* 2 Vols. Reprinted Chicago: Rio Grande Press, 1965.

Clarke, Dwight. *Stephen Watts Kearny: Soldier of the West.* Norman: University of Oklahoma Press, 1966.

Conkling, Roscoe and Margaret. *The Butterfield Overland Mail 1857-1869.* 2 Vols. Glendale: Arthur Clark, 1947.

Cooke, Philip St. George. *The Conquest of New Mexico and California.* Albuquerque: Horn and Wallace, 1964.

Emory, William. *Notes of a Military Reconnaissance.* Albuquerque: University of New Mexico Press, 1951.

Faulk, Odie. *Destiny Road.* New York: Oxford University Press, 1973.

Faulk, Odie. *The U.S. Camel Corps.* New York: Oxford University Press, 1976.

Lingenfelter, Richard. *Steamboats on the Colorado.* Tucson: University of Arizona Press, 1978.

North, Diane. *Samuel Peter Heintzelman and the Sonora Exploring and Mining Company.* Tucson: University of Arizona Press, 1980.

Ormsby, Waterman. *The Butterfield Overland Mail.* San Marino: Huntington Library, 1955.

Pumpelly, Raphael. *Pumpelly's Arizona.* Tucson: Palo Verde Press, 1965.

Tyler, Daniel. *A Concise History of the Mormon Battalion in the Mexican War.* Chicago: Rio Grande Press, 1964.

Wallace, Edward. *The Great Reconnaissance: Soldiers, Artists, and Scientists on the Frontier, 1848-1861.* Boston: Little, Brown and Co., 1955.

Young, Otis E. *The West of Philip St. George Cooke*. Glendale, CA.: A. H. Clark Co., 1955.

CHAPTER 8—TURBULENT TIMES: THE INDIAN WARS

Altshuler, Constance Wynn. *Chains of Command: Arizona and the Army 1856-1875*. Tucson: Arizona Historical Society, 1981.

Arnold, Elliott. *Blood Brother.* New York: Duell, Sloan and Pearce, 1947.

Bailey, L. R. *The Long Walk, A History of the Navajo Wars*. Los Angeles: Westernlore Press; 1964.

Bailey, L. R. *Indian Slave Trade in the Southwest*. Los Angeles: Westernlore Press, 1966.

Bourke, John. *On the Border with Crook*. Chicago: Rio Grande Press, 1962.

Brandes, Ray. *Frontier Military Posts of Arizona*. Globe: D. S. King, 1960.

Browne, J. Ross. *Adventures in Apache Country*. New York: Harper, 1869.

Clendenin, Clarence. *Blood on the Border.* New York: Macmillan, 1969.

Cremony, John. *Life Among the Apaches*. San Francisco: A. Roman, 1968.

Davis, Britton. *The Truth about Geronimo.* New Haven: Yale University Press, 1963.

Debo, Angie. *Geronimo.* Norman: University of Oklahoma Press, 1976.

Hunt, Aurora. *Major General James H. Carleton*. Glendale, CA. A. H. Clark Co., 1958.

Johnson, V. W. *The Unregimented General: Nelson Miles*. Boston and New York: Houghton Mifflin, 1962.

Kerby, Robert Lee. *The Confederate Invasion of New Mexico and Arizona*. Tucson: Westernlore Press, 1981.

Leckie, Robert. *The Buffalo Soldiers*. Norman: University of Oklahoma Press, 1967.

Schmitt, Martin ed. *The Autobiography of George Crook*. Norman: University of Oklahoma Press, 1960.

Summerhayes, Martha. *Vanished Arizona*. Philadelphia: Lippincott Co., 1908.

Thrapp, Dan. *Conquest of Apacheria*. Norman: University of Oklahoma Press, 1967.

Utley, Robert. *Frontiersmen in Blue.* New York: Macmillan Co., 1967.

Utley, Robert. *Frontier Regulars.* New York: Macmillan Co., 1973.

CHAPTER 9—MINING IN ARIZONA

Allen, James B. *The Company Town in the American West.* Norman: University of Oklahoma Press, 1966.

Arizona Bureau of Mines. *Gold Placers in Arizona.* Bulletin 168. Tucson: University of Arizona, 1961.

Arizona Bureau of Mines. *Artzona Lode Gold Mines and Gold Mining.* Bulletin 137. Tucson: University of Arizona, 1967.

Bailey, Lynn R. *Bisbee: Queen of the Copper Camps.* Tucson: Westernlore Press, 1983.

Burns, Walter Noble. *Tombstone.* New York: Grosset and Dunlap, 1929.

Byrkit, James. *Forging The Copper Collar.* Tucson: University of Arizona Press, 1982.

Canty, J. Michael and Greeley. *History of Mining in Arizona.* Tucson: Mining Club of the Southwest Foundation, 1987.

Cleland, Robert G. *A History of Phelps Dodge.* New York: Knopf, 1952.

Crampton, Frank. *Deep Enough.* Denver: A. Swallow, 1956.

Dunning, Charles, and Peplow, Edward. *Rock to Riches.* Phoenix: Southwest Publishing Co., 1959.

Egerton, Kearney. *Somewhere Out There.* Glendale, AZ.: Prickly Pear Press, 1974.

Gilbert, Bill *Weltering Man: The Life of Joseph Walker.* New York: Atheneum, 1983.

Lingenfelter, Richard. *The Hardrock Miners.* Berkeley. University of California, 1974.

Love, Frank. *Mining Camps and Ghost Towns.* Los Angeles: Westernlore Press, 1974.

Mitchell, John D. *Lost Mines and Buried Treasures Along the Old Frontier.* Glorieta, N.M. The Rio Grande Press, 1954.

Myers, John M. *The Last Chance: Tombstone's Early Years.* New York: E.P. Dutton and Co., 1950.

North, Diane. *Samuel Peter Heintzelman and the Sonora Exploring and Mining Company.* Tucson: University of Arizona Press, 1980.

Sonnichsen, C. L. *Colonel Greene and the Copper Skyrocket.* Tucson: University of Arizona Press, 1974.

Young, Herbert V. *The Ghosts of Cleopatra Hill.* Jerome: Jerome Historical Society, 1964.

Young, Herbert V. *They Came to Jerome.* Jerome: Jerome Historical Society, 1972.

Young, Otis E. *How They Dug the Gold.* Tucson: University of Arizona Press, 1967.

Young, Otis E. *Western Mining.* Norman: University of Oklahoma Press, 1970.

Young, Otis E. *Black Powder and Hand Steel.* Norman: University of Oklahoma, 1976.

CHAPTER 10—LEGENDS IN LEVIS: THE COWBOYS

Adams, Ramon. *The Old-Time Cowhand.* New York: Macmillan Co., 1961.

Coolidge, Dane. *Arizona Cowboys.* New York: E. P. Dutton, 1938.

Frantz, Joe and Choate, J.E. *The American Cowboy: The Myths and the Reality.* Norman: University of Oklahoma Press, 1968.

Hughes, Stella. *Hashknife Cowboy.* Tucson: University of Arizona Press, 1984.

Hunt, Frazier. *Cap Mossman: Last of the Great Cowmen.* New York: Hastings House, 1951.

Moore, Dan. *Log of a Twentieth Century Cowboy.* Tucson: University of Arizona Press, 1965.

Proctor, Gil. *The Trails of Pete Kitchen.* Tucson: D.S. King, 1964.

Rak, Mary Kidder. *Cowman's Wife.* Boston and New York: Houghton Mifflin, 1934.

Rak, Mary Kidder. *Mountain Cattle.* Boston and New York: Houghton Mifflin, 1936.

Rollins, Philip A. *The Cowboy.* Albuquerque: University of New Mexico Press, 1979. (Reprint).

Santee, Ross. *Cowboy.* Lincoln: Bison Books, University of Nebraska Press, 1977. (Reprint).

Sharp, Bob. *Big Outfit: Ranching on the Baca Float.* Tucson: University of Arizona Press, 1974.

Sharp, Bob. *Bob Sharp's Cattle Country.* Tucson: University of Arizona Press, 1985.

Trimble, Marshall. *The CO Bar Ranch.* Flagstaff: Northland Press, 1982.

Wagoner, Jay. "History of the Cattle Industry of Southern Arizona." Tucson: University of Arizona Social Science Bulletin #20, 1952.

CHAPTER 11—OUTLAWRY AND JUSTICE

Boyer, Glenn. ed. *I Married Wyatt Earp (The Memoirs of Josephine Marcus Earp)*. Tucson: University of Arizona Press, 1976.

Breckenridge, Billy. *Helldorado*. Boston and New York: Houghton Mifflin, 1928.

Burrows, Jack. *John Ringo: The Gunfghter Who Never Was*. Tucson: University of Arizona Press, 1987.

Dedera, Don. *A Little War of Our Own: The Pleasant Valley War Revisited*. Flagstaff: Northland Press, 1988.

Forrest, Earle. *Arizona's Dark and Bloody Ground*. Caldwell, Idaho: Caxton Printers, 1936.

Haley, J. E. *Jeff Milton: A Good Man with a Gun*. Norman: University of Oklahoma Press, 1958.

Hunt, Frazier. *Cap Mossman: Last of the Great Cowmen*. New York: Hastings House, 1951.

Krakel, Dean. *The Saga of Tom Horn*. Laramie: Powder River Publishers, 1954.

Lake, Stuart. *Wyatt Earp: Frontier Marshal*. Boston and New York: Houghton Mifflin, 1931.

Miller, Joseph. ed. *The Arizona Rangers*. New York: Hastings House, 1972.

Monaghan, James. *The Last of The Bad Men: The Legend of Tom Horn*. New York: Bobbs-Merrill Co., 1946.

Myers, John M. *The Last Chance: Tombstone's Early Years*. New York: E. P. Dutton, 1950.

Myers, John M. *Doc Holliday*. Boston and New York: Houghton Mifflin, 1955.

Powell, Donald. *The Peralta Grant*. Norman: University of Oklahoma Press, 1960.

Rosa, Joseph. *The Gunfighter: Man or Myth*. Norman: University of Oklahoma Press, 1969.

Rynning, Tom. *Gun Notches*. New York: Frederick A. Stokes, 1931.

Sonnichsen, C. L. *Alias Billy the Kid (Brushy Bill Roberts)*. Albuquerque: University of New Mexico Press, 1955.

Trimble, Marshall. *Arizona Adventure*. Phoenix: Golden West, 1982.

Trimble, Marshall. *Arizoniana*. Scottsdale: Reata Publishing Co., 1988.

Woody, Clara T. and Schwartz, Milton. *Globe, Arizona. (Pleasant Valley War)*. Tucson: Arizona Historical Society, 1977.

CHAPTER 12—STEEL RAILS ACROSS ARIZONA

Myrick, David. *Railroads of Arizona*. 3 volumes. Berkeley and San Diego: Howell North Books, 1975, 1980, 1983.

Sayre, John. *Ghost Railroads of Central Arizona*. Boulder: Pruett Publishing Co., 1985.

Trimble, Marshall. *Roadside History of Arizona*. Missoula: Mountain Press, 1986.

CHAPTER 13—TERRITORIAL POLITICS 1863-1912

Goff, John. *Arizona Biographical Dictionary*. Cave Creek: Black Mountain Press, 1983.

Sacks, Ben. *Be It Enacted: The Creation of a Territory*. Phoenix: Arizona Historical Foundation, 1964.

Wagoner, Jay. *Arizona Territory: 1863-1912*. Tucson: University of Arizona Press, 1970.

Wagoner, Jay. *Arizona's Heritage*. Salt Lake City: Peregrine Smith, 1977.

CHAPTER 14—LIFE IN THE TERRITORIAL YEARS

Brooks, Juanita. *Jacob Hamblin, Mormon Apostle to the Indians*. Salt Lake City: Westwater Press, 1980.

Cozzens, Samuel. *The Marvellous Country*. Minneapolis: Ross and Haines, Inc. 1967. (Reprint).

Gressinger, A. W. *Charles Poston*. Globe: D.S. King, 1961.

Gustafson, A.M., ed. *John Spring's Arizona*. Tucson: University of Arizona Press, 1966.

Hensen, Pauline. *Founding a Wilderness Capital*. Flagstaff: Northland Press, 1965.

Herner, Charles. *The Arizona Rough Riders*. Tucson: The University of Arizona Press, 1970.

Hodge, Hiram. *Arizona as It Was*. Chicago: Rio Grande Press, 1965.

Jennings, James. *The Freight Rolled*. San Antonio: The Naylor Company, 1969.

Lynch, Richard. *Winfield Scott: A Biography of Scottsdale's Founder.* Scottsdale: City of Scottsdale, 1978.

McClintock, James. *Mormon Settlements in Arizona*. Phoenix: Privately published, 1921.

Myers, John M. I, *Jack Swilling*. New York: Hastings House, 1961.

Peplow, Edward. ed. *The Taming of the Salt.* Phoenix: Salt River Project, 1979.

Peterson, Charles. *Take Up Your Mission: Mormon Colonizing Along the Little Colorado River.* Tucson: University of Arizona Press, 1973.

Powell, John Wesley. *The Exploration of the Colorado River and Its Canyons.* New York: Dover, 1961.

Quebbeman, Frances. *Medicine in Territorial Arizona.* Phoenix: Arizona Historical Foundation, 1966.

Rochlin, Harriet and Fred. *Pioneer Jews: A New Life in the Far West.* Boston: Houghton Mifflin Co., 1984.

Rockfellow, John. *Log of an Arizona Trailblazer.* Tucson: Acme Printing Co., 1933.

Ruffner, Budge. *All Hell Needs Is Water.* Tucson: University of Arizona Press, 1972.

Ruffner, Budge. *Shot in the Ass With Pesos.* Tucson: Treasure Chest Publications, 1979.

Rusho, W.L. and Crampton, C. Gregory. *Desert River Crossing: Historic Lee's Ferry on the Colorado River.* Salt Lake City: Peregrine Smith Inc., 1975.

Schmitt, Jo Ann. *Fighting Editors.* San Antonio: The Naylor Company, 1958.

Smalley, George. *My Adventures in Arizona.* Tucson: Arizona Pioneers Historical Society, 1966.

Smith, Dean. ed. *Arizona Highways: The Road to Statehood.* Phoenix: Arizona Highways, 1987.

Sonnichsen, C. L. *Billy King's Tombstone.* Caldwell, Idaho: Caxton Printers, 1942.

Tinker, George. *Northern Arizona and Flagstaff in 1877.* Glendale, CA.: A. H. Clark Co., 1969.

Theobald, John and Lillian. *Arizona Territory Post Offices and Postmasters.* Phoenix: Arizona Historical Foundation, 1961.

Trimble, Marshall. *In Old Arizona.* Phoenix: Golden West, 1985.

Trimble, Marshall. *Arizoniana.* Scottsdale: Reata Publishing Co., 1988.

Wagoner, Jay. *Arizona Territory: 1863-1912.* Tucson: University of Arizona Press, 1970.

Walker, Dale. *Death Was the Black Horse* (Later issued as *Buckey O'Neill: The Story of a Rough Rider*). Austin: Madrona, 1975.

Wampler, Vance. *Arizona: Years of Courage.* Based on the Life and Times of William H. Kirkland. Phoenix: Privately published, 1984.

CHAPTER 15—THE BABY STATE

Clendenin, Clarence. *Blood on The Border.* New York: Macmillan, 1969.

Mason, Herbert M. *The Great Pursuit.* New York: Random House, 1970.

Smith, C. C. *Emilio Kosterlitzky.* Glendale: A.H. Clark Company, 1970.

CHAPTER 16—THE 1920s AND 1930s

Wagoner, Jay. *Arizona's Heritage.* Salt Lake City: Peregrine Smith, 1977.

Wyllys, Rufus K. *Arizona, The History of a Frontier State.* Phoenix: Hobson and Herr, 1950.

CHAPTER 17—HARNESSING THE GREAT RIVERS

Cross, Jack L. ed. *Arizona: Its People and Resources.* Tucson: University of Arizona Press, 1972.

Johnson, Rich. *The Central Arizona Project: 1918-1968.* Tucson: University of Arizona Press, 1977.

Mann, Dean. *The Politics of Water in Arizona.* Tucson: University of Arizona Press, 1963.

Peplow, Ed. ed. *The Taming of the Salt.* Phoenix: Salt River Project, 1970.

Smith, Karen. *The Magnificent Experiment: Building the Salt River Reclamation Project - 1890-1917.* Tucson: University of Arizona Press, 1986.

CHAPTER 18—POLITICS IN ARIZONA SINCE STATEHOOD

Goff, John. *George W.P. Hunt and His Arizona.* Pasadena: SocioTechnical Publications, 1973.

Goldwater, Barry M. *With No Apologies: The Personal and Political Memoirs of United States Senator Barry M. Goldwater.* New York: Morrow, 1979.

Goldwater, Barry, with Jack Casserly. *Goldwater.* New York: Doubleday and Co., 1988.

McFarland, Ernest W. *Mac: The Autobiography of Ernest W. McFarland.* Phoenix: Privately published, 1979.

Shadegg, Stephen C. *Arizona Politics.* Tempe: Arizona State University, 1986.

Udall, Morris K. *Too Funny To Be President.* New York: Henry Holt and Co., 1988.

CHAPTER 19—RECENT ARIZONA HISTORY

Goff, John. *Arizona: An Illustrated History of the Grand Canyon State.* Northridge, CA.: Windsor Publications, 1988.

Luckingham, Brad. *The Urban Southwest: A Profile History of Albuquerque, El Paso, Phoenix, Tucson.* E1 Paso: Texas Western Press, 1982.

Trimble, Marshall. *Diamond in The Rough: An Illustrated History of Arizona.* Norfolk: Donning Co., 1988.

Wagoner, Jay. *Arizona's Heritage.* Salt Lake City: Peregrine Smith, 1977.

Urban Growth in Arizona: A Policy Analysis. Morrison Institute for Public Policy. School of Public Affairs. Arizona State University.

Periodicals that provide useful and important information on current events include: *Arizona Highways Magazine; Arizona Trend; Phoenix Magazine; The Business Journal; Arizona Business Gazette; Arizona Yearbook: A Guide to Government in the Grand Canyon State (annual); Tucson Magazine; Scottsdale Magazine; Tempe Magazine; Mesa Magazine; Arizona Living; Arizona Capitol Times.*

INDEX

Page numbers in italics refer to maps, illustrations or photos.

Aero Corporation, 250
Agriculture, 214, 216, 266
    Indians, 22, 45, 49
Air conditioning, 290-291
Air transportation, 250-251
Ajo, 124, 129, 130-131, 146
Alarcón, Hernando, 49, *55*, 58-59
Ali, Jadji (Hi Jolly), 96
Allande, Pedro, 70, 71
Allen, William C., 219
Allyn, Joseph P., *195*
American Mining and Trading
    Company, 130
Amundsen, Andrew, 218
Anasazi Indians, 10-11, *12*, 17, 19,
    34
Animal life, 4, 9
Anza, Juan Bautista de, 56, 67, 68,
    69
Apache County, *209*
Apache Indians, 9, 19, 28-33, 47,
    48, 78, 137, 138
    ceremonies, 32
    hostilities, 29-31, 66, 70-71, 74,
    75, 76, 104-105, 132, 159-160
    language, 20
    marriage, 31
    regional names, 29
    religion, 32
    wars of, 111, 113, 114, 115,
    116121, 159-160
Apache Pass, 97, 111, 112

Arissona, 65
Arizona Canal, 216-217, 259
Arizona Cardinals, 306
Arizona Cattle Company, 161
Arizona Diamondbacks, 305
Arizona Gazette, 238
Arizona Improvement Company, 217
Arizona Lumber and Timber
    Company, 225, *226*
Arizona National Guard, 236, 243,
    244, 263, 292-293, *293*
Arizona Rangers, 150, 178 183, *178*
*Arizona Republican (Arizona
    Republic)*, 248, 303
Arizona State Museum, 8
Arizona State University, 297
Arizona Strip, 2, 221-222
Arkansas River, *55*, 77, 83, *106*
Armijo, Manuel, 83
Army Corps of Topographical
    Engineers, 47, 82, 91,
    301
Arpaio, Joe, 283-284
Ash Fork, *190*, 192
Ashley, James, 194
Ashurst, Henry F., 268, 271,
    278-279
Athabascan language group,
    20, 28-29
Atlantic and Pacific Railroad, 161,
    220, 225
Aubry, Felix, 76

Aubry, Francois X., 92
Aubry Route, *192*
Awatovi, 38, 58, 63
Ayer, Edward, 225
AzScam scandal, 277
Aztec Land and Cattle
    Company, 162, *165*

Babbitt, Bruce, 281-282,
    282
Babbitt Brothers, 162, 281
Ballinger, Jesse D., 219
Banters, Jennie, 145
Barnum, "Silent Tom," 204-205
Barrett, James, 109
Bartlett, John Russell, 88
Bascom, George, 112
Basketmakers, 10
Baylor, John, 107
Beale, Edward, 47
Beale, Ned (Fitzgerald), 85,
    95-96, 97
Becknell, Bill, 76
Behan, Johnny, 169, 170
Bent's Fort, 83, *106*
Bering Strait, 8, 29
Berry, Rachel Allen, 235
Big Dry Wash, Battle of, 118
Bill Williams Mountain, 80, 82
Bill Williams River, *12, 39,* 82, *110,
    124, 192, 209*
Bisbee, 6, 123, *124,* 129, 130, 137-
    143, 146, 181, 208, *209,* 229
    Deportation of 1917, 142
    drilling contests, 232-233
Bisbee, DeWitt, 140-141
Black Mesa Range, 2, 33-34
Blacks
    cowboys, 224-225
    in military, 224, 240
Blevins, John, 173
Bolin, Wesley, 281, 283
Bosque Redondo, 23, *106,*
    113-114
Bostwick, Joe, 182
Bradshaw Mountains, 47, 49, 79,
    112, 126, 127, 190, 191
Brady, Pete, 125, 130
Brewery Gulch, 141
Brocius, "Curly Bill," 169, 171
Brodie, Alexander, 206

Buffalo Soldiers, 224
Bullock, Tom, 189
Bush, George, 285, 286
Bush, Nellie Trent, 235-236, 263
Butler, John C., 292
Butterfield, John, 98
Butterfield Overland Mail, 97, 98,
    100, *192*
Byrne, T.D., 138

California, 106
    war with Mexico, 82, 83, 84, 88
California Column, *106*
Calles, Plutarco, 242
Camels, 95-96, *96*
Camino del Diablo, *59, 67*
Camp Calhoun, 90
Camp Date Creek, *110*
Camp Grant, *110,* 114-115
Camp Reno, *110*
Camp Verde, 47
Campbell, Tom, 244, 261, 267, 269
Canyon de Chelly, 1, 2, 5, *12,* 22,
    23, 78, 113
Canyon Diablo, 187, *188*
Canyon del Muerto, 22, 113
Cardenas, Lopez de, *55,* 58
Carleton, James, 78, 79, 108, 111,
    112, 113, 126, 194, 196, 200
Carlos III (King), 66
Carr, Eugene A., 118
Carranza, Venustiano, 242
Carson, Kit, 22-23, 75, *76,*
    77-78, 80, 84, 85, 113
Carter, Jimmy, 281
Casa Grande, *12, 16*
Cashman, Nellie, 210-212, *211*
Castillo, Alonzo del, 54, 56
Castro, Raul, 281, 283
Cattle
    ranching, 158-164, 254
    rustling, 151-152, 160-161, 168,
        171-172, 178, 179
Cenozoic Age, 5, 6
Central Arizona Project, 262, 265,
    266, 271, 302
Cerbat Mountains, 47
Cerro Colorado, *125*
Chacon, Augustin, 179-180
Chambers, Reed, 245
Charbonneau, Baptiste, 85

Chase, Hal, 146
Chavez, Manuel, 108
Chemehuevi Indians, 21, *39*, 50
Chenowth, J.A., 204
Chevrolet, Louis, 237
Chi-muc-tah, 85
Chihuahua Desert, 4
Chiricahua Mountains, 1, 97
Chivington, John, 108
Christmas (town), 137
Church, William, 132
Chuska Mountains, 1
Civil War, 78, 90, 91, 107-111
Civilian Conservation Corps, 254
Clanton, Billy, 169, 170, 205
Clanton, Ike, 169, 171, 205
Clanton, Newman H., 169
Clark, William Andrews, 144
Clarkdale, 190
Cleveland, Grover, 121
Clifton, 124, 129, 130, 131-133,
    146, *209, 229*
Clum, John, 117, 169
Cochise, 100, 104, 111, 112, 115-
    116
Cochise County, 10, 169, 171, 178,
    203, *209*
Cochise Culture, 10, 11, 17
Coconino County, *209*
Cocopah Indians, *39*, 48,
    49-50, 51
Colorado, 88
Colorado Plateau, 6, 262
Colorado River, 12, *39*, 47, 50, *55,
    56*, 58, 90, 91, 93,
    94-95, *106, 110, 124*, 125, 126,
    184, *192, 209*, 261
    gold in, 125
    railroad across, 185
Colorado River Compact, 271
Colorado River reservation, 50
Colorado Volunteers, *106*, 108
Colt, Sam, 167
Colter, Fred, 261-262
Comanche Indians, 22, 114, 132,
    167
Conde, Pedro Garcia, 88
Congress, *124*
Cooke, Philip St. George, 83, 85
Coolidge Dam, 263
Cooper, Andy, 173

Copper, 129, 131-132, 134, 135,
    138-143, 146, 248, 254
Copper Queen Mining Company,
    139, 140, 142, 223
Corbin, Bob, 276
Cornelia Copper Company, 131
Coronado, Francisco Vasquez de,
    34, 53, *54, 55*, 56,
    57-58, 59
Coronado Expedition, 49, 53, 54,
    55, 58, 60
Cortés, Hernán, 53
Cotton, 246-247, 248, 254
Cowboys, 147-164, *147, 149, 154,
    163*
    clothing, 150-155
    horses, 157-158
Cozzens, Samuel W., 220
Crabb, Henry, 104
Cremony, John, 111
Crook, George, 115, *115*, 116, 117,
    118, 119-121
Cross, Ed, 200
Crowe, Frank, 262
Crown King, 191, 193
Cuba, 205
Cushing, Frank Hamilton,
    13-14

Dams, 225, 259, 261-267
Davis-Monthan airport, 251
Davis, Jefferson, 95, 107
Davis, W.H., 78
Day, Henry Clay, 282
Depression, 253-254, 257, 272, 291
Deserts, 1, 2-3, 4
Detroit Copper Company, 132
Diamond, Nathan and Isaac, 223
Díaz, Juan, 69
Díaz, Melchior, 49, *55*, 59
Dobie, J. Frank, 158
Dodge, Henry Chee, 23
Dominguez, Francisco, 68
Dorantes, Andres, 54
Douglas, James, 132, 134, *135*, 140,
    143, 144, 279
Douglas, Lewis, 279
Douglas, "Rawhide" Jimmy, 144, .
    279
Douglas, 181, 229, 239
Downing, Bill, 183

Drilling contests, 145-146,
    231-233, *232*
Dripping Springs Mountains, 137
Duffield, Milton B., *195*
Dunn, Jack, 138
Dunn, Tom, 185
Duppa, Bryan Philip Darrell, 214-
    215

Earp, Josie Marcus, 223
Earp, Morgan, 170, 205
Earp, Virgil, 169, 170, 205
Earp, Wyatt, 169, 170-171, *170*,
    205, 223
Echavarria, Natalie, 223
Education, 254
Ehrenberg, 95, *124*, 126, 130, *192*
El Paso, 88
Emory, William, 84, *84*, 89
Epitaph, 169
Escalante, Silvestre, *56*, 68
Espejo, Antonio de, 34, 56, 60
Espinol, Luisa, 223
Esteban (slave), 54, 57

Fannin, Paul, 271
Farfán, Marcos, 34, *56*, 60
Farnsworth, C.H., *180*
Favorite, "Whispering Jim,"
    204-205
Fay, Dorothy, 238
Fenner, Hiram, 237
Fitzpatrick, Thomas, 77
Flagstaff, 18, *209*, 220, 225, 298,
    301
Fleury, H.N., *195*
Florence, 203, *209*
Forests, 1, 3-4
Fort Bowie, *110*, 112
Fort Breckinridge, 104
Fort Buchanan, 91, 104, *110*
Fort Crittenden, *110*
Fort Defiance, 90-91, *110*
Fort Huachuca, *110*
Fort McDowell, 47, *110*, 212
Fort Mohave, 49, 91, *110*
Fort Sumner, 23
Fort Union, 108
Fort Verde, *110*, 116
Fort Yuma, 49, 80, 89, 90, 93, *110*,
    185

Foster, W.K., *180*
Fremont, John C., 77, 84

Gadsden, James, 89
Gadsden Purchase, 89-90, *106*, 194
Gage, Almon, 195
Galiuro Mountains, 1, 245
Gálvez, Bernardo de, 72
Gambling, 52, 229, 297, 304
Ganz, Emil, 223
Garcés, Francisco Tomas, 47, 48,
    49, *56*, 66-68, 69
Garcia, Hilarion, 90, 100
Gatewood, Charles, 120
Germany, 243
Geronimo, 117, 118-121, *120*, 160,
    205
Gila City, 124, 125
Gila County, *209*
Gila River, *12, 39 , 40, 55, 56, 76*,
    84, 86, 88, 89, *106, 110, 124,
    125, 192, 209*, 216, 263
    gold in, 125, 184
Gila Trail, 86, 88, 89, 93, 97, *192*
Gilleland, John, 172
Glanton, John, 93
Glendale, 303
Globe, 118, *124*, 133-137, 146, *209*,
    216, 229
Gold, 80, 86, 93, 112, 122, 138,
    141, 143, 191, 224
    placer, 79, 125, 127
    rush, 125-127
Goldberg, Hazel, 208
Goldwater, Baron, 223-224
Goldwater, Barry, 208, 224, 266,
    271, 272, 279,
    287-289, *288*
Goldwater, Joe, 126, 223
Goldwater, Michael, 126, 223
Goodwin, John, *195*, 195,
    197-198
Gordon, Frank, 276
Graham family, 172-175
Graham County, *209*
Gran Quivira, 59
Grand Avenue Expressway,
    303
Grand Canal, 15
Grand Canyon, 1, 2, 7, *12*, 37, 47,
    48, 94

Grant, Ulysses, 115
Grasslands, 3, 4
Gray, Andrew B., 88, 89, 97
Grazhoffer, Johann, 65
Great Basin, 4
Great Plains, 4
Great Spanish Flu Epidemic, 246
Green River *55, 106*
Greenlee, *209*
Greenway, Isabella Selmes, 279, 279-280
Greenway, John C., 131, 280
Griffin, James, 84
Guevavi, 39
Gulf of California, 2
Gulf of Mexico, 55
Gunfight at OK Corral, 170-171
Gunfighters, 166-183
Gurley, John, 195

Halcro, Joe, 139
Hamblin, Jacob, 217, *218*
Hamblin Road, *192*
Hardyville, 95, *192*
Harte, Bret, 166
Hassayampa River, *39*, 79, *110, 124,* 126, *127, 224*
Haury, Emil, 14
Havasupai Indians, *39,* 48
Hawikuh, *57*
Hawkins, Lee, 145
Hayden, 137
Hayden, Carl, 44, 104, 268, 277-278, *277,* 279, 289
Hayden, Trumbull, 104
Hayes, Ira, 293, 294, *295*
Hayes, Rutherford B., 42
Hays, John Coffee, 167
Heintzelman, Sam, 200, *201*
Heintzelman Mine, 104
"Hell's Gate," 91, 117
Hensley, Cindy, 285
Herrera, Silvestre, 292, *292*
Hidalgo, Miguel, 74
Hohokam Indians, 10, 12, 13, 14-17, 19, 41
Holbrook, 209
Holliday, John "Doc," 170, 171
Hooker, Henry Clay, 161
Hoover Dam, 1, 262
Hoover, Herbert, 262

Hopi Indians, 22, 33-40, *39,* 50, *56,* 60
ceremonies, 36-37, 58
family traditions, 35
Great Pueblo Revolt of 1680, *34,* 35
hostilities, 34, 62-63
language, 20
Old Oraibi, 34, 35
reservations, 1
Spanish interactions, 38, 58, 61, 62, 68
Horn, Tom, 120-121
Horses, 156
breeding and introduction of, 156-157
mustangs, 156, 157
Howard, Oliver, 115, 116
Howell, William T., 198-199, 264
Howell Code, 198, 264
Hualapai Indians, *39,* 47
Hualapai Mountains, 47
Hull, Jane Dee, 276-277
Hunt, George W.P., 242, 261, 262, 267-269, *270*
Hunter, Sherod, 107, 108-109

Indians *(See also* specific tribes)
arts and crafts, 10, 16, 17-19, 38, 40, 51
athletic activities, 15
ceremonial traditions, 27-28, 32, 36, 37, 41, 52
clothing, 43-44
community property concept, 37
death, 26-27, 33
family structure and traditions, 25-26, 33, 35, 42-43, 46, 48
farming, 22, 45, 49
forced relocation, 22-23, 42
hostilities, 22, 29-31, 34, 57, 66, 71, 74-76, 90-91, 104-105, 113-114, 118, 132, 159-160
Apache Pass, 111-112
atrocities against, 112-115
with Spanish, 62-73
housing, 10, 11, 13, 15, 19, 22, 50
language groups, 20-21
marriage customs, 26, 31, 35, 43, 44

medicine man, 28, 32, 62
migration, 8-9, 29
missions and missionaries, 35, 38, 51, 61-73, 117
Paleo Indians, 8-19
psychics (hand tremblers), 27
religion, 10, 20, 23-24, 27, 31-32, 41-42, 45-46
reservations, 1, 23, 24, 33, 42, 45, 46, 47, 49, 50, 51, 52, 116-117
scalphunting, 75
slaves, 75, 115
Spanish influence, 38
taboos, 26, 33
tribal government, 30, 43-44, 46
in World War II, 294
Industrial Workers of the World (IWW), 142
Industry, 250, 296-299
Irrigation, 213-214, 216, 259-267
prehistoric, 14-15, 17
Isaacson, Jacob, 223
Ives, Joseph C., 91, 92, 93-94, 97
Ives route, *192*

"Jackass Mail," 97
Jackson, David, 76
Jaeger, Louis J.F., 93
Jeffords, Tom, 115-116
Jerome, Eugene, 143
Jerome, 6, 123, *124*, 129, 130, 143-146, 229
Jesuits, 65-66
Jews, 222-224
Johnson, George, 93-94
Jones, Hugh, 139
Jones, Robert T., 270
Juan, Mathew, 245, *245*

Kalbab Plateau, 2, 7
Kansas, *106*, 168
Kearny, Stephen Watts, 77, 83, 84, 85, *106*, 264
Kennedy, John F., 281, 287
Kent, Edward, 264
Kern, Dr. Ben, 81
Kern, Richard, 81-82
Kibbey, Joseph H., 264
Kingman, 6, *124*, *209*

Kinishba, *12*
Kino, Eusebio, 49, *56, 63, 64,* 63-64, 65, 15g
Kinsley, Edward, 162
Kirker, James, 75, 80
Kirkland, Bill, 100-101, 160
Kiowa Indians, 78, 113
Kitchen, Pete, 160
Kleindienst, Richard, 274
Korrick, Sam, 223
Kosterlitzky, Emilio, 180-181

Lake, George, 219
Lake Mead, 262
Lamy, Jean Baptiste, 103
La Paz, 124, *125*, 126, *192*
Law, the, 66, 166-183
Arizona Rangers, 178-183
guns carried by, 166-168
hangings, 177, 179-180
Pleasant Valley War, 171-175
Leach, Jesse, 97
Leach Road, *192*
Lead, 141
Leatherwood, Bob, 186-187, 203
Lehner, Ed, 8
Leisure activities, 227-234, *227*, 302
Leroux, Antoine, 47, 76, 82, 85, 9l, 92
Lesinsky, Charles and family, 131, 132
Lewisohn brothers, 134, 136
Levin, Alex, 223
Lincoln, Able, 93
Lincoln, Abraham, 195
Lindbergh, Charles A., 251
Little Colorado River, 2, 7, *12, 39, 56, 110, 125, 192, 209*
Little Colorado River Valley, 218-220
Lockwood, Lorna, 235-236, *236*
Lopez, Martin "Red," 239
Lount, Sam, 216, 291
Luis, 65
Luke, Frank Jr., *244*, 244-245
Lumber, 225

MacArthur, Douglas, 292
McCain, John, 285-287, *286*
McCleave, William, 109
McClendon, Ben, 224

McClintock, Jim, 206
McCormick, Margaret, 196
McCormick, Richard, 195, 196, 198
McCoy, Hank, 139
McCrackin, Jackson, 198
McDowell, Irvin, 184-185, 186
McFarland, Ernest W., 271-272, 278, 281
McKinnon, Angus and Rod, 143
McLawry, Tom and Frank, 169, 170, 205
McPhee, John, 257-258
Machcbeuf, Joseph, 103
Mader, Harry, 146
Magma Copper Company, 137
Magoffin, James, 83
Manning, Reg, 1
Mangas Coloradas, 111, 112, 117
Manifest Destiny, 82
Marcus, Josephine, 170
Maricopa, 216, *192*
Maricopa County, 204, 205, 209, 215
Maricopa Indians, *39*, 48, 50-51
Maricopa, Phoenix, and Salt River Railroad, 189
Marion, John, 198
Marshall, James, 86
Marvellous Country, The, 220
Maurel, Andre, 135
Mayer, Joseph, 223
Mecham, Evan, 273-277, 284
Melczer, Joe, 208
Mendoza, Antonio, 54-55
Merriam, Clinton Hart, 3
Merrill, Philemon, 221
Mesa, 221, 256
Mesa Tribune, 256
Mesilla, 90, 107
Mesilla Valley, 88, 194
Mesozoic Age, 5-6
Metcalf, Bob, 131
Mexico, *106*
    Gadsden Purchase, 89-90
    Germany's role, 243
    loses Texas, 82, 88
    Revolution of 1810, 73, 74
    Revolution of 1910, 51, 222, 239-243
    Treaty of Guadalupe Hidalgo, 88

war with United States, 75, 82, 83-86, 88
Mexico City, 57
Miami (AZ), 135, 136-137, 146
Miami Copper Company, 136
Miles, Nelson, 119-120, 121
Mills, Billy, 40
Miner, (Prescott), 198
Ming, Daniel Houston, 164
Mining, 104, 122-146
Mission of San Jose de Tumacacori, *39, 72,* 73
Mission of San Xavier del Bac, *39*, 64, 66, *67*, 72-85
Missionaries and missions, 35, 38, 51, 54, 60, 61-73, 117
    Mormons, 219
    Spanish, 56, 60, 61-73
Mississippi Valley, 4
Missouri River, *55*
Moeur, Ben, 236, 263, 269-270
Mofford, Rose, 276, 281, 283-285, 284
Mogollon, Juan Ignacio, 18
Mogollon Indians, 10, 11, *12*, 13, 17-18, 19
Mogollon Rim, 6, 262
Mohave Indians, *39*, 48-49, 50, 51, 78
Mojave County, 201, *209*
Mojave Desert, 4
Montana, 168
Montezuma Castle, *12*, 18
Monument Valley, 2, 6, *12*, 22
Morenci, *124*, 129, 131-133, 146
Moreno, Matias, 69
Mormons, 51, 83, 201, 217-222, 276
    missions, 219
    Mormon Battalion, 85-86, *86, 106*
    Mormon War, 219
    polygamy, 221-222
Mormon Cattle Company, 161
Mossman, Burt, 179-180, 181
Motor vehicles, 237-238, 248
    road races, 237-238
Mount Graham, 1
Mowry, Sylvester, 125, 199-200, 200
Mowry, *125*

Mule Mountains, 137
Mule Pass, 137, 138, 139
Munds, Frances Willard, 235
Murphy, Frank, 190-191, 193
Murphy, Nathan Oakes, 179
Murphy, Patrick, 252-253
Murphy, William J., 216-217

Naco, Sonora/Arizona, 8, 229, 240, 240, 241, 251-253
Na-ti-o-tish, 118
Navajo Code Talkers, 293, *294*
Navajo County, *209*
Navajo Indians, 9, 19, 21-28, *25*, *39*, 50, 78
 ceremonies, 27-28
 epidemics, 23
 hostilities, 22, 90-91, 113-114
 housing, 22-23
 language, 20
 Long Walk, 23, 113
 religion, 23-24, 27
 reservations, 1, 23, 24
 in World War II, 293-294, *294*
Navajo National Monument, 10
Neal, Bill and Ann, 225
Nevada, *106*, 201
Newlands Act, 259
Newman, "Black Jack," 136
New Mexico, 6, 69, *106*, 168, 206-207
 civil government in, 83-84
 Civil War, 107-112
 Pueblo Revolt of 1680, 63
 Territory of, 90-105, 194
 war with Mexico, 82, 88
Newspapers, 238-239
Nixon, Richard, 280, *286*
Niza, Marcos de, 57
Nock-ay-del-klinne, 118
Nogales, 223, 242
Northern Arizona University, 226, 298

Oak Creek Canyon, 5
O'Connor, John, 282
O'Connor, Sandra Day, 282-283, *283*
O'Conor, Hugo, 69-70
Old Dominion mine, 134

Old Nana, 118
Old Oraibi, 33, *39*
Old Spanish Trail, *106*
Oldfield, Barney, 237
Olson, Lute, 306
Oñate, Juan de, 29, 34, 48, 49, *56*, 60
O'Neill, Ralph, 245
O'Neill, William O. "Buckey," 205, *206*
Osage Indians, 81
Osborn, John, 270, 271
Osborn, Neri, 270
Osborn, Sidney P., 270
Ostrich Farms, 236-237
Oury, Bill, 160
Owens, Perry, *172*, 173

Pah-Ute County, 106, 201, 202
Painted Desert, 1, 2
Pais Indians, 20
Paiute Indians, 21, *39*, 51
Paleo Indians, 8-19
Paleozoic Age, 5
Palma, Salvador Carlos Antonio, 69
Papago Freeway, 303
Papago Indians, *39*
Papago Park, 295
Parke, John G., 91, 97
Parker, Fleming, 176-177
Parker Dam, 263
Parsons, Ed, 242
Patayan Indians, 10, 12, 19
Pattie, James Ohio, 48, 78-79, 80
Patton, George, 294
Peabody, Endicott, 230-231
Pearce, 229
Pecos River, 22, *55*
Pershing, John J., 143, 243
Phelps Dodge and Company, 132, 133, 134, 140, 141, 142, 143, 144
Phillips, John C., 269
Phoenix, *124*, 178, 189, 190, *192*, 203, 208, *209*, 229, 249, 265, 290, 300, 301, 302, 303, 304
 airport, 251
 background, 212-217
 capital, 203-204, 217
 growth, 290
 industry in, 250, 296-297

Phoenix Coyotes, 306
Phoenix Gazette, 303
Phoenix Suns, 306
Pico, Andres, 85
Pierce, Franklin, 89
Pima County, 201, *209*
Pima Indians, 17, 21, 39, 40-44, 48,
    51, 159
    reservation, 247
    and US government, 42
Pimeria Alta, 63-65, 66
Pinal County, 202, *209*
Pinal Creek, 133-134
Pinal Mountains, 1, 136
Pinaleno Mountains, 1
Pipe Spring National Monument, 51
Pizarro, Francisco, 53
Plan of San Diego, 243
Planchas de Plata, 65, 125
Plant life, 3, 4
Platte River, *55*, 79
Pleasant Valley War, *165*,
    171-175, 205
Politics, 169, 182, 207
    since statehood, 267-289
    territory, 195, 198-199, 202, 205
Polk, James, K., 82
Popé, 62-63
Population, 2, 201, 214, 216, 249,
    254, 290, 297,
    298-299, 301
    Indian, 23, 33, 40, 43, 45, 47,
    49, 51, 52
Porras, Francisco, 61-62
Poston, Charles Debrille,
    101-103, 104-105, 125, 130,
    195, 199, *199*, 200)
Power, Jeff, 245
Power, Tom and John, 245-246
Precambrian Age, 5
Prehistoric era, 8-19
    animal life, 9
Prescott, 79, 122, *126*, *165*, 176,
    189-190, *192*, 209, 216
    territorial capital, 196-197, 198,
    202-203, 298, 301
Prescott Miner, 114
Prohibition, 249-250, *250*
Prostitution, 135, 228-229
Pruitt, John Henry, 244, 245
Pueblo Indians, 11, 21, 61, 62, 63

Pueblo Revolt of 1680, 34, 35, 62-63
Pulliam, Eugene, 303
Pyle, Howard, *271*, 271,
    272-273, 279

Quayle, Dan, 284
Quechan Indians (*See* Yuma
    Indians), 49, 51

Rainfall, 4-5, 8
Railroads (*See also* specific line
    names), 79, 89, 97, 132, 140,
    144, *184*, 184-193, 210, 216
Ray, 137, 146
Reagan, Ronald, 283, 287
Real estate, 248-249, 258
Reavis, James Addison, 258
Redbird, Ida, 51
Red River, *55*
Rehnquist, William, 282, 283
Remington, Frederic, 156
Resorts, 254-256
Rhodes, John, *271*, *280*,
    280-281, 285
Rich Hill, *125*, 126
Ricketts, L.D., 134
Ringo, Johnny, 169, 171
Rio Grande, 7, *55*, *56*, *106*
Riordan brothers, 225-226
Rio Salado Project, 301-302
Ritter, Tex, 238
Roadways, 238, 302-304
Roberts, Jim, 172, *172*, 174-176
Roberts, Tom, 111
Rocky Mountains, 4
Rogers, Will, 263, 268
Ronstadt, Linda, 223
Roosevelt, Franklin D., 279
Roosevelt, Theodore, 121, 143, 205,
    207
Roosevelt Dam, 134, *260*,
    261-262
Rosenzweig, Isaac, 223-224
Rucker, John A., 138
Ruelas, Felix, *158*
Ruffner, George, 176, 177
Ruffner, M.A., 143
Russell, Charley, 148
Ruxton, George Frederick, 81
Rynning, Tom, 180, 181
Safford, *209*, 221

St. David, 221
St. James, Lewis 145
St. Johns, *209*
St. Joseph (Joseph City),
    219-220

Salado Indians, 10, 19
Saloons, *227-228,* 229
Salt River, *12, 39, 55, 56,* 76, *106,*
    110, 124, 192, 209, 216
Salt River Project, 259, *260,* 261
Salt River Valley, 4, 13, 40, 51, 212,
    214, 220, 258, 261, 264, 302
Sandige, John, 249
San Francisco Mountains, 2, 7
San Francisco Peaks, 3, 7, *12,* 36,
    37, 61
San Pasqual, 85, *106*
San Pedro River, 2, 8, *12, 39,* 85,
    110, 124, 192, 209
San Pedro Valley, 129
San Simon River, 2
Santa Anna, Antonio Lopez de, 74,
    83
Santa Catalina Mountains, 1
Santa Cruz, 209
Santa Cruz River, 2, *12, 56, 110,*
    124, 192, 209
Santa Cruz Valley, 104
Santa Fe, 56, 61, *106*
    capital of territory, 206
    war with Mexico, 83
Santa Fe Compact, 261, 265, 271
Santa Fe Railroad, 92, 140, 144,
    187-188, *188,* 189, *192, 203,*
    291
Santa Fe Trail, 76, 83, *106,* 132
Santa Rita, *125*
Santa Rita Mountains, 1
Sawyer, Frenchy, 214
Schieffelin, Ed, *128,* 129, 169
Scott, Winfield, 83
Scottsdale, 259
Sea of Cortez, *55, 56, 106*
Seligman, 189, 190
Serra, Junipero, 67
Sharlot Hall Museum, 196
Shaver, Ellen, 216
Sheep, 254
Shotwell, A.J., 130-131
Sibley, Henry, 78, 107-108

Sieber, Al, 118, 143, 260
Sieber, Arnold, 141
Sierra Madre, 4
Sierra Nevada, 4, 79
Sierra Vista, 301
Silver, 101, 112, 122, 127-129, 130,
    135, 138, 141, 143, 202
Silver Queen, 137
Silver Belt, 136
Silver King, 128, 137
Sinagua Indians, 10, *12,* 18-19
Sisson, Tom, 245, 246
Sitgreaves, Lorenzo, 47, 82,
    91-92, 97
Sitgreaves Route, *192*
Slaughter, John, 171
Slidell, John, 82
Smith and Wesson, 167-168
Smith, Jed, 48
Smith, Jedediah, 75
Smith, John, Y.T., 212-213
Smith, Lot, 219
Smith, Marcus, A., 268
Smith, Mark, 269
Smith, Thomas, "Peg Leg," 76, 79-80
Smith's Station, 212, 213
Snively, Jake, 125
Solomon, Isador, 223
Sonora, 75, 104
Sonoran Desert, 3, 4
Southern Pacific Railroad, 97, 140,
    184-186, 188, 189, *192,* 203,
    216
Southworth, Harriet Fay, 238
Spain, 53
    conquistadores, 53-60
    exploitation of Indians,
        62-63, 65-66, 68-72
    Mexico, 74
    missionaries in New World, 56,
        60
    war with Moors, 53
Spanish-American War, 205-206
Squaw Peak Expressway, 303
Stagecoach travel *(See also* wagon
    roads), 98-99, 184
Stanford, Rawghlie, 267, 270
Stanley, John Mix, 84
Statehood (AZ), 205, 206-208, 235
    early years, 235-247
State seal, 139

Steamboats, 50, 90-95, *95*, 184
Steen, Enoch, 90, 101
Steinfeld, Albert, 223
Stevens, J.N. and Jay, 131
Stinson, Jim, 172
Stinson, Katherine, 235
Stoneman, George, 86, 97
Sugarfoot Jack, 113
Sullivan, John L., 224
Superior, *124*, 137, 146
Swain, John, 224-225
Swilling, Jack, 13, 109, *213*, 213, 215
Swilling Irrigation Canal Company, 213
Symington, J. Fife, 275-276

Taft, William Howard, 207
Taos, 62
Taylor, Zachary, 83, 167
Teal, John, 111-112
Tempe, 203
Territorial status, 194-208
Territory of Arizona, 90, 210
Tewa, 35, 52, 63
Tewanima, Louis, 40
Tewksbury family, 172-175
Texas, 82, *106*, 168
   and Mexico, 82, 88
Texas Rangers, 167
Theater, 230
Thompson, W. Boyce, 137
Thorpe, Jim, 40
Tiguex, *55*, 56, 59
Time, 278
Tohono O'odham Indians (Papago), *12*, 17, 21, 44-46, 48, 159
Tombstone, 117, 122, 123, *124*, 129, *130*, 168-169, 170, 186, 211, 229
Tonto Creek, *39*, *110*, *124*, *209*
Tonto National Monument, *18*, 19
Topete Revolution, 252
Tourism, 225, 256-257, 298, 299
Tovar, Pedro de, 34, 55, 58
Trapping, 75-78, 80
Truman, Harry S., 279, 292
Tuba City, 6
Tubac, *39*, 65-66, 74, 124
   in 1850s, 101-103, 105

Tucson, *39*, 69, 70, 74, 90, 97, 101, *165*, 178, 182, 186, *192*, 195, 198-203, *209*, 211, 216, 229, 265, 297, 300, 301, 304
   airport, 251
   bid for capital, 195, 198
   during Civil War, 108, 109, 114-115
   industry in, 250
   Royal Spanish Presidio, *70*, 69, 71-72, 74-75, 85, 100
Turco, El, 59
Turley, Stan, 277-278
Turnbull, James, 93
Tuzigoot, *12*, 18-19
Twain, Mark, 122, 123, 133

Udall, Morris, 281
Udall, Stewart Lee, 281
United Verde, 143, 144, 146
Utah, 88, *106*
Ute Indians, 22
Ute-Aztecan language group, 21, 33

Vaca, Cabeza de, *54*, 55
ValTrans, 304
Van Dyke, Cleve, 136
Van Dyke, John C., 3
Vargas, Diego de, 63
Ventana Cave, *12*
Verde River, *12*, 19, *39*, 76, *110*, *124*, *192*, *209*, 262
Verde Valley, 18, 60, 143
Victorio, 117, 129
Villa, Francisco "Pancho," 240, *241*, 241-243
Vulture, 124

Wagon roads, 86-87, 95-96, 97-99
Walker, Joseph R., 76, 79, 80, 126
Walker, William, 89
Walnut Canyon, 19
Walpi Village, *34*
Warren, George, *138*, 138-139
Wattenberg, Jurgen, 295
Weaver, Pauline, *(Pauline)*, 76, 85, 114, 125, *125*, 126
Weaver Mountains, 126
Weaver-Peeples party, 224

Weekly Arizonian (Tubac), 200
Wheeler, Harry, 182, 240
Whipple, Amiel, 47, 88, 89, 91, 92, 97
White, Ammi, 109
Wickenburg, Henry, 127
Wickenburg, 216
Williams, 80
Williams, Jack, 271
Williams, "Old Bill," 76, 80-81
Wilson, Woodrow, 242, 243, 244, 269
Winslow, 187, 219, 220
Women, 66, 235, 238
    prostitution, 141, 145, 227-229
    Suffrage, 207, 235
    Sonoran, 102
Woodhouse, Sam, 91
Woolsey, King, 113, 133, *165*
World War I, 142, 144, 239, 244, 246
    effect on economy, 246-247
World War II, 292-297
Wyoming, 88, 168

Yankie, Joe, 131
Yaqui Indians, 51-52
Yavapai County, 201, *209*
Yavapai Indians, *39*, 46-47, 48, 112, 116
Yosemite National Park, 79
Young, Brigham, 199, 218
Young, Ewing, 48, 76, 77, 80
Young, John, 161-162
Yuma, 3, 5, 50, *56*, 59, 95, *124*, 184, 185, *192, 209*, 216, 297, 301
Yuma County, 201, *209*
Yuma Crossing, 39, 90, 93, 297
Yuma Depot, 110
Yuma Indians, *39*, 48, 51, 59, 92. 93
Yuma Revolt of 1781, 69
Yuman language group, 20, 33

Zander, C.M., 270
Zeckendorf, William, 223
Zimmerman, Arthur, 243
Zimmerman Note, 243
Zinc, 141
Zuni Indians, 34